Martianus Capella
and the Seven Liberal Arts

VOLUME II

NUMBER LXXXIV OF THE
Records of Civilization: Sources and Studies

Martianus Capella
and the
Seven Liberal Arts

VOLUME II

THE MARRIAGE OF PHILOLOGY AND MERCURY

TRANSLATED BY

William Harris Stahl and Richard Johnson

with E. L. Burge

COLUMBIA UNIVERSITY PRESS

NEW YORK 1977

LIBRARY OF CONGRESS CATALOGING IN PUBLICATION DATA

Martianus Capella.
  Martianus Capella and the seven liberal arts.

  (Records of civilization: sources and studies, no. 84)
  Translation of De nuptiis Philologiae et Mercurii.
  Bibliography: v. 1, p.
  CONTENTS: v. 1. The quadrivium of Martianus Ca-
pella: Latin traditions in the mathematical sciences, 50
B.C.-A.D. 1250, by W. H. Stahl, with a study of the alle-
gory and the verbal disciplines, by R. Johnson with E. L.
Burge.—v. 2. The marriage of Philology and Mercury,
translated by W. H. Stahl and R. Johnson, with E. L.
Burge.
  I. Stahl, William Harris. II. Johnson, Richard, 1929-
III. Series.
PA 6511. M3Me   186   76-121876
ISBN 0-231-03254-4 (v. 1)
ISBN 0-231-03719-8 (v. 2)

Columbia University Press
New York   Guildford, Surrey
Copyright © 1977 Columbia University Press

Foreword

THIS IS a translation into English prose of a work written in mingled Latin verse and prose. The verse passages of the original are, in this translation, set off from the rest of the text by indention at the left margin.

Books I, II, III and V were translated and annotated by me.

Book IV was translated and annotated by E. L. Burge.

Books VI, VII, VIII and IX were first translated and annotated by William Harris Stahl, but had not been fully revised at the time of his death. They were revised and prepared for publication by the late Carl Boyer of Brooklyn College and by myself, with assistance from Anna Griffiths, W. T. H. Jackson, and (for Book IX) Edward A. Lippman of Columbia University.

This translation has worked from the text of Martianus edited by Adolf Dick (Teubner, Leipzig, 1925; rep. 1969). James Willis is preparing a new edition for Teubner, and conjectures many emendations, some of which he has published. The translators—I in particular—have had the benefit of his advice and suggestions, and his opinions are often to be found in the notes. However, these are not to be regarded as other than interim opinions, relatively few in number, pending the publication of Willis's edition. This translation should be regarded as a translation of the Dick edition with some suggestions about variant readings, and with no responsibility borne by Dr. Willis or his publisher.

It has been a moving tribute to William Harris Stahl that so many and diverse people have so readily cooperated to ensure the publication of his last scholarly work. I should like to add my personal deep appreciation of the extraordinary assistance given by Columbia University Press and Michelle Marder Kamhi over the years of preparation of this book.

R. JOHNSON

Canberra, A.C.T.
January 15, 1977

Contents

The Marriage of Philology and Mercury

BOOK I

The Betrothal

[1] Sacred principle of unity amongst the gods, on you I call;
you are said[1] to grace weddings with your song; it is said that a
Muse was your mother. You bind the warring seeds of the world
with secret bonds and encourage the union of opposites by your
sacred embrace.[2] You cause the elements to interact reciprocally,
you make the world fertile; through you, Mind is breathed into
bodies by a union of concord which rules over Nature, as you
bring harmony between the sexes and foster loyalty by love. Fair
Hymen, you are the main object of the Cyprian's care;[3] Desire,
inflamed by Venus, glows on your face. Perhaps[4] because dancing
has pleased you, Bacchus being your father; or perhaps because
you sing at weddings, which are the province of your mother; or
perhaps because the three Graces granted to you, their kinsman,
the task of garlanding the thresholds blooming[5] with spring flow-

[1] This sort of appeal to vague authority is common in Martianus; cf. §§ 4, 45,
188-89.

[2] This opening hymn is based on the concept of the universe as composed of
varying elements or "seeds" brought into fruitful harmony and coherence by
mutual attraction—here personified as Hymen, a god of love and marriage. The
concept owes something to Empedocles, but is elaborated by Plato (e.g.,
Timaeus 32c; *Gorgias* 508a) and especially by Neoplatonic cosmology (e.g.,
Macrobius *Commentary on the Dream of Scipio* 11. 2. 18). These lines also
recall Claudian's description of Hymen as a god of marriage, in a marriage
hymn possibly dating from A.D. 399 (*Carmina minora* 25, lines 31-55).

Like many of the allegorical passages in the work, this hymn is in verse in
the original Latin. Such verse passages have been translated into prose, but are
set off from the rest of the text by indention at the left margin.

[3] *Maxima cura*: a phrase used by Venus to describe Aeneas' son Ascanius in
Vergil *Aeneid* 1. 678; and by Arethusa to describe her sister Cyrene's son
Aristaeus in Vergil *Georgics* 4. 454.

[4] For this style of invocation, with a series of alternative reasons for invoking the god concerned, cf. §§ 39, 149; and Apuleius *Metamorphoses* 6. 4;
11. 2.

[5] Martianus: *comere vernificis florentia limina sertis*; cf. Vergil *Aeneid* 4. 202:
pingue solum et variis florentia limina sertis.

ers—for some such reason, Calliope is glad to have you bless the beginning of her poem concerning the wedding of a god.

[2] While I was repeatedly reciting these verses of Hymen and pondering some original composition unimagined hitherto, Martianus[6] interrupted me. He could not abide that a gray-haired man living in retirement[7] because of his advanced years should chatter silly trifles, and he said: "Father, why is it that you are in a hurry to recite before revealing your subject, and, like a sleepy priest, you chant a hymn before you open the entry and the portals? Tell us, rather, the burden and the meaning of your utterance."

I said to him:[8] "Surely you are joking; do you not recognize like the dawn the opening passage of the work you see me reciting? Since the poem is addressed to Hymen, is it not clear that my theme is a marriage? If, however, your question is serious, when you ask from what source my ideas have flowed, I shall unfold to you a story which Satire[9] invented in the long winter nights and taught me by the dimming lamplight—that is, unless its length discourages you."

[3] There was a time when on all sides amongst the gods the

[6] This appears to be not only the author's name but also that of his son.

[7] The phrase *incrementis lustralibus decuriatum* literally means something like "multiplied by ten with fivefold increases." Commentators have taken this to mean "a man fifty years old." *Decuriatum*, however, can be applied to a man retired from office or military service. The translation given is deliberately vague; the general idea of the dignity due to age is clear enough. The possible implications of this passage are further discussed by W. H. Stahl above, Vol. I, p. 11, n. 10.

[8] This passage of dialogue echoes Apuleius *Metamorphoses* 1. 6. Martianus' son begins: '*Quid istud, mi pater. . . .*' and Martianus describes his reply: '*Ne tu*' inquam '*desipis. . . .*' Apuleius' narrator begins: '*Mi Socrates, quid istud?*' . . . and the reply comes: '*Aristomene,*' inquit, '*ne tu . . . ignoras.*'

[9] *Satura*. The Latin term means a dish of mixed ingredients, a stew; it became the name of a literary form invented by early Latin writers—a mixture of prose and verse on a miscellany of topics. This is the genre satire; one type of satire became purely verse (e.g., the satires of Horace, Persius, Juvenal); the other, Menippean satire, retained the mixture of prose and verse—this is what Martianus is writing. The caustic tone which is implied in the modern word "satire" was not essential to the ancient genre, but was present in the writing of Lucilius and Juvenal, in particular, and from the latter was taken over into European satirical writing.

sacred weddings of a numerous generation were being celebrated;[10] the noble children of the gods and the celestial multitude of their beloved descendants were also for their part winning the embraces and pledges of the dwellers in heaven. The fruit of marriage especially delighted the great gods, and the human race in its chatter spread the news through the streets of the gift[11] that had been given to the world. The poets, who were disciples of the Thracian lyre player [Orpheus] and the blind Maeonian [Homer], old and eloquent, published epic poems and lyrics about the marriages; they sang that amongst the delights of heaven nothing pleased Jove more than his wife alone. Old priests are encouraged by ready credence to give their message when the omens suggest it; and ready credence was given to the message of the poets that when Jupiter, unappeased despite many sacrifices, denies anything to the hesitant prayers of men worried by doubts and fears, it comes to pass, when prayer is addressed to his wife, when he has with dispatch passed a sentence and the hand of the Parcae is waiting to carry out his order, he cancels it when his wife gently persuades him and mollifies him with her embraces.

[4] Not only the king of the gods was thought to be under feminine domination; this was also said of Dis and Portunus [Neptune], while it was regarded as beyond question that Gradivus [Mars] was aflame with love for his wife Nereia, the daughter of Nereus. Aesculapius felt a similar passion; and Saturn, the melancholy elder of the gods, was moved in the same way by his wife Ops, Cybele,[12] when he caressed her. Janus with both his faces admires the Argive goddess;[13] and they say that the queen of Memphis [Isis], so loved her husband that she was beset by unending grief and preferred[14] never to find him.

---

10 This paragraph forms an interesting contrast to Arnobius *Adversus nationes* 4. 19-21, where Arnobius says that the pagans debased their own deities by anthropomorphically ascribing marriages, adulteries, etc. to them.

11 This translates the text edited by Dick (*idque deditum mundo*). Willis accepts Grotius' *diditum* for *deditum;* the translation would then be "spread to the world the news of this."

12 Ops, the Roman equivalent of the Greek Rhea, the Great Mother, was syncretized with Cybele.

13 The text is corrupt; Dick reads *Argionam.* "The Argive goddess" ought to mean Juno.

14 Isis' husband Osiris was slain and torn apart by his brother; Isis sought and

[5] The Cyllenian [Mercury], then, was moved and excited by this story, by the reciprocity of love among the gods; at the same time he saw what was clear to many people—love and marriages being universally celebrated. He too decided to get married. His mother had encouraged him in this inclination when, on his yearly journey through the zodiac, he greeted her in the company of the Pleiades. She was concerned about him, especially because his body, through the exercise of wrestling and constant running, glowed with masculine strength and bore the muscles of a youth perfectly developed. Already with the first beard on his cheeks, he could not continue to go about half naked, clad in nothing but a short cape covering only the top of his shoulders—such a sight caused the Cyprian great amusement. With all this in mind he decided to marry.

[6] Because of the importance of the venture, he pondered a great deal on whom he ought to marry. He himself ardently desired Wisdom, because she was prudent and holy, and purer and fairer than the other maidens. However, she was his sister's foster sister[15] and seemed to be inseparably devoted to her, and seemed therefore to have espoused virginity herself; he accordingly decided not to marry her, as this would offend Pallas. In the same way, the splendid beauty of Prophecy inflamed his desires. She was nobly born, being the elder daughter of Forethought, and her farsighted and penetrating wisdom commended her to him. But at that very time, as it happened, she went of her own accord to young Apollo and, unable to endure her inordinate passion, she became his lover.

[7] He wanted then to ask for Psyche, the daughter of Entelechia and Sol,[16] because she was extremely beautiful and the gods had

---

collected the pieces for burial; her grief was such that she would have been happier never to have found him. That seems to be the implication of Dick's reading: *contenta sit.* Willis suggests: *nusquam eum non tentaverit invenire;* the sense would then be "sought everywhere to find him."

The text of this entire passage is badly corrupted; the syntax is also extremely involved. From the beginning of § 3 to the end of the second sentence in § 5 is, in the Latin, one sentence; the principal verb is *instituit* [decided]; the author (let alone the reader) gets lost a number of times in the course of the sentence.

15 Mercury's sister is Athena, goddess of learning and wisdom.

16 In ancient philosophicoreligious thought, disseminated in Italy especially by Stoicism, fire was regarded as the primary element, from which the others were created; hence Sol, the sun, was regarded as the creator. This philosophy is here

taken great care over her education. On the day of her birth the
gods, being invited to a celebration, had brought her many gifts.
Jupiter, in fact, had placed on her head a diadem which he had
taken from his favored daughter Eternity; Juno had added a band
for her hair, made from a gleaming vein of pure gold. Even the Tritonian [Athena] loosed from her tunic the flame-red veil and breast-
band and, herself a virgin holy and wise, draped the virgin in the
very mantle from her own bosom. The Delian also, carrying his
laurel branch, showed her with that wand of foresight and prophecy
the birds, the bolts of lightning, the motions of heaven itself and
the stars. Urania with gentle kindness gave her a gleaming mirror
which Wisdom had hung in Urania's rooms amongst her gifts—a
mirror in which Psyche could recognize herself and learn her origins.[17] The craftsman of Lemnos kindled for her ever-burning
flamelets; she would not then be oppressed by gloomy shadows
and blind night. Aphrodite had given to all her senses every kind
of pleasure; she had spread ointment on Psyche, garlanded her with
flowers, taught her to appreciate and enjoy perfume and to delight
in the sweetness of honey; she had implanted in her also a desire for
gold and jewelry, a taste for wearing rich ornament. When she
rested, Aphrodite brought her rattles and bells with which one lulls
a baby to sleep; and then, to make sure that she was never without
amusement and delectation, Aphrodite assigned Pleasure to stimulate
desire in her by intimate titillation. The Cyllenian himself gave her a
vehicle with swift wheels in which she could travel at an astonishing
speed, although Memory bound it and weighed it down with golden
chains.[18] So the Arcadian [Mercury], his earlier hopes frustrated,

---

blended with the Aristotelian distinction between potentiality (represented by
Sol, the creative element) and actuality (*Entelechia* is the Aristotelian term for
actuality); the human soul (Psyche) is thus represented as the actualization of
the divine potentiality, an incarnation of the divine Fire. When one considers
that Apollo is to Martianus also the god of the sun (see § 8 and n. 19), as is
Vulcan (Mulciber)—see §§ 48, 49; and the corresponding reference to Weinstock—without any syncretism between them, one has some measure of the
theological confusion of Martianus and his contemporaries.

17 Urania is the Muse of astronomy. The soul (Psyche) was believed to take
its origin amongst the stars.

18 Kopp interprets the gifts of Mercury as intellect and imagination, which can
carry the soul swiftly far and wide; memory may be said to bind and stabilize
intellect.

sought in marriage Psyche, wealthy as she was in the gifts of
heaven and richly adorned by the gods. But Virtue, almost in tears
and clinging fast to the Cyllenian, confessed that Psyche had been
snatched from her company into the hand of Cupid the flying
archer, and was being held captive by him in shackles of adamant.

[8] So the happiness of the destiny he had planned eluded Mercury, because of the marriages of these maidens; and there did not
readily seem to be anyone else who might fittingly be chosen as
the Thunderer's daughter-in-law. Virtue therefore suggested that
he give the matter further thought; he ought not decide anything
without the advice of Apollo; he was not meant to wander far
from his company, since, as Mercury traveled through the signs of
the zodiac, Apollo never permitted him to be further than one
month's journey away from himself.[19] And so it was decided that
he go to his brother, wherever he might be.

[9] Then, as usual, he gave his caduceus to Virtue, so that she
could penetrate the secret parts of the world with him, and with
equal swiftness could break into the more remote quarters of heaven.
He himself bound on his feet his golden sandals[20] and they made
a thorough search for Apollo. They looked for him in temples
where oracles poured forth in evasive ambiguity and where, by
the slaughter of animals and the separation of their entrails, the
viscera declared foreordained events; and in places where it was the
custom for a lottery to be drawn and for prophecies to be told.[21]

[10] But in these leading shrines and these deserted caves they
found nothing of Apollo except only a few leaves of withered
laurel and half-torn fillets which, behind the sybil in the cave of
Cumae, worms and rot were devouring. Even through the paths
of air where Apollo usually guided the varied flights of birds and

---

[19] Martianus later says (§ 880) that the planet Mercury's distance from the
sun does not exceed 22° and that the sun traverses one sign of the zodiac (that
is, 30°) in one month.

[20] Martianus: *Ipse pedibus talaria nectit aurea, . . .* ; cf. Vergil *Aeneid* 4.
239-40: *et primum pedibus talaria nectit aurea, quae. . . .*

[21] In this passage the phrases *fissiculatis extorum prosiciis* and *sagaci eum in-
vestigatione disquirunt* echo Apuleius *De deo Socratis* 6. 134: *extis fissiculandis*
and *Metamorphoses* 6. 2: *anxia disquisitione . . . requirit;* also Firmicus Maternus
Mathesis 2. 29. 3: *sagaci . . . inquisitione.*

the cries they uttered, and formed omens in their fleeting wings,[22] they looked for him without success. Indeed the Pythian, distressed by contact with those who sought his advice, had long ago given up his reputation as a prophet.[23] They pursued him to Helicon, Delos, Lycia. In one place they found old laurel and withered ivy, in another a rotting tripod, sandals stiff with mildew, and an account of prophecies lying between them.

[11] At length they learned by rumor that the rock of Parnassus rejoiced[24] in the presence of Phoebus, although from there too it was said that he had later moved to an Indian mountain's secret crag, shrouded in perpetual clouds. Yet Mercury and Virtue visited the Cirrhaean retreat[25] and the sacred cave's prophetic hollows. In it there stood about all the impending vicissitudes of the ages, in their order: the fortunes of cities and nations, of all their kings, and of the entire human race. Some were seen in flight because the measure of their course had been completed; some were standing in full view, and many were approaching, while in the intervening distance some faded away, so that an uncanny haze, like a dense fog, seemed to envelop them. Amidst these extraordinary scenes and these vicissitudes of Fortune, a sweet music arose from the trees, a melody arising from their contact as the breeze whispered through them; for the crests of the great trees were very tall and, because of this tension, reverberated with a sharp sound; but whatever was close to and near the ground, with drooping boughs, shook with a deep heaviness of sound; while the trees of middle size in their contacts with each other sang together in fixed harmonies of the duple [2.1], the sesquialtera [3:2], the sesquitertia [4:3] also, and even the sesquioctava [9:8] without discrimination, although semitones came between. So it hap-

---

22 Martianus: *quibus formare solitus et volucrum diversos meatus et oscinum linguas et praepetis omina pennae . . .* ; cf. Vergil *Aeneid* 3. 361: *et volucrum linguas et praepetis omina pennae.*

23 Martianus: *dedignatur 'augur' Pythius nuncupari;* cf. Horace *Odes* 1. 2. 32: *augur Apollo.*

24 Martianus: *quod Phoebo gaudet Parnasia rupes;* cf. Vergil *Eclogues* 6. 29: *nec tantum Phoebo gaudet Parnasia rupes.*

25 The ancient town of Cirrha, on the Gulf of Corinth, was near Delphi and served as its port. Although Mercury and Virtue find Apollo near Delphi, and there is no mention of their departure thence until § 26, it is obvious that Martianus is here creating an allegorical picture with no reference to the actual topography around Delphi.

pened that the grove poured forth, with melodious harmony, the whole music and song of the gods.

[12] As the Cyllenian explained this, Virtue learned that in heaven also, in the same way, the spheres either produce harmony or join in the accompaniments; so it is not strange that the grove of Apollo should be so full of harmony, when the same god, in the sun, modulates the spheres of the heavens also. So it happens that in one place he is called Phoebus, and in another Auricomus [the golden-haired]; [13] (for the august head of the sun, streaming and surrounded with flaming rays, is like a gleaming head of golden hair). For this reason he is also called Sagittarius [the Archer]; and hence Vulnificus [the one who wounds]—because he can penetrate what he strikes with the darts of his rays.

[14] The Cyllenian also showed to Virtue some rivers flowing down from heaven which, he said, they had to cross to reach the god whom they were trying to find. The streams swept along in multicolored billows.[26] The first stream, a wide and far-spread body of leaden color, eddied with a cloudy swirl and its currents were extremely cold and sluggish.[27] Within it, another one, like milk or a white light, steady in movement and calm in every way, was rolling its silvery waves.[28] The third one was sulphurous, and with breathless swiftness was twisting currents headlong and crashing in their haste, flashing with their torrent of red flame.[29] The next one was golden and flashing, gleaming with sparkling flames.[30] It was joined on either side by some tributary streams, and mingled the different rivers to a moderate temperature. Within shone a river purer than amber,[31] with a crowd of people standing beside it who wanted this more than the other rivers of the Destinies; some of these people were allured by its fragrant perfume; others were charmed by the sound of gentle melody from its waves. Many were

[26] The seven rivers represent the seven planets, and their different colors and other properties derive from this identification.

[27] This represents the planet Saturn, whose course, being long, appears slow.

[28] Martianus: *undas volvebat argenteas;* cf. Apuleius *Metamorphoses* 4. 6: *evomebat undas argenteas.* Apuleius is describing a stream in the lair of some bandits; Martianus is referring to the course of the planet Jupiter.

[29] This represents the planet Mars.

[30] This refers to the sun.

[31] *Electro purior;* cf. Vergil *Georgics* 3. 522: *purior electro.* The phrase refers to the planet Venus.

thirsting to taste a drink of its delicious stream, while some people wanted the water to bathe and soothe themselves and to be immersed in it. There were besides two narrower streams hurrying along with a tighter curve inside the others; each of these added a little of its own character to a mixture from other sources as it was blended with the other streams close by.[32] For one,[33] hastening along at an excessive speed, frequently halted and reversed its course; while the other,[34] which carried in itself the source of all waters,[35] wandered on a winding course and bubbled over with the elemental seeds of water.

[15] These streams of variegated hue encircled the aforementioned Destinies of events and of nations with windings at first immense. But then the different speeds and rushing force of the waves, lapping each Destiny with surprising violence, dragged them headlong downward with rapid eddies; one stream would often pour them into another, and that Destiny which the latter had long buffeted the former would either return to the bank or sink in the river. Yet those blue or crimson whirlpools did not carry off all the Destinies in their whirls. Frequently the gleaming water of the white stream bore up on a tall crest those that had been suddenly snatched away; at another time too it bore them suspended in a high wave and cast them into that surging crimson stream, or spewed them forth into the leaden river, to be swallowed up by its dark abyss. Thus the people in the hands of the Destinies were tossed about in the welter of the rivers, for none of the rivers flowed directly without any whirlpool or eddy and free from the immission of some other stream.

[32] The "two narrower streams" represent the moon and Mercury. Each of them has a comparatively tight orbit. The reference to a blending of characteristics is not easy to explain. In the case of the moon the reference may be to the fact that its light is the reflection of the sun. With respect to Mercury, Kopp refers to Ptolemy (*Tetrabiblion* 1. 4) and Manilius (*Astronomicon* 1. 870), suggesting that Mercury and Venus were readily confused at evening. Kopp also refers to Pliny (*Natural History* 2. 18) for the belief that color was altered by altitude, so that the colors of the planets, which are extremely high, could appear to blend.

[33] Mercury.

[34] The moon.

[35] Translating Dick's *originem*. Willis accepts Eyssenhardt's *auriginem;* the sense of the phrase would then be "a certain watery pallor."

[16] Virtue followed the Cyllenian and crossed all the rivers by herself without fear, for although the waves crashed about her and buffeted her they could not make her fall. Once on the other side of the rivers, which led on to some retreat[36] of Phoebus, Mercury halted with Virtue; and then they saw Latona's son [Apollo], sitting on a great and steep height with four closed jars[37] in front of him, of different appearance and different metals, which he was opening and inspecting one by one. As far as could be told, one seemed made of hard iron, another of gleaming silver, and the third of soft dark lead[38]; but the one nearest the god was made of translucent glass, and glittered like the sea. Each contained a different one of the four seeds and elements of creation.

[17] The iron jar, which was called Mulcifer's [Vulcan's] Whirlwind, gave out a blazing flame drawn from the kindling of the torrid zone itself. The second one, made of silver, had a smooth luster, and shone with the mildness[39] of a spring sky; this they called Jove's Smile. The one made of heavier metal was full of stormy winter and biting cold and frost; and this was called Saturn's Ruin. But the one made of the glittering sea and placed at the right hand of the god himself was full of the seeds of all the air; they called this one Juno's Bosom.

[18] Out of each of these jars in turn Apollo drew what was sufficient for his purposes. For when the world pleased him and he provided it with the healthy breezes of life-giving wind, he compounded elemental seeds of air, which he drew from the beneficent silver jar. But when he threatened dread pestilence on those mortals who deserved it, he compounded (as with the air) blasts of fire or destruction by freezing cold, and sent them forth to afflict the world.

[19] Virtue observed the god commingling the elements and,

[36] Translating Dick's *receptaculum*. Willis accepts *spectaculum*; the sense would then be "leading on to a sight of Phoebus."

[37] Cf. Homer *Iliad* 527-33, where Achilles speaks of Zeus' having two urns, from one of which he draws afflictions for men and from the other of which, blessings.

[38] The phrase *liventis plumbi* is borrowed from Vergil *Aeneid* 7. 687.

[39] *temperie renidebat*. Yet in § 27 *aëria Temperies renidebat* seems to have no possible meaning except "the region of Air shone"—certainly not "the mildness of Air shone."

taking particular note when he was blending the beneficent breezes, she recited, with Mercury's approval, the verse of the blind poet:[40]

Long-haired Phoebus dispels the cloud of Pestilence.

Mercury told her that by this line the plague could be averted if the recitation of the verse was first humbly addressed to him [Mercury]; but it had to be submitted to the Clarian [Apollo] as he played his lyre with his smooth hair plaited with bands of laurel.

[20] When the Pythian [Apollo] saw them approach from afar, conversing thus, and realized from the first glance the reason for their coming, he rose from the throne on which he was sitting and bade the Muses meet them. Although they seemed to hasten in service to Maia's son [Mercury], they moved with measured pace.[41] When his brother had been brought to sit with him and join him in his work, Phoebus first began:

[21] "When their minds tremble with apprehension in perilous times, or their destiny is unknown and unsettled with the future insecure, let the race of men consult the gods, because anxiety without knowledge of the truth makes them hesitant, uncertain prospects weary them; but to us foreknowledge is permitted, for us there is no hesitation. What the gods decide[42] is law; heaven's decisions cause us no wistfulness, for necessity is whatever is pleasing to us. But because you have not yet settled upon a choice, you want to have my advice. You thus associate me with all your desires, and you make up your mind with my advice.

[40] This is obviously a reference to Homer, and the verse sounds as if it might well come from *Iliad* 1, where Apollo sends a plague upon the Greek army. However, it does not occur in Homer; it is a prophetic utterance of the religious charlatan Alexander of Abonoteichus (late 2d cent. A.D.), recorded by Lucian in his *Alexander the False Prophet* (36), and it was concocted during the plague which swept through the Roman Empire about A.D. 165. "One could see this utterance everywhere," says Lucian, "written over doorways as a protection against the plague." Martianus seems unaware of the true origin of the quotation.

[41] The term *ratis incessibus* [measured pace] applies to the Pythagorean numerical proportion that produces harmony; the implication is that the beauty of the Muses' movements is based on their conformity to Pythagorean ratios.

[42] Martianus: *Quod superi voluere licet;* cf. Ovid *Metamorphoses* 8. 619: *quicquid superi voluere peractum est.*

[22] "There is a maiden of ancient lineage, highly educated and well acquainted with Parnassus; upon her the constellations shine in close proximity; no hidden region can conceal from her the movements of the stars through Tartarus, nor can thunderbolts hide from her the will of Jove: she beholds under the sea the nature of wave-born Nereus. She knows your circuits through the several kingdoms of your brothers: ever watchful, with unsparing toil she penetrates the secrets of knowledge, so that with her patient learning she can anticipate all that it is given to gods to foreknow. Indeed, very often she has rights over us,[43] impelling gods under compulsion to obey her decrees; she knows that what no power of heaven can attempt against Jove's will, she can attain. Sublimity may cost dear: and the crowning consideration is that either of you is a fitting match for the other."

[23] Virtue was delighted at these words of Apollo, recognizing that he proposed for marriage a paragon of a maiden; nevertheless, to be sure that there was no detraction from the dignity of the prospective brides mentioned earlier, she asked this one's name. When she learned that it was Philology whose espousal Apollo was urging, she was seized with such joy and enthusiasm that she behaved with less severity of deportment than was her wont. She called to mind that Philology was her own kinswoman, a patroness of Prophecy, who had been so well commended, and most generous to Wisdom in giving her valuable ornaments. In addition, said Virtue, Psyche, who at first lived a primitive sort of existence,[44] has been so refined by Philology that whatever beauty and embellishment Psyche had she acquired from the polish Philology gave her; for the maiden had shown Psyche so much affection that she strove constantly to make her immortal. Therefore they must not delay—and indeed she knew that the Cyllenian was swift in action. Having heard the words of Apollo, Maia's son replied:

[24] "Lord of the laurel, splendor of the gods, certain it is that our concord comes from our kinship, and that you, my fel-

[43] Martianus: *in nos / ius habet illa, deos urgens . . .* ; cf. Ovid *Heroides* 4. 12: *regnat et in dominos ius habet ille deos.*

[44] Martianus: *ferino more versantem;* cf. Ovid *Metamorphoses* 4. 722-23: *more ferocis / versat.* When one remembers that "Psyche" means "soul," the allegory here is clear: Philology, learning, is the agent of civilization; it gives the soul its beauty—indeed, its immortality.

low-god, bring to pass whatever you and I together find to approve. I am never more ready to give up my own will, more happy to obey orders than when your caution and judgment prompt me to obey the Delian oracle.

"I think it is sacrilege to regard the Delian utterances as ambiguous, and I forgo my own decision, whatever it was. It is therefore all the more appropriate that the Arcadian [Mercury] gladly obey these celebrated pronouncements when he is ordered to enter into matrimony. Try then, Delian, to ensure that the Thunderer should give the same decision, that he should give willing approval; for you are used to moving his will, you are alert to influence his predispositions; get him to approve your commands; I pray that his holy will has shone upon what has begun."

[25] As Mercury said this, Virtue remarked, "Really, each of you ought rather to persuade Jove; for Apollo is aware of his plans, while you are his aide in his commands; Apollo knows his mind, you prepare his utterance. When Phoebus urges him he generally yields; to you he usually bares his heart. Furthermore, it is ordained that you should never be separated; and although Mercury in his course is often outstripped by the speed of Apollo's chariot and is overtaken while delaying in his station, and finally hastens forward of Apollo, yet while he is catching up, his advance is so counterbalanced that he is happy to be constantly returning to Apollo.[45] As dutiful sons, then, go together to meet your Jove. Indeed, it is certain that he will yield, half closing his eyes at Phoebus' brilliance, and in agreement with Stilbon [the planet Mercury] he will be delighted at the marriage bond."[46]

[26] When she had said this, Virtue, in attendance on Mercury as he went before her, was wafted up toward heaven by the draft from the movement of his caduceus. But the Delian's augural birds halted for him in front of his chariot, in order that he might ascend and be carried up by them if he wished. Often while shaping future events he had foreshadowed them with these birds. Mercury began to go forward, with his winged hat and sandals propelling him;

---

[45] See §§ 854, 857, 879, and 882, where Martianus assumes for Mercury and Venus heliocentric motions with positions sometimes ahead of and sometimes behind the sun.

[46] The last sentence refers to the occultation of Jupiter when in conjunction with the sun.

but as Phoebus mounted the chariot, the escort of Muses who closely attended him was carried by a gleaming white swan melodiously singing.[47]

[27] Then the whole world could be seen joining in celebration; for Tellus[48] had seen Mercury the god of Spring flying upward and was bright with flowers, and the region of Air[49] shone without clouds in the sight of Apollo. The upper spheres and the seven planetary spheres produced a symphony of the harmonious notes of each, a sweeter song than usually heard; indeed they had sensed the approach of the Muses, each of whom, after traversing the spheres, took her position where she recognized the pitch that was familiar to her. For Urania was attuned to the outermost sphere of the starry universe, which was swept along with a high pitch. [28] Polymnia took over the sphere of Saturn; Euterpe controlled that of Jove; and Erato, that of Mars, which she entered; while Melpomene held the middle region, where the sun enhanced the world with the light of flame. Terpsichore joined the golden Venus; Calliope embraced the Cyllenian's sphere; Clio set up as her lodging the innermost circle—that is, the moon's, whose deep pitch reverberated with deeper tones. Only Thalia[50] was left sitting on earth's flowery bosom, because the swan which was to carry her was indisposed to carry its burden or even to fly upward and had gone to find the lakes which were its home.

[29] Meanwhile Phoebus had gone beyond the airy regions, when suddenly his headband was transformed into rays of light, the laurel which he was carrying in his right hand burst into a glow of cosmic splendor; and the birds which were drawing the Delian chariot turned into swift jets of flame. In the guise of the sun he shone forth brightly, his mantle gleaming red, the threshold of

---

[47] This whole passage is very similar to the description of the ascent of Venus to heaven in Apuleius *Metamorphoses* 6. 6.

[48] The earth.

[49] See n. 39 on § 17 above.

[50] There are nine Muses, to whom are allocated the spheres of the five visible planets, the sun, the moon, the outermost sphere, and the earth. Thalia is the Muse of comedy, and there may be some allegorical significance in her remaining on earth while the more serious Muses ascend; but she has rejoined her sisters by § 126. Kopp regards Thalia as a patroness of flowers and thus explains her staying on the "flowery" earth.

the starry heavens open. The Cyllenian, too, was transformed into a glimmering planet.

[30] Thus enhanced by this transformation into celestial bodies, they were carried through Gemini, a sign kindred to them, and they shone forth in the majestic sky and soon sought the palace of the Thunderer. "When they had gone in and been granted an audience,"[51] the Clarian saw that his father was keeping close to Juno's company, and he knew that she was a strong defender and supporter of marriage; this first omen gladdened him, and thus he addressed them gently, to win Juno's favor, knowing that the decision of her husband depended on her judgment:

[31] "I, an overgrown youth trembling at my father's commands, would be hesitant and of little confidence in approaching the Thunderer alone to urge the marriage of his son, were it not that marriages amongst the gods and the fond warmth of their unions promise a favorable outcome. Which of the gods would not be willing to seek a marriage if he had as his confidante Juno,[52] who promises her support and will sponsor the bride? By your blandishments secure your husband's approval and ensure that Persuasion[53] favor our efforts. [32] We turn now to you, Father, almighty Lord, master of our destiny: (for the chorus of the Parcae weighs the fortunes of men, but you weigh those of the gods, your will is before all foreknowledge, you bear in your mind whatever is to affect the gods; necessity springs from your will,[54] your decision is binding on the future, even last-minute desires of yours demand accomplishment); it is you I implore, by that divine majesty which is the source of your beneficence, O Celestial Serenity, Supreme Holiness, truly the father of the gods;

---

51 The line is quoted from Vergil *Aeneid* 1. 520.

52 Martianus: *Iunone thalamos quis rogare conscia nollet decorum . . .* ; cf. Ovid *Heroides* 12. 87: *Conscia sit Iuno sacris praefecta maritis.*

53 *Suada;* here used as a proper noun for a personification, the word occurred at the end of § 3 as an adjective describing Juno, though rendered as a verb in the translation. The sense might be ". . . that you, as Persuasion, favor our efforts"; but the Latin verb is third person, not second.

54 Martianus' theology is somewhat inconsistent. In § 21 he says: "Necessity is whatever is pleasing to us [the gods]"; here in § 32 he reduces necessity to the will of Jove, to whom the other gods are subject; and in § 22 he speaks of Philology (i.e., learning) as having power over the gods, able to compel them and even to overcome the will of Jove.

grant to your child that he may increase the number of your descendants, sparkling in the starry skies. Your child, the sacred bond between you and Maia, begs you to let him marry this cultivated maiden. [33] But if your parental anxiety[55] restrains you, it is reasonable that you and your spouse summon a conclave of the gods with jurisdiction to ratify the marriage, so that the marriage of your son may take place according to divine law, and propriety may always mark the marriages of the immortals."

[34] When the Delian had stopped, Jupiter turned to his wife and asked her will. She was pleased with the idea for many reasons; first, because she was asked by Phoebus, who usually brought her calmness[56] and who had made her daughters the Muses (whom he had educated) ascend into their parents' sight; furthermore, Juno did not normally oppose marriages,[57] and she was fond of the Cyllenian because he had been nourished at her breast and had drunk there the draught of immortality, so that she bore toward him a mother's feelings; the Clarian inclined her feelings still more with his prayers, because he had laid her under obligation to him with many acts of friendship. So she urged that the marriage take place quickly, before the Cyllenian enticed and inflamed by the Cyprian, was impelled to father a brother for Hermaphroditus.[58]

[35] It worried Jove a little that the charms of a wife might make the Cyllenian slothful and indolent, drowsy and languid; he might regard himself as being on a honeymoon and refuse to go as messenger at the orders of Jupiter. [36] "I know," he said, "that for a long time he has been afire with love for Philology, and in his passion for her has taken into his household several Disciplines[59] related to her, and that, simply to please the girl, he has acquired a most elegant diction and refinement of speech and can play the lute and golden lyre well. Furthermore, he has a wonderful magic

---

[55] Martianus: *Sed te parentis cura si stringit pia;* cf. Ovid *Heroides* 8. 15: *At tu, cura mei si te pia tangit, Oreste.*

[56] Remigius explains that the sun shining (Apollo) means calm weather and air (Juno).

[57] One of Juno's offices was as *Pronuba;* that is, the sponsor of a bride.

[58] The son of Hermes (Mercury) and Aphrodite (Venus).

[59] The seven liberal arts, whom Mercury gives to Philology as handmaidens (see § 218 below); they speak each on her own subject in Books III-IX.

in painting, and as a sculptor in bronze or marble he brings life[60] into the features; the whole effect is excellent—everything that contributes to the perfection of a young man." Jupiter said that he had therefore delayed the lovers for a little while, though they had for a long time been joined by the bonds of mutual love; so that Mercury should not hasten into marriage on a youthful impulse and then, when he should have to go on his travels, lose something of his constancy, through the languor of these many nights[61] of love. [37] "Yet still," said Juno, "it is fitting that he should be married to the very maiden who would not tolerate his dozing off even if he wanted to rest. Is there anyone who claims he does not know the wearisome vigils of Philology, the constant pallor that comes from her studies at night? For who is there who discusses the heavens, the seas, seething Tartarus, for whole nights at a time, and traverses in her careful research the homes of all the gods—who considers the constitution of the world, the girding circles, the parallels, the oblique circles and colures, the poles and climates[62] and rotations, and the multitude of the stars themselves—unless it is this slender girl, Philology, who is devoted to these pursuits? How often have the gods complained of her importunate summonses, when in the dead of night, the silence of first sleep, she compels them from their rest to come to her, heedless of their protestations?[63] [38] So far from being impeded and delayed by this girl, the Cyllenian will be encouraged by her to move and stir his wings and seek the utmost limits of the world. Why then, Your Majesty, is their marriage deferred, when in return for the single wit of Atlas's descendant I offer you two vigilant emissaries?"

[39] Juno was sitting close to Jove, but he was a good deal higher and bent his head to listen. While she was saying this to

---

[60] Martianus: *cum vivos etiam vultus aeris aut marmoris signifex animator inspirat;* cf. Vergil *Aeneid* 6. 847-48: *Excudent alii spirantia mollius aera / (credo equidem), vivos ducent de marmore vultus.*

[61] Following Dick's text: *tot is noctibus.* Willis accepts *totis noctibus;* the meaning would then be "entire nights." Martianus is here referring to anomalies in Mercury's orbit when the planet is in station or retrogradation.

[62] Reading *climata* with Grotius, instead of Dick's *limmata.*

[63] Kopp explains this as a reference to the literary and rhetorical custom of summoning the gods to witness or to aid a speaker or writer.

him, glittering Pallas glided gradually down from some place of pure and shimmering light and, flying overhead so that she seemed to stand on the very forehead of Jove, she finally settled on a higher level. When Jupiter saw her, close by and almost touching him, as he sat higher than his wife, he spoke to her: "O maiden, my noblest flesh and blood, how timely you come to be concerned in the hopes of Maia's son!—whether you come down at the entreaty of the Delian, or whether it would not be possible for Jove to form a plan without your help, or whether you came to give our agreement the appearance of unanimity.[64] At any rate, you ought to know that the Cyllenian is asking for the hand of Philology in marriage. I have not yet made up my mind, and I am waiting for your advice. I know how the ceaseless efforts of this girl have always been agreeable to you, and how she has always striven to be counted as one of your attendants; it is only right then that you yourself should determine whatever decision you in your providence will make about her marriage."

[40] Then Pallas blushed[65] with virginal modesty and covered her eyes with the mantle which she wore over her shining head and in a soft voice deprecated the suggestion that a virgin's advice should be asked on marriage, particularly the marriage of one whom she would wish always to remain a virgin because of their commitments to each other. Besides, she refused to give approval in this way, because she was thought to be so much without experience of any kind of union that Arithmetic herself would show that Pallas neither was begotten from any intercourse nor herself begot anything.[66] Then, aloof in her virginity, she unveiled her seven-rayed crown[67] so as to have no part in mating and procreation. But since

[64] See § 1, n. 4.

[65] Martianus: *virginalis pudoris rubore suffusa;* cf. Vergil *Georgics* 1. 430: *at si virgineum suffuderit ore ruborem.*

[66] Pallas is identified with the number seven in ancient arithmology; seven is not the product of any multiplication, nor does it produce by duplication or other multiplication any number within the decad (that is, under ten); see § 738 and the footnotes thereon.

[67] The allegory here is obscure. Because of the identification of Pallas with the number seven, it is appropriate for her to have a seven-rayed crown, without further allegory. However the crown has been taken by Remigius as referring to the seven liberal arts. Why does she unveil it? The Latin following clearly means "so as to have no part . . .", but there seems to be no logical connection,

Jupiter had hoped for her advice and demanded it, she advised that the married gods and elder goddesses should be summoned to a meeting to decide the issue; indeed it was an advantage to the Cyllenian that the mightiest gods should approve his union as a reward for services performed. Furthermore, it added dignity to Jove's decision when it was published in the presence of an assembly of the gods; and the bride herself could not marry a god unless, with the approval of the divine council, she ceased to be a mortal. The Tritonian used many such arguments, and both of the royal couple agreed.

[41] And soon the scribe of Jove was ordered to summon the deities, each in his own rank, according to the customary procedure, and especially those senators[68] amongst the gods who were called the companions[69] of Jove himself. Jupiter did not allow their names to be known, but kept them a sacred secret; because they were bound by mutual promises in every respect, he gave the group a name derived from their union [consentes]. [42] Jupiter himself asked his son Vulcan to come, although Vulcan never came down from his glittering throne. Amongst the others to be invited were the most powerful associates of Jove himself, those who with the Thunderer make up the Twelve and whose names are included in the couplet of Ennius:

Juno, Vesta, Minerva, Ceres, Diana, Venus, Mars,
Mercury, Jove, Neptune, Vulcan, Apollo;[70]

[43] also the other seven, who are not named among the Twelve. After these there had to be summoned a great many inhabitants of

---

unless it be that the seven arts are themselves virgins. Remigius, again, explains the second half of the allegory: Wisdom (Pallas) is concerned with learning (Philology), not necessarily with expression (Mercury); hence, while Pallas does not oppose their union, she takes no part in it. This seems an acceptable allegorization, but appears to have no connection with the unveiling of the crown.

[68] Cf. Seneca Quaestiones naturales 2. 41. 2.

[69] Penates: cf. Arnobius Adversus nationes 3. 40; Macrobius Saturnalia 3. 4. 6. For a similar assembly of gods, cf. Ovid Metamorphoses 1. 167-76; Apuleius Metamorphoses 23.

[70] The fragments of Ennius are collected and translated by E. H. Warmington in Remains of Old Latin, Vol. I (Cambridge, Mass., 1956). This couplet is 11. 60-61.

heaven, exalted in keeping with their rank, and the whole com-
munity of the gods except those outside the pale.[71] [44] Without
delay Jove's guardsmen hurried through all the quarters of heaven.
Indeed, the individual gods generally inhabited separate areas, and
although throughout the whole zodiac some of them had given names
to one or two abodes, naming them after animals, they usually lived
not in these but in other quarters.

[45] For the whole heaven is said to be divided into sixteen regions.[72] In the first[73] of these regions, they say, are the homes not
only of Jupiter but of the gods of the council, the god of welfare,
the household gods, Janus, the secret gods of goodwill, and the
god of night. [46] In the second region—besides the home of Jupiter, which towers there, since he is wealthy in every way—there live
Mars Quirinus and Lars the warrior; Juno also has her home there,
as do Fons, the Lymphae [goddesses of waters], and the nine gods
of lightning.[74]

[47] Jupiter decided that from the third region only one should
be invited. In that region were the homes of Jove of the second rank
[Neptune] and Jove god of wealth and Minerva; but all of them were
already in the presence of Jove. Who would invite Discord and Strife
to the holy wedding, especially when these goddesses were perpetual
enemies of Philology herself? And so from that region only Pluto
was invited, because he was the uncle of the bridegroom. [48]
From the fourth region came the goddess of primary matter,[75] and

[71] Such deities are mentioned in § 47.

[72] Cf. Pliny the Elder *Natural History* 2. 143. For a full discussion of the
religious lore in §§ 45-60, and its correlation with §§ 150-68, see S. Weinstock,
"Martianus Capella and the Cosmic System of the Etruscans," *Journal of Roman
Studies*, XXXVI (1946), 101-29.

[73] North; see Weinstock, p. 104. The regions are numbered in sequence from
north to east, south, west, and back to north, but in a spiral descent to earth, not
on one level; see Weinstock, p. 106. Thus they correlate with the account in
§§ 150-68.

[74] For this interpretation of *dii Novensiles*, see Weinstock, p. 107, citing
Arnobius *Adversus nationes* 3. 38.

[75] Weinstock's suggestion for *Lynsa silvestris* (p. 110). It is a daring interpretation, but accords with the "theology" of the passage and with Martianus'
fondness for oblique references. Any measure of certainty seems quite impossible.

Mulciber,[76] and Lar of the sky,[77] as well as the Warrior and Goodwill. [49] From the next region, traversing the domains of the royal couple, were invited Ceres, Tellurus,[78] and Vulcan, the father of earth, and Genius. [50] And you were invited from the sixth region, you sons of Jove, Pales and Goodwill; as well as Swiftness, the daughter of the sun; for Mars Quirinus and Genius were invited above. [51] From the seventh region were invited Liber and Pales of the second rank. After long deliberation, Jupiter decided also to invite Deceit, from the same region, because she had often been in complicity with the Cyllenian himself.

[52] The eighth region was passed over, because everyone from that region had been invited already, and only the child of Spring[79] came from there. [53] The Genius of Juno of Hospitality[80] was summoned from the ninth region. [54] And you, Neptune and Universal Lar,[81] and Neverita,[82] and you, Consus,[83] came from the tenth region. [55] From the next region came Fortune and Health and Goodwill the Shepherd; but the Manes [gods of the underworld][84] were not allowed to come, because they could not come into the sight of Jupiter. [56] From the twelfth region only Sancus

---

[76] Vulcan, who is mentioned again in § 49; thus this is the area of the sun, the East (see Weinstock, pp. 111-12).

[77] The recurrence of the unidentifiable *Lares* in this passage is one of its particular problems; see Weinstock, pp. 109-10.

[78] This is the only use in Latin of this name; Augustine (*City of God* 7. 23) quotes Varro in referring to this god as Tellumo.

[79] *Veris fructus:* literally, "the fruit of Spring"; the commentators do not agree on the interpretation of this appellation; see Kopp, *ad loc.*

[80] Weinstock (p. 127) explains this as a periphrasis for the wife of Neptune, and refers to § 81.

[81] Weinstock (p. 114) equates this figure with the *genius universalis* [universal guardian] of § 152; he states that it "would then represent the world soul of Platonizing cosmogonical narratives."

Kopp explains this second occurrence of Neptune (cf. § 47) by reference to his double role as a god of seas and of lakes.

[82] This name does not occur elsewhere in Latin; Lewis and Short identify it as a sea-goddess; there is no evidence for this.

[83] Consus is identified by Weinstock (p. 127) with Equestrian Neptune (*Poseidon Hippios*).

[84] According to Weinstock (p. 165): the good Manes; i.e., the Lares and Lemures (cf. §§ 160-62).

was invited. [57] From the next region the Fates were invited; but the other gods[85] of the Manes stayed there. [58] From the fourteenth region Saturn and his daughter Juno of the heavens were invited, of course. [59] From the fifteenth came Vejovis [Vediovis] and the lower-class gods.[86] [60] From the last region Nocturnus [god of night] and the Janitors [gods of the portals of earth] were invited in the same way. [61] When the gods had been summoned from all the quarters of heaven, the others whom they called the Unzoned,[87] were invited and urged to come by the Cyllenian himself.

[62] And then the patron deities of the elements and those who care for the public welfare and the things of the mind, and the whole host of heavenly powers who had all been forthwith invited by the command of Jove (and which of Numa's many successors could name them all?)[88] thronged into the great hall of heaven with its shimmering stars. [63] Then Janus stood on the threshold, and Jove's guard stood before the royal portals; Fame, serving as a herald, called out the names of all those who were to enter. [64] Inside the royal council chamber stood the woman called Adrastea,[89] who was whirling with a speed beyond recall a celestial urn and the divine destiny, while relentless Necessity[90] was catching the lots in her robe as they fell from the whirling globe. [65] Clotho, Lachesis, and Atropos, who by their study of true and correct writing recorded the decisions of Jove—being the librarians of the gods and the keepers of their archives—when they saw that the senate and council was being summoned and that the Thunderer himself was donning his magisterial

[85] According to Weinstock (p. 105): the evil Manes; i.e., the Larvae and Maniae (cf. §§ 163-64).

[86] For this interpretation of *dii publici,* see Weinstock, pp. 105-106.

[87] *Azonos.* This refers to gods of such status and importance that their influence is not restricted to a particular area of the heavens; hence, perhaps, the personal invitations by Mercury, instead of the authoritative summons by Jupiter; cf. Servius on *Aeneid* 12. 118.

[88] This seems to be the sense of Dick's text, but the text is seriously corrupt here. Willis suggests *quas Numae multus successor indigitat* [which Numa's many successors invoke]. Numa Pompilius was the second king of Rome, and was renowned for piety and religious lore.

[89] The daughter of Jupiter and Necessity, Adrastea rewards men for good deeds and punishes pride and arrogance.

[90] *Imarmene:* a Greek name, meaning "fated" or "destined."

lieved that he could become a young man. [71] His wife, a full-bodied matron of great age, ever so prolific and surrounded by her offspring, wore over her colorful and flowery dress a mantle of green, on which was the whole range of precious stones and metals and all the crops and produce of the fields in generous profusion. [72] With her came Vesta, who was the same age as she.[99] Vesta had been the nurse of Jove himself, and was said to have fondled him on her lap, and so she did not hesitate to kiss the head of the king. [73] Behind them was summoned golden Sol, with his radiant[100] sister. As soon as he began to approach the entrance, an intense purple glow preceded him, and the glory of his rosy brilliance lit the whole court of the palace and dimmed its other splendors. When he was about to enter, the first rays from his revered head shone before him, so that Jupiter himself stepped back a pace and was blinded by the intense glory of the godhead;[101] but the spheres and globes which he held in his right hand shone with the reflection of a light akin to their own. [74] But Juno, spectacular in ornaments of many colors and resplendent in the light of her varied jewels, was dazzling in her serene radiance. [75] Sol's head was encircled with a gleaming crown which glowed with the fire of twelve burning stones. Over his forehead were three stones—ruby, cat's-eye and onyx—which, by the flashing of their beams of light, hid his awesome face from the recognition of those looking on; they say that the first was taken to become the brain of Cancer, the second the eyes of Leo, the third the forehead of Gemini. Three other stones shone on either side of the crown, of which one was called beryl, the second

---

follows immediately on the close of the preceding year, when the sun returns in its tracks. It is not clear what Martianus means by saying that the number of days in the year is signified in the spelling of the dragon's name; the medieval commentators interpret this by claiming that the dragon's name is Greek, *Tex*, the letters of which have a numerical value totaling 365—but there is no such Greek word or name.

98 The reference is to Saturn, who represents winter.

99 Vesta is an earth-goddess; see Augustine *City of God* 7. 16 and 24 (based on Varro). But cf. below, §§ 168, 215, and n. 110 of Book II.

100 *candida:* an epithet applied to the moon in Vergil *Aeneid* 7. 8.

101 Pierre Courcelle regards this scene as based on the rituals of the cult of Hecate; *Les Lettres grecques en occident de Macrobe à Cassiodore*, 2d ed. (Paris, 1948), p. 203.

emerald, the third jasper; amidst the greenness, like light impregnated by sea, a certain deeper charm shone forth upon his countenance. On either side of sapphire were set *dendritis* and striped jasper. These stones by their colors gave greenery to the earth at fixed seasons of the year, which Spring and Autumn were said to bring regularly in their service to the deity. The back of the crown was set with *hydatis* [a water-colored stone], diamond, and crystal; these originated in the floods of Winter. You would think that the hair of the god himself had been sprinkled with gold dust and gilded.[102]

[76] As he entered, his face shone like a boy's, in mid-course he looked like a young man out of breath, while at the end of his course he seemed a declining old man;[103] there are some who think he has a dozen different appearances. His body was all fiery, his feet bore wings; his cloak was scarlet, thickly flecked with gold. [77] In his left hand he carried a glittering shield, in his right a flaming torch, while his shoes glowed like bronze. Beside him Luna reflected on her soft and gentle face the light of her brother's brilliance. [78] Behind them entered the brothers of Jove, one of whom was always greener than the ocean, the other sallow from shadowy darkness.[104] [79] Each of them wore on his head a garland suited to the kingdom that he governed; [80] for one garland was white as surf, the same hoary color as foam; the other was ebony with the blackness of subterranean night. The latter god was much richer than his brother, and was wealthy through the constant acquisition of whatever things come into being. The other, because of the extent and bulk of his body, was naked, and spat back the wealth that he engulfed. [81] Their wives were very different; the naked one

---

[102] Remigius understands the crown of Sol to represent the year, and the twelve stones to symbolize the twelve months, in four groups of three to match the four seasons: the first three for summer, the next for spring, the third for autumn, the last for winter. He explains at considerable length the characteristics of each stone and its aptness for the zodiacal sign and time of year with which it is matched.

The identification of the stones *dendritis* and *hydatis* is uncertain. Remigius suggests amber for the former.

[103] Cf. Macrobius *Saturnalia* 1. 18. 10.

[104] Neptune, the god of the sea; and Pluto, the god of the underworld.

brought with him the nurse of all things, the hostess of the gods;[105] the other brother had a young girl,[106] overjoyed at the accessions that came to them; she so readily gave the fruits of the earth to those who asked her that mankind swore by a great deity to pay her back one per cent.[107]

[82] Then the sons of the Thunderer himself entered, the first of whom was a young man of ruddy complexion who came forward to eat everything and to drink even blood; the next one was compliant and agreeable and held a sickle in his right hand, in his left the soporific bowl; he was being carried in, far-gone in wantonness. His steps were unsteady, his legs tripped each other, and he reeked of wine.[108] [83] Behind these came twins[109] identical in features—but one shining with the light of the morning star; the other, of the evening star. [84] Behind them came the god of incredible strength,[110] always ready to overthrow opposition; with sidelong glance Juno observed his amazing muscles and the gaping maw of his Cleonaean lion skin. [85] Together with them came two fair women:[111] one said to be the mother of all conception; the other a virgin. The latter had a bow and a quiver; the other, a garland of plaited roses in the form of an X.[112] You would love to see her in her splendor, to hear her murmuring sweet blandishments, draw her to you scented with the perfume of her eager breast, kiss her, fondle her body, sigh with desire of her. Yet, although she is reckoned to be mother of all

105 Neptune's wife is called Amphitrite, among other titles; she is a goddess of water, whether salt or fresh; she is called the nurse of all things, since water is the support of all things; and she is called hostess of the gods, because the stars, who are regarded as gods, are received into the ocean at their setting.

106 Pluto's wife is Proserpina, a fertility goddess.

107 Scotus and Remigius explain that the earth gives back a hundredfold the seed sown in it, and therefore men dedicated one per cent of their crops as sacrifice, which seemed enough to ensure the goodwill of Proserpina. Grotius (cited by Kopp, *ad loc.*) concurs with this explanation, and quotes Ovid in support.

108 The first of the sons is Mars; the second, Bacchus.

109 These are Castor and Pollux, the zodiacal sign Gemini.

110 Hercules.

111 Venus and Diana.

112 *Decussatim* occurs elsewhere only once in Vitruvius and once in Columella; it is derived from the Latin *decem* [ten] and means "in the form of a ten"; hence "in the form of an X."

love and pleasure, to this same goddess man used to attribute the patronage of modesty.[113] [86] Kindly Ceres was seen with them, a most venerable woman, nurse of earth and nurse of men. [87] There also came a craftsman, a cripple[114] who was thought to be the son of Juno, though he was called by Heraclitus the one who slows down the whole world.[115]

[88] And then the most talkative of girls came flaunting and jumping about with nimble lightness, constantly unstable,[116] extravagant now one way, now the other; some call her Sors, some Nemesis, many Tyche, and others Nortia. She carried in her ample bosom the honors and decorations of the whole world, and conferred them on some people, distributing them unexpectedly; while like a girl she plucked the hair of others, beating[117] others on the head with a rod; while the same people she had formerly flattered she wounded with frequent blows[118] of her knuckles on their heads. [89] She soon saw the Fates observing everything that was going on in the council chamber of Jove; she ran to their books and notes, and with reckless boldness helter-skelter snatched up what she saw: so that some things, suddenly starting from their place, upset, as it were, the due order of things; but others, which were common knowledge through a providential system of cause and effect, she could not render unforeseen, and therefore she claimed them as due to her own efforts. Others came along in a crowd behind her. [90] Jupiter then sat down[119] on his throne and ordered them all to be seated in order of

[113] Venus was of course identified with the Greek goddess Aphrodite, who had the two titles Urania and Pandemus. Plato in his *Symposium* regarded the first as representing spiritual love; the second, physical love. This separation was not evident in the ancient cult, but Martianus was presumably referring to the Platonic concept.

[114] Hephaestus (Vulcan).

[115] Translating Dick's *demorator*. This word is not found elsewhere in Latin, and may not be the correct reading. Willis suggests *moderator;* the sense would then be "the one who regulates . . .".

[116] *fluibunda*. This word is not found elsewhere in Latin. The woman is a goddess of fate or destiny, therefore capricious and erratic.

[117] The diction echoes phrases of Roman comedy (e.g., Plautus *Rudens* 1118).

[118] Martianus: *ictibus crebris verticem complicatisque in condylos digitis vulnerabat;* cf. Apuleius *Metamorphoses* 6. 22: *convulneraris assiduis ictibus crebrisque terrenae libidinis foedaveris casibus.*

[119] Martianus: *Iuppiter tunc solio resedit;* cf. Vergil *Aeneid* 1. 506: *Solioque alte subnixa resedit.*

merit. Seats of flame supported the starry host; a boy wearing a crown[120] gave the signal for silence with his finger held to his lips. "All fell silent, and were hushed with concentration."[121] [91] Then Jupiter began:

"People of the stars, my well-known beneficence compels me to bring before you my most secret decision, and it suits me to make public a matter that required only a silent act of will; otherwise, I would be able to lay before you accomplished facts carried out at my commands, and no rival would desire by unlawful endeavor to overthrow the commands of the father of the gods. A judgment of woe is better kept hidden: silence suppresses the inexpressible thoughts, lest, being uttered, they disturb our hearts with sorrow. But when a father has joyful news to tell, and by his binding assent will publicly join his children in a firm union, it is pointless not to want his appropriate sentiments to be known. And so I want to tell you, deities, my dear kinfolk, the news of my son's betrothal. Indeed, I think it right that the gods should at the beginning put their seal of approval on the course that is to be followed. [92] You know that Maia's son has in my heart the place due to a celebrated son. I have good reason for the love I bear him; he is accustomed to pluck his father's heartstrings. For he is my trust, my speech, my beneficence, and my true genius, the loyal messenger and spokesman of my mind, the sacred Nous.[122] He alone can give the number of the gods, he alone can know the glittering stars, the dimension of the heavens and their depth; he knows the number of the ebb tides, how great are the flood tides the ocean sweeps along its shores; he knows the bond that joins the contrary elements, and I, the father, enforce those bonds through him—perhaps Duty[123] alone will reckon what rewards this obedience will pay. For though he often flies up in front

---

[120] Harpocrates, the Egyptian god of silence. Cf. Catullus 74. 41; Varro *De lingua latina* 5. 57; Augustine *City of God* 18. 5. Martianus: *puer ad os compresso digito salutari silentium commonebat;* cf. Ovid *Metamorphoses* 9. 692 (depicting an Egyptian scene): *quique premit vocem digitoque silentia suadet.*

[121] A quotation from Vergil *Aeneid* 2. 1.

[122] A reference to the Neoplatonic concept of Mind as a divine emanation of the divine One.

[123] *Pietas* is personified as the goddess of duty, who assesses the reward for Mercury's obedience.

of the team of Phoebus, does he not slip back again into his role of attendant?[124] Furthermore, he is so devoted to the honors of his uncles, that it is hard to say who has the stronger claim on him. Years spent in devoted service argue that he should be allowed duly to marry; and besides, his youthful vigor is an added incentive to marriage. [93] The girl who has taken his fancy is extremely learned and his equal in study; she is earthborn, but destined to rise to the stars; often in her swift circuits she outstrips Mercury and encompasses the terrestrial globe.[125] That her earthly upbringing may be no obstacle to this noble girl, O gods, we must consider and remember that your childhood rattles are kept on earth,[126] which temples conceal in their inner sanctuaries. Let them start their married life in equality, as is fitting, and let them add to the number of stars with descendants of mine."[127]

[94] When Jupiter had finished, the whole assembly of gods was called together to vote, and they all shouted that the marriage should take place forthwith; and to Jove's opinion they added their own, that those mortals whose elevated lives and high deserts had raised them to desire heaven and to acquire a taste for celestial affairs, should be coopted into the number of the gods; [95] and soon, amongst others whom the Nile or Thebes proffered—Aeneas, Romulus, and others who afterward won a place among the stars through the fame of their learning—should be specifically named inhabitants of heaven, so that after their bodily life they should become members of the court of heaven.[128] [96] When Jove had approved this, a certain dignified and striking woman called Philosophy was ordered to have this decree of the heavenly assembly cut on bronze tablets and published in heaven and on earth. [97] Then Juno an-

---

[124] A reference to the heliocentric motions of Mercury; cf. § 25 above.

[125] That is, intellectual power, personified by Philology, is faster than the movements of the planets.

[126] A picturesque reference to the ancient belief that most of the gods spent their infancy and childhood on earth; cf. Arnobius *Adversus nationes* 4. 21.

[127] Kopp likens Jupiter's speech here to his speech to the gods at the deification of Hercules in Ovid *Metamorphoses* 9. 243-58.

[128] Cf. Cicero *De natura deorum* 1. 38; Augustine *City of God* 18. 21. Egypt generally and the river Nile in particular were regarded as the places of origin of many ancient gods; Thebes in Greece was particularly associated with Bacchus. This whole passage is comparing the new Roman gods with the older Greek and Egyptian ones.

nounced that because of the marriage of these celebrated young people and the ceremonies that had to be performed, all that assembly
of gods was to reassemble at dawn on the next day in the palace
which formed the principal home of Jove the arbiter in the Milky
Way. At the end of these proceedings, the king himself arose from his
throne, and all that number of gods dispersed to their own celestial
homes and orbits.[129]

[129] The gods are identified with stars and planets; cf. § 29 and § 186; also
Augustine *City of God* 7. 7, citing Varro.

BOOK II

The Marriage

[98] When Phoebus had set, Night with her starry reins began to climb the limpid heavens, summoning the glittering constellations.[1] Then old Boötes kindled the lofy Plaustra [the Wain], and the stars of Draco fierce with coils shone out: Orion now flamed forth in golden armor, drawing in his sultry ascent gleaming Sirius; and that glowing figure too who was arrayed with the flowers of the Nysaean [Bacchus] was crowned with a circlet of varied light.[2] Meantime Rumor sped through the trembling ears of the maiden, while Jove's palace was filled[3] with a great shouting.

[99] At length, when she learned the decrees of the gods, Philology, wakeful though the night was now far advanced, pondered long and anxiously[4] with great concern. First she must enter the heavenly assembly, and she must be examined by Jove without preparation, and she must migrate to the heavens and to the gods' way of life. [100] Then again, she was to be united to the Cyllenian, whom admittedly she had always desired with a remarkable passion, but whom she had barely glimpsed while she was picking blooms amongst certain select little herbs[5] and he was running back after being anointed for exercise. What is this? Was she anxiously wondering whether this grand marriage was in her own interest?[6] She

[1] Martianus: *fulgentia sidera Phoebo;* cf. Manilius *Astronomica* 1. 652: *fulgentia sidera ponto.*

[2] This is the Corona Ariadnes.

[3] Martianus: *magno dum complet tecta boatu;* cf. Vergil *Aeneid* 2. 679: *gemitu tectum omne replebat;* also *Aeneid* 7. 502: *atque imploranti similis tectum omne replebat.*

[4] Martianus: *multa secum ingenti cura anxia retractabat;* cf. Ovid *Metamorphoses* 9. 275: *longis anxia curis.*

[5] According to Remigius, the meaning of the allegory is that Philology beholds Mercury, or eloquence, while she is engaged in mastering the rudiments of grammar and literary studies: in other words, we discover and attain eloquence only through the study of the basic liberal arts.

[6] This passage recalls Vergil's picture of Dido, queen of Carthage, contemplating union with Aeneas in Book 4 of the *Aeneid.*

had a fear,[7] not without substance, that after she had ascended to the sky, she would forgo altogether the myths and legends of mankind, those charming poetic diversities of the Milesian tales.

[101] And so, first she sought from numbers to discover whether a marriage would be beneficial and whether the winged swiftness of the celestial whirlwind[8] would unite with her by a suitable bond in the harmony of marriage. [102] She soon counted up on her fingers the number of letters in her own name and that of the Cyllenian—not the name which the conflicting stories of different nations had given him, not the name which the different rituals of peoples, varying according to the interests and cults of each place, had created, but that name which Jove himself had settled upon him by a celestial proclamation at his birth and which the faulty research of man had claimed was made known only through the ingenuities of the Egyptians. She took from each end of his name the bounding element that is both the first and the perfect terminus of number.[9] Next came that number which is worshiped as Lord in all temples, for its cubic solidity.[10] In the next position she took a letter which the Samian sage regarded as representing the dual ambiguity of mortal fate.[11] Accordingly, the number 1218 flashed forth. [103] Diminishing

---

[7] Martianus: *non cassa opinatione formidat;* cf. Arnobius *Adversus nationes* 1. 31: *rumoris cassi opinatione;* and Apuleius *Metamorphoses* 8. 5: *cassa formidine.*

[8] Martianus: *aetherii verticis pennata rapiditas;* cf. Apuleius *Metamorphoses* 6. 30: *pinnatam Pegasi vincebas celeritatem.*

[9] Grotius first discerned that Martianus is referring to the Egyptian god Thouth, who was identified with Mercury; the whole passage is based on the numerical value of the Greek letters in the name θωύθ. The letter at the beginning and the end of the name, the "bounding element," is θ, which in Greek numeration represents 9. Nine is the terminus of the series 1 to 9, the decad; it is the first such terminus, being prior to that in 19, 29, and so on; it is the perfect terminus, because it is the square of 3, which is itself one of the most highly regarded numbers in ancient numerology. (For further explication, see W. H. Stahl's Introduction, above, Vol. I, pp. 36-37.)

[10] This refers to the number 800, which in Greek is represented by the letter ω; since 8 is the cube of 2, and 100 is the square of 10, their product would obviously be extremely important to numerologists.

[11] The "Samian sage" is Pythagoras: the letter alluded to is the Greek Y, whose forked shape represents the parting of ways and symbolizes the choice between good and evil in human life; its numerical value is 400. See Servius on *Aeneid* 6. 136; Jerome *Letters* 107. 6; Lactantius *Institutiones divinae* 6. 3. 9.

this figure by the rule of nine, by substituting units for the tens, she cleverly reduced it to the number three.[12] [104] Her own name, which was set out in numeral form as 724, she reduced to the number four;[13] these two numbers (three and four) are marked by a harmonious relationship with each other. [105] For the number three is certainly perfect, because it may be rationally arranged as a beginning, a middle, and an end; it alone both makes a line and defines the surfaces of solids (for solids are defined by length and depth);[14] furthermore, the triplication of the number three is the first to yield a cube from the odd numbers. Who does not know the threefold harmonies in music? And an odd number is attributed to masculinity. All time changes in a threefold sequence;[15] the number three is also the seedbed of perfect numbers, namely of six and of nine, by different forms of connection.[16]

[106] It is therefore properly associated with the god of rationality. But Philology, because she is herself a most learned woman, although she is reckoned amongst the female (even) numbers, yet is made perfect by complete computation. For the number four with its parts makes up the whole power of the decad itself[17] and is therefore perfect and is called quadrate, as is the Cyllenian himself, with whom are associated the four seasons of the year, the regions of heaven, the elements of earth.[18] [107] That celebrated oath of old Pythagoras, who did not refrain from swearing "by the tetrad"— what does that signify except the number of perfect ratio? Within itself it contains the one, the dual, the triad, and is itself the square of two, within which proportions the musical harmonies are produced.

[12] See Varro De lingua latina 9. 86. The "rule of nine" was known to classical mathematicians. When any number is divided by 9, the remainder is the same as that left when the sum of the digits in the original number is divided by 9. In this instance, 1218 divided by 9 leaves a remainder of 3; likewise the sum of 1, 2, 1, and 8—that is, 12—when divided by 9 leaves a remainder of 3.

[13] The sum of the numerical values of the letters in the name Philologia in Greek amounts to 724; applying the same procedures as with the name Thouth, we arrive at the number 4.

[14] Dick would delete this parenthesis from the text.

[15] Past, present, and future.

[16] That is, multiplication by 2 and by 3, an even and an odd number.

[17] All the numbers from 1 to 10 are made up of the numbers from 1 to 4 or some addition or multiplication amongst them. Furthermore, $1+2+3+4=10$.

[18] Cf. Macrobius Commentary on the Dream of Scipio 1. 6. 40-44; and Saturnalia 1. 19. 14-15.

For the ratio three to four is called the epitritus in arithmetical calculation, and it is named the fourth by musicians. Within it lies the
ratio three to two, which is a hemiolius, and these two numbers produce the secondary concord called a fifth. The third harmony is
called the octave by musicians and is produced by a double ratio
that is in the proportion of one to two. And so the number four, being
perfect, contains all the concords within its parts, and by the distribution of harmonies it brings together the whole range of songs.
Thus, in her examination of agreement among numbers, the clever
maiden was delighted. [108] Then she joined them with each other,
and three joined to four makes the heptad [seven]. But this number is the perfection of the celestial rationality, as the fullness of
sevens testifies. For what else is shown by the passage of the fated
climacteric, by the circuits and movements of the planets, and by the
viability of the fetus in the seventh month in the darkness of the
womb?[19] Furthermore, three times three makes nine, while four
doubled gives eight. But the proportion nine to eight gives the ratio
of the *epogdous* [major ninth][20] and it has the same value in number
as the full octave has in music, which [octave] produces the full
tone—that is, a sustained tone of a consonant unity. As a result, there
was no intermediate number to upset the harmony and sequence,
and the numbers suited each other by their congruent juxtaposition.

[109] Thus the numbers represented by their names were in concord. Therefore the concord established between them bound their
nuptial union with a true proportion, so that the maiden delighted in
a marriage so advantageous to herself; but being circumspect, she
was disturbed for another reason. For although having no misgivings
about her mental capacities, she began to fear for her appearance,
her form and physical substance; not without reason was she in a
state of trepidation at the spheres of celestial flame[21] through which

19 The climacteric, or change of life, was believed to occur in the male in the
fifty-sixth year, and 56 is the product of 7 and 8, two significant numbers; there
are seven planets; the seventh month of gestation was regarded as marking the
viability of the human fetus; Martianus brings all this evidence to attest the importance of the number seven, cf. Macrobius *Commentary* 1. 6. 45-83. For a
fuller discussion of the arithmological passages in Martianus, see W. H. Stahl's
comments above, Vol. I, pp. 152-54.

20 Cf. Macrobius *Commentary* 2. 1. 20.

21 Martianus: *flammarum caelestium globos;* cf. Vergil *Georgics* 1. 473:
flammarumque globos; and *Aeneid* 3. 574: *globos flammarum.*

she must pass, the fires of burning stars which she must endure, though her limbs were still those of a mortal and exhausted because of their meager thinness. [110] But against this she prepared a certain ointment of the old man of Abdera[22] in which she put many herbs and green shoots[23] mixed in. A magic preparation of the Colchian herb "hundred heads" is given a special power by the inclusion of a tuft of *adamantis*;[24] she was putting this up as some defense against the fires of heaven and the neighborhood of the gods to protect her appearance from the radiance of beauty.[25] Then, in the reflection of the moon, she smeared the dewy fluid[26] on her body.

[22] Democritus, the atomistic philosopher of the fifth to fourth centuries B.C., who was represented in later Greek writing as a magician; see Albin Lesky, *History of Greek Literature*, tr. James Willis and Cornelis De Heer (London, 1965), p. 340; cf. Pliny *Natural History* 24. 156,160.

[23] Martianus: *lapillis surculisque permixtis;* cf. Apuleius *Metamorphoses* 2. 5: *surculis et lapillis.*

[24] The text of this passage is corrupt and the meaning obscure; as Kopp says "it awaits its Oedipus." *Fiducia*, something in which one trusts, I have translated as "a magic preparation." Colchis, the home of Medea, was renowned for magic and for herbs. Martianus' words *in centum voces continuata* [extended to a hundred voices] I have taken to be a periphrasis for the herb *centum capita* (*eryngium campestre*), described by Pliny (*Natural History* 22. 20) as having antivenin, medicinal, and aphrodisiac properties and being of interest to Magi and Pythagoreans. Pliny (24. 157-67) also describes other plants of interest to Pythagoras, Democritus, and Magi; one of these is *adamantis* (*ibid.,* 162), whose two characteristics are that it cannot be crushed and that it tames lions; *impressio*, which I have translated as "inclusion," can mean a squeezing or crushing. Pierre Boyancé interprets this passage as a reference to mystic rituals of Neopythagoreanism; see "Une allusion à l'oeuf Orphique," École française de Rome. *Mélanges d'archéologie et d'histoire*, LII (1935), 95-96. Kopp regards the reference to "a hundred" as a clumsy erudite pun, since one tradition regards Medea's mother as Hecate, and *hecaton* is the Greek word for "a hundred." I have based my translation of this sentence on Boyancé, and my translation of the next on Kopp's paraphrase of it.

[25] Philology appears to be preparing an ointment which will protect her from the heat and brilliance through which she must travel, just as Medea prepared an ointment to render Jason invulnerable to fire and thus to protect him from the fire-breathing bulls; or as Phoebus anointed Phaëthon with such an ointment to protect him, a mortal, as he drove the chariot of the sun (Ovid *Metamorphoses* 2. 122-23). Since Philology applies the ointment to her body in the moonlight, there is obviously a connection between this magic and the moon.

[26] Martianus: *irrorati liquoris allinibat unguentum;* cf. Ovid *Metamorphoses* 1. 371: *libatos inroravere liquores.*

[111] While the maiden was arranging this, her attendant Periergia,[27] whether sent by the maiden's mother or by her own concern (for she was her foster sister), perceived what she was doing. [112] When she peeped through the chinks of the door and saw Philology making these arrangements, she began to rebuke another of her handmaids—whose name was Wakefulness[28] and who acted as guard within the bedroom—because she had not allowed the maiden even a little sleep[29] to preserve her beauty, although Wakefulness herself was able to do all these things if Philology commanded her. [113] For she claimed that she had already gone around to many places and had found out what skills, what dress and ornaments her dowry-slaves should assume. It was also not unknown to her what the bridegroom himself was doing, what was happening at Jove's palace, whether Leucothea was lighting her torch and her ruddy light, whether the oarsmen of the sun were awake and the horse of Phosphoros [the daystar] was being groomed. She added innumerable details of this kind, which she had noted by diligent scrutiny.

[114] Suddenly Philology's mother, Phronesis [Wisdom], burst into[30] the privacy of the bedroom. When Philology saw her she ran to her and kissed her bosom reverently and told her of the aids she had prepared; but the mother stripped her daughter of the clothing and ornaments in which she would have had the courage to enter the society of the gods. She gave her a dress and robe white as milk, which seemed made of that fleece from the precious shrub in which, they say, the sages of India and the inhabitants of the mountain of shadow are clothed, and of threads of shining cotton, as much as that country produces.[31] Then she placed on her head a virginal

27 The word *periergia*, in Greek or Latin, means overelaboration, the taking of excessive pains, and is used by Quintilian in reference to rhetorical style (*Institutiones Oratoriae* 8. 3. 55). It is interesting to note that the term, which in Greek and in Quintilian is pejorative, was apparently highly regarded by Martianus, as reflected in his own labored style and in his use of the term to personify a kinswoman of Philology.

28 *Agrypnia* [Sleeplessness, or Wakefulness] is mentioned again in § 145.

29 Martianus: *paululum conivere;* cf. Apuleius *Metamorphoses* 1. 11: *paululum coniveo.*

30 Martianus: *secretum cubiculi repente Phronesis mater irrupit;* cf. Apuleius *Metamorphoses* 9. 2: *cubiculum . . . protinus inrupissem.*

31 The fleece mentioned may be silk: it was believed to grow on trees, and the

crown, which shone brightly with the luster of its central gem, from which gleamed forth, cut deep into the stone, like the Trojan Palladium, a maiden wearing a helmet and with her face shielded. [115] The mother thoughtfully also took off the belt which she was wearing and put it on Philology, to make her more appropriately dressed, so that she should not be without the adornments of Phronesis herself. Furthermore, she tied on her feet slippers of pleated papyrus so that no carrion[32] should defile her feet. The maiden's hands were filled with an incense box, shining and heavy with spice.

[116] And now Aurora, with the modesty befitting a goddess, began to hide the stars with her rosy gown, while kindly day flashed upon the darkness, Dione shone with jewels, and in one gold star Phosphoros appeared. Then glittering frost congeals on the gentle dew, the flocks batter the sheepfold to get to their morning pasture,[33] while worry gnaws and beats at weary[34] hearts, and sleep, driven out, flees to Lethean shores.

[117] Before the door, sweet music with manifold charms was raised, the chorus of assembled Muses singing[35] in well-trained harmony to honor the marriage ceremony. Flutes, lyres, the grand swell of the water organ blended in tuneful song and with a melodious ending as they became silent for an appropriate interval of unaccompanied singing by the Muses. Then the entire chorus with melodious voices and sweet harmony outstripped the beauty of all the instrumental music, and the following words were poured forth in notes of sacred song:

"Ascend into the temples of heaven, maiden, deserving of such a marriage; your father-in-law Jupiter asks you to rise to the lofty stars."

[118] Then, while the others kept quiet a moment, Urania began:[36]

---

brahmins of India were said to wear it—or it may be the produce of the cotton tree mentioned by Pliny (*Natural History* 12. 21). "The inhabitants of the mountain of shadow" cannot be clearly identified.

[32] It was a common ancient belief that dead bodies of humans or animals defiled sacred things; cf. Varro *De lingua latina* 7. 84; Servius on *Aeneid* 4. 518; Ovid *Fasti* 1. 629.

[33] This picture and its diction recall to some extent Vergil *Georgics* 3. 318-26.

[34] Martianus: *pulsant pectora;* cf. Lucan *Pharsalia* 7. 128: *pectora pulsant.*

[35] As at the wedding of Psyche in Apuleius *Metamorphoses* 6. 24.

[36] Compare the content of this hymn with that of 22 above. Urania is usually regarded as the Muse of astronomy.

"With trust in the divine will and without disputing, behold the assemblies of the stars and the sacred vaults of the heavens; you formerly studied what cause whirled the interdependent spheres, now as their leader you shall assign causes to their sweeping motions. You shall perceive what is the fabric that connects their circuits, what bond encompasses them, and what huge spheres are enclosed within a curving orbit; you will see what drives on and what delays courses of the planets, which rays of the sun inflame the moon or diminish its light, what substance kindles the stars in heaven, and how great are the bodies which heaven spins around, what is the providence of the gods, and what its mode of operation. Ascend into the temples of heaven, maiden, deserving of such a marriage; your father-in-law Jupiter asks you to rise to the lofty stars."

[119] Then sang Calliope:[37]

"Always a friend to the favoring Muses, for you Magnesian[38] rivers and the fountain of the Gorgonian horse[39] have poured your drink, for you the Aonid peak,[40] green with garlands, puts forth its leaves, while Cirrha[41] prepares violets; you know how to chant prophecies to the sweet Muses and to play the lyre of Pindar, and at your word the strings and the sacred plectrum know how to pour forth the Thracian song. Light of our lives, praise always our sacred songs and approve the music that we play. Ascend into the temples of heaven, maiden, deserving of such a marriage; your father-in-law Jupiter asks you to rise to the lofty stars."

[120] Thus sang Polymnia:[42]

"You have been exalted and, though recently of mortal blood, are now endowed with godhead; at last you reap the rewards of

---

[37] Calliope is usually regarded as the Muse of heroic and epic poetry.

[38] Magnesia is a peninsula in northeastern Greece closely associated with Mount Olympus, the Vale of Tempe, and the region of Pieria, all haunts of the Muses.

[39] The Gorgonian horse was Pegasus; the fountain, Hippocrene—the inspiring fountain of the Muses—which burst forth where Pegasus struck the ground with his hoof. The phrase clearly echoes Juvenal Satires 3. 18.

[40] Aonia was a region of Boeotia. The reference is probably to Mount Helicon, sacred to Apollo and the Muses.

[41] The ancient seaport for Delphi; cf. above, § 11.

[42] Polymnia is usually regarded as the Muse of mime, though this hymn deals mainly with rhythm and scansion.

your efforts: the shining sky, the abodes of the gods, and the companionship of Jove. You are used to combining and dispersing a variety of sounds according to the rules of rhythm, to assessing then which syllable, marked with the macron, is pronounced with circumflexion, which with the mark of brevity the micron curves; to assessing melodies and tones and tunes and all such knowledge, and all that can, when the mind is urged to it, gain the heights of heaven. Ascend into the temples of heaven, maiden, deserving of such a marriage; your father-in-law Jupiter asks you to rise to the lofty stars."

[121] Thus sang Melpomene:[43]

"You are accustomed to sing tragic songs for the theater, or wear the boot of comedy and echo the songs which under your care we offered when sweet music aided us; now to you, maiden,[44] our champion and our expositor, made immortal by the theme of your song, to you I sing. For I am happy to adorn your bridal chamber, and may my garlands be acceptable in your service. May you ever seem worthy of an Olympian wedding, ever fairer than the other gods. Ascend into the temples of heaven, maiden, deserving of such a marriage; your father-in-law Jupiter asks you to rise to the lofty stars."

[122] Thus sang Clio:[45]

"You sound forth in the guise of the rhetorician and set free by your passion the man accused, you link together contrary sentiments, building up sophisms by heaping together arguments, now binding something together by the rule of grammar, clever at using your gift of fine speech to play with words that by their double meaning destroy the ordinary sense; now gaze upon the starry threshold of the sky and enjoy the holy whiteness of heaven, for it is precious to see that in its true light. Ascend into the temples of heaven, maiden, deserving of such a marriage; your father-in-law Jupiter asks you to rise to the lofty stars."

[123] Next spoke Erato:[46]

[43] Melpomene is usually regarded as the Muse of tragic drama; Martianus appears to associate her with comedy also.

[44] The diction echoes Vergil *Aeneid* 8. 514.

[45] Clio is usually regarded as the Muse of history; Martianus associates her with rhetoric.

[46] Erato is usually regarded as the Muse of lyric and love poetry.

"O famous maiden, to whom the palace of the Thunderer is open, source of the arts, rightly is the world subject to you, since it was from the beginning apprehended by your rational principles. Why the sacred lightning flashes, whence the echoing thunder[47] sounds, what drives the moisture through the opening of the sky when the storm clouds gather, what is brought back by the clearness of spring when the rain clouds march away, why the circle of the year spins round to end all the hurrying centuries—we avow that secrets unknown to others are known to you alone. Ascend into the temples of heaven, maiden, deserving of such a marriage; your father-in-law Jupiter asks you to rise to the lofty stars."

[124] Then sang Terpsichore:[48]

"I am delighted, dear maiden, that through this honor you gain a sight of the stars! Your industry and the genius of your nature have won this for you. That wakeful concentration[49] of yours bestowed this honor on your lucubrations. Having toiled day and night[50] on the sacred writings, and knowing the future and being ready to learn, you have understood what the Stoics offer in their sacrifices when the flame puffs from the kindling. For without misgivings, with unhesitating utterance, you anticipate what the smoke tells on the flaming altars of the Sabaeans, what message is brought by air thick with the ash of incense, or what the sure signs foretell by prophetic voices. Ascend into the temples of heaven, maiden, deserving of such a marriage; your father-in-law Jupiter asks you to rise to the lofty stars."

[125] Then Euterpe[51] began:

"O maiden, our guide to skillful prophecy, who could ascend to heaven and bring down to pure souls the sacred teachings by which they were able to know themselves, and by which they dis-

---

[47] The diction echoes Vergil *Aeneid* 2. 692; and, more closely, Calpurnius *Eclogues* 1. 86. The hymn as a whole recalls Vergil *Georgics* 2. 475-82; Ovid *Metamorphoses* 15. 68-72; and Claudian *Panegyric on the Consulship of Flavius Manlius Theodorus* 100-12. The tone of all these passages recalls Lucretius, perhaps especially *De rerum natura* 5. 55-109. Presumably the exposition of the secrets of nature was a cliché among classical versifiers.

[48] Terpsichore is usually regarded as the Muse of dance.

[49] Martianus: *cura vigil;* as in Ovid *Ars amatoria* 3. 411.

[50] Martianus: *perdia pernoxque;* cf. Apuleius *Metamorphoses* 5. 6: *et perdia et pernox.*

[51] Euterpe is usually regarded as the Muse of flute music.

cerned and saw with a clear light the decrees of fate and the
countenances of the spirits, and who allotted stars to be the minds
of Plato and Pythagoras,[52] and who has ordered ephemeral creatures to behold the decree of heaven with all obscurity removed:[53]
rightly ascend to the senate of the Thunderer, you who alone are
fit to be married[54] to Mercury. Ascend into the temples of heaven,
maiden, deserving of such a marriage; your father-in-law Jupiter
asks you to rise to the lofty stars."

[126] Then Thalia[55] spoke:

"O blessed maiden, who take up the marriage bond amid such a
singing of the stars, and with such approval from the universe become a daughter-in-law[56] of the Thunderer: of which god are
you to become the wife? He alone on wandering wing, alert for
sudden storms, flies out beyond the stars of the universe, and when
he has crossed the straits on high, returns to Tartarus. He alone is
able to wield his famous staff before the chariot and white
horses[57] of the high father; he alone gladly restores the fortunes
of Osiris[58] as he falls, whom the father of the gods knows to be
weighed down by the life-giving seed[59] he has discovered; to Mercury his stepmother gladly gave her milky breast;[60] his powerful
caduceus[61] counteracts dread poison; and when he speaks, all

[52] In Neoplatonism and certain other forms of ancient belief, the minds and
souls of man came from stars and returned to become stars.

[53] Martianus: *nube remota;* as in Marius Victor *Alethia* 1. 402.

[54] Martianus: *foedere iungi;* cf. Vergil *Aeneid* 4. 112: *foedera iungi.*

[55] Thalia is usually regarded as the Muse of comedy.

[56] Martianus: *nurus addero Tonanti;* cf. Statius *Achilleid* 1. 655: *nurus addita
ponto.*

[57] Martianus: *ante currum / et candidos iugales;* cf. Vergil *Aeneid* 7. 280:
currum geminosque iugalis.

[58] See Book I, n. 14. After the discovery of Osiris' dismembered body, Isis
reassembled the fragments with the aid of Thouth, the Egyptian counterpart of
Mercury.

[59] Osiris in Egyptian mythology gave the world barley, a staple food in Egypt
(Diodorus Siculus *Bibliotheca historica* 1. 14. 1; 1. 15. 56).

[60] Juno suckled the infant Mercury.

[61] Mercury's staff. He is said to have separated with this staff two snakes
that he found fighting (Hyginus *Astronomica* 2. 7). This is allegorized as the
power of eloquence in settling quarrels, which is Martianus' theme here. Editors
refer to Vergil *Eclogues* 8. 71; Ovid *Metamorphoses* 7. 203; and other passages
which express the ancient belief that serpents could be destroyed by magical

venom is dissolved. He is learned among the gods; but this girl is still more learned. Now, now the arts are blessed, which you two so sanctify that they allow men to rise to heaven and open to them the stars and allow holy prayers to fly up to the clear sky. Through you the mind's intelligence,[62] alert and noble, fills the uttermost depth, through you proven eloquence brings everlasting glory. You bless all subjects, and you bless us, the Muses."

[127] While the Muses thus wove their web of song, now singly, now in unison, and in turn repeated their sweet melodies, there came into the maiden's quarters and her bedroom some matrons dressed with commendable sobriety, their faces beautiful without artifice but glowing with the charm of simplicity. One of them, scrupulous in her careful examination,[63] who checked everything with analytical care, was said to be called Prudence. [128] Her sister gave to all their due, and to no one what had not been deserved; she was said to bear the name Justice. [129] The third was praiseworthy for her restraint and contempt of gifts, and from her self-control she received the name Temperance. [130] The last one was very brave and always steadfast in bearing all hardships, ready too with strength of body to undertake all labors; her name was Strength. They approached to embrace and kiss Philology; but when they saw her in her bedroom, cowering full of fear, shunning the light of day, and numb with hesitancy, they turned her body and head into their full view and made her show her face.

[131] After these, there entered a dignified woman,[64] with flowing hair, who was very proud of the fact that through her Jupiter permitted anyone to ascend to the heavens.[65] When the maiden saw

---

incantations; but this seems inappropriate here. Martianus' language is typically tortuous (lit. "by his powerful wand dread poison is amazed; all venom makes a twin orb for him when he speaks"); yet the last two clauses seem to imply reconciliation rather than destruction.

[62] *Nus* [Nous]: this word, which commonly means the divine Mind (Neoplatonic terminology), is not found with the simple meaning of "intelligence" elsewhere in Latin.

[63] Martianus: *circumspectione cautissima;* cf. Apuleius *Metamorphoses* 11. 19: *cautoque circumspectu.*

[64] Philosophy.

[65] See Cicero *De natura deorum* 2. 62, and *De legibus* 2. 19, for the belief that humans may be admitted to heaven and the company of the gods for exceptional merit.

her, she ran to her with the deepest affection, inasmuch as the new-comer herself had prophesied, with certain confidence based on knowledge, that Philology would ascend to heaven, and now the woman had been sent to Philology by Maia's son himself [Mer-cury] to conduct her to the marriage. [132] Besides, three splendid girls of equal beauty in face and bearing, clasping each other's hands and wearing garlands of roses, approached the maiden. One of them kissed Philology on the forehead on the smooth skin between the eyebrows, the second embraced her face, the third her waist; the first that "she might breathe joy and honor into her eyes,"[66] the second laid grace upon her tongue, and the third gave her gentle-ness of spirit. They were called the Graces, and they bestowed charm on whatever they touched. After they had filled the maiden with light, they mingled with the Muses and broke into the rhythmic movements[67] and steps of the wedding dance. [133] Then they all danced together, with a great booming of tambours and ringing of cymbals, so much that the sound of the Muses was to some extent drowned by the booming sound of the tambours. To this accom-paniment a palanquin was brought in, bedecked with stars, to which they sang their loud songs with the ritual of the mysteries, as was the custom when a goddess-bride was entering the bond of celestial matrimony. [134] There stood before her a woman of reverend countenance, shining with holy and celestial light in all the dignity of a priestess. All the company, when they saw her, paid homage to her glorious majesty as the guardian of all the gods and of the world; her name was Immortality. "O maiden!"[68] she said, "the father of the gods has commanded that you be carried to the courts of heaven in this royal palanquin, which no earthborn creature may touch,[69] not even yourself before you drink this cup."

[135] With these words,[70] she lightly felt with her right hand

---

[66] Martianus: *ut laetos oculis afflaret honores;* cf. Vergil *Aeneid* 1. 591: *et laetos oculis adflarat honores.*

[67] The scene is reminiscent of Horace *Odes* 1. 4. 6-7.

[68] Martianus: *Et 'heus,' inquit, 'virgo';* cf. Apuleius *Metamorphoses* 9. 33: *Et 'heus,' inquit, 'puer.'*

[69] Martianus: *nulli fas attractare terrigenae;* cf. Vergil *Aeneid* 2. 719: *attrectare nefas.*

[70] *Et cum dicto.* This is an unusual phrase, also used by Apuleius (*Metamor-phoses* 2. 5, and elsewhere).

Philology's heartbeat and breast; when she found that it was greatly swollen with some inner fullness, she said: "Unless you retch violently and void this matter which is choking your breast, you will never attain the throne of immortality at all." The girl strained hard and with great effort vomited up the weight she was carrying in her breast. [136] Then that nausea and labored vomit turned into a stream of writings of all kinds. One could see[71] what books and what great volumes and the works of how many languages flowed from the mouth of the maiden. There were some made of papyrus which had been smeared with cedar oil, other books were woven of rolls of linen, many were of parchment, and a very few were written on linden bark. [137] There were some written with a sacred ink, whose letters were thought to be representations of living creatures;[72] when Immortality saw the writings of these books, she ordered them to be inscribed on certain imposing rocks and placed inside a cave within the sanctuaries of the Egyptians, and she called these stones *stelae*[73] and ordained that they should contain the genealogies of the gods.

[138] But while the maiden was bringing up such matter in spasms, several young women, of whom some are called the Arts, and others the Disciplines, were straightway collecting whatever the maiden brought forth from her mouth, each one of them taking material for her own essential use and her particular skill. Even the Muses themselves, especially Urania and Calliope, gathered countless volumes into their laps. In some of these books the pages were marked with musical notation and were very long; in others there were circles and straight lines and hemispheres, together with triangles and squares and polygonal shapes drawn to suit the different theorems and elements; then a representation joined together the limbs of various animals into a particular species. There were also

---

71 Martianus: *Cernere erat;* cf. Vergil *Aeneid* 6. 596: *cernere erat.*

72 Presumably the Egyptian hieroglyphs (see Tacitus *Annals* 11. 14). The belief that learning, especially in religious matters, originated with the Egyptians, was widespread in the Greek and Roman world, and finds frequent expression in Herodotus *Histories* (esp 2. 4,50-51,77,82) and Diodorus Siculus *Bibliotheca historica* 1. 9. 6; 1. 10. 2. Martianus has already subscribed to this belief in § 102; see also Book I, n. 128.

73 Cf. Diodorus Siculus *Bibl. hist.* 1. 27. 2-6, where the steles of Isis and Osiris are described.

books which contained the harmonies of music and the notations of rhythm and some pieces for singing.

[139] After the maiden had with travail brought forth from deep inside herself all that store of literary reproduction, worn out and pale with exhaustion,[74] she asked help from Immortality, who had witnessed such a great effort. The latter said: "Drink this so that you may be borne up and rise to heaven reinvigorated."[75] [140] From her own mother, Apotheosis, who had come with her and who was already blessing the books which had flowed from the mouth of Philology, touching them with her hand and counting them, Immortality took a smooth, living sphere and gave it to the maiden to drink from. It had the appearance of an egg[76] inside, but its outside shone, being anointed with saffron; within that, it seemed transparent with void and a white humor, and then something more solid at the center. When Philology received this, being extremely thirsty after such physical ordeals and the seething of her mind, once the secrets of the sphere had been revealed and she had discovered its extreme sweetness, she drank it in a draught:

and straightway her limbs are strengthened with new vigor,
her fragile thinness passes, the power of earth leaves her,
and there comes to her the immortality of heaven,
free from the laws of death.

[141] But when the goddess saw that Philology had drunk the cup of immortality, in order to show her by the symbol of a wreath that she was leaving earth for heaven and had been made immortal, she crowned the maiden with the wildflower whose name is Everlasting; she ordered her to rid herself of all that she had put on her body as a mortal to protect herself against the power of heaven,

[74] Martianus: *exhausto pallore confecta;* cf. Apuleius *Metamorphoses* 5. 22: *marcido pallore defecta.*

[75] Much of the diction in this solemn scene echoes the very bawdy scene in Apuleius *Metamorphoses* 2. 16; however the occasion closely resembles *ibid.* 6. 23, where Jupiter gives Psyche the cup of immortality at her wedding to Cupid.

[76] For the mystical significance of the egg in ancient religion, see Macrobius *Saturnalia* 7. 16. 2-8; and W. K. C. Guthrie, *Orpheus and Greek Religion* (London, 1952), pp. 92-94; on this passage in particular, see the article by Boyancé mentioned above, n. 24; he interprets this as a Neopythagorean ritual.

reminding her that those were trifles[77] of a transitory and mortal nature. Her mother took all these things away from her after she realized that she had risen beyond earthly concern. [142] Then Philology first of all made an offering to Immortality with a preparation of spice and with her own box of incense, and then made a thank offering to her mother with much sacrifice, because she herself would not now behold Vedius[78] and his wife, as Etruria[79] used to tell her; nor did she fear the Eumenides, those Chaldean manifestations; nor would Apotheosis (the mother of Immortality) burn her with fire, nor bathe her with water;[80] nor would she chastise the image[81] of her soul according to the teaching of some Syrian;[82] nor would she by dying first, according to the ritual of old Colchis, consecrate an immortality bound up in the hands of Charon.[83]

[143] Meantime, although she had been ordered to get into the palanquin, she thought it extremely difficult, not to say impossible, since it seemed to be at a very great height. Consequently, to achieve this, she summoned the faithful ward whom she loved above all others, and with his support she overcame all the difficulty of the ascent; but he, whom she called Labor, not only lifted her right into the palanquin, but swiftly traversed heaven with his mistress. [144] He had for company a brilliant boy, who was not the son of the pleasure-loving Venus[84] but was nevertheless called by philosophers Amor; together they did not delay in supporting the palanquin from the forward end. [145] For at the rear, Attention and Wakefulness,

[77] minima. Willis suggests munimina; the sense would then be "defenses."

[78] Vediovis, i.e., Pluto.

[79] Much of Roman religion was drawn from Etruscan beliefs.

[80] Typical examples of forms of purification; see Kopp, ad loc.

[81] See Servius on Aeneid 4. 654 for the belief that, besides body and soul, man has his "shade" or simulacrum, a slightly corporeal image of the body which survives for some time after death; cf. Franz Cumont, After Life in Roman Paganism (New York, 1959), pp. 166-69.

[82] Probably the Neoplatonist Iamblichus; cf. § 172.

[83] This piece of Martianic tortuousness seems to mean that Philology, unlike Pelias (king of Colchis and Medea's father), will not die and pass through Charon's hands to immortality of an inferior kind; rather, she will pass directly to immortality with the gods.

[84] The speech of Pausanias in Plato's Symposium (esp. 180d-181c) distinguishes two types of love, one noble and one sordid. This distinction, with varying interpretations of each type, persists throughout antiquity; cf. Apuleius Apologia 12 and De Platone 2. 14.

servants dear to the maiden, carried her. Thus Immortality had ordered, that each sex should be able to rise to heaven with Philology. Immediately before her as she ascended went a procession of Muses singing together and the awesome assembly of her companions we have described. [146] But Periergia followed, accompanied by her other servants and her bridal attendants, carefully examining and investigating everything. So the retinue with the maiden approached the summit of the citadel of the sky.

[147] Suddenly it was announced that Juno, sponsor of divine marriages, was approaching, and in front of her were coming Concord, Faith, and Modesty; [148] as for Cupid, her lure of physical pleasure, although he always flew in front of Juno, yet he did not dare to be amongst those to meet Philology.

[149] When the goddess came into the bride's sight, and, as was the custom with a virgin, Philology had made an offering of spices, she spoke to the goddess in these words: "Fair Juno, although the heavenly host has given you a different name, and we call you Juno because of your help,[85] from which we also name Jove; or we call you Lucina,[86] because you give light to those being born, and it is appropriate to name you Lucetia—for it is not necessary for me to invoke the names Fluvonia, Februalis, and Februa, since I am a virgin and have suffered no physical pollution; mortal brides ought to summon you to their marriages as Iterduca and Domiduca, as Unxia or Cinctia, in order that you may protect their journeys and

---

[85] The Latin verb "to help" is *juvare*.

[86] For the manifold epithets of Juno, cf. Augustine *City of God* 7. 3, based on Varro. *Lucina, Lucetia:* derived from *lux* [light]. *Fluvonia:* derived from *fluere* [to flow] and connected with the menstrual flow. It was believed that this flow ceased during pregnancy because it was diverted to nourish the fetus; hence, Juno Fluvonia is a patroness of pregnancy, and inappropriate for a virgin to invoke. See Festus *De verborum significatu* (ed. Lindsay), 42 M; and Augustine *loc. cit.* My thanks are due to Professor G. W. Clarke for assistance with this explanation. *Februalis, Februa:* derived from *februare* [to purify]. *Interduca, Domiduca:* derived from *ducere* [to lead] on a journey (*iter*) or home (*domus*). *Unxia:* derived from *ungere*, or *unguere* [to smear, to anoint]. *Cinctia:* derived from *cingere* [to encircle, to bind]. *Opigena:* derived from *ops* [strength, aid] and *gignere* [to beget, to bring forth]. *Poplona:* apparently derived from *populus* [the people]; though Lewis and Short derive *Populonia* from *populari* [to devastate, to lay waste]. *Curitis:* derived from *curis* [a spear].

bring them into the abodes that they desire; and, when they anoint the doorposts, you should fix a favorable sign thereon; and you should not leave them when they put aside their girdle in the bridal chamber; those whom you protect in the crisis of childbirth will call you Opigena; the common people ought to call you Poplona, and in their battles ought to call upon Curitis; now I call upon you as Hera, named from your kingdom of the air;[87] grant my request to know what goes on in the vastness of the sky and in these fields of living souls glowing with conflicting atoms, and which of the deities is said to fly here. I am not asking about that lower level of air, which is traversed by birds, which the crest of Mount Olympus soars above, which is barely ten stades high; I mean the higher air. I think it is now legitimate to see whatever I had understood from my reading *Peri eudaimonias* [about blessedness]."

[150] Juno did not disdain the prayers of the maiden in her ascent, but led her into the citadels of the sky and from there showed her the main different kinds of spirits. "Those," she said, "whom we see up there of a fiery or flaming substance, those who wander from the ether itself and from the circuit of the celestial sphere even to the solar sphere, are called gods, and elsewhere they are called inhabitants of heaven, and they dispose the secret workings of hidden affairs. They are the purer ones: the entreaties of human anxieties do not trouble them at all; they are said to be free from suffering.[88] In that region Jove is indubitably king. [151] Between the pathway of the sun and the orb of the moon are the deities of the second stage of blessedness, those of almost equal power, through whom prophecies and dreams and portents are disposed. These, by the soothsayer's art, divide certain prophetic entrails and utter sounds and speak through foretelling omens. Often to those who question them they give advice, either by the course of a star or by the thunderbolt or by some unprecedented sign. [152] Since each one of them serves some one of the gods above, by the power of the superior gods and by the obeisance of the inferior ones a

[87] The Latin Juno is identified with the Greek Hera. In Greek script, the same three letters form the name Hera and the word for air.

[88] Augustine (*City of God* 7. 6) quotes similar views of Varro; cf. also Cicero *De natura deorum* 2. 3. 7; Apuleius *De deo Socratis* 6. 132-34; and 16. 154-56. The theology of this speech is discussed at length by Robert Turcan, "Martianus Capella et Jamblique," *Revue des études latines*, XXXVI (1958), 235-54.

universal guardian is assigned to all men, a particular Genius[89] to
each individual, whom they have called the Supervisor because he
is to supervise all that is to be done; prayers are made to the Genius
of a people when the universal guardian is invoked, and each individual owes obedience to his own supervisor. The spirit is called a
genius because he is immediately assigned to a person at the moment
when the person is generated. As a guardian and most loyal kinsman,
he protects the minds and spirits of all men; [153] and because he
announces to a higher power the secrets of their thoughts, he can
also be called an angel.[90] [154] The Greeks called them all *dae-
mones*, from the Greek word for 'distributing,'[91] and in Latin they
call them *medioximi*.[92] As you see, they are all of a less clear and
brilliant nature than the superior gods, yet they are not so corporeal
as to be visible to men. [155] Here, then, the Lares live; here, after
their union with their bodies, live those purer spirits who, if they
are borne aloft by outstanding merits, often even leap beyond the
flaming ramparts and the orbit of the sun. [156] There is a space
between earth and moon,[93] and this space is itself divided into parti-
tions, but the upper section contains those whom they call demigods
and who are generally known in Latin as *Semones* or *Semidei*.[94]
These have celestial souls and godlike minds and are born in
human form for the good of the whole world. [157] Often by some
miracle they gave proof of their celestial nature; as when the night,
in service at the conception of Hercules, doubled its length,[95] or

[89] Cf. Augustine *City of God* 7. 13 (quoting Varro) and Apuleius *De deo
Socratis* 15. 151; also mentions of Genius in §§ 46-60 above.

[90] Etymologically, the word *angel* means "messenger."

[91] *apo tou daiomenou.* That is, from the Greek verb *daiomai.* Cf. Chalcidius
Commentarius in Platonis Timaeum 132; Servius on Vergil *Aeneid* 3. 111.

[92] The intermediate gods; cf. Apuleius *De Platone* 1. 2.

[93] Cf. Lucan *Pharsalia* 9. 5-9; Apuleius *De deo Socratis* 6. 132ff.; Servius on
Aeneid 8. 275.

[94] There seems to be no significant difference of terminology between these
demigods (*Semidei*) and those mentioned in § 160 (*hemithei*)—except that the
first term is Latin, the second Greek. Turcan (pp. 246-47) explains this as an
attempt by Martianus' source (probably Cornelius Labeo) to include Etrusco-
Roman religious figures and concepts within a Greek framework borrowed from
Iamblichus.

[95] Martianus: *geminatae noctis;* cf. Seneca *Agamemnon* 815: *geminavit horas
roscidae noctis.* Jupiter, in begetting Hercules, prevented the dawn from
breaking and doubled the length of the night.

when the same infant strangled the serpent and showed the power of his divinity; or when Tages[96] sprang from the furrows and immediately demonstrated the ritual of his family and the vessel. Hammon appeared with the horns of a ram[97] and showed his clothing of wool and showed to the thirsty people the water of a fountain.

[158] What am I to say of those who first showed to mortals the uses and outstanding advantages of natural products? For instance, Dionysus' discovery of the vine at Thebes; and, among the Egyptians, Osiris' discovery of the use of wine as a drink; Isis taught the cultivation of grain in Egypt; and Triptolemus, in Attica; and the same Isis pointed out the use and cultivation of flax. Italy ascribes to Pilumnus[98] the milling of different grains. Greece ascribed medicine to Asclepius. [159] Other humans of this kind were created to practice divination and foreknowledge, such as Carmentis in Arcadia, who got her name from the songs she poured out as prophecies,[99] or the Erythraean sibyl who is also the Cumaean sibyl, or the Phrygian. You know that there were not ten of these sibyls, as they say, but two—namely, Herophila, a Trojan, daughter of Marmensus; and Symmachia daughter of Hippotensis, who was born at Erythrae but prophesied at Cumae. For this power of divination Amphiaraus and Mopsus[100] were celebrated.

[160] From the middle of the region of the air down to the borders of the mountains and the earth, roam the demigods and Heroes, who are called Heroes because the ancients called the Earth Hera. And there are the Manes, too—that is, guardians assigned to the

---

[96] Tages was the son of a god and taught divination to the Etruscans; according to Etruscan legend, he sprang from the earth when a ploughman one day ploughed too deep a furrow; cf. Cicero De divinatione 2. 50. The reference to the ritual and the vessel is obscure, and the text seems to be corrupt at this point.

[97] Hammon, or Ammon, was an epithet of Zeus as worshiped in Egypt and Libya; Zeus Ammon was represented with ram's horns. See Herodotus Histories 4. 181; Macrobius Saturnalia 1. 21. 19.

[98] The name is derived from pilum [a pestle]. Cf. Servius on Aeneid 9. 4; 10. 76; Varro, cited in Nonius Marcellus De compendiosa doctrina 12. 528; and in Augustine City of God 6. 9.

[99] The name is said to be derived from carmen [a song, a prophetic chant]. She is said to have been the mother or grandmother of Aeneas' contemporary Evander and to have prophesied the Trojan settlement in Italy; cf. Ovid Fasti 1. 461-538; Servius on Aeneid 8. 51.

[100]Cf. Apuleius De deo Socratis 154.

human body—who have flowed[101] from the seeds of parents. [161]
Next, all this expanse of air[102] below the moon is under the power
of Pluto, who is also called Summanus, being as it were the chief
(*summus*) of the Manes. Here Luna, who is foremost in this air, is
called Proserpina. [162] But those Manes, since they are assigned to
bodies at the very moment of conception, are attracted by the same
bodies also when life is ended; and, remaining with them, are called
Lemures.[103] If they have profited by honorable conduct in the preceding life, they become Lares of homes and cities; [163] but if
they were corrupted by the body, they are called Larvae and Maniae.
There are then good Manes as well as fell, whom the Greeks distinguish as good and bad daemons. [164] In these regions also are the
lesser Manes and their overseers Mana and Mantuona, gods whom
they also call the Dark Ones; then too Fura and Furinna[104] and
Mother Mania[105] and the Furies and other fell deities live here.

[165] Around the sphere of the earth itself, air, set in motion by
the heat above and the exhalations and moisture below, striking the
souls with a certain turbulence as they come out of the bodies, does
not allow them to fly forth easily. [166] Hence the poet in his
sagacity alludes to the Pyriphlegethonian region; and, tossed in this
everlasting uproar, the wicked souls which Vedius has condemned,
are dashed. [That is, Pluto, whom they also call Dis and Vejovis.][106]
[167] Where the earth is inaccessible to men it is crowded with the
ancient beings who inhabit the woods and forests, the groves, lakes,
springs and rivers—the beings called Pans, Fauns,[107] Fones, Satyrs,

[101] The name is derived from an old Latin word *manus* [good], but Martianus
appears to derive it from *manare* [to flow, to trickle].

[102] Cf. Varro, cited in Augustine *City of God* 4. 10.

[103] Cf. Augustine *City of God* 9. 11; Apuleius *De deo Socratis* 152-53; Nonius
Marcellus 135.

[104] A very obscure Italic goddess, according to Varro *De lingua latina* 6. 19;
Cicero (*De natura deorum* 3. 46) connects her with the Eumenides (the Furies).

[105] Originally a deity requiring human sacrifice. See Macrobius *Saturnalia*
1. 7. 35.

[106] This parenthesis is bracketed by Dick as not part of the original text.

[107] Martianus: *Panes, Fauni, Fones, Satyri, Silvani, Nymphae. . .* ; cf. Ovid
Metamorphoses 1. 192-93: *sunt rustica numina, nymphae / faunique satyrique et
monticolae Silvani*; also Ovid *Ibis* 81-82: *Fauni Satyrique Laresque / fluminaque
et nymphae. . . .*

foretelling the secrets of the future;[131] [191] or Lyceus,[132] because you annul the actions of the night; the Nile reveres you as Serapis; and Memphis, as Osiris; differing cults revere you as Mithras, Dis, Horus, and Typhon; [192] you are fair Attis, and the bountiful youth with the curved plough,[133] and Hammon from parched Libya, and Phoenician Adonis. Thus the whole earth invokes you under different names. [193] Hail, true face of the gods,[134] countenance of the Father; your number is 608, and your three letters form the holy name and sign of Mind.[135] Father of Mind, allow us to rise to the heavenly assemblies and come to know the starry sky in the power of your sacred name."

[194] After this speech she was bidden to pass through the abodes of the gods. But when she ascended a half tone she was delayed by the circle Pyrois,[136] where Jove's greatest son was. [195] From this circle the river Pyriphlegethon was seen to flow to the lower regions. [196] When she had crossed this (for it was no effort[137] to cross the space of a half tone), she came to the brightness of Jove's planet, whose circle rang with Phrygian sound.[138] There was a planet whose temperature gave life,[139] a constellation flashing with a healthy brightness and gentle gleam; its light, glowing with a mixture of warmth and moisture, was such that it shone with the

---

131 The Greek name for the sun god is simply the Greek adjective φοῖβος [bright]; contrary to Martianus' explanation, it has no connection with prophecy.

132 This title, which is also Greek, may be connected with the stem λυκ- or λευκ-, Latin *luc-* [light]; with this whole passage, cf. Macrobius *Saturnalia* 1. 17. 33, 36-37; 1. 20. 18; 1. 21. 1, 9, 11, 13, 19.

133 Osiris. Cf. Vergil *Georgics* 1. 19; Tibullus *Carmina* 1. 7. 24-32.

134 Martianus: *Salve vera deum facies;* cf. Vergil *Aeneid* 8. 301: *Salve vera Iovis proles.*

135 *Phre* is an Egyptian sun-god; in Greek script φρη has the numerical value 608. Because of the closeness of φρη to φρῆν [mind], it was possible by ancient standards of etymology to presume a connection between the sun and the divine Mind, which suited Neoplatonic cosmology.

136 Mars. "The circle of Pyrois" would be the normal English, but Martianus appears to use the nominative case and give the name to the circle.

137 Martianus: *Neque enim labor fuerat;* cf. Vergil *Aeneid* 11. 684: *Neque enim labor;* both phrases begin parentheses.

138 Dick accepts Kopp's addition of *phrygio,* based on Pliny *Natural History* 2. 84, where Pliny says that "Saturn moves with a Dorian sound, Jupiter with Phrygian." Dorian and Phrygian are two of the modes of ancient music.

139 Jupiter, whose location between the heat of the sun and the cold of Saturn, caused it to be regarded as temperate.

peace which good fortune brings. That was truly Jove's planet; he himself was said to have gone to the celestial senate and the rule of the gods, lighting up all the quarters of the universe. [197] When she went an equal distance beyond this circle, from her lofty position she saw the creator of the gods, stiff with cold and with chill hoar-frost clinging to him; she tried to circle round the planet, which rang with Dorian sound.[140] Saturn himself wore now the face of a dragon, now the gaping jaws of a lion, now a crest made of the teeth of a boar. In his raging fury he caused horror and destruction, and his power was reckoned to exceed all others according as the size of his circle exceeded theirs. At length, terrified by the swords and drums, the maiden fled from an encounter she could not endure.

[198] From there they rose with great effort one and a half tones; in that distance they reached the globe of the celestial sphere itself and the periphery studded with stars. [199] Thus they were worn out with complete exhaustion after so many stades—an ascent of six tones. When they noticed that all that they had traversed gave forth a concord of the whole octave in full and perfect harmony, they were refreshed, and rested a little after their mighty efforts.

[200] Philology herself leaped down from the palanquin and saw enormous fields of light, the springtime of heavenly peace; she discerned at one moment the many varied aspects of the decan gods; at another moment she wondered at the eighty-four attendants standing by in the heavens;[141] she saw besides the shining orbs of a multitude of stars, and the constitution of the celestial circles and their intersections;[142] [201] she beheld the very sphere which contains the outermost periphery, driven on at astonishing speed, and the poles, and the quivering axis which from the highest point of heaven pierces the depth of earth and itself makes the whole mass and fabric of heaven revolve; [202] she was aware that the god who was the father[143] of such a work and so great a system had withdrawn even from the very acquaintance of the gods, for she knew that he had

---

[140] See n. 138 above; this is the planet Saturn.

[141] Robert Turcan here discerns a clear influence of the theology of Iamblichus; see "Martianus Capella et Jamblique," *Revue des études latines*, XXXVI (1958), 237-39.

[142] Circles like the ecliptic, the zodiac, the Milky Way, and the colures, since they run slantwise or at right angles, intersect the parallels.

[143] This is presumably the "Father Unknown" mentioned in § 185 above.

passed beyond the felicity that is itself beyond this world, and he rejoiced in an empyrean realm of pure understanding. On her knees[144] beside the wall of the outer periphery, concentrating the whole attention of her mind, she prayed long in silence, [203] and according to ancient ritual, uttered certain words with her inner voice, words varying in number according to the practice of different peoples, words of unknown sound, made up of alternating combinations of letters. In these words she paid reverence to the presiding deities of the world of pure understanding, and to their ministers, to whom the powers of the sensible world owe veneration, and to the entire universe contained by the depth of the infinite Father; [204] then she invoked those certain three gods[145] and the others who shine on the seventh day and night. [205] She prayed also, according to the mysteries of Plato, to those powers Once and Twice *hapax kai dis epekeina*,[146] to the Maiden of the Source.

[206] With these prayers she long besought with her whole heart the flower of the fire[147] and that truth which arises from nonexistent things (the uncreated truth); then she seemed to perceive that she had earned deification and worship. [207] The incandescence of a milk-white river gradually flowed down from the burning stars. [208] Full of joy and thanksgiving she turned toward the Galaxy, where she knew that Jove had assembled the divine senate. There was the abode of Jove, which, astonishing in size, encompassed the periphery of the universe, surpassed in its brilliant beauty the shin-

---

144 The diction and the scene recall the depiction of Psyche in Apuleius *Metamorphoses* 6. 3.

145 The Neoplatonic One, Mind, and World Soul; cf. Plotinus *Enneads* 5. 1. 1; and Kopp, *ad loc.*; also Macrobius *Commentary* 1. 14. 6-9.

146 See Pierre Courcelle, *Les Lettres grecques en occident de Macrobe à Cassiodore*, 2d ed. (Paris, 1948), p. 202 and nn. 7-10, for references and a summary of this discussion; Martianus is here expressing a Chaldaean element in Neoplatonism which ascribes the origin of all things to Hecate (under the title of *Dis epekeina*, which I have translated as "twice") and the Originators (*Plegaioi Pateres*), under the title of *Hapax epekeina*, which I have translated as "Once"); in numerology these are the monad and the dyad, the numbers one and two, from which all numbers—and therefore all things, according to ancient numerological belief—are derived.

147 The purest part of the flame; hence, the substance from which souls are made.

ing of the stars, and in the strangeness of its situation cut across the starry circle.[148] Moreover, it shone so brightly that one would think it made of silver. There glowed refulgent walls and a white-edged roof, [209] and Jupiter was now sitting there[149] with Juno and all the gods, on white benches placed on a great dais, waiting for the nuptial party to approach. He heard the voices of the Muses and the sweet strains of varied songs as the maiden drew near, and so he ordered the Cyllenian to come forward.

[210] Liber [Bacchus] and the Delian, the Cyllenian's fondest and loyal brothers, and Hercules, Castor and Pollux, and Gradivus [Mars], and all the divine progeny of Jove were in attendance on him. [211] The guardians of the elements followed the progress of Maia's son, as did a glorious assembly of angelic beings and the souls of the ancients who had attained celestial bliss and had earned temples in heaven. [212] Linus, Homer, and the Mantuan poet[150] were to be seen there, wearing crowns and chanting their poems; Orpheus and Aristoxenus were playing their lyres; Plato and Archimedes made golden spheres rotate. [213] Heraclitus was afire, Thales was soaked with moisture, and Democritus appeared surrounded with atoms. Pythagoras of Samos was cogitating certain celestial numbers. Aristotle with the utmost care was seeking Entelechia throughout the heights of heaven. Epicurus was carrying roses mixed with violets and all the allurements of pleasure.[151] Zeno was leading a woman who practiced foresight, Arcesilas was examining the neck of a dove, and a whole crowd of Greeks were singing discordantly; yet, loud as they were, they could not be heard through the harmonious songs of the Muses.

[214] As the Cyllenian approached and entered, the whole senate of the gods rose in honor, to his exaltation. Jupiter himself sat him

---

[148] With this description of the Milky Way, cf. Macrobius *Commentary* 1. 15. 1-7.

[149] Martianus: *in suggestu maximo . . . residens;* cf. Apuleius *Metamorphoses* 3. 2: *sublimo suggestu magistratibus residentibus.*

[150] Vergil.

[151] Heraclitus believed that all things were derived from fire; Thales believed, from water; Democritus, from atoms; Pythagoras, from numbers. Aristotle emphasizes the distinction between potentiality and actuality (*entelecheia*). Epicurus taught that pleasure was the supreme good and the guiding principle of conduct. Belief in a "paradis des intellectuels" was common in the fourth century; see Courcelle, pp. 35, 199, 204.

down next to himself, with Pallas on Mercury's right. [215] After a brief interval, Philology was brought in, surrounded by the Muses, with her mother walking ahead of her. As she entered and poured out that scented box of perfume upon Vesta, the nurse of the gods, and on Vesta's servant, the whole celestial array delighted in the Arabian fragrance, and shared it out amongst themselves. [216] Jove ordered the maiden to sit down at his side; but she, ever modest, preferred to sit where she had seen the Muses sitting, away from the company of Pallas. [217] Then her mother arose and asked of Jove and all the gods that whatever Maia's son had prepared in the way of a dowry should be handed over in the sight of all, and then that a gift should be given by the maiden, and after that, let them permit the recital of the Papian and Poppaean laws.¹⁵² [218] In reply to this most reasonable plea, the senate of the gods decreed that the offerings should be approved in the full assembly of heaven. Now Phoebus arose, without usurping his brother's duty, and he began to bring forward, one by one, chosen members of the Cyllenian's household, women who shone with a beauty in every way equal to their raiment.

[219] Reader, we have covered a great part of the story made up of such long and interconnected tales, and the dawn, pressing close upon us, makes the lantern flicker in the half-light; if the dawn were not touching the rooftops with purple,¹⁵³ making them beautiful with its first breath as it rises and cleaves the windows with light, page after page would make my story longer to cover every aspect. [220] So now the mythical part is ended; the books which follow set forth the arts. With true intellectual nourishment they put aside all fable and for the most part explain serious studies, without however avoiding entertainment. Now you know what will follow, given the goodwill of the heavenly powers and the Muses and the lyre of Latona's son [Apollo].

---

152 The Roman codifications of marriage laws in the time of Augustus (A.D. 9).
153 Martianus: *ac ni rosetis purpuraret culmina Aurora;* cf. Apuleius *Metamorphoses* 6. 24: *Horae rosis et ceteris floribus purpurabant omnia.*

BOOK III

Grammar

[221] Once again in this little book the Muse prepares her ornaments and wants to tell fabricated stories at first, remembering that utility cannot clothe the naked truth; she regards it as a weakness of the poet to make straightforward and undisguised statements,[1] and she brings a light touch to literary style and adds beauty to a page that is already heavily colored.[2]

[222] "But," I cried, "in the previous book notice is given that the myths have been put away and that the precepts in the volumes which follow are a work of those Arts which tell that which is the truth."

But with a laugh she joked at this and said: "Let us tell no lies, and yet let the Arts be clothed. Surely you will not give the band of sisters naked to the bridal couple? Surely they will not go like that before the senate of the Thunderer and the heavenly gods? To say no more about embellishment, what is to be the program?"

"Surely let them speak on their own teachings, and let them be clothed in incorporeal utterance."

"Now you are deceiving me and are not consistent with your promise; why do you not admit that your work cannot be composed except by the use of imagery?" With these words the Muse got the better of me: "Are you running away?" "I am joining in the game."

[223] So Latona's son [Apollo] moved forward from her former place one of the servants of Mercury, an old woman indeed but of great charm, who said that she had been born in Memphis[3] when

---

[1] This expresses the literary principles which Martianus himself appears to be following.

[2] Martianus: *multo illitam colore:* cf. Ovid *Medicamina* 97-98: *Tempore sint paruo molli licet illita vultu, / haerebit toto multus in ore color.*

[3] The old woman is *Grammatice* [Grammar]. Mercury is said to have invented languages for mankind (Hyginus *Fabulae* 143). His Greek name Hermes is taken to be akin to *hermeneutes* [an interpreter]; hence, the idea that he "found

Osiris was still king; when she had been a long time in hiding, she was found and brought up by the Cyllenian [Mercury] himself. This woman claimed that in Attica, where she had lived and prospered for the greater part of her life, she moved about in Greek dress; but because of the Latin gods and the Capitol[4] and the race of Mars and descendants of Venus, according to the custom of Romulus [i.e., Roman custom] she entered the senate of the gods dressed in a Roman cloak.[5] She carried in her hands a polished box, a fine piece of cabinetmaking, which shone on the outside with light ivory, from which like a skilled physician the woman took out the emblems of wounds that need to be healed. [224] Out of this box she took first a pruning knife with a shining point, with which she said she could prune the faults of pronunciation in children; then they could be restored to health with a certain black powder[6] carried through reeds, a powder which was thought to be made of ash or the ink of cuttlefish. Then she took out a very sharp medicine which she had made of fennelflower and the clippings from a goat's back, a medicine of purest red color, which she said should

---

and brought up" Grammar. The idea that various disciplines originated in Egypt was common (cf. §§ 102, 330). Pseudo-Servius (on *Aeneid* 4. 577) records a tradition that Mercury, having fled to Egypt after slaying Argus, there invented letters and numbers and was known by the Egyptians as Theuth (Thouth). On this whole subject, see Cora E. Lutz, "Remigius' Ideas on the Origin of the Seven Liberal Arts," *Medievalia et humanistica*, X (1956), 32-49, esp. 34-35.

4 Martianus refers to this allusively, saying *Olium caput* [lit., the head of Olus]. The Capitoline hill in Rome was said to have got its name from the discovery there of a human head (*caput*) when foundations were dug by order of Tarquin for the temple of Jupiter (Varro *De lingua latina* 5. 41; Livy 1. 55; Dionysius of Halicarnassus *Roman Antiquities* 4. 59-61). The Romans consulted an Etruscan soothsayer called Olenus on the significance of the discovery (Pliny *Natural History* 28. 15). By the time of Arnobius the head was attributed to Olus Vulcentanus (Arnobius *Adversus nationes* 6. 7; cf. Servius on *Aeneid* 8. 345), so that the name *Capitolium* was thought to be derived from the phrase *caput Olium*; it is in fact a diminutive from *caput* (cf. *capitulum*, meaning "little head") and referred originally to the temple of Jupiter built on the summit of the Saturnian (or Tarpeian) hill by the Tarquinii; this name for the temple was extended to the whole hill.

5 *paenula*. This appears to have been the official dress of an orator or a teacher. See Tacitus *Dialogus* 39; Augustine *Confessions* 1. 16. 25.

6 I.e., ink.

be applied to the throat when it was suffering from bucolic ignorance and was blowing out the vile breaths of a corrupt pronunciation.[7] She showed too a delicious savory, the work of many late nights and vigils, with which she said the harshness of the most unpleasant voice could be made melodious. [225] She also cleaned the windpipes and the lungs by the application of a medicine in which were observed wax smeared on beechwood and a mixture of gallnuts and gum and rolls of the Nilotic plant [papyrus]. Although this poultice was effective in assisting memory and attention, yet by its nature it kept people awake. [226] She also brought out a file fashioned with great skill, which was divided into eight golden parts joined in different ways, and which darted back and forth—with which by gentle rubbing she gradually cleaned dirty teeth and ailments of the tongue and the filth which had been picked up in the town of Soloe.[8]

[227] She is reckoned to know by the effort of frequent calculations these arcane poems and manifold rhythms. Whenever she accepted pupils, it was her custom to start them with the noun. She mentioned also how many cases could cause faults or could be declined accurately. Then, appealing to her pupils' powers of reasoning, she firmly held the different classes of things and the words for them, so that the pupils would not change one name for another, as often happens with those who need her attention. Then she used to ask them the moods of the verbs and their tenses and the figures,[9] and she ordered others, on whom complete dullness and inert laziness had settled, to run through the steps and to climb upon as many works as possible, treading on the prepositions or conjunctions or participles, and to be exercised to exhaustion with every kind of skill. [228] Some of the gods called this woman, so clever in so many ways, Iatrice,[10] others called her Genethliace,[11] be-

---

[7] The language and content of Cicero In Pisonem 13 and Lucilius Satires 1. 136, seem to underlie this passage.

[8] I.e., solecisms.

[9] In ancient grammatical theory, verbs and nouns have two figures—simple and compound.

[10] The name is derived from the Greek word for a physician or surgeon. The allegory in §§ 224-27 likens Grammar to a medical practitioner.

[11] The name is derived from the Greek word for birthday. It is hard to see

cause of the different aspects of her work; she is also skilled at restoring the truth, and neither Pallas nor Maia's son himself would deny that she can assist in faults of pronunciation. Yet it seemed inappropriate that she should enter as a doctor in Roman dress. So she was asked for her name and her profession and an explanation of her whole field of study.

[229] As if it was normal for her to explain what had been asked and easy to tell what was wanted of her, she modestly and decently folded back her cloak from her right hand and began: "In Greece I am called *Grammatice,* because a line is called *grammé* and letters are called *grammata* and it is my province to form the letters in their proper shapes and lines. For this reason Romulus[12] gave me the name *Litteratura,* although when I was a child he had wanted to call me *Litteratio,* just as amongst the Greeks I was at first called *Grammatistice;* and then Romulus gave me a priest and collected some boys to be my attendants. Nowadays my advocate is called *Litteratus,* who was formerly called *Litterator.* This is recalled by a certain Catullus, a poet not without charm, when he says 'The Litterator Sylla renders you his service.'[13] Such a man was called by the Greeks *Grammatodidaskalos.*

[230] My duty in the early stages was to read and write correctly; but now there is the added duty of understanding and criticizing knowledgeably.[14] These two aspects seem to me to be shared with the philosophers and the critics. Two of these four functions may be called active, and two contemplative, since indeed we are active when we write or read anything, but we are engaged in the contemplation of the result when we understand or assess what has been written, although these four functions are all linked by a certain

---

its relevance here, unless it is that Grammar is the source of all learning; yet cf. § 894, where a different personage is called Genethliace.

12 Fischer, citing Augustine *De ordine* 2. 12. 35, identifies this as Varro; see Balduinus Fischer, *De Augustini disciplinarum libro qui est de dialectica* (Jena, 1912), pp. 13-14. One may perhaps regard Romulus as a personification of early Latin and see the priest in the next sentence as Varro.

13 Catullus *Carmina* 14. 9.

14 "Grammar" in antiquity not only meant the study of linguistic forms but also embraced the study and appreciation of literature. Hence, Grammatice admits that her duties are shared by the philosophers and literary critics, each of whom has an interest in the forms of verbal expression.

affinity, just as is shown to happen in other studies also. For the actor understands at the beginning what is the efficacy of acting, and the astronomer does certain things in order to know through them what he ought to demonstrate. The geometrician combines those functions, in that he both writes and comprehends the shapes of the theorem, assisted by sure calculation.

[231] I have four parts: letters, literature, the man of letters, and literary style. Letters are what I teach, literature is I who teach, the man of letters is the person whom I have taught, and literary style is the skill of a person whom I form. I claim to speak also about the nature and practice of poetry. Nature is that from which speech is formed. Practice occurs when we put that material into use. To these we add the matter, so as to know what we must talk about. Speech itself is taught in three steps; that is, from letters, syllables, and words.[15]

[232] In respect of letters, two questions arise. Letters are either natural or artificial. The names of letters are formed into speech by the operation of nature; artificial formation has laid down their written forms to the end that people in each other's presence could use one form, those absent another.[16] From the point of view of the writer they are called mute, from the reader's they are called voiced,

---

[15] For ancient methods of teaching grammar, see Henri-Irenée Marrou, *A History of Education in Antiquity*, tr. G. Lamb (New York, 1956), pt. II, chap. VI. The method started from the elements—i.e., the letters—and proceeded to syllables, words, phrases, clauses, and sentences, in a manner more tidy than practical or effective. Martianus, in this tradition, begins with an elaborate study of letters, their connections and pronunciations; then treats syllables, their connections and pronunciations, with special attention to final syllables, which are important in Latin as an inflected language. In discussing "words," he concentrates on analogy; that is, the consistent similarity between corresponding forms of different words which are morphologically analogous (or which, as we might say, are of the same declension or conjugation). He concludes with one paragraph on anomaly; that is, exceptions to these analogies. The principles of analogy and anomaly are treated at length by Varro *De lingua latina* 8-10. For a good brief survey of ancient grammatical study and the ways in which it differs from modern linguistic study, see Robert Henry Robins, *Ancient and Mediaeval Grammatical Theory in Europe* (London, 1951).

[16] This remarkably roundabout sentence appears to mean that letters (i.e., sounds) used in speech are natural, letters used in writing are artificial. People use speech in each other's presence, writing to communicate with those absent. See Robins, pp. 13-14.

if indeed the latter can be taken in only by hearing and the former only by sight.[17]

[233] There are some letters which can form a complete sound by themselves, others which by themselves can form none. For there are the vowels, of which the Greeks say there are seven, early Latin[18] says six, later usage five—rejecting *y*, as a Greek letter. These vowels in Latin can be long or short, acute, grave, or even circumflex in accent, combined and separated without losing their names. Sometimes single vowels form syllables, sometimes they accept consonants and certain vowels on either side, sometimes they change themselves, in recent times they follow themselves with pleasing effect. For instance, *a* often changes into *e*, as *capio* gives *cepi*; sometimes into *i*, as in *salio, insilio*; sometimes into *o*, as in *plaustrum, plostrum*; or into *u*,[19] as in *arca, arcula*. The letter *e* changes first into *a*, as in *sero, satum*; or into *i*, as in *moneo, monitus*; or into *o*, as from *tegendo* comes *toga*; or into *u*, as from *tego* you get *tugurium*. Similarly, the vowel *i* changes into *a*, as in *siquis, siqua*; into *e*, as in *fortis, forte*; into *o*, as in *qui, quo*; into *u*, as in *ibi, ubi*. In the same way the letter *o* changes into *a* as in *creo, creavi*; or into *e*, as in *tutor, tutela*; or into *i*, as in *virgo, virginis*; or into *u*, as in *volo, volui*. Again, *u* likewise changes into *a*, as in *magnus, magna*; into *i*, as in *telum, teli*; into *o*, as in *lepus, leporis*; into *e*, as in *sidus, sideris*. The changed letters can be linked with letters on either side, or on one side only, or on none; and sometimes they end some parts of speech, and sometimes they do not.

[234] To begin with, *a* takes the letters *v* and *i* on either side of itself: we say *aurum* and *varus* and *Ianus* and *Aiax*. It takes *e* on one side only, as *Aeneas*; but it does not take *o* beside it at all. It ends masculine nouns, like *Iugurtha*; feminine, like *dea*; and neuter nouns in the singular (but only Greek ones) like *toreuma, peripetasma*; and in the plural, Latin nouns like *monilia*; in verbs it ends the imperative mood, as in *canta, salta*. [235] The vowel *e* has the force of two Greek letters; when it is short, it is the Greek *epsilon*, as

---

[17] It was normal in antiquity to read aloud. Hence, while a writer would not voice his writing, the reader would voice it.

[18] Martianus here uses the name *Romulus*; cf. above, n. 12.

[19] Latin has the one letter *v* for the functions of English *u* and *v*. I have used the two English letters as seemed appropriate in each instance.

in *ab hoc hoste;* and when it is long, it is the Greek *eta,* as in *ab hac die.* Then especially it takes a circumflex accent. It takes the two vowels *i* and *v* on either side, as in *Euro, Veientano,* and *eia, iecore.* It ends neuter nouns, such as *monile,* and Greek feminine nouns such as *Calliope,* and pronouns such as *ille, iste;* it ends numerals of every gender, such as *quinque,* although the numeral is indeclinable; it also ends verbs in the imperative mood, such as *sede, curre,* and in the infinitive mood, such as *scribere, scripsisse.* [236] The letter *i* takes all vowels on either side: it takes *a,* as when we say *ianuariae* and *Aiax;* the examples given above have shown how it takes *e;* it is joined to *o* in the names *Iovis* and *Oinone,* and *oisus* is also used—that is the archaic form of *usus;* and it takes *v,* as in *iuvando* and *vita.* Sometimes this vowel makes a double syllable;[20] it ends nouns of every gender, such as *frugi;* and numerals of every gender, such as *viginti;* and verbs in the indicative mood, such as *novi, memini;* in the imperative, such as *sali, veni;* and in the infinitive, such as *iaculari, luctari.* [237] I have noted above with what vowels the letter *o* is juxtaposed, and in what positions. It ends masculine nouns, such as *Cato;* feminine nouns, such as *Iuno;* numerals of all genders, such as *octo;* the active verb, such as *canto, laudo* (it is found in the imperative mood only in the form *cedo*); and it can end an adverb, such as *subito;* or a preposition, such as *pro.* [238] The letter *v* is juxtaposed with every other vowel on either side, except that *o* does not precede it. *V* [*u*] alone of vowels, when it occurs twice consecutively, does not form a double vowel but conjoins as if with a consonant, as in *vulgus, vulcanus.* It ends articles,[21] such as *tu,* and neuter nouns like *genu, cornu;* but it does not end any verb.

[239] So much for vowels. I was instructed to expound all the letters, not only the vowels. It is beyond dispute that the remaining letters, which now follow, are consonants. They are divided into semivowels and mutes; I shall set out the list of each. [240] The

---

[20] E.g., *Graii.*

[21] *Articulos.* The word *tu* is of course a pronoun. However, the term *articulus* in Latin grammar may be used loosely to describe words which have no major syntactical function but serve connective, intensive, and other minor functions. Personal nominative pronouns are seldom essential in Latin syntax, since the inflexion of the verb shows clearly enough who or what the subject is; hence, such a pronoun may be loosely termed an *articulus;* cf. §§ 249, 260.

letter *f*, which is the first of the semivowels, precedes only two consonants, *l* and *r*, as in *flavus* and *frugi*. In juxtaposition with vowels, it will not take *i* and *v* preceding it, and it is never the final letter of a word.[22] [241] The letter *l* has three different sounds. It gives a thin sound when it is doubled, as in *sollers*, *Sallustius*; a sound of moderate degree when it ends nouns, as in *sol*, *sal*; again it gives a light sound when it precedes vowels, as in *lapis*, *lepus*, *liber*, *locus*, *lucerna*; and a full sound[23] when it is preceded by the letters *p*, *g*, *c*, *f*, as in *Plauto*, *glebis*, *Claudio*, *Flavo*. *L* never precedes any semivowel or mute. It substitutes for *d* in a prepositional prefix when *a* precedes it, as in *allidit*, *alligat*.[24] When the preposition *in* is prefixed, the *l* is kept, as in *illepidus*, *illotus*.[25] It takes vowels on either side, and it is the final letter of some nouns: in the masculine *sol*; in the feminine *Tanaquil*; in the neuter when *a*, *e*, *i* precede it, as in *bidental*, *mel*, *sil*. It is also the final letter of adverbs, as in *semel*.

[242] The letter *m* can equally well be at the beginning, the middle, or the end of words, as in *mores*, *umbra*, *triticum*. It precedes only *n* amongst the consonants, as in *Memnon*; and it is preceded only by *s*, as in *Sminthius*; and it is sometimes changed into *n*, as when we say *nunquis*.[26] It is the final letter of neuter nouns like *aurum* and *argentum*, and of indeclinables like *nequam*, and of the masculine gender's accusative singular and genitive plural,[27] and of participles, verbs, and adverbs, such as *tractum*, *legam*, *cursim*; and of numerals of all genders, such as *novem*, *decem*.

[243] The letter *n* receives a fuller value as the first or the last of a word, as in *Nestor*, *tibicen*; and a slighter value in the middle of a word, as in *mane*, *damnum*. Amongst the consonants, it follows the letter *m*, as in *Memnon*; and it precedes *s*, as in *fons*, *mons*. It is assimilated into *m* when *b*, *p*, or *m* follow it, so that we say *im-*

---

[22] Martianus uses *finitiva* for "final" and *sermo* for "word"—both are unusual usages.

[23] This would appear to give four different values to *l*, instead of three as just mentioned. However the Latin suggests that the "light" sound is regarded as identical with one of the two preceding sounds.

[24] *Adl-* becomes *all-*.

[25] *Inl-* becomes *ill-*.

[26] For *numquis*.

[27] E.g., *bonum*, *bonorum*; the examples appear to have been lost from the text.

buit, impulit, imminet.[28] It is the final letter of some nouns: masculine, such as *tibicen;* Greek feminine nouns, such as *Siren;* neuters, such as *culmen.*

[244] The letter *r* accepts vowels on either side of it. Of the consonants, it precedes only *s,* as in *sors, fors;* and occasionally the double letter *x,* as in *arx.* It is converted into *l* and *n* and *s,* as *niger* into *nigellus, femur* into *feminis, gero* into *gessi.* It can be the final letter of masculine nouns after any vowels, as in *par, pater, vir, nitor, fur;* of feminine nouns after *e* and *o,* as in *mulier* and *soror;* and of neuter nouns after all vowels except *i,* as in *calcar, piper, marmor, sulphur.* It can be the final letter of verbs and adverbs, as in *venor, vador, ter.*

[245] Some people have not regarded *s* as a letter; Messala said it was a kind of hiss. It accepts the letter *p* on either side, as in *spado, psittacus;* and it accepts *c, q,* and *t* after it, as in *Scaurus, squama, stella.* It is more often converted into other letters, such as *l* when we say *modus* and *modulus;* or *n* in the case of *sanguis, sanguinis;* or *r* in *flos, floris;* or *d* in *custos, custodis;* or *t* in *nepos, nepotis.* It can be the final letter of masculine and feminine nouns after any vowel and of neuter nouns after *a, o, u,* as in *vas, os, nemus.* To *s* the emperor Claudius added *p* or *c,* because of the Greek letters *psi* and *xi,* as in *psalterium, sacsa (saxa).* [246] No one thinks *x* is a letter, because it is a double letter. It is made up of *g* and *s,* as in *rex, regis;* or of *c* and *s* as in *pix, picis,* or *nux, nucis.* It sometimes changes into *v,* as in *nix, nivis;* or into *ct,* as in *nox, noctis.* It is never an initial letter in Latin, but may be in Greek, as in *Xanthus.* It is juxtaposed with any vowel in masculine nouns, such as *Aiax, frutex, calix, velox, Pollux,* and in feminine nouns, such as *fax, lex, lodix, celox, lux;* it is never the final letter of a neuter noun.

[247] Having dealt with the semivowels, we must examine the mutes. These are so called because, unless vowels occur in association with them, their sound ceases at its beginning within the mouth. [248] *B,* first of all, accepts any vowel on either side of it, and it precedes the consonants *l* and *r,* as in *blaesus* and *brevis.* It is converted into *c,* as in *succurrit;* into *f,* as in *sufficit;* into *m,* as in

28 For *inbuit, inpulit, inminet.*

summittit; into *p,* as in *supponit;* into *s,* as in *sustulit.*[29] It is never a final letter, except of the three prepositions, *ab, ob, sub.* [249] C accepts vowels on either side of it, and it precedes certain consonants; namely, *l, t, r, m, n,* as in *clarus, tectum, crus, Acmon, Cnidus.* It is the final letter of the pronouns[30] *hic, haec, hoc,* and of adverbs, such as *sic, huc, hic. C* alone of the mutes lengthens the preceding vowel and is treated as a double letter, as in *hic, hoc, hac.*[31] [250] D accepts vowels on either side of itself. It precedes the letter *r* in *Drusus,* but never precedes the letter *m* in Latin, though it sometimes does in Greek, as in *Dmolus;* also *n,* as in *Ariadne.* It is converted into *c,* as in *accidit;* into *g,* as in *aggerat;* into *l,* as in *allegat;* into *p,* as in *apponit;* into *r,* as in *arripit,* into *s,* as in *assidet;* into *t,* as in *attinet.*[32] It may be the final letter of neuter pronouns, such as *istud, illud;* and of prepositions, as in *apud.* [251] G precedes any vowel and follows the letter *a,* as in *aggere;* whenever *g* is doubled, *a* is preceding it. G precedes the letter *r,* as in *grave; l,* as in *gladius; n,* as in *ignis.* It changes into *c,* as in *rego, rector.* It is never a final letter. [252] It is beyond doubt that *h* is the symbol of the aspirate; when it occurs it is an addition to a vowel, as in *hospes* and *heres.* It changes into *x,* as in *traho, traxi.* The Greeks divided it into two—its right half the sign of the aspirate, its left signifying the contrary.[33] [253] *K* is thought sometimes to be a notation, some-

29 For *subcurrit, subficit, submittit, subponit, subtulit.*

30 Lit., "of the articles which are called pronouns"; see above, n. 21.

31 Priscian *Institutiones grammaticae* 1. 44 (Heinrich Keil, ed. *Grammatici Latini,* 8 vols., Leipzig, 1855-1880; repr. Hildesheim, 1961; II, 34) says that *c* is the only mute before which, as a final letter, long vowels occur, and brings forward as examples *hoc, hac,* and the adverbial *hic.* Martianus, on the other hand, claims that the letter *c* is regarded as a double letter, which (according to normal principles of Latin pronunciation) makes the preceding vowel long. Priscian is correct as to *hac,* where the vowel is long, being ablative; Martianus is right as to *hoc* (from *hodce*) and the pronominal *hic* (by analogy with *hoc*); see Carl Darling Buck, *Comparative Grammar of Greek and Latin* (Chicago, 1933), p. 225.

32 For *adcidit, adgerat, adlegat, adponit, adripit, adsidet, adtinet.*

33 Greek has no letter *H.* Every Greek word which begins with a vowel has a symbol above the vowel to indicate whether the vowel is aspirated or not—' for aspirate,' for nonaspirate. These are what Martianus describes as the two halves of the letter *H* (" = *H*). Perhaps he describes as the "right half" (Ⱶ) what we regard as the left half, because he considers the letter as facing him; i.e.,

times a letter, for the letter *c* can certainly perform all its functions except these: *kapita, kalendae, kalumniae.*

[254] *P* accepts vowels on either side of itself, and precedes the letter *r*, as in *prandere; l,* as in *placere; t,* as in *Ptolemaeus; s,* as in *psittacus; n,* as in *Sipnus;* it is never a final letter. [255] Some people used not to consider *q* to be a letter, and they would be right, if only it were not so evident in *aequus* and *equitatus.* It never occurs without two vowels in association, of which the first is always *u;* the other vowels may then follow, as in *quartus, questus, Quirites, quotus, equus.* It is made up of *c* and *u* and so is a double and composite sound, and double-*q* does not occur. It is not preceded by any particular letter,[34] and it is never a final letter. [256] *T* accepts vowels on either side of itself, as in *coniunctiones* and *praepositiones.* It precedes *l* in *Tlepolemus, m* in *Tmolus, n* in *potnia, r* in *Troia* It can be the final letter of neuter nouns, such as *caput, sinciput, lact.* It ends articles,[35] such as *quot, tot;* verbs, such as *legunt;* an adverb and an interjection, such as *ut, attat.* [257] *Z* comes from the Greeks, although they themselves at first used the Greek sigma; they used to say *Sethum,* which now they call *Zethum;* they also consider it a double letter. It is made up of *t* and *s,* and being obviously a double letter it never occurs twice consecutively. It precedes the letter *m,* as in *Zmyrna.* [258] Out of all these, 18 letters meet all the requirements of a piece of composition. I am satisfied to include *y* amongst the vowels; without it one cannot write *Hyacinthus* or *Cyllenius.* This gives us a total of six vowels and 12 semivowels and mutes. [259] For if *h* is treated as an aspirate symbol; and *q* and *k* are unnecessary; and *x,* being a double letter, lacks the simplicity prerequisite for the basic letters; and *z* is excluded from Latin; then, as I said, 18 letters remain.

[260] All these letters, including those classed as unnecessary or not genuine, are formed by the sound of any single voice; and in

---

with the "right half" facing his left. On the other hand, the text could be defective. Priscian *Institutiones grammaticae* 1. 47 (Keil, II, 35-36) describes the right half as the "smooth-breathing," the left half as the aspirate. The replacement of *levis* or *exilis* (smooth) before *nota* in Dick's line 20 (which would then mean: "its right half the sign of the smooth-breathing") would restore consistency with Priscian's sense and text.

34 *Nullam singularem litteram comprehendit.*

35 These are indeclinable correlative adjectives; see above, n. 12.

the harmony of the voice they have uncovered the various elements of the concord of nature.

[261] We utter *A* with the mouth open, with a single suitable breath. We make *B* by the outburst of breath from closed lips.

C is made by the back teeth brought forward over the back of the tongue.

D is made by bringing the tongue against the top teeth.

E is made by a breath with the tongue a little depressed.

F is made by the teeth pressing on the lower lip.

G, by a breath against the palate.

H is made by an exhalation with the throat a little closed.

I is made by a breath with the teeth kept close together.

K is made with the palate against the top of the throat.

L is a soft sound made with the tongue and the palate.

M is a pressing together of the lips.

N is formed by the contact of the tongue on the teeth.

O is made by a breath with the mouth rounded.

P is a forceful exhalation from the lips.

Q is a contraction of the palate with the mouth half-closed.

R is a rough exhalation with the tongue curled against the roof of the mouth.

S is a hissing sound with the teeth in contact.

T is a blow of the tongue against the teeth.

U is made with the mouth almost closed and the lips forward a little.

X is the sibilant combination of *C* and *S*.

Y is a breath with the lips close together.

Z was abhorrent to Appius Claudius, because it resembles in its expression the teeth of a corpse.

[262] The rules of literacy, the primary study, which usually are spread over many volumes, are quickly brought into a small compass: in it we see what any letter connects together by its association on either side; on which side it accepts or demands an accompanying letter; how a letter customarily is altered by the laws of transformation and thus accepts a different name; what sounds of the mouth or movements of the tongue or outbursts from the lips form the letters. Now we must survey the syllable, composed of letters in combination: how it is accented; when it is long or short. I shall survey these two points, since the preceding study of the letter has at the same time taught the con-

nections. The order of studies takes this as the next matter to be dealt with, if that meets with your divine approval."

[263] While Grammar was saying this, and Jupiter and the Delian were urging her forward, Pallas spoke up: "While Literature here is hurrying on to discuss the connection of syllables, she has passed over the historical aspect." At this objection by the maiden goddess, Grammar in great agitation answered: "I know I must pass over a great deal, so as not to incur the distaste of the blessed by getting entangled in details. So I shall perform my purpose, hastening along the shortest ways, to avoid getting lost, hidden in thick undergrowth or a dense mass of briars.

[264] A syllable is a combination of letters which makes and is heard as a single sound. It is agreed, as I said, that it has three aspects: its connection, its accentuation, and its length. [265] There are four kinds of connection, two natural and two historical. They are natural when each syllable is examined to see whether it is joined on one side or on both or on neither, and whether letters which cannot by themselves come together may be united when some other letter is combined with them—as with *m* and *n*, which cannot combine of themselves, but can when a vowel is added, as in *amni* and *somno*—we may pass over these kinds of connection, since they have been dealt with in our discussion of letters [266] The historical type of connection occurs in dealing with letters which can be combined of themselves, when different modes of speech join them differently and with different numbers of letters. For we write the first syllable of *Musae* with two letters, but the Greeks write it with three.[36] Lucilius joins *a* and *e* in the dative case, saying *huic Terentiae, Orbiliae;* but in the genitive he joins *a* and *i*, and so does Lucretius often; and Vergil, as in *aulai, pictai*.[37] [267] There are, moreover, two kinds of connection when we join syllables in a manner to fit a rhythmical foot or verse, so that two letters suddenly vanish into one, as in *synaliphe* (for *synaloephe*), or when certain letters are dropped from a word, as in *ec(th)lipsis*.

[268] So much for connections; now let us look at accentuation, a topic which the Greeks call *peri prosodion* [pitch]. This has three divisions: each and every syllable is either grave or acute or circum-

---

36 The Greek spelling is *Mousai*.
37 Vergil *Aeneid* 3. 354 (*aulai*); 9. 26 (*pictai*).

flex;[38] and just as no sound exists without a vowel, so is none without an accent. The accent, as some have thought, is the soul of a sound, the seedbed of music, because every melody comes from the accents and weight of sounds; and so it has been called 'accent' from *adcantus* [tuning]. [269] Every utterance in Latin, whether simple or compound, has one sound that is either acute or circumflex; none can ever have two acute or circumflex sounds, but two grave sounds are common. The acute is on the first syllable when you say *Caelius*, on the second in *Sallustius*, on the third in *Curiatius*, and a circumflex on the first when you say *caelum;* the penultimate is never acute when short by nature, but the preceding syllable, the third from the end, may be acute whether short or long, as in *Cicero, Caelius*. The circumflex stands only on the penultimate syllable, and only when that syllable is long by nature and the final syllable short, as in *Galenus*. If the final syllable is long, or the penultimate is long by position and not by nature, even when the final syllable is short, the penultimate bears an acute accent, as in *Galeni, Camilli*. It is a peculiarity of the circumflex accent that it falls only on syllables long by nature, whereas the acute accent is found on both long and short syllables. Every voiced sound must have either an acute or a circumflex accent, even if the sound be a monosyllable; monosyllables do not have the grave accent. Every monosyllabic word, if it is short or long by position, has the acute accent, as in *far, ars;* if it is long by nature, it bears the circumflex, as in *lux, mos*.

Disyllabic words have an acute accent on the first syllable when both syllables are short, as in *citus;* or when both are long by position, as in *sollers;* or when the final syllable is long by position, as in *cohors* If, however, the first syllable is long by nature and the final syllable short, then the first syllable bears the circumflex, as in *luna;* if the final syllable is long by position or by nature, the first syllable bears the acute accent, as in *codex, docte;* in a disyllabic word the grave accent will never be found on the first syllable.

In a trisyllabic word, if the middle syllable (which we call the

---

[38] These terms refer to the pitch of the voice; the acute is a pitch rising above the normal, grave is the normal, and circumflex is a dual pitch which rises and falls back to normal within the one vowel sound (as in the English word "air"). Pitch and stress (the normal English manner of accenting words) generally coincide. See Leonard Robert Palmer, *The Latin Language* (London, 1964), pp. 211-14.

penultimate) is short, it will always be pronounced with a grave accent, and the syllable immediately before it, the third from the end, will have an acute accent, as in *Catulus;* but if the middle syllable is long, its accent depends on whether it is long by nature or by position. If it is long by nature and the last syllable is short, the middle syllable has the circumflex, as in *Cethegus, Mancinus;* if the middle syllable is long by nature and the final syllable is long, the middle syllable has the acute accent, as in *Catoni, Ciceroni;* if the middle syllable is long by position it will have the acute accent, whatever the length of the final syllable, as in *Catullus, Catullo, Metellus, Metello.* [270] Those pronouns which may be declined in two ways —that is, with the middle syllable of the genitive case either shortened or lengthened, like *ipsius* and *illius*—vary their accentuation accordingly; if their second syllables are shortened, their first syllables have the acute accent, as in *ípsius, íllius;* if their middle syllables are long, the first syllables have the grave accent, the second syllables the circumflex, as in *ipsîus, illîus.* So the first syllables have the acute accent when the middle ones are short; the middle ones when long have either acute or circumflex: acute when the last syllables are long, circumflex when these are short. [271] The words *tenebrae, latebrae, manipli* differ from the former examples in this: that the former examples have their consecutive consonants in separate syllables,[39] whereas these three words, though their penultimate syllable is long by position, have no consonant at the end of the second syllable, but have two at the beginning of the third.[40] So it comes about that the middle syllable produces the nouns *tenebrae* and *latebrae* with an acute accent on the first syllable;[41] but *maniplos*

---

[39] E.g., *Ca-tul-lus, Sal-lus-ti-us.*

[40] *Te-ne-brae, la-te-brae, ma-ni-pli.*

[41] The text is corrupt here, and I have rendered Dick's text as literally as I can. Diomedes (*Ars grammatica* 2; Keil, I, 432) and Priscian (*De accentibus* 12; Keil, III, 521) explain the point much more clearly, thus: Words of three syllables with the penultimate syllable long have an acute accent on that syllable, except when the length of the penultimate results from its position as being followed by a mute and a liquid (as in *tenebrae*, where the middle *e* is long only because it is followed by the mute *b* and the liquid *r*); in these cases the accent customarily goes onto the antepenultimate—i.e., the first syllable. In Latin verse scansion, vowels naturally short but followed in the same word by a mute and a liquid may be scanned long or short to suit the meter. There seems to be no reason why this should not apply to *manipli* also.

and *fenestras* have an acute accent on the penultimate syllable: some scholars have thought that that kind of penultimate syllable is always short, because it is not closed with a consonant; some, that it is long, because, although it is not closed with a consonant, the next syllable begins with two consonants, and because the natural softness of the letters *l* and *r* make syllables now long, now short. But no Latin word of two or more syllables has an acute accent on the final syllable; and a word never has a circumflex on the final syllable unless the antepenultimate syllable is long by nature, as in *ergo* and *pone*.[42]

[272] The true pronunciation of individual sounds is frequently altered or even lost by their context in speech. Those sounds are lost which are carried onto a succeeding sound, as, in the case of prepositions, in the phrase *ante urbem;* here *ante* loses its acute accent on the first syllable; similarly with *post muros*. Words change their accents when *-que*, *-ve*, and *-ne* are suffixed; when *-que* is a copulative conjunction, and *-ve* an expletive one, as in *Latiumque augescere vultis* and *stimulove meum cor* in the *Pelopidae* of Accius. The acute accent will never move from the first syllables to the last except in the case of suffixed particles, which have the effect of rendering acute the final syllables of words to which they are suffixed.

When Greek nouns are brought into Latin, they are pronounced according to our rules unless they remain in their Greek forms. Thus, if *Olympus* and *Caucasus* are pronounced as Latin words, it is clear, from the principles set out above, on which syllables they should bear the acute or circumflex accent. But if they remain in their Greek form (in the case of foreign words, we agree to this rule), then they nevertheless must keep the acute accent on the middle syllable in the oblique cases, since we hear Greeks themselves pronouncing them in no other way. [273] The acute accent is signified by a stroke ascending from the left to the right thus ´; the grave descends from left to right, thus `; the symbol of the circumflex is a semicircle placed above the letters themselves ^. We some-

---

[42] The archaic Latin preposition *ergo* [for the sake of] is distinguished from the common conjunction *ergo* [therefore] by accenting the last syllable, contrary to the general rule; similarly, *pone* the adverb [behind] is distinguished from the imperative verb *pone* [put!] by accenting the last syllable—not, however, with a circumflex as Martianus says, but with an acute accent; see Diomedes *Ars grammatica* 2 (Keil, I, 433).

times call accents *fastigia* [gables], because they are placed on top of letters; sometimes *cacumina* [summits], *toni* [tones], or *soni* [sounds]; and the Greeks call them *prosodiae* [pitches]. It is worth knowing that all three accents can occur in a single word, such as *Argìlêtum*.

[274] I think I have given a sufficient outline of what the accents are on the syllables and in what circumstances they are modified; now I shall explain the lengths of syllables. Each syllable is either short or long or common. It is short when the vowel is short and nothing following helps to make it long, or when the syllable ends with a short letter or form.[43]

[275] A syllable is rendered long in two ways, by nature and by position: by nature when the vowel itself is long, or when[44] the syllable has a circumflex accent or an acute on the penultimate, or when the vowel is a monosyllabic word, or when the syllable contains a diphthong, or when the first syllable, of any word, even in some other compound form, does not change its vowel or accent;[45] by position, when a short vowel is followed by two consonants, either in the same syllable or in the next syllable or shared between the two syllables, or by a double consonant in either syllable. [276] The double consonants are *x* and *z;* sometimes *i* and *c* can be considered double consonants, as when *i* comes between vowels, as in *aio, Troia;* or when *c* does, as in *hoc erat alma parens.*[46] These are the types of consonant or double consonant which can make short vowels into long syllables if they occur at the end of the same word. If they occur in the following phrase, the consonants do not lengthen the preceding syllable, although Vergil would contest this, saying *arma virumque cano / Troiae,*[47] and again *fontesque/*

---

[43] By "a short form" Martianus presumably means a vowel short by nature followed by one consonant.

[44] The text here is corrupt. A vowel must be long to carry a circumflex accent or an acute accent as the penultimate syllable, so that *aut cum* [or when] is inappropriate here; Willis suggests *ut cum* [as when], which would make better sense.

[45] This appears to be an elliptical way of saying that if a syllable in a word is long, and the word is compounded with another without changing its form (e.g., *circum, circumflecto*), the syllable remains long.

[46] Vergil *Aeneid* 2. 664.

[47] Vergil *Aeneid* 1. 1. The last syllable of *cano* must be scanned long to fit the meter.

fluviosque voco.[48] [277] The diphthongs are *ae, oe, au, eu, ei;* there are no diphthongs without these syllables.

[278] There are eight ways in which syllables may be common. The first is when a short vowel is followed by two consonants, the second of which is a liquid: for then it is long, as in *vasto Cȳclopis in antro;*[49] or short, as in *vastosque ab rupe Cȳclopas.*[50] The second way is when a short vowel is followed by two consonants, the second of which is *h:* for then it is long, as in *terga fatigamūs hasta;*[51] or short, as in *quisquĭs honos tumuli.*[52] The third way is when a short vowel is followed by two consonants, the first of which is *s:* for then it is long, as in *undē spissa coma;*[53] or short, as in *ponitĕ spes sibi quisque.*[54] The fourth way is when a short syllable ends a period: for at the break it is long, as in *nam tibi, Thymbre, capūt Euandrius;*[55] or short, as in *hoc capŭt o cives.*[56] On another occasion a diphthong can make a common syllable: long, as in *musāe Aonides,*[57] short, as in *insulăe Ionio in magno.*[58] For when it is followed by a vowel, a diphthong can become short, as in *sudibusve prăeustis.*[59] Again, when a long vowel is followed by another vowel, it can be long, as in *Ō ego infelix, quem fugis;*[60] or short, as in *sub Iliŏ alto.*[61] Again when a pronoun ends with the letter *c* and is followed by a vowel, it can be

---

[48] Vergil *Aeneid* 12. 181. The last syllable of *fontesque* must be scanned long, whereas the last syllable of *fluviosque* must be short. The only difference between them is that the first is followed by two consonants (*fl*), the second by only one (*v*).

[49] Vergil *Aeneid* 3. 617.

[50] *Ibid.,* 647.

[51] *Ibid.,* 9. 610.

[52] *Ibid.,* 10. 493.

[53] This example occurs in meter in the verses *De syllabis* of the grammarian Terentianus Maurus (Keil, VI, 358, line 1103), where *scissa* is used for *spissa.* The example occurs in several other grammarians (refs. in Keil, *ad loc.*), but not in surviving Latin poetry.

[54] Vergil *Aeneid* 11, 309.

[55] *Ibid.,* 10. 394. In the complete line a caesura occurs after *caput.*

[56] *Ibid.,* 12. 572.

[57] Dick cites Silius Italicus *Punica* 11. 462; and 12. 408: Silius uses merely the word *Aonides,* not the phrase.

[58] Vergil *Aeneid* 3. 211.

[59] *Ibid.,* 7. 524.

[60] A variant reading of Horace *Epodes* 12. 25: *O ego non felix quam tu fugis.*

[61] Vergil *Aeneid* 5. 261.

long, as in *hōc erat alma parens;*[62] or short, as in *solus hĭc inflexit sensus.*[63] Again, when a short vowel is followed by *z*, it can be long, as in *Mēzenti ducis exuvias;*[64] or short, as in *nemorosa Zacynthos.*[65]

I have discussed the nature of the three kinds of syllables;[66] it remains to discuss final syllables, which are authoritative for the grammarian and define the role of the word.[67] First I must deal with the noun. [279] When the nominative singular ends with *a*, the letter is short, as in *Catilina, Iulia.* When it ends with *e*, this is long in Greek words, as *Euterpe.*[68] The final letter *i* is long, as in *frugi.* The final *o* is short in Latin nouns, as in *Cato.*[69] The final *u* is short, as in *cornu.* The final *al* is short, as in *tribunal; el* is short, as in *mel; il* is short, as in *vigil*, except in the one Ẹtruscan word *Tanaquil.* *Ol* is long, as in *sol; ul* is short, as in *consul.* When the nominative singular ends with *m*, the syllable is short, as in *tectum*, although an example of this seldom occurs, because an *m* between two vowels is elided to avoid mytacism.[70] The final *an* is long, as in *Titan; en* is short in neuter nominatives such as *carmen*, but long in other genders, as in *lien, Siren.* The ending *on* is long, as in *Memnon.* The ending *ar* is long only in monosyllables such as *Nar, far.* The ending *er* is short in Latin nouns such as *puer*, with the single exception of the nonosyllable *ver*; but in Greek nouns such as *aer* it is long. The ending *ir* is short, as in *vir*; the ending *or* is short, as in *auctor.* The ending *ur* is short, as in *murmur*, with the single exception of the monosyllable *fur.* The ending *as* is long in Latin nouns such as *facultas, paupertas;* and in Greek nouns it is short only in those instances when the genitive ends in *dos*, as in *Arcas, Arcados.* The nominative singular ending *es* is long in Greek nouns such as *Anchises;* in Latin nouns of the fifth declension it is long, as

---

62 *Ibid.*, 2. 664.

63 *Ibid.*, 4. 22.

64 *Ibid.*, 11. 7.

65 *Ibid.*, 3. 270.

66 I.e. long, short, and common.

67 In Latin, being an inflected language, the final syllables of words are of major importance in defining the syntactical function of the word.

68 Dick and Kopp postulate a lacuna at this point, and would add: "short in Latin words, as in *sedile.*"

69 There may be a lacuna here: "long in Greek nouns, as in *Dido.*"

70 Mytacism is the excessive use of the letter *m.*

in *dies;* in the third declension it is long in those instances where
the genitive singular has no more syllables than the nominative, such
as *labes, labis;* or where the genitive singular has more syllables but
keeps the long *e* in the antepenultimate syllable, as in *quies, quietis.*
If the *e* of the nominative changes to *i* in the genitive, as in *miles,
militis,* or if the *e* in the genitive is short, as in *seges, segetis,* then
the *e* of the nominative is short, except in *Ceres, pes,* and words like
these. The nominative ending *is* is short, as in *agilis.* The ending *os*
is short in those Latin nouns in which the genitive's antepenultimate
syllable is not naturally long, such as *os, ossis.* In Greek words the
nominative termination *os* is short when the genitive ends in a diphthong, as in *Delos, Delou.* The ending *us* is short, as in *doctus,* but
it becomes long if the genitive has more syllables than the nominative and has a long *u* in the antepenultimate syllable, such as *virtus,
virtutis,* and in one indeclinable word, *pus.* Nominatives ending in
t have short final syllables, as in *caput.* Only two nouns end their
nominatives with *c,* namely *allec,* where the final syllable is long,
and *lac,* whose inflection is disputed. [280] The genitive singular
is long when it is similar to the nominative, as in *senatus;* or when
it has a diphthong, as in *Iuliae;* or when it ends in *i,* as in *docti;*
in other instances it is short. The dative singular is long . . . ,[71]
as in *Pompeio;* in Greek words it is short if it ends in the letter
i, as in *Palladi.* The accusative singular in Greek words is short only
when it ends in *a* or *on,* as in *Thesea, Delon;* but in Latin words it
is short, as in *doctum.* The vocative singular ending in *a* in Latin
nouns or in feminine Greek nouns is short, as in *tabula, Musa;*
but in masculine Greek nouns it is long, as in *Aenea.* The vocative
ending *e* in Latin words is short, as in *docte;* in Greek nouns it is
long, as in *Tydide,* except in those nouns which have the Greek
nominative ending *os,* such as *Phoebos, Phoebe.* The vocative ending
i in Latin nouns is long, as in *Mercuri;* in Greek nouns it is short,
as in *Nai.* The vocative ending *o* in Latin nouns is short, as in *Cato,*
although Vergil feels otherwise; in Greek nouns it is long, as in
Dido. The vocative ending *u* is short, as in *cornu;* vocatives which
end in consonants follow the rule for pronunciation of the nominative, with the exception of Greek nouns, in which the vocative often
differs in length from the nominative because of the difference be-

---

71 The phrase "in Latin words" appears to have dropped out of the text.

tween the two languages, as in the noun *Diomedes*.[72] The ablative singular is always long, except when it ends in *e*, at least in those nouns which are of the third declension, as in *a pariete*. [281] The nominative and vocative plural in the masculine and feminine genders are long, as in *fluctus, terrae;* in neuters they are short, as in *fata;* in Greek nouns they are short when they end in *es* or *a*, as in *rhetores, poemata;* in other instances they are long, as in *musae*. The genitive plural ending is short, as in *doctorum*, though in Greek nouns following the Greek declension, such as *Philaenon*, it is long. The dative and ablative plural ending in *is* is long, as in *doctis;* the ending in *bus* is short, as in *nominibus;* if the noun is declined as in Greek and the dative plural ends in *in*, as in *Arcasin*, the ending is short; otherwise it is long. The accusative plural in masculine and feminine nouns is long, as in *doctos, Iulias;* in neuter nouns it is short, as in *moenia;* but in Greek nouns, if the accusative plural ending is *as* and the noun's genitive singular ending is *os*, then the accusative plural ending is short, as in *Arcados, Arcadas;* otherwise it is long, as in *Musas*.

[282] In all pronouns the nominative singular is short, except the two monosyllables *tu* and *qui*. In the genitive singular, *i* or *ae* at the end of the word are pronounced long, as in *mei, meae;* otherwise they are short, as in *illius*. The dative singular ending is always long, as in *nostro*, except in *mihi, tibi, sibi*, which are regarded as either long or short. The accusative singular ending is short, as in *illum*, with the exception of *me, te, se*. The vocative singular is the same as the nominative singular. The ablative singular is long, as in *ab illo*. The nominative and accusative plural are short only when they end in *a*, as in *nostra*. The genitive plural is always short, as in *illorum*. The dative and ablative plural ending *is* is long, the ending *bus* is short.

[283] In all verbs, their moods, tenses, numbers, persons, and conjugations, this is the standard rule: whatever part ends in *a*, that ending is long, as in *canta*. The ending *e* is short, as in *lege*, unless it is in a verb of the second conjugation, such as *doce;* then it is long. A part ending in *i* is always long, as in *nutri*. The ending *o* is short, as in *audio*, although the authorities disagree on this: Vergil makes the first person singular of the first conjugation long, as in

---

[72] The nominative is *Diomedēs* (-ηs), the vocative *Diomedĕs* (-ες); Latin has only the one letter *e* to represent the two Greek letters eta and epsilon.

canto quae solitus[73] and *terra tibi mando.*[74] However, monosyllables such as *do, flo, sto* are long. The ending *u* is long. . . .[75] The ending *am* is short, as in *legebam.* The ending in *r* is short, as in *loquor.* The endings in the letter *s* are long if the penultimate letter is *a* or *e*, as in *amas, doces,* with the exception of the monosyllable *es* and its compounds, such as *ades;* but if *i* is the letter before the *s*, it is short, as in *legis, legitis;* except that the second person singular of the present indicative in the third conjugation[76] is long, as in *nutris, audis,* and the same part of the verb *volo, vis;* if the letter before *s* is *u*, it will be short, as in *nutrimus.* The ending in *t* is short, as in *legit.* The ending in *c* is long, as in *produc.* Participles, although they are inflected through cases, are pronounced by principles completely different from those for the pronunciation of nouns.

[284] Monosyllabic adverbs like *huc*, or their compounds like *illuc*, are all long, except *bis* and *ter;* for other adverbs the ending in *a* is long, as in *una;* the ending in *e* is long, as in *docte, pulchre,* except in those cases where the adverb has no comparative or superlative, such as *rite*, or those in which the comparative is defective, such as *bene*, . . . *impune.*[77] The ending in *i* is long, as in *heri*, except for *ibi* and *ubi* and their compounds like *sicubi*, and for *quasi* also. The endings in *o* of adverbs which are not derived from other parts of speech are short;[78] if they are derived from other parts of speech, as in *falso*, the endings are long, although the authorities differ. Endings in *u* are long, as in *noctu;* those in *l* should be short, as in *semel;* those in *m, n, r* are short, as in *cursim, forsan, fortiter;* those in *s* are long only when the *s* is preceded by *a*, as in *alias;* those in *c* are long, as in *illuc.*

[285] In participles, the nominative singular ending is always

---

73 Vergil *Eclogues* 2. 23.

74 *Ibid.*, 8. 93.

75 The example appears to have dropped out of the text.

76 Martianus includes in the third conjugation the two now commonly called the third and the fourth; he distinguishes them as "third conjugation, short" and "third conjugation long." See § 311.

77 *Impune* does have a comparative and a superlative. By comparison with the grammarians Victorinus and Servius, it would appear that a phrase such as "or those not derived from adjectives, like" has dropped out of Martianus' text between *bene* and *impune*.

78 Dick postulates the loss of an example here.

short,[79] as in *lecturus;* the genitive and dative singular endings are long, as in *lecturi, lecturo,* except in the present tense, where the genitive ending is short, as in *amantis.* The accusative and vocative endings are definitely short, as in *lecturum, lecture;* the ablative singular ending is short only when it ends in *e,* as in *amante, legente.* The nominative and accusative plural endings in participles of the masculine and feminine genders are long, as in *lecturi, lecturos, lecturae, lecturas;* in neuters they are short, as in *lectura.* The genitive plural ending is short, as in *lecturorum.* The dative and ablative plural endings in *is* are long; those in *bus* are short.

[286] The endings of copulative, disjunctive, and expletive conjunctions are short unless their position makes them long. Causal and rational conjunctions ending in *a,* such as *propterea, interea,* have their endings long, except for *ita* and *quia;* those which end in *i,* such as *si,* have their endings long, with the sole exception of *nisi;* those which end in *n* have the ending long if *i* precedes the *n,* as in *sin;* otherwise the endings are short. All other conjunctions are regarded as having short endings.

[287] Prepositions ending in *a,* such as *contra, extra,* and the monosyllabic *a,* are the only prepositions with long endings. Prepositions governing the ablative case all have short endings, except for those monosyllables which either consist of a vowel or end in a vowel, such as *e, de.* Prepositions which govern more than one case are certain to have short endings.

[288] Interjections are long if they are monosyllables like *heus;* but if they are of two or three syllables, since they have the appearance of one of the other parts of speech, their length is determined by the standard applying to the part of speech they resemble, as in the case of *papae.*

These, then, are the rules to be observed in pronouncing the final syllables in all the parts of speech, except with respect to diphthongs and to words long by position.

[289] The topic of syllables has now been quickly covered;

[79] This can apply only to future and perfect participles, not to present participles. Dick, following Johann Jürgensen ("De texto Martiani Capellae libro," *Commentationes philologae seminarii philologiae Lipsiensis,* 1874, pp. 57-96), deletes the phrase *temporis futuri* [of future time], which in some manuscripts qualifies "participles."

we must come on to words. This is the proper order for such matters, and this topic in turn will divide into two. First we must discuss *proportio*, which the Greeks call *analogia* [analogy]; and then what the scholars commonly call *anomala* [anomalies], the innovations which set the rule aside; in them half of our speech consists, or rather, the consistency of our speech is injured; these I shall discuss within the scope of one small book, and as far as your taste for serious topics will permit.

[290] Analogy, which in Latin is called *proportio*, is the observance of agreement between similar words. In the first place, all Latin nouns end in one of twelve letters: the five vowels, the six semivowels, and one mute, *t*, as in *caput*.

A, the first of the vowels, ends masculine nouns such as *Catilina*, *Iugurtha*, feminine nouns . . .[80] such as *advena*, Greek feminines such as *Helena*, *Andromacha*, and pronouns such as *altera*, *sola*, *illa*. In these, if you substitute *ius* for the *a* ending, you get the genitive singular, *alterius*, *solius*, *illius*; if you substitute *i*, you get the dative, *alteri*, *soli*, *illi*. Greek neuters like *poema*, *toreuma*, have identical endings in three cases of each number; they add *tis* to form the genitive singular, omit the *s* to form the dative, and end the ablative with a short *e*; in the dative and ablative plural they keep the form of the genitive singular, although they can also add the *bus* ending.

[291] Those Latin nouns which end with a short *e*, such as *monile*, *sedile*, are neuter. Besides those cases which have identical endings (as being neuter)[81] these words have identical dative and ablative endings (*huic monili*, *sedili*, and *ab hoc monili*, *sedili*); the reason is that an ablative ending in *e* would make four cases identical, which the declension of neuter nouns does not permit. Nouns which end with a long *e* in the nominative, being Greek feminine nouns like *Agave* and *Autonoe*, should be declined in the Greek manner so that their nominative, dative, vocative, and ablative are all identical, with the genitive ending in *s* and the accusative in *n*.

---

[80] Grotius and subsequent editors note a lacuna here; *advena* is not feminine but common in gender, so that the words "such as *Musa*, common nouns . . ." have clearly dropped out of the text after "feminine nouns"—the example of course need not be *Musa*.

[81] I.e., nominative, vocative, and accusative.

However, the Greek feminine nouns which change their *e* ending to *a*, as *Andromache* to *Andromacha*, are declined in the same way as the Latin nouns ending in *a*.

Latin nouns ending in *i* are of every gender and are indeclinable, like *frugi*, *nihili*. *Gummi* and *synapi*, however, are exotic nouns of neuter gender and only singular number; their case endings are identical, except for the genitive, which has an *s* (*synapis*, *gummis*); nevertheless it is correct to say *haec gummis*.

[292] No neuter nouns end in *o*; nouns with this ending are either masculine, like *Cicero*, or feminine, like *Juno*, *hirundo*, or of common gender, like *homo*. The declension of such nouns takes two forms: either they keep the *o* in the oblique cases, as in *unio*, *unionis*; or they change it to *i*, as in *cupido*, *cupidinis*; *crepido*, *crepidinis*; in both instances they become a syllable longer in the oblique cases, except for the vocative singular. Although *caro* is declined contrary to this analogy, custom has preserved it and *Anio* also; in their declension they are unique, and follow no exemplars, for their genitives are *huius carnis*, *Anienis*. *Duo* and *ambo* are always plural, and therefore should not be included amongst the categories I mentioned above; they follow their own particular declensions. Nouns ending in *o* of Greek origin but later Latinized, such as *leo*, *draco*, are declined like *Cicero*, *Milo*; those which have kept their earlier form, like *Io*, *Ino*, are declined in the Greek way, with their genitives *Ius*, *Inus*, accusatives *Iun*, *Inun*,[82] and so on for the other cases, although it is customary to say *hanc Io*. *Turbo* as a proper noun is declined like *Cicero*; but if it means 'the force of the wind' or the child's toy[83] it is declined like *cupido*.

[293] Only neuter nouns end with the letter *u*; for instance, *cornu*, *veru*, which in the plural is *verua*. Earlier writers also used *specua*. The declension of the plural is quite certain in these nouns; the first three cases are the same, as usual in neuter nouns, the dative and the ablative end in *bus*, and the genitive adds *um* to the ablative singular. There is dispute about the genitive singular, which some end in *us*, others in *is*; also about the dative singular, which some end in *i*, as in *cornui*, *genui*; but some follow archaic writers

---

[82] Strictly, these should be transliterated as *Ious*, *Inous*, *Ioun*, *Inoun*; but the normal Latin transliteration of Greek represents the diphthong *ou* as *u*.

[83] *Turbo*, the word for "whirlwind," was also used as the name for a spinning top.

and make the dative the same form as the ablative, *huic genu, cornu;* the grounds for this are, that we say in the plural *genubus, cornubus,* and when the last syllable is omitted the remainder is the dative singular form, as happens in *civibus* and *suavibus.* Just as in *genibus* and *cornibus* the letter *i* has been substituted for the letter *u,* so do we say *optimus* and *maximus* when the forms used to be *optumus* and *maxumus.* However, some scholars say *genuis* and *cornuis* for the genitive singular, though the genitive ought not have more syllables than the dative and the ablative. Although *senatus* and *exercitus* are of a different declension, yet one ought to say *genus* and *cornus* for the genitive singular, on the model of *senatus* and *exercitus.* Besides, any nouns or participles which end their genitive singular in *is* have one syllable more in the dative plural, as in *Catonis, Catonibus;* on this principle, if the genitive singular be *genuis, cornuis,* the dative plural would be *genuibus,* to make an extra syllable.

[294] Nouns ending in *l* have two forms. The first includes masculine nouns like *Hannibal, Hasdrubal,* and comprises Carthaginian names almost entirely, except for our name *Sol;* it also includes feminine nouns like *Tanaquil,* an Etruscan name, and common nouns like *vigil, pugil,* which are all of the same declension. The other class is of neuter nouns such as *mel, fel,* which differ from the first class in being monosyllables and in doubling the *l* in the oblique cases. Those who say *proconsule* as a nominative, with the *e* ending, have in view the nature of the preposition *pro,* which is used only with an ablative. They do not take the view that when one says *proconsul* one is using not two words but a composite noun like *procurator, propugnator;* the fact that these nouns can form verbs like *procuro, propugno,* where the preposition is absorbed into the verb, while *proconsul* forms no such verb (though we do have the verb *consulo*), in no way renders the example invalid. If one should say *proconsule* as the nominative, then the noun would be indeclinable; but one ought to follow the custom and say *proconsul,* so that the noun can be declined in the same way as the other nouns ending in *l,* like *vigil, mugil, pugil,* where the genitive plural is *mugilum* and *pugilum;* for if the nominative were *mugilis,* like *agilis,* the genitive plural would be *mugilium,* like *agilium.*

[295] M is the ending of neuter nouns like *caelum, scamnum.* Note that nouns which have *i* before the last syllable, like *lilium, folium,*

ought to double the *i* in the genitive singular and the dative and ablative plural, as in *lilii* and *liliis;* for the genitive has either the same number of syllables as the nominative, as in *scamnum, scamni;* or more syllables, as in *caput, capitis;* but never fewer syllables. Besides, the dative ending in *o* changes the *o* to *i* to form the genitive, as *scamno* to *scamni,* but usage and the authority of earlier writers prefer to say *ingeni* and *consili* and *imperi* in three syllables.

It is disputed whether one ought to say *vasum* or *vas,* since all neuter nouns whose nominative singular ends in something other than *m* form their dative and ablative plural in *bus;* for instance, *monile, monilibus; genu, genibus; pecus, pecoribus; nomen, nominibus; marmor, marmoribus.* On this principle, *vas* ought to form *vasibus* and, in the genitive, *horum vasum;* for all neuter nouns which end their ablative singular with *e* have in the genitive plural the same number of syllables as in the ablative singular, for instance, *a nemore, nemorum; capite, capitum.* However, the declension of *vas* is an anomaly; in the singular the nominative is *vas,* genitive *vasis,* dative *vasi,* ablative *a vase;* while in the plural it is declined like *scamna.* Nevertheless, Lucretius has the genitive *vasi,* in *rarique facit lateramina vasi.*[84]

[296] *N* is the final letter of masculine nouns like *flamen, pecten,* and of neuter nouns like *omen, flumen,* and of nouns common to both masculine and feminine genders, like *tibicen, fidicen*—though some authors disagree with this, using *tibicinam* and *fidicinam.*[85] All these nouns follow the same clearly defined declension. *Gluten* is similar to these, though Sallust uses *glutinum.* Some feminine nouns seem similar, such as *Siren.* There is another kind of masculine noun, such as *lien, rien,* which keeps the *e* before the final *n,* but in other respects declines just like the examples cited. *Ren* is a nominative singular which has no other case in use except the ablative. Greek nouns ending in *n* have before the *n* the letters *a, e, i, o,* as in *Alcman, Cephen, delphin, Phaëthon;* of these, those which end in *an, en, in* follow the declension of the examples above, like *fulmen, numen, fidicen;* those which end in *on* and in Greek retain the long *o* throughout their declension, such as *leon,* keep the *o* long in Latin also and are declined like *Cicero, Scipio;* those which in

---

[84] Lucretius *De rerum natura* 6. 233, where modern editors in fact read *vasis.*

[85] I.e., using in the accusative a feminine form which would postulate the feminine nominatives *tibicina, fidicina.*

Greek change the long *o* of the nominative to a short *o* in the other cases, such as *Amphion, Creon, Agamemnon,* in Latin lose the *n* in the nominative and are declined like those Latin nouns which shorten the final vowel of their stems in the oblique cases, such as *virgo, turbo.* Those which in Greek add *t* to the nominative do the same in Latin, as *Phaëthon, Phaëthontis.*

[297] Nouns which end in *ar,* like *Caesar, lar, far, par, impar,* follow a single formation, except that neuter nouns double the *r* in the oblique cases, as *far, farris* [*grain*]. Poetic license uses a plural with these nouns, although there is no plural for those nouns whose quantity we measure by weight or extent, like *aurum* [gold], *plumbum* [lead], *triticum* [wheat], *oleum* [oil]. . . .[86] So people are mistaken when they say *parium,* because these nouns have the same ending in the first three cases of the plural, as in *hi Caesares, hos Caesares, o Caesares,* and the accusative cannot have *i* before the final *s* if the genitive has *r* before the *u* of its ending.[87] But those who say *parium* appear to be considering the nominative plural of the neuter;[88] and since the nominative plural is *paria,* like *suavia,* they say for the genitive plural *parium,* like *suavium.*

[298] There are six variations on the ending *er:* the first when the genitive has the same number of syllables as the nominative and ends in *i,* as *aper, niger, macer,* giving *apri, nigri, macri;* the second like *tener, lacer, puer,* giving *teneri, laceri, pueri;* the third like *imber, uter,* which is to this extent different from the foregoing, that the genitive singular ends in *s* and the dative in *i,* yet they are not like the second type longer than the nominative, and the genitive plural ends in *ium;* the fourth type is like *mater, pater, frater,* which form their dative plural not in *is* (*apris*) like the first type but in *ibus* (*fratribus*), while at the same time this type does not lengthen by a syllable in the oblique cases like the second type, and has the genitive plural ending *um;* for we say *patrum, fratrum,* not (as in the third type) *utrium, imbrium.* Besides, this fourth type

---

[86] Because the transition here is so abrupt, Dick supposes a lacuna in which Martianus discussed genitive plural endings in *um* and *ium* and accusative plural endings in *is.*

[87] What Martianus appears to mean is that *parium* is incorrect because nouns with an *ium* genitive plural have an *is* accusative plural, whereas those nouns with an *ar* nominative all have an *es* accusative plural.

[88] *Parium* being an adjective.

has the same ending in the three cases *hi patres, hos patres, o patres,* while *imber* and *uter* have *hos imbris* and *utris.* The fifth type is that of *passer, anser, later, mulier,* which differs from the second type in that the second type forms its genitive ending in *i,* and it is longer by one syllable than the nominative (as in *gener, generi*), while the fifth type has the longer genitive but its ending is in *is* (as in *passer, passeris*). There are other differences as well. The natural classification of *piper* and *cicer* is in this fifth type, for they are declined like *passer* in the singular, and they occur only in the singular. The sixth type is that of *neuter* and *uter;* it forms *neutrius* and *utrius,* and its declension is that of the pronouns which have the genitive ending in *ius* and the dative in *i;* these genitive and dative endings are common to all genders.

There is only one type with the nominative ending *ir,* that of *vir.* There are two types with the ending *or;* one lengthens the *o* in the oblique cases, as in *sopor, soporis; color, coloris;* the other has the *o* short, as in *arbor, arboris;* they are declined in the same way. In former times the genitives *Castoris* and *Hectoris* were pronounced with the *o* long, but nowadays we make them short, since the Greeks pronounce them short. There are two types with the nominative ending *ur;* the first, like *satur,* has the genitive ending *i,* as in *saturi;* while the second has the genitive ending *is,* as in *sulphur, sulphuris; augur, auguris.* Of the neuter nouns with the nominative ending *ur,* some keep the *u,* as in *sulphur, sulphuris;* others lose it as in *ebur, eboris.*

[299] There are eight types with the nominative ending in *s;* one type has *a* before *s,* like *Maecenas, civitas;* one has *e,* like *verres, moles;* or *i,* like *panis;* or *o,* like *custos, nepos;* or *u,* like *vetus, Ligus;* or *r,* like *iners;* or *n,* like *serpens;* or *p,* like *praeceps.* The type with *a* before *s* has two forms: The first like *Maecenas, Laenas;* the second like *nostras, Privernas,* which differ from the first form in that they are common to all genders and ought to have in the genitive plural the letter *i,* which is frequent in the nominative, accusative, and vocative plural of neuter nouns. Thus we say *nostratium, Privernatium,* since the nominatives are *nostratia, Privernatia;* we also say *praegnatium, optimatium,* because these have their accusative plural in *i, optimatis, praegnatis,* although the older writers used *praegnatum, optimatum; praegnas* can be both feminine

and neuter in gender. *As* and *mas*, being monosyllables, are not bound by the analogy, but follow their own forms of declension, giving *assis* and *maris* for the genitive singular, and *assium* and *marium* for the genitive plural. *Fas* and *nefas* are indeclinable.

[300] There are three kinds of Greek nouns which, when used in Latin, end in *as:* the first, like *Olympias, Pythias,* form their genitive *Olympiadis, Pythiadis;* the second, like *Pallas, Thoas, Atlas,* form it *Pallantis, Thoantis, Atlantis;* the third, like *Aeneas, Pythagoras, Lichas,* form it *Aeneae, Pythagorae, Lichae,* following the declension of those Latin nouns which have their genitive in *ae* and their nominative in *a,* like *Catilinae* from *Catilina.* These nouns, being Greek, keep the *s* in the nominative, although some Greek nouns, like *Nicia, Mela,* lose it in the nominative; in these nominatives one ought to follow customary usage.

[301] There are five kinds of nouns ending in *es:* the first have their nominative, vocative, and accusative plural the same, but the genitive plural ends in *um,* as *Hercules, proles,* give *Herculum, prolum.* The second kind differs from the first in that the genitive plural ends in *ium* and the accusative plural in *is* as with *nubes, rupes, cautes;* there are no masculine nouns in this class. The third kind might have some differences of declension amongst themselves but are considered one class because the nouns agree in adding an extra syllable in the oblique cases; such nouns are *Ceres, bipes, merces;* there are no masculine nouns in this class except Greek nouns like *Chremes, Laches.* The fourth kind differs from the third in changing *e* into *i* in the oblique cases, whereas the third kind retains the *e;* and whereas the third kind has the *e* long in the nominative singular, the fourth kind has it short, as in *hospes, antistes, ales, comes.* The fifth kind differs from the fourth in that the genitive has an extra syllable and ends in *i,* which is the same as the dative, while the accusative ends in *em* and the ablative in long *e;* the addition of *rum* to this makes the genitive plural. The nominative plural is identical with the nominative and vocative singular, while the dative and ablative plural ends in the syllable *bus,* as in *facies, dies, spes, acies. Rei* and *spei* are customarily pronounced short, perhaps because these nouns are monosyllabic.

[302] Of the nouns ending in *is,* some add a syllable in the oblique cases, others do not, at least in the singular. There are two kinds of

these latter; the first includes masculine nouns, like *scrobis, mensis* (although Lucan says *exigua scrobe*),[89] feminine nouns,[90] and nouns of common gender like *canis, iuvenis*, the declension of which is clear. The second kind differs from the first in that the ablative ends in *i*, the accusative in *im*, as in the only two masculine examples, *Ligeris* and *Tiberis*, and the feminine ones, *clavis, pelvis, turris, sitis, tussis*. Their diminutives show clearly that in their declension all these are pronounced with a long *i*. So as often as we are in doubt over the pronunciation of a noun, let us look at its diminutive. Of those which add a syllable there are two kinds: one keeps the *i* short, and this includes masculine nouns like *sanguis, pulvis, lapis*, and feminine nouns like *cuspis, cassis*; it makes no difference that in their declension one group keeps the *i* while the other converts it to *e* (in the ablative), nor that one ends its genitive singular in *dis*, the other in *ris*. The second kind has the letter *i* long in the nominative, as in *glis, lis, Samnis*, and keeps it so in the oblique cases, while in the genitive plural we use *i* before the final *um*, as in *glirium, litium, Samnitium*, as distinct from the first kind's *lapidum, cuspidum, cassidum*.

[303] Nouns ending in *os* can be said to form one class, since there is little difference between them. Though they all lengthen by a syllable in the oblique cases, they differ in that some convert the *s* of the nominative to *t*, some to *d*, some to *r*, as seen in *nepos, nepotis; custos, custodis;* masculine monosyllables like *flos, floris, ros, roris*, or a neuter one like *os, oris*. In *ossibus*, however, the nominative is *os* by usage and contrary to principle, since it does not have *r* in the genitive; but the nominative *ossum* is impossible, since neuter nouns with the nominative singular ending in *m* do not admit the syllable *bus* in the plural; so in the monosyllable the analogy does not apply.

[304] There are six kinds of nouns ending in *us*. In the first the genitive ends in the single *i*, the vocative in *e:* for instance, the genitive of *Marcus Sextus* is *Marci Sexti*, the vocative *o Marce Sexte*. The second kind differs from the first in that the genitive ends in double *i* and the vocative ends in *i:* for instance, *Antonius Iulius* gives the genitive *huius Antonii Iulii* and the vocative *o Antoni Iuli;* otherwise the second kind is the same as the first. The third kind had

[89] *Civil War* 8. 756. The feminine form of the adjective makes it clear that Lucan regards the noun as feminine; so do a number of other classical writers.

[90] It seems likely that examples have here dropped out of the text.

the same form in the nominative and the vocative, and the genitive
is spelled the same but pronounced with a long ending; the dative
ends in *ui*, the ablative in *u*, the accusative in *um*, as with *senatus*,
fluctus, exercitus; in the plural these nouns have long *us* in the
nominative, the accusative, and the vocative; the genitive ends in
uum; the dative and the ablative in *bus*. The fourth kind adds a
syllable in the oblique cases, but the nouns have minor variations
amongst themselves; some keep the letter *u*, pronounced short;
others have it long, as in *Ligus, Liguris; palus, paludis; virtus, virtutis*.
Some change the *u* to *e*, as *vetus, veteris; Venus, Veneris;* some to
o, as *nemus, nemoris;* but these follow the same declension. Although
laus and *fraus* are monosyllables containing diphthongs, they are in
this same class, because they also add a syllable in the oblique cases.
The fifth kind is the class of pronouns which end in *us*, such as
unus, solus, totus; they are declined thus: *unus, unius, uni, unum,
unus, ab une, uni, unorum, unis, unos, uni, ab unis*. The sixth kind
ends in *eus*, like *hinnuleus, eculeus*, and in the vocative the *e* is
repeated, as in *eculee, hinnulee;* though some people prefer to use
the Greek vocative in *eu*, as in *Tydeu*.

   [305] Neuter nouns ending in *is* are indeclinable, like *tressis, sexis*.
There are two kinds of neuter nouns ending in *us*. The first has the
genitive in *i* and has no plural: for example, *vulgus, pelagus*. Lucretius says *viri* from *virus*,[91] although it would be more correctly left
uninflected. The second kind includes those nouns which add a syllable in the oblique cases and end the genitive singular in *ris*, such as
genus, nemus; some of these change the *u* of their nominative ending
to *e*, as *olus, oleris; ulcus, ulceris;* some change it to *o*, as *nemus,
nemoris; pecus, pecoris*. There is some doubt whether *fenus* and
stercus change their *u* to *e* or to *o*, since nouns like *vulnus, genus,
funus*, ending in the syllable *nus*, change the *u* to *e;* and we do use
the word *feneratus*. The example of *penus* does not affect the issue,
since its place is amongst the doubtful kinds of noun. Again, earlier
writers used *stercoratos agros*, not *sterceratos*.

   [306] Nouns ending in *ns* or *rs* are all of one kind, except that of
those ending in *rs* some end their stem in the oblique cases in *d*, like
socors, socordis; some in *t*, such as *sollers, iners*. Their declension
is the same in all cases of the plural except the genitive and the accu-

---

[91] *De rerum natura* 2. 476.

sative; some, like *Mars* and *Arruns*, end the genitive plural in *um* and the accusative in *es;* some, like *sapiens* and *patiens*, end the genitive plural in *ium* and therefore end the accusative in *is*. Most nouns of this group are common to all three genders, and the letter *i*, which appears in the nominative plural neuter, is found also in the genitive of the other genders with which the noun is common.

[307] Only a few neuter nouns end with the letter *t*, such as the indeclinable *git*, and *caput* and *sinciput*. Some people, when they say *lac*, add *t*, because it does form the genitive *lactis;* but Vergil writes *lac mihi non aestate novum non frigore defit;* [92] indeed no nouns in Latin end in two mutes, and for this reason archaic writers used *lacte* as the nominative.

[308] Of the nouns which end in the letter *x*, some (amongst which are all the common nouns) end their genitive plural in *ium*, and therefore have their accusative in *is;* but most end their genitive plural in *um* without the antecedent *i*, and therefore have their accusative in *es*. In all other details both kinds agree; in the singular, all end the nominative in *x*, the genitive in *is*, the dative in *i*, the ablative in *e*, and add to this *m* to form the complete accusative; in the plural the dative and ablative end in the syllable *bus*. On the points where they differ, some earlier writers used *astrocum* and *ferocum;* if one follows them, there appears to be only one class of nouns ending in *x*. Any vowel may precede the *x*, as in *capax, frutex, pernix, atrox, redux*. Some of these nouns pronounce the last syllable of the nominative long, some short; some nouns follow the same practice as each other in the nominative, but differ in the oblique cases. *Pax* and *rapax*, *rex* and *pumex*, *nux* and *lux* differ in pronunciation of the nominative; but *nix* and *nutrix*, *nox* and *atrox* give the same value to their corresponding vowels in the nominative, but different values in the oblique cases.[93] We should note that in the declension of these nouns some change the *x* to *g*, some to *c:* for *lex* makes *legis;* *grex, gregis;* but *pix* makes *picis;* and *nux, nucis*. The *x* always changes to *c* in the genitive of nouns that are not monosyllabic, as in *frutex, fruticis; ferox, ferocis*. By exception, *supellex, senex*, and

---

[92] *Eclogues* 2. 22.

[93] E.g., the genitive singular forms of *nix* and *nox* (*nivis* and *noctis*) have their penultimate syllables long, whereas those of *nutrix* and *atrox* (*nutricis, atrocis*) have them short.

nix are declined contrary to the general rule: *supellex* adds two syllables to its stem in the oblique cases, which is against the rule;
senex remains disyllabic in the genitive as in the nominative, although
all other nouns ending in *x* add a syllable; and *nix* changes its stem
ending not to *c*, like *pix*, nor *g*, like *rex*, but to *v*, although a consonant may not change to a vowel.

The form of the genitive plural is derived from the ablative singular. If the ablative singular ends in *a* or *o*, the ending of the genitive
plural adds *rum* to that; if the ablative singular ends in short *e*, the
genitive plural ending is *um*; if the ablative singular ends in long *e*, the
genitive plural ending is *rum*; if the ablative singular ends in *i*,
the genitive plural ending is *ium*; if the ablative singular ends in *u*, the
genitive plural ending is *uum*. The dative and ablative plural end
either in *is* or in *bus*—these are well-worn school precepts; when they
end in *is* the syllable is long, when in *bus* it is short.

[309] After that survey of the rules for nouns, it is proper to
come on to those for verbs. There are five kinds of verbs: active,
passive, neuter, common, and deponent. The active end in *o* and
signify action, such as *lego* [I read], *scribo* [I write]; the passive
end in *r* and signify that one is acted upon, as with *scribor* [I am
written], *legor* [I am read]; the neuter [intransitive] end in *o* and do
not signify complete action or complete passivity; such are *sudo*
[I sweat], *dormio* [I sleep]; in these, I do not know whether someone is acting or being acted upon. Common and deponent verbs both
end in *r*, but the difference between them is this: the common verb
may have both active and passive meanings, for we say *osculor te*
[I kiss you] and *osculor a te* [I am kissed by you]; but the
deponent verb has either an active meaning, as in *luctor* [I grieve],
or a passive, as in *morior* [I die]. There is also the impersonal verb,
such as *sudatur, curritur*,[94] which is so called because although it may
apply to any person it has no particular person as its subject.

[310] Verbs have five moods, although some people have said
they have six, some seven, some eight, some nine, and a few ten.
Those who say five name these: indicative, imperative, optative, conjunctive, infinitive—which is also called constant. Those who say six

---

[94] Literally, "it is sweated"; "it is run"—idiomatically, "there is sweat"; "there
is running."

add the permissive, those who say seven add the impersonal, those who say eight add the interrogative, those who say nine add the subjunctive and distinguish it from the conjunctive, those who say ten even add the hortative; but these unnecessary additions are against all reason.

[311] There is no disputing that there are three conjugations (*syzygiae*, as the Greeks call them), which in active and neuter verbs are distinguished in the second person of the present tense. As often as the last syllable of this ends in *as*, it is the first conjugation; in *es*, the second conjugation; in *is*, the third: for example, *cantas, vides, audis*. *Audis* would exemplify the 'third conjugation, long,' while the 'third conjugation, short' would be as in *curris*.[95] Verbs of all these conjugations, in the first person singular of the present indicative active, permit only three vowels to precede the last letter; namely, *e, i, u*, as in *sedeo, lanio, irruo;* but any consonant may precede except *f, k*, and *q*: for example, *libo, voco, cado, lego, traho, impello, amo, cano, scalpo, curro, lasso, peto, nexo*. To these are added *i* and *v* when used as consonants, as in *aio, adiuvo*. *F* is not excluded when we say *triumfo*, though this comes from Greek and is better written with *ph;* besides this example, from the fact that we say *faris* and *fatur* people postulate a first person of the verb, *for*.[96] There is also some doubt about the letter *q*, for we do say *eliquo* and *aequo*, and in words of this kind the letter *u* has the value of neither a vowel as in *irruo* nor a consonant as in *adiuuo*.

[312] In declining all these conjugations there are thirty-six forms apart from the defective, the impersonal, and the inchoative. Verbs of the first conjugation, whether they end with no other vowel preceding the *o* or with any vowel preceding it, have four forms. Verbs of the second conjugation have seven forms. Verbs of the 'third conjugation, short' have twenty forms; those which end their first person singular present indicative with *io* have six forms; those that end this part with *uo* have two forms; those that end this part with *o* with no vowel preceding have twelve forms. Verbs of the 'third conjugation, long,' which end their first person singular present

---

[95] Modern students of Latin conventionally regard these as the fourth and third conjugations, respectively.

[96] This is a defective verb of which the first person singular of the present indicative (by which a Latin verb is usually denoted) is not found in use.

indicative with *io,* have five forms. Any verbs of any conjugation whose first person singular present indicative ends with *o* with any other vowel preceding or with no vowel preceding has its declension included in this number of forms, which I shall discuss one by one.

[313] Verbs of the first conjugation end the first person singular present indicative with *o,* either with no other vowel preceding, such as *amo, canto;* or with *eo,* such as *commeo, calceo;* or with *io,* such as *lanio, satio;* or with *uo,* such as *aestuo, continuo.* Verbs of the first conjugation end the second person present imperative with long *a,* as *ama* from *amo, canta* from *canto.* They end the infinitive by adding *re* to the imperative, keeping the vowel long, as in *amare* from *ama, cantare* from *canta.* Again, in the first conjugation, verbs which end their perfect indicative by adding *vi* to the imperative, keeping the syllable long (as in *commeo, commea, commeavi,* and *lanio, lania, laniavi,* and *satio, satia, satiavi*), end the imperfect by adding *bam* to the imperative, as in *commeabam* from *commea, laniabam* from *lania, aestuabam* from *aestua.* The first conjugation ends its pluperfect by adding *veram* to the imperative, as in *commeaveram* from *commea, laniaveram* from *lania, aestuaveram* from *aestua.* In this conjugation *bo* added to the imperative ends the future indicative, as in *commeabo* from *commea, laniabo* from *lania, aestuabo* from *aestua.*

[314] Verbs which end their first person singular present indicative with *o* with no preceding vowel appear in the perfect and pluperfect indicative in four different ways. The rule of the first is similar to the preceding verbs which in the first person singular present indicative have a vowel immediately before the last letter of the stem, as in *amo, ama, amavi, amabam, amaveram, amabo, amare.* The second way changes the *o* to *i* and lengthens the penultimate vowel in the perfect and the antepenultimate vowel in the pluperfect, as in *adiuvo, adiuvi, adiuveram.* The third way follows a rule similar to the first but separates and omits the *a,* as in *seco, seca, secui, secabam, secueram, secabo, secare;* it makes *secui* in the perfect and *secueram* in the pluperfect. The fourth way appears through reduplication of the syllable, as in *sto, sta, steti, stabam, steteram, stabo, stare;* similar to this is *do, da, dedi, dabam, dederam, dabo, dare,* where the letter *a* is shortened, contrary to the rule applying in the formation of *dabam, dabo, dare.*

[315] Verbs of the second conjugation end the first person of the present indicative with *eo*, as in *video, vides; moneo, mones*. They end the present imperative second person with long *e*, as in *video, vide; moneo, mone*. The infinitive is formed by adding *re* to the imperative, keeping the syllable long, as in *vide, videre; mone, monere*. The perfect and pluperfect indicatives are conjugated in seven different ways. The first is the regular form: the perfect is formed by adding to the imperative ending (keeping the syllable long) the letters *vi*, as in *deleo, dele, delevi*; the pluperfect is formed by adding *veram* to the imperative ending, as in *dele, deleveram*. The second way is by changing the *eo* ending of the first person present indicative to *i*, as in *sedeo, sedi*; and for the pluperfect, *sederam*. The third way is when *eo* changes to *ui*, as in *caleo, calui; moneo, monui; calueram, monueram*. The fourth way is when *eo* changes to *i* and the consonant preceding *eo* changes to *s*, as in *mulgeo, mulsi, mulseram*. The fifth way is when *eo* changes to *i* and the consonant preceding *eo* changes to *x*, as where *luceo* and *lugeo* both form *luxi, luxeram*. The sixth way is when the part is formed by reduplication, as in *spondeo, spopondi, spoponderam*. The seventh way is when the perfect tenses are of passive form, as in *audeo, ausus sum, es, est; ausus eram, eras, erat*. Verbs of the second conjugation form the imperfect indicative by adding *bam* to the imperative ending, keeping the syllable long, as in *vide, videbam; mone, monebam*. They form the future by adding *bo* to the imperative ending, keeping the syllable long, as in *vide, videbo; mone, monebo*.

[316] Verbs of the third conjugation, short, in the first person present indicative either end in the letter *o* with no other vowel preceding it, as in *lego, legis; peto, petis*; or end in *io*, as in *rapio, rapis; facio, facis*; or in *uo*, as in *induo, irruo*. Verbs of this conjugation, which end the first person singular present indicative in *o* with no preceding vowel, end the second person singular present imperative in short *e* with the same consonant preceding the ending as in the present indicative, as in *lego, lege; peto, pete*; those verbs of this conjugation which end in *uo* retain the *u* with the *e* of the imperative, as in *induo, indue; irruo, irrue*. Verbs of this conjugation end their infinitive by adding *re* to the imperative, keeping the *e* of the imperative short, as in *lege, legere; pete, petere*. [317] Those verbs of this conjugation which end their first person present indicative in *io* form their perfect and pluperfect tenses in one of six ways.

The first way is to follow the rule of the third conjugation, long, making the *i* of the imperative long and adding for the perfect the syllable *vi*, for the pluperfect *veram*, as in *cupio, cupivi, cupiveram*. Sometimes the *v* is omitted and in the perfect the *i* is repeated (*cupii*), while in the pluperfect it is pronounced short (*cupieram*). The second way is to omit the *o* of the first person singular present indicative and to lengthen the preceding syllable, either altering the vowel or leaving it, as in *facio, feci; fugio, fugi;* in the pluperfect the *i* is replaced by *e*, and the syllable *ram* is added, as in *feceram, fugeram*. The third way is when the *io* ending is turned into the ending *ui*, as in *elicio, elicui, elicueram;* the fourth way is by dropping the *io* ending and the preceding consonant and pronouncing the word with a double *s*, as in *percutio, percussi, percusseram;* the fifth way uses *x* instead of *ss*, as in *aspicio, aspexi, aspexeram;* the sixth way reduplicates a syllable, as in *pario, peperi, peperam*. [318] Verbs of this conjugation which end the first person singular present indicative in *uo* form their perfect and pluperfect in two ways. The first is by changing the *o* of the present indicative to *i*, as in *induo, indui, indueram;* the second uses *x*, as in *instruo, instruxi, instruxeram*. [319] Verbs of this conjugation which end their first person singular present indicative in *o* with no preceding vowel form their perfect and pluperfect indicative in twelve ways. The first is the same as the third conjugation, long, as I showed above in dealing with those verbs of the third conjugation, short, whose first person present indicative ends in *io;* for as *cupio* forms *cupivi* and *cupiveram*, so *peto* forms *petivi* and *petiveram*. Sometimes also the *v* is omitted and the *i* repeated, as in *petii, petieram*. The second way is to change the *o* of the present indicative to *i*. . . .[97] to change the *o* of the present indicative to *i* and lengthen the preceding syllable, either altering its vowel or preserving it, omitting also any penultimate consonant which closed the syllable in its original form; for instance, *ago, egi, egeram; lego, legi, legeram;* or, as instances of those which omit consonants, *frango, fregi, fregeram; fundo, fudi, fuderam*. The fourth way is to omit the penultimate consonant of the present stem and shorten the preceding vowel, as in *findo, fidi, fideram; scindo, scidi, scideram*. The fifth way is to substitute *ui* for the *o* of the present indicative, as in *molo, molui, molueram; colo*,

---

[97] There is clearly a lacuna here where an example has dropped out; e.g., *cudo, cudi, cuderam*. The next sentence would begin: "The third way is. . . ."

colui, colueram. The sixth way is to substitute *si* for the *o*, as in *carpo, carpsi, carpseram; scribo, scripsi, scripseram.* The seventh way is to omit the *o* and turn the preceding consonant into double *s*, as in *meto, messui, messueram.* The eighth has a similar omission, of *o*, a single *s*, and the preceding vowel long, as in *trudo, trusi, truseram.* The ninth uses *x*, as in *expungo, expunxi, expunxeram; ungo, unxi, unxeram.* The tenth reduplicates the first syllable, as in *pungo, pupugi, pupugeram; curro, cucurri, cucurreram.* The eleventh way reduplicates the final syllable of composite verbs, as in *trado, tradidi, tradideram; reddo, reddidi, reddideram.* The twelfth way uses a passive form, as in *fido; fisus sum, es est; fisus eram, eras, erat.* [320] All these verbs of the third conjugation, short, end their imperfect indicative by adding the syllable *bam* to the imperative, with the same consonant or vowel to end the stem as in the first person singular present indicative; for instance, *lege, legebam; pete, petebam.* The exceptions are those verbs which have *i* before the *o* of the present indicative; for they form their imperfect ending by inserting *i* before the imperative ending, lengthening the *e* and adding *bam*, as in *rapio, rape, rapiebam.* Verbs of this conjugation form the ending of the future indicative by dropping the *e* of the imperative form and adding the syllable *am*, as in *lege, legam; pete, petam; indue, induam.* The exceptions are those verbs which have *i* before the *o* of the present indicative; to form the future they change the *e* of the imperative to *i* and add the syllable *am*, as in *rapio, rape, rapiam; facio, face, faciam.*

[321] Verbs of the third conjugation, long, in the first person singular present indicative end either in *eo*, as in *adeo, adis; prodeo, prodis;* or in *io*, as in *audio, audis; nutrio, nutris.* Verbs of this conjugation in the second person singular present imperative end in long *i*, as in *adeo, adi; prodeo, prodi; audio, audi; nutrio, nutri.* In the infinitive mood they end by adding *re* to the imperative, keeping the *i* long, as in *adi, adire; prodi, prodire.* Verbs of this conjugation which end their first person present indicative in *eo* end their perfect by adding *vi* to the imperative, as in *adeo, adi, adivi,* and the pluperfect by adding *veram*, as in *adiveram;* but usage for the sake of brevity frequently omits the *v* and in the perfect reduplicates the *i*, as in *adii, adieram; prodii, prodieram.* The ending of the imperfect is formed by adding *bam* to the imperative, as in *adibam, prodibam.*

[322] However, those verbs of this conjugation which end their first person present indicative in *io* form their perfect and pluperfect in five ways. The first is like that mentioned above: *nutrio, nutrivi, nutriveram, nutrii, nutrieram;* and *audii, audieram,* as when Vergil says *audieras et fama fuit.*[98] Only the imperfect form differs from the example above; for all the verbs of this conjugation which end their present indicative first person in *io* form their imperfect in the same way, by adding long *e* before the final syllable, as in *audiebam, veniebam, operiebam;* although earlier writers used these without the letter *e,* as when Vergil says: *nutribat Tyrrhusque pater, cui regia parent / armenta.*[99] The second way is to omit the *u* of the present and to lengthen the preceding syllable, as in *venio, veni, veneram.* The third way is to substitute *ui* for *io,* as in *operio, operui, operueram.* The fourth way is to omit *io* and change the preceding consonant to *s,* as in *sarcio, sarsi, sarseram.* The fifth uses *x,* as in *vincio, vinxi, vinxeram.*

[323] Verbs of this conjugation which end their present indicative in *eo* form their future ending in the one way, by adding *bo* to the imperative, as in *adeo, adi, adibo; prodeo, prodi, prodibo.* Those verbs which end their present indicative in *io* add *am* to the imperative to form the future, as in *audio, audi, audiam; nutrio, nutri, nutriam.* Terence, however, uses the *bo* ending, so that there appear to be two alternative formations; for he says: *iam scibo, ubi siet.*[100]

[324] Of those verbs which have a present indicative ending in *eo* there are some which, though differing in their present forms, have an identical perfect form, as for instance *luceo* and *lugeo:* for the perfect of both is *luxi.* Similarly, *cernit* and *crescit* have the perfect form *crevit.* There are other verbs which, though sharing a common first person singular present indicative, are of two different conjugations, such as *pando* and *mando;* for they form both *pandas* and *pandis,* both *mandas* and *mandis.*

Verbs sometimes govern a single case, like the genitive as with *misereor tui,* or the dative as with *suadeo tibi,* or the accusative as with *moneo te,* or the ablative as with *utor illo;* sometimes they

---

98 *Eclogues* 9. 11.
99 *Aeneid* 7. 485. The verb in Vergil is in fact plural—*nutribant.*
100 *Adelphi* 361: *iam hinc scibo ubi siet.*

govern two cases, like the genitive and . . .[101] the accusative and ablative as with *fungor hanc rem* and *fungor illa re.*

Those are enough examples of analogy. The forms that are
not included above must certainly be reckoned as anomalies. I shall
discuss these very briefly to show that some words have acquired a
usage inconsistent with their form or have abandoned a usage
proper to it.

[325] When *reus* and *deus* are similar in the nominative singular,
why do we say *hi rei* in the plural for one and, inconsistently, *hi
di* for the other, when we ought to say *dei*—especially when no genitive should be longer by two syllables than its nominative, as happens when we say *deorum?* When *Thoas, Aeas,* and *Aeneas* are
similar, why do two form the genitives *Thoantis* and *Aeantis,* yet
Aeneas forms not *Aeneantis* but *Aeneae?* When we say *hic biceps*
and *triceps,* why is the genitive form two syllables longer, contrary
to the norm, so that we say *bicipitis* or *tricipitis,* and not *bicipis* or
tricipis? How does it happen that *aliger, frugifer, accipiter* have all
the case terminations, but *Iuppiter* has only two? When *sanctus, pius,*
and *bonus* are all similar, why do we say *sanctior* but not *piior?* Why
do we say *sanctior, sanctissimus,* but not *bonior, bonissimus?* When
Vergil says *fandi atque nefandi,*[102] why do we form *nefarius* from
nefando but not *farius* from *fando?* Why can *seiunctus* lose its prefix
and form *iunctus,* while if you take *se* away from *securus* and *sedulus*
you cannot use what is left? When we may say, in the plural, *singuli
viri, singulae mulieres, singula scrinia,* why may we not say, in the
singular *singulus vir, singula mulier, singulum scrinium?* When the
verbs *venor, piscor,* and *aucupor* are similar, why do we form from
them the nouns *venator* and *piscator,* yet not *aucupator* but *auceps?*
Why does *volo* have no imperative? Why does the verb *fare* have no
first person singular in the present indicative? Why does *soleo* have no
perfect tense? When *canta* and *lava* are similar, why does one form
cantavi but the other not form *lavavi?* Again, *corusca* forms *coruscavi,*
but *tona* does not form *tonavi.* Why does *ego* have no other case?

---

[101] Dick postulates a lacuna here, since Martianus lists three cases instead of
two. By comparison with the corresponding passage in Charisius *Institutiones
grammaticae* 5 (Keil, I, 295, line 29), Dick supposes that an example dealing with
the genitive and the accusative has dropped out. The example given illustrates
a verb which governs both the accusative and the ablative.

[102] *Aeneid* 1. 543.

When *calceatus, armatus, togatus,* and *penulatus* all seem the same, why do we say *calceo* and *armo* and cannot say *togo* and *penulo?* Adjectives whose nominative singular ends in *us* all form the adverb with a long *e* ending, as *doctus* forms *docte; avarus, avare; parcus, parce;* then why do *bonus* and *malus* have the *e* of the adverb short in *bene* and *male?* When we form the adverb *habiliter* from *habilis,* why do we not form *faciliter* from *facilis?* Again, when we say *difficulter,* why can we not say *faculter?* When from *audax* we form *audacter,* why do we form from *verax* not *veracter* but *veraciter?* Why do we say *singulatim* but not *binatim* or *ternatim?* There are innumerable things of this kind which I could mention if I did not have to hurry on to other topics."

[326] When Grammar had said this as if she were merely introducing her subject, Minerva intervened, because of the boredom that had come upon Jove and the celestial senate, and said: "Unless I am mistaken, you are getting ready to go back to the elements and begin telling us about the eight fundamental parts of speech, adding also the causes of solecisms, the barbarisms, and the other faults of speech which celebrated poets have discussed at length; you will also discuss tropes, metaplasms, schemata, figures, and all the faults which flow, as it were, from the fountain of embellishment, illustrating either the misconception of the writer who does not understand them or the labored ornamentation of the pedant. If you bring such matters from the elementary school before the celestial senate, you will nip in the bud the goodwill you have won by this display of knowledge. If you were to take up a discussion of rhythm and meter, as you would venture to do with young pupils,[103] Music would surely tear you apart for usurping her office. The teaching you have given us will be well-proportioned and complete if you keep to your own particular subjects and do not cheapen them by commonplace and elementary instruction."

The Delian and his spouse nodded in approval of these words of his sister, and they made Grammar walk across to the attendants of Philology. Then the Clarian introduced another of the women who would form part of the nuptial exchange of gifts.

103 Quintilian (*Institutiones Oratoriae* 1. 4. 4) urges the teacher of literature to discuss meter and rhythm, though he regards this as strictly within the province of music.

BOOK IV

Dialectic

[327] Into the assembly of the gods came Dialectic, a woman whose weapons are complex and knotty utterances. Without her, nothing follows, and likewise, nothing stands in opposition. She brought with her the elements of speech; and she had ready the school maxim which reminds us that speech consists in words which are ambiguous,[1] and judges nothing as having a standard meaning unless it be combined with other words. Yet, though Aristotle himself pronounce his twice-five categories, and grow pale[2] as he tortures himself in thought; though the sophisms of the Stoics beset and tease the senses, as they wear on their foreheads the horns they never lost[3]; though Chrysippus[4] heap up and consume[5] his own pile,[6] and Carneades match his mental power through the use of hellebore,[7] no honor so great as this has ever befallen any of these sons of men, nor is it chance that

---

[1] Cf. pseudo-Augustine *De dialectica* (Migne, *PL*, Vol. XXXII, col. 1415): *Atque rectissime a dialecticis dictum est, ambiguum esse omne verbum.* The writer has explained that any word can be put into all kinds of contexts (e.g., into questions on meter or history or poetry) and that until the utterance is complete a hearer cannot tell how to interpret any individual word. Pseudo-Augustine quotes Dialectic's "school maxim" from a discussion in Cicero's *Hortensius*, now lost.

[2] Cf. § 37, where Philology grows pale with nocturnal study.

[3] This refers to the sophism: "What you have not lost, you have; you have not lost horns from your head; therefore you have horns on your head." See Diogenes Laertius 7. 187.

[4] A celebrated stoic philosopher of the third century B.C., author of numerous logical works, including a book on the sorites—"the heap." See Diogenes Laertius 7. 192. Cf. Persius 6. 80.

[5] Reading *consumat* with Dick. Some earlier editions prefer *consummat* [put the finishing touches to].

[6] The sorites.

[7] Carneades, a skeptic philosopher of the second century B.C., is said to have used hellebore, a purgative drug, to make his mind keener and more subtle before disputing with Chrysippus (a chronological impossibility). See Valerius Maximus 8. 7. 5.

so great an honor has fallen to your lot: it is your right, Dialectic, to speak in the realms of the gods, and to act as teacher in the presence of Jove.

[328] So at the Delian's summons this woman entered, rather pale but very keen-sighted. Her eyes constantly darted about; her intricate coiffure seemed beautifully curled and bound together, and descending by successive stages,[8] it so encompassed the shape of her whole head that you could not have detected anything lacking, nor grasped anything excessive.[9] She was wearing the dress and cloak of Athens, it is true, but what she carried in her hands was unexpected, and had been unknown in all the Greek schools. In her left hand she held a snake twined in immense coils; in her right hand a set of patterns[10] carefully inscribed on wax tablets, which were adorned with the beauty of contrasting color, was held on the inside by a hidden hook; but since her left hand kept the crafty device of the snake hidden under her cloak, her right hand was offered to one and all. Then if anyone took one of those patterns, he was soon caught on the hook and dragged toward the poisonous coils of the hidden snake, which presently emerged and after first biting the man relentlessly with the venomous points of its sharp teeth then gripped him in its many coils and compelled him to the intended position. If no one wanted to take[11] any of the patterns, Dialectic confronted them with some questions; or secretly stirred the snake to creep up on them until its tight embrace[12] strangled those who were caught and compelled them to accept the will of their interrogator.

[329] Dialectic herself was compact in body, dark in appearance,

---

[8] The Latin here, *deducti per quosdam consequentes gradus,* applies equally well to a logical argument "deduced through certain successive steps" as to Dialectic's symbolic hairstyle.

[9] Remigius remarks that this may refer to the requirements of a good definition; cf. § 340. More probably it simply refers to the rigor and completeness of logical argument.

[10] *Formulae.* The reference may be to inference patterns (*schemata*), or perhaps to certain attractive-seeming propositions which, when combined with further admissions (the hook), could lead to an opponent's overthrow (the snake).

[11] *Assumere,* a common word for the granting of a proposition to serve as a premise in dialectical argument.

[12] *Complexio,* a philosophical term (Greek: *symploké*) for the interweaving of subject and predicate terms into a proposition; or, as here, for the union of premises in a syllogism. See also § 344, where it is translated as "embracing."

with thick, bushy[13] hair on her limbs,[14] and she kept saying things that the majority could not understand. For she claimed that the universal affirmative was diametrically opposed to the particular negative,[15] but that it was possible for them both to be reversed by connecting ambiguous terms to univocal terms;[16] she claimed also that she alone discerned what was true from what was false,[17] as if she spoke with assurance of divine inspiration. [330] She said she had been brought up on an Egyptian crag[18] and then had migrated to Attica to the school of Parmenides, and there, while the slanderous report was spread abroad that she was devoted to deceitful trickery, she had taken to herself the greatness of Socrates and Plato.

[331] This was the woman, well-versed in every deceptive argument and glorying in her many victories, whom the Cyllenian's two-fold serpent, rising on his staff, tried to lick at, constantly darting its tongues,[19] while the Tritonian's [Athena's] Gorgon hissed with the joy of recognition. Meanwhile Bromius [Bacchus], the wittiest of the gods, who was completely unacquainted with her, said: "Surely this woman comes from the sands of panting Libya,[20] as her braided

---

[13] Martianus: *Dumalibus hirta setis;* cf. Ovid *Metamorphoses* 13. 850: *Hirtae . . . saetae*. The word *dumalis* is not found elsewhere in Latin.

[14] This is the meaning of Dick's text following the better manuscripts. One manuscript reads *hirsuti*, which would be translated as "her cloak [rather than complexion] was dark and covered with thick, prickly hair."

[15] See § 401.

[16] This sentence remains opaque. If *vertier* (here translated as "reversed") means "converted" rather than "overthrown," the first part taken alone is nonsense, since it is precisely these two kinds of propositions which cannot be converted *simpliciter*. In this case, the second part ("connecting ambiguous terms to univocal terms") may refer to some fallacious way of effecting the conversions. If *vertier* means "overthrown," there may be a reference to the "fallacy of four terms," where an ambiguous middle term is used in different senses in the premises of a syllogism. It is hard not to suspect the text.

[17] Cf. Cicero *Academica* 2. 91.

[18] See Raymond Klibansky, "The Rock of Parmenides," *Mediaeval and Renaissance Studies*, I (1941-1943), 178-86. The original text may, however, have had *urbe* [city] instead of *rupe* [crag].

[19] Martianus: *Cum . . . anguis assurgens allambere feminam crebris linguarum micatibus attemptaret;* cf. Silius Italicus *Punica* 6. 223: *Lingua micat motu atque assultans aethera lambit.*

[20] Martianus: *ex harenis Libyae anhelantis;* cf. Lucan *Pharsalia* 1. 368: *per calidas Libyae sitientis harenas.*

hair and her fondness for venom suggest. Otherwise we must believe that she is a Marsian sorceress[21]: she is so well recognized by snakes, and they show their fondness for her in their slimy way. Apart from this, we may deduce from that concealed hook that she is proven a most alluring charlatan,[22] and an inhabitant of the distant parts of Marsia." [332] When he had said this and several of the gods had laughed as much as was seemly, Pallas, rather shocked, restrained them as they were starting to make jokes, reminding them that this was a woman of perfect sobriety, something which had been wholly denied to some of the gods; and even amongst her sisters, who were estimable women, she was the most sharp-witted, and could not be scorned when she uttered her assertions. But Pallas ordered Dialectic to hand over those items which she had brought to illustrate her sharpness and her deadly sure assertions, and told her to put on an appearance suitable for imparting her skill. [333] Grammar was standing close by when the introduction was completed; but she was afraid to accept the coils and gaping mouth of the slippery serpent. Together with the enticing patterns and the rules fitted with the hook, they were entrusted to the great goddess who had tamed the locks of Medusa.[23] Thus Dialectic stood revealed as a genuine Athenian, a daughter of Cecrops, by the beauty of her hair and especially because she was attended by a crowd in Greek dress, the chosen youth of Greece, who were filled with wonder at the woman's wisdom and intelligence. But, for assessing virtue as well as practicing it, Jupiter considered the levity of the Greeks inferior to the vigor of Romulus [i.e., the Romans], so he ordered her to unfold her field of knowledge in Latin eloquence. [334] Dialectic did not think she could express herself adequately in Latin;[24] but pres-

---

[21] The Marsi, an Italian tribe, had a reputation for sorcery, poisoning, and snake-charming; see Horace *Epodes* 17. 29; and *Satires* 1. 9. 29; Pliny *Natural History* 25. 11; Silius Italicus *Punica* 8. 495-501. The reputation may originate in their claim to be descended from Circe; see Pliny *Natural History* 7. 14-15.

[22] Cf. § 424.

[23] Athena bore the representation of Medusa's head on her shield to commemorate her slaying of the Gorgon (Euripides *Ion* 989-97) or her part in helping Perseus to do so (Lucan *Pharsalia* 9. 655-77). See H. J. Rose, *A Handbook of Greek Mythology*, (London, 1958), pp. 30, 271-72.

[24] A commonplace in Latin philosophical writing. Cf. Lucretius *De rerum natura* 1. 136-39; Cicero *Academica* 1. 18; Seneca *Epistles* 58. 1.

ently her confidence increased, the movements of her eyes were confined to a slight quivering, and, formidable as she had been even before she uttered a word, she began to speak as follows:

[335] "Unless amid the glories of the Latin tongue the learning and labor of my beloved and famous Varro had come to my aid, I could have been found to be a Greek by the test of Latin speech, or else completely uncultivated or even quite barbarous. Indeed, after the golden flow of Plato and the brilliance of Aristotle it was Marcus Terentius' labors which first enticed me into Latin speech and made it possible for me to express myself throughout the schools of Ausonia. [336] I shall therefore strive to obey my instructions and, without abandoning the Greek order of discussion, I shall not hesitate to express my propositions in the tongue of Laurentum [i.e., Latin.] First, I want you to realize that the toga-clad Romans have not been able to coin a name for me, and that I am called Dialectic just as in Athens: and whatever the other Arts propound is entirely under my authority. [337] Not[25] even Grammar herself, whom you have just heard and approved, nor the lady renowned for the richness of her eloquence,[26] nor the one who draws various diagrams on the ground with her rod,[27] can unfold her subject without using my reasoning.

[338] Indeed there are six canons on which the other disciplines rely, and they are all under my power and authority. The first concerns terms; the second, complete utterances; the third, propositions; the fourth, syllogisms;[28] the fifth, criticism; that is, of poets and their works; while the sixth concerns the style suitable for orators. [339] Under the first heading, one inquires what genus is, what is species, difference, accident, property, definition, the whole, the part, the difference between division and partition, and what is meant

[25] The words *nam* at the beginning of this sentence and *quis dubitat* at the end in Dick's text should be omitted. See Jacobus [James A.] Willis, *De Martiano Capella Emendando* (Leiden, 1971), p. 28.

[26] Rhetoric.

[27] Geometry.

[28] The terminology of the first four divisions: *de loquendo, de eloquendo, de proloquendo, de proloquiorum summa* is found also in the book *De dialectica* attributed to Augustine, and is almost certainly Varronian. The first four divisions correspond to Aristotle's works on logic; the remaining two to his *Poetics* and *Rhetoric*.

by equivocal, univocal, and (to coin a word) plurivocal. You should put up with the strangeness of my language, since you have compelled a Greek to treat the subject in Latin. [340] The first part of my discipline considers the proper senses of words, the transferred senses of words, and the number of ways the sense can be transferred; it considers also substance, quality, quantity, relation, place, time, attitude, state, activity, passivity, opposition, and how many modes of opposition there are. [341] In the second part, which I have called 'On Complete Utterance,' one investigates what is a noun, a verb, and the result of combining these; which of these is the subject part of a sentence, and which is the predicate part; what is the extent of the subject and of the predicate; how far the noun and the verb are taken;[29] and how far a complete sentence can be a proposition. [342] Next comes the third part, on propositions. In this one studies, so far as is sufficient for the purpose of today's brief exposition, the differences in propositions as regards quantity, quality; what is the universal, the particular, the indefinite; which are affirmative, which negative; what is their individual force, and how they are related to one another. [343] Then follows the fourth part, on the syllogism. In this we inquire what is a premise, a conclusion, a syllogism, a related conclusion; a categorical syllogism, a conditional syllogism, and the difference between the two; how many figures of the categorical kind there are and what they are; whether they adhere to a fixed order and, if they do, what is the explanation of that order; how many moods they each have and whether these moods adhere to a fixed order and, if they do, what is the explanation of that order; and, finally, how many fundamental and necessary moods of the conditional syllogism there are; what is the order of those moods, and what is the difference between them. These are the matters which I think are sufficient for our present understanding and exposition.

Therefore, going back to the beginning, in order to survey the whole subject I shall first explain[30] what is meant by *genus*.

---

[29] I.e., taken as identical with these parts.

[30] Sections 344-54 correspond in subject matter to Porphyry's *Introduction* (3d cent. A.D.) to Aristotle's *Categories* and deal with what came to be called the *quinque voces* [the five terms, or predicables]. This became the standard order of exposition among the medieval logicians.

[344] *Genus* is the embracing of many forms[31] by means of a single name, as, for example, *animal:* its forms are *man, horse, lion*, and so on. But some forms sometimes fall under genera in such a way that they themselves can comprise a genus with other forms subsumed under it. For example, the genus *man*, which is a form in relation to *animal*, is a genus to *barbarian* or *Roman*. Genus can extend right down to the point where on dividing it into its forms you reach the individual. For example, suppose you were to divide *men* into *males* and *females;* likewise, *males* into *boys, youths* and *old men;* the likewise, *boys* into *infants* and *those who can speak*. If you wished to divide *boy* into *Ganymede* or some other particular boy, that is not a genus, because you have arrived at the individual. We ought to use the genus which is closest to the matter in hand, so that if we are discussing *man*, we ought to take *animal* as the genus because it is closest to our subject. For if we take as our genus *substance*, that is true in logic but is too wide for our needs.

[345] *Forms*, we say, are the same as *species*. *Forms* are those things which being subordinated to a genus retain[32] its definition and name: *man, horse, lion*, since they are forms of *animal*, can each be called an *animal* and a *corporeal living being;* both the name and the definition are recognized as being those of the genus.

[346] *Difference* is a distinction adequate for the matter under discussion.[33] For example, if one is asked what is the difference between a man and a horse, it is enough to say that a man has two feet and a horse four. However, we ought to be aware that, because there are many differences in individual cases, we are able to distinguish any given thing in different ways, as often as we can discover in it more and more points of difference. For if we want to divide the genus *animal*, we can divide it into *sexes*, since some are masculine, some feminine; we can divide it into *age groups*, since some are

---

[31] The word *forma* is regularly used by Martianus for our "species"; cf. § 345. In this translation it is usually rendered as "species," except in this and the following paragraph.

[32] That is, the definition and name of the genus can be truly predicated of the species. *Corporeal living being* (*corpus anima participans:* lit., "body sharing in soul") is here taken as the definition of animal. Cf. Plato *Timaeus* 77b.

[33] Martianus here makes no distinction between *differentia* meaning "*any* difference" and meaning "a *specific* difference" based on a comprehensive scheme of classification. In § 353, however, only the latter meaning will make sense of the passage.

infant, some young, some old; we can divide it by *sizes*, since some
are small, some large, some of medium size; we can divide it by
their various *modes of motion*, since some walk, some crawl, some
swim, some fly; or by their different *habitats*, since some live in
water, some on land, some in the air, others, it is said, in fire;[34] or
by the sound of their *cries*, since some talk, some growl, some bark,
some howl. But let us be sure that these individual divisions are
complete and that all the members are included within the individual divisions. For male animals can include those recently born,
small, walking, terrestrial, two-footed, and speaking. Therefore, of
the possible distinctions, you ought to use that which is appropriate
to the matter under discussion. For if you are to speak about mankind in a complimentary manner, you will have to divide animals
into the rational and the brute, so that it may be more readily understood how great a value nature has placed on mankind amongst all
the animals—since to men alone she has given the power of reason to
come to knowledge of herself.

[347] *Accident* is something found only in a given species[35] but
which does not always occur in that species. For example, *rhetoric*
occurs only amongst men, but it can fail to occur amongst them,
so that although someone may be a man he need not be an orator.

[348] *Property*[36] is what is found only in a given species and always occurs in it, so that it marks off the given thing from the generality of things; for example, *laughter* in man. For no one can
laugh unless he is a man, and there is no man who cannot laugh
when he wants to, so far as is in his nature. Difference is distinguished from property in this, that difference distinguishes something only by reference to the subject under discussion, whereas
property distinguishes from everything. For when we want to distinguish man from lion by difference, and say that the lion is wild
but man is gentle, clearly we make a distinction relevant only to the
subject in question. For in saying *The lion is wild, but man is gentle,*

---

34 The inclusion of "two-footed" in the list two sentences later suggests that
a division based on numbers of feet may have been dropped from the text here.

35 The phrase limiting *accident* to a given species seems unique to Martianus.
Normally *black* and *white* would be understood as accidental qualities of man,
but of course they apply to many other kinds of things as well. Martianus was
perhaps trying to bring his definition into symmetry (however false) with the
definition of *property;* and his example did nothing to make his error evident.

36 I.e., *proprium* [peculiarity].

we have not distinguished man from other tame animals, nor the lion from other wild animals. But when we call man an animal capable of laughter, we have thereby distinguished him from the generality of all other living things.

[349] *Definition* is the clear and brief explanation of any involved concept. In definition three things must be avoided: signifying what is false, what is too wide, or what is too narrow. We signify something false as follows: *Man is an immortal, irrational animal.* For although man is truly an animal, it is false that he is immortal or irrational. We signify too much when we say: *Man is a mortal animal.* For although this is brief, it is too wide, since it is true of all animals. We signify something too narrow when we say: *Man is a grammatical animal.* For although there is no animal except man with a knowledge of grammar, yet not every man has a knowledge of grammar. The full definition is *Man is a rational, mortal animal.*[37] For by adding the word *mortal* we have distinguished him from the gods, and by adding *rational* we have distinguished him from the beasts.

[350] A *whole* is that which sometimes lends its name but never its definition to two or more parts within itself. This is found only in individuals. For example, when we refer to a given man and consider his various limbs as his parts, we understand that the man himself is the whole, since we have decided on a particular man, and that the definition and name of that whole man cannot descend to his parts. For we cannot say that an arm or a head by itself is a man, nor can the separate limbs take the definition that belongs to man himself. Yet we must notice that sometimes it is possible to say *all* instead of *the whole*, but with a difference of meaning. For a whole is recognized in single items, but *all* is applied to a plurality. For when we say *man*, meaning Cicero, because Cicero is one person the appropriate term is *the whole;* but when we mean 'mankind,' because that can include the unskilled and the skilled, men and women, the better term is *all*.

[351] *Parts* are those which are understood to be present in a whole and of which the whole consists.

---

[37] This definition is a commonplace. See, e.g., Apuleius *Peri hermeneias* 271 (ed. Thomas, p. 182, line 12); pseudo-Augustine *De dialectica* 9 (Migne, *PL*, Vol. XXXII, col. 1416). It introduces an inconsistency, however, with Martianus'

[352] *Division* ought to be carried to the point at which we reach the individual; this comes when we reduce genera through their differences to cover a smaller number of items, and then we subordinate species to these in such a way that the separate species themselves can each be genera with other species subordinate to them.[38] For instance, if we want to make a first brief division of *animal,* we can proceed by differences, because some animals walk, some crawl, some swim, some fly. Again, we can make genera of these divisions, so that we say that walking animals are a genus and we subordinate species to it, because some are human, some beasts. Of these again there can be other species, through which, if need be, it will be possible to reach the individual. This ought not to be done in every statement, but only in minute argument. In a speech[39] we can divide in this way when the obscurity of our subject requires it; if the subject is not obscure, the theory of division should be applied and incorporated but ought not to be very apparent.

[353] In *partition,* specific differences[40] do not often occur, and without them partition can be limitless, if we wish to reach what cannot be further divided. For if we name a particular man as a whole and wish briefly to enumerate his parts, there are no differences of parts available, and we are forced to use the names of the particular parts, so that we say the head, the feet, and the rest. If we want to group these briefly, the fact that there are no specific differences means that we cannot group the particular items; the fact that they are so many means it will be impossible, or else a very long task.

---

claim three sentences earlier that all animals are mortal. If *animal* is defined in this way, the distinction between man and the gods becomes unnecessary.

[38] *Division* in the technical sense, where it applies to a species or a genus but not to an individual, corresponds to our *subdivision.*

[39] Here, as in many other places, Martianus' preoccupation with dialectic as the practical art of disputation, rather than as the theoretical study of formal logic, is evident.

[40] *Differentiae,* interpreted in a narrower sense than in § 346. Martianus does not, of course, mean that there are no differences between the right arm and the left leg, for example, but that in dealing with the parts of a whole it is easier to deal with the individual parts than with groupings of parts. Such groupings as might occur to us—limbs, organs, vessels and so on,—are not based on a full scheme of classification which is at once exclusive and exhaustive. To draw up

[354] Between *division* and *partition* there is the difference that in division we proceed by species, in partition by parts. Species are what are subordinate to a genus and can retain its definition and name. Parts are those which are included in a whole, and they can never take the definition of the whole but sometimes can take its name. For we can take one and the same thing as both a genus and a whole, but with a certain difference of force. For instance, if we wish to divide *man* into youth, old man, and child, we have a genus and its species; but if we want it to be partitioned into head, feet, and hands, we have a whole and its parts. This is because youth, old man, and child, which as we have said are species, can take[41] the name and definition of man, so that an old man may be called a man and a rational, mortal animal; and so may a child, and also a youth. But the head and the feet, which as we have said are parts, cannot take the definition or name of man, because a head cannot be said to be an animal capable of laughter,[42] nor can the feet or hands.

[355] The *equivocal*[43] occurs when many things have one name, but not the same definition; for instance, *lion*. For *lion* is applied to an actual lion, a picture of a lion, and the zodiac sign Leo, so far as the word goes, but as far as the definition is concerned, the actual lion is defined in one way, the painted lion in another, and the zodiac sign in another again.

[356] The *univocal* occurs when there is one name and one definition for two or more items; as, for instance, *clothing*. For

---

one, and so determine the right distinguishing characteristics for each group, would be "impossible, or else a very long task."

[41] I.e., can have the name and definition of man truly predicated of them.

[42] The Aristotelian tradition settled on no definition of man as *the* correct one. For purposes of illustration, as here, any plausible definition would do.

[43] The next two paragraphs are derived ultimately from the opening of Aristotle's *Categories*. However, the resemblances are much greater to the logical works attributed to Augustine. In Martianus the technical terms are given in a Latin form (*aequivoca* [equivocals], *univoca* [univocals]), whereas in pseudo-Augustine they are given in the Greek form used by Aristotle (*homonyma, synonyma*). As Aristotle was concerned with the things signified, rather than with the words that signified them, he has no term corresponding to Martianus' *plurivoca* [plurivocals], which pseudo-Augustine calls *polyonyma*. In the second sentence of § 355 compare Martianus: *ut leo . . . verus et pictus* with pseudo-Augustine *De decem categoriis* 2 (Migne, *PL*, Vol. XXXII, col. 1421): *ut homo . . . pictus et verus.*

both a cloak and a tunic have the name of clothing and can take
its definition. Therefore the univocal is recognized in the genera,[44]
which give their name and definition to their subordinate species.

[357] The *plurivocal* occurs when one thing is known by many
names; as, for instance, a sword: for *gladius, ensis,* and *mucro* all
signify the same thing.[45]

[358] Words are *proper* to things when they are the natural and
appropriate terms for them, as *lapis* [stone], *lignum* [wood], and
so on.[46]

[359] Words are *transferred* [i.e., are used metaphorically] when
they are changed in some way, either from necessity or for imagery:
from necessity, as when we say *vites gemmare* [the vines are forming gems; i.e., are budding] or when we say *laetas segetes* [the crops
are in good heart; i.e., are abundant].[47] Here, since the proper
word is lacking, we have used one transferred from another context:
we cannot say that vines do anything except form gems, or that crops
are anything except in good heart. But for imagery we say *fluctuare
segetes* [the crops are rippling]; we can say something else—that
they are moving—but since that is not decorative, we use a word
proper to another subject.

[360] Words have a transferred sense in three ways: through
similarity, or contrariety, or difference;[48] through similarity, as are
those which are included in the tropes of grammar, like the one I

---

[44] Reading: *ergo hoc univocum in generibus esse intelligitur, quae et nomen
et definitionem dant formis suis.* See Willis, pp. 29-30.

[45] Martianus: *quando multis nominibus una res dicitur, ut gladius: nam et
ensis et mucro idem significant;* cf. pseudo-Augustine (as cited above, n. 43):
cum multa nomina unam rem significant . . . ut ensis, mucro, gladius. The same
example, without the technical term, is found in Quintilian *Institutiones
Oratoriae.* 10. 1. 11 ff.

[46] With §§ 358-60, cf. §§ 509-12.

[47] The expressions quoted are everyday Latin idioms, used, as Cicero remarks
(*Orator* 80-81), even by countryfolk. The examples are standard; cf. also Cicero
De oratore 3. 155; Quintilian *Institutiones Oratoriae* 8. 6. 6; Julius Victor
Rhetorica 20 (ed. Halm, p. 431).

[48] The structure and content of this paragraph correspond closely to the
similar treatment in pseudo-Augustine. Martianus: *per similitudinem . . . ut
verborum habeant propinquitatem, . . . per contrarium, per differentiam;* cf.
pseudo-Augustine *De dialectica* 6 (Migne, *PL,* Vol. XXXII, col. 1412): *Voca-
bulum translatam . . . similitudine, . . . quadam vicinitate . . . hinc progressio . . .
usque ad contrarium.*

have already mentioned: 'the crops are rippling.' Of this kind also are those which signify the part by the whole or the whole by the part in such a way that there is some appropriately close relationship between the words. It has been found desirable to include these under the heading of similarity. Words are used through contrariety when they are understood in a sense contrary to what we say, as when we call the Fates the *Parcae* although they are not merciful,[49] or when use the word *lucus* [grove] although it does not transmit light.[50] Grammarians call this *antiphrasis*. Words are transferred through difference when they are taken from other words without any reason, as if we were to call a man who was neither hard of body nor stupid of mind *lapis* [stone]. It is not appropriate to use these words; for it is stupid to bring forward words which either have no meaning or are transferred too far from their proper meaning. It is, however, right to use words that are proper, or similar, or contrary.

[361] Before I speak about substance,[51] there are some things that need to be explained: everything that we say[52] is either a *subject* itself, or *of a subject,* or *in a subject,* or both *of* and *in a subject.*[53]

---

[49] A derivation from *parcere* [to spare] is assumed by Martianus. In fact, their name is derived from a root which means "to weave" (cf. *plico*) and refers to their function of weaving the web of life.

[50] Martianus: *Lucum, cum non luceat; cf.* pseudo-Augustine (as cited in n. 48): *Lucus . . . quod minime luceat.* The derivation from *lux* [light] is probably correct, but not the explanation. Originally the word may have referred to a clearing.

[51] The exposition from here to § 387 is based ultimately on the *Categories* of Aristotle. Some small sections read like a literal translation of the Greek, but a great deal of Martianus' account reads like an expanded paraphrase of certain sections of Aristotle. One suspects that Martianus is following a commentator rather than the original text, whether in Greek or Latin translation. See Lorenzo Minio-Paluello, "The Text of the *Categoriae:* The Latin Tradition," *Classical Quarterly,* XXXIX (1945), p. 66.

[52] This is a commentator's attempt to improve upon Aristotle, to make his classification of "things there are" (*Categories* 1ᵃ 20) into a classification of terms.

[53] This opaque terminology is abbreviated from Aristotle's "said of" and "[present] in." J. L. Ackrill explains this well: "What is 'said of' an individual, X, is what could be mentioned in answer to the question 'What is X?', that is, the things in direct line above X in the family-tree, the species (e.g. man or generosity), the genus (animal or virtue), and so on" (*Aristotle's 'Categories' and 'De Interpretatione,'* trans. with notes by J. L. Ackrill [Oxford, 1963], p. 75).

A *subject*[54] is itself not attributed to anything else in such a way that it is dependent on it for its existence, but other things are attributed to it; as, for instance, *Cicero* (not the name, but what is signified by that name). Something is *of a subject*[55] when it is said of the subject itself and gives to it its definition and name; as, for example, *man:* for Cicero is a man and is a rational, mortal animal. So both the name and the definition, which is of the subject, have been predicated of the same subject; and thus what is said *of the subject* is found in its genera and species. [362] Something is *in a subject* when it gives neither its name[56] nor its definition to the subject but is understood to be in the subject itself in such a way that it cannot exist without the subject;[57] as, for instance, *rhetoric:* for a subject cannot take the name and definition of rhetoric. For Cicero is not rhetoric, nor is Cicero the science of speaking well; but rhetoric is understood to be in Cicero, although he himself cannot be called rhetoric. Something is both *of a subject* and *in a subject* when it is of a subject with regard to one thing and in a subject with regard to another; as, for example, *discipline:* for with regard to rhetoric, discipline is of the subject; with regard to Cicero, it is in the subject. A *primary substance*, therefore, is a subject; a *secondary substance* is what is said of a primary substance. For instance, *Cicero* is a primary substance, *man* and *animal* are secondary. Now all the following cate-

---

Ackrill similarly explains (p. 74) that what are "present in" a subject are individuals in categories other than the category of substance: "Presumably Aristotle has in mind the occurrence in ordinary Greek of locutions like 'heat in the water', 'courage in Socrates'." Martianus' four classes are thus (i) subjects—that is, individuals in the category of substance; (ii) species and genera in the category of substance; (iii) individuals in the other categories; (iv) species and genera in the other categories.

[54] Dick's text here reads: *Subiectum est prima substantia, quod* . . . [A subject is a primary substance which . . .]. The words "primary substance" spoil the exposition and are probably a gloss such as I have given in the preceding note.

[55] Aristotle himself gives no explanation of this phrase.

[56] This contradicts the possibility envisaged by Aristotle in *Categories* 2ª 28 ff. The change may reflect the greater ease with which Latin forms abstract nouns. Thus the category member would be termed, for example, "whiteness" (*candor*), rather than simply "white" (*to leukon*) as in Greek.

[57] Martianus omits Aristotle's further condition that what is *in a subject* must not be a *part* of the subject. The exemplification which follows is not due to Aristotle.

gories are understood to be in a subject; so let us look at them one by one.

[363] A *quality* is that in accordance with which we say what a thing is like; for instance, *whiteness*. It can be understood that a quality is in a subject,[58] since whiteness necessarily is in something, without which it cannot exist; the thing itself in which the whiteness exists is a subject.

A *quantity* is that in accordance with which we say how much a thing is; for instance, *a length of two feet*. This also must necessarily be in a subject.

The *relative* is what is so called in relation to something; for instance, *father, brother*. These are undoubtedly in a subject. For necessarily these names relate to something else. There are also some relative terms whose correlates will be evident in the mind.[59]

Place is what we call such expressions as *in Rome;* Rome is a substance, this bears reference to Rome itself.[60] *Time* is, for instance, *yesterday, recently, at evening*. The things by whose movements time is reckoned, are substances; for instance, the sun, by whose course we understand time, and those bodies which give us understanding of interval. *Attitude*[61] is, for instance, *is-lying, is-sitting*. *State* is, for instance, *having-shoes-on, having-armor-on;* man is

[58] Martianus' attempt to show the dependence of each of the other categories upon substance does not correspond to anything in Aristotle's preliminary listing and exemplification of the categories (*Categories* 1b 25 ff). Pseudo-Augustine reflects a critical tradition in which quality, quantity, and attitude are in a substance, whereas place, time, and state are separate from substance (*De decem categoriis* 8; Migne, *PL*, Vol. XXXII, col. 1425).

[59] Martianus means that some correlates have no names: the understanding comes before the word, which may have to be coined. Cf. § 379, and Aristotle *Categories* 7a 5.

[60] Lit., "this happens to (is an accident of) Rome itself." Presumably Martianus means that one can say *X is in Rome* only if something has happened to Rome; namely, that *X* is there. It is far from clear that Rome would be considered a substance by Aristotle, however. A serious Aristotelian point might be made that although there might be positions (i.e., points in space) without there being substances, we could not specify the coordinates for any position without reference ultimately to some material object (i.e., substance).

[61] The words for *attitude* and *state* are quite general in both Greek and Latin. Aristotle's examples, given also by Martianus, show that he conceived of the categories with a particular man as subject, and of these categories with the narrow meanings of "posture" and "clothing." The Latin terms could equally well be so translated here.

the substance, these bear a reference to him. *Activity* is, for example, cutting, burning. *Passivity* is, for example, *being cut, being burned*.

[364] A *primary substance,* then, is what is not inseparably in a subject and is not predicated of any subject. "Inseparably" has been added to the definition[62] for this reason—that every primary substance, though it may be in some locality, nevertheless can be separated and move from that locality; for example, Cicero is understood to be in the senate house in such a manner that he can go from there to some other place. And a part of a primary substance, though in the whole substance, is not inseparable from it, for our arm can be separated from our body, either in fact or in thought.[63] Rhetoric, on the other hand, is in the mind of Cicero in such a way that, even if by some chance it ceased to be there, we do not understand that it is going somewhere else; for when it has begun to be in Cicero's mind we do not consider it has come from elsewhere.

[365] A *secondary substance*[64] is, as has been said, what is predicated of primary substance, as *man* is predicated of Cicero, and *animal* is predicated of man and Cicero. Whatever is the genus of a primary substance is understood to be a secondary substance. Therefore it is common to all substances not be *in* a subject, but primary substance is not *of* a subject either. Substance cannot be extended or reduced; that is, it cannot admit of a more and a less. If no man is more a man than any other man, and no particular man will be more a man tomorrow than he was yesterday, so in different species a horse is not more a horse than a man is a man. But in discussing substances we must be careful to compare within the same class; that is, to compare a primary substance with a primary, a secondary with a secondary. For the primary substance more directly signifies

[62] The addition of "inseparably" to Aristotle's definition (*Categories* 2ª11), and the justification which follows, is due to a commentator. Aristotle had already explained that whatever is *in a subject* is incapable of independent existence (a point against Plato's Ideas), and Martianus had included this in § 362.

[63] Aristotle may hint (*Categories* 8ᵇ15), but he does not say, that parts of the body are capable of independent existence. His doctrine in other passages (*Metaphysics* 1035ᵇ23; *De anima* 412ᵇ20; *Politics* 1253ª20) is that a hand, for example, in separation from the organism of which it is a part, is not strictly a hand at all.

[64] Again, this section reads as if made up of short quotations from Aristotle interleaved with longer sections of commentary.

the thing; secondary substance involves the possibility of confusion with other things. When I say *Cicero*, I signify a definite individual; when I say *man*, it is uncertain whom I mean, because we are all subject to this title. Thus it happens that primary substance is more truly substance than is secondary substance; for primary substance more directly identifies the thing. [366] The concept of more or less a substance cannot apply, therefore, among substances within the same class. Again, substance has no opposite; for there is nothing opposite to man, or horse. If someone says that Clodius was the opposite of Cicero, he means not that the substances were opposed to each other but that the qualities in them were opposites, such as evil opposed to good, vice to virtue, injustice to justice. It is clearly a property of substance that one and the same substance can accept opposite qualities by variation within itself. Thus a stone can be now white, now black, and not cease to be the same stone; and Cicero, at first foolish, later wise, does not cease to be the same Cicero.

[367] A *quality*,[65] as I have said, is that in accordance with which we are said to be of a certain kind. Of qualities, one sort is that in which a certain disposition and habit of mind is understood; as, for instance, in all the acquired disciplines—philosophy, grammar, rhetoric, and the rest—which so take root in the mind that it is difficult for them to be lost from it. Amongst this sort, some are perfect, some imperfect; if someone has studied grammar yet often makes mistakes, one cannot refer to the habit [of grammatical knowledge], but only to the disposition. Not every disposition is regarded as a habit, but every habit is regarded as being a disposition. [368] A second sort is what we call the 'affective' qualities, like sweet or bitter, hot or cold; not that the corresponding substances are affected by anything from these qualities, but that they compel our senses to be affected. For heat compels the person who comes in contact with it to be affected, as sweetness compels the person who tastes it. Again, there are the qualities which have been implanted in us by some natural affection, in accordance with which each of us is said to be pale or ruddy, without any sudden cause making us

[65] Sections 367 and 368 read like a condensed version of Aristotle, except that Martianus' second species of quality is Aristotle's third, and vice versa. The discussion of *athletic* in § 369, however, is a commentary on Aristotle's *Categories* 9[a]14 ff. and 10[a]34 ff.

pale or ruddy. These are more rightly called *affections* than qualities,[66] if we are not said to be of a certain kind because of them. For it does not follow that he who grows pale is a pale person, that he who loves is a lover, that he who is drunk is a drunkard. The former instances are affections; the latter, qualities. [369] There is a third kind of qualities which are understood not from what actually exists in an individual case but from what can exist; for instance, we say that wood is breakable, not because it is already broken, but because it can be broken. Again, we speak of a body as *athletic*[67] in two senses: both as one that has been athletically trained and as one so formed by nature that it is well-suited to athletics even though it has not in fact been athletically trained. The former kind of body is rightly called athletic from its athletic skill, because the skill is ingrained in it; but there does not exist any name for the quality itself from which the adjective has been derived and named to apply to a body which is able to be athletically trained but is not so yet. Therefore we must recognize that some substances are said to be what they are from qualities for which there are no names. For though we speak of *good* as derived from goodness, we do not speak of *best* as derived from 'bestness.'[68] In the same way *athletic*, which we understand from the fact that a body can acquire athletic skill, does not have a definite name for the quality from which it is seen to be so called, yet we agree that it is so called from a quality. [370] The fourth kind of quality covers those according to which we understand the shapes and configurations of things, such as *square, round,*

[66] Aristotle too appears to exclude temporary affections (or "passions") from the category of quality; e.g., in *Categories* 10ᵃ10. His introduction to the subject (9ᵃ28) shows, however, that this is not necessarily his intention. Martianus or his source (cf. Ackrill, pp. 106-7) takes the defining phrase "said to be of such and such a kind" as referring to permanent characteristics, and so appears to exclude temporary affections completely.

[67] *palaestricum*—lit., "capable of wrestling."

[68] The example has been well adapted for Latin. In Greek, "good" (*agathos*), with a different stem from that in the word "goodness" (*arete*), is a sufficient example. Aristotle had earlier made the point, needed for clarity, that most terms of qualities which are predicated of substances are named derivatively from the qualities themselves. For instance, when we say X *is generous* the term *generous* is derived from the quality *generosity*. But sometimes the words do not have the same derivation, or (as with the word translated as *athletic*) a suitable noun for the quality may not be available.

beautiful, ugly,[69] and the like. Quality accepts the idea of a more and a less, but not in every instance. For nothing square is more square than any other square thing; but something can be said to be more white than another white thing. And it is a question often discussed, whether one person may be said to be more just than another.[70] But there appear to be many who have given careful thought to the question and say that the qualities themselves cannot accept the idea of a more and a less, but only the items named after them. For instance, justice is in itself one single perfect concept, so that we cannot say *This is more justice than that,* but we can say *This man is more just than that.* Similarly, we cannot say *This is more health than that,* but we can say *This man is more healthy than that.* So it happens that substance[71] does not accept the idea of a more and a less, but qualities can accept it through substances. Again, quality can have a contrary, but not in every case; for although infirmity is the contrary of health, there is no contrary for square or round. It must be noted that when anything is contrary to a quality it must itself be a quality: for instance, sweetness is a quality; therefore bitterness is a quality; and so on.

[371] *Quantity*[72] is of two kinds, discrete or continuous: discrete, as of number or speech;[73] continuous, as of a line or time. There is

[69] The last two examples are not found in Aristotle, and their propriety is questionable.

[70] This sentence is omitted in one manuscript, and Dick proposes its exclusion "not unwillingly as an inept gloss." Perhaps, however, the sentence reflects a Stoic critique of Aristotle's claim (*Categories* 11ª1) that "undoubtedly . . . one man is called . . . more just than another."

[71] It is not clear whether *substance* here means the subject in which the qualities inhere (for example, the man who is just); or the quality itself (for example, justice). The context suggests the latter, but the meaning is probably the former. Martianus, or his source, has finished his discussion, based on Aristotle, *Categories* 10ᵇ26-11ª14, of the extent to which qualities admit of degrees, and he now restates the doctrine of § 365.

[72] Like the section on quality, Martianus' discussion of the category *quantity* reads largely like an abridgment of Aristotle. In § 373 only one of Aristotle's several examples is given, but this is elaborated with explanatory commentary.

[73] Aristotle explains (*Categories* 4ᵇ32) that spoken language is a quantity, being measurable into long and short syllables. Aristotle's procedure in his whole chapter on quantities is strange, in that he is concerned not so much with quantitative predicates (e.g., two-feet-long) as with a classification of the primary things which are quantitatively measurable (e.g., lines). It would seem that he

another division of quantity, whereby one form of it has its parts in a certain position while the other does not. For a line is understood by the position of its parts, since one can say which part of it is where, and it is seen to have a left and a right. But number or speech or time have none of these, although they can have order so that there is in them something that is first and second and last and midmost, but nothing which is understood as being in any place. [372] Quantity has no contrary whatever. For what can be contrary to a two-foot length or a three-foot length? If anyone were to say that *greater* and *smaller*, which seem to be words of quantity, are contraries, he should realize that it is not quantity which is indicated.[74] If he says that something is greater, it seems to be contrary to that which is less. But if I ask: 'Greater than what?' and he replies: 'Than three feet long,' it is clear that there is no contrary. For things which are said to be greater or less are clearly said to be so in a relative sense. For whatever is greater when compared to a less is less when compared to a greater. If therefore greater and less are contraries, we are compelled to admit to an absurdity, that contraries can apply to the same thing at the same time. Again we are compelled to accept another absurdity, that one and the same thing can be contrary to itself, if one thing compared to different quantities can be at the same time both greater and less. [373] Quantity does not accept the idea of greater and less; for five is not more five than two is two, and two are not more two than any other two, and they will not be any more two tomorrow than they are today. It is a distinguishing characteristic of quantity that according to it we speak of equal and unequal, just as it is a characteristic of quality that according to it we speak of similar and dissimilar, although with different things it is possible to abuse and misapply either term.[75]

---

has either glossed over or rejected the distinction made in the preceding sentence, partly because of a desire to avoid classing lines, etc. as substances. Speech, presumably, is the primary owner of such quantitative predicates as *iambic*, *dactylic*, and so on.

[74] That is, these belong to the category of relation.

[75] The final clause corresponds to nothing in Aristotle, but is strikingly like Ackrill's comment (p. 98) on the same passage: "an examination of the uses of 'equal' and 'unequal' (in Greek or English) soon shows the inadequacy of this as a distinguishing mark of those things Aristotle counts as quantities."

[374] *Relation*[76] is the term used when the thing we are discussing is *of* some other thing, or can be referred *to* some other thing in some way; as, for instance, *son* cannot be understood without *father* or *mother*, *slave* without *master*, and vice versa. [375] There are three kinds of relation: either *of* something, as in the case of *son;* or *to* something, as in the case of *neighbor;* or *in comparison with* something, as in the case of *double,* since it is double in comparison with something *single.*[77] All relatives have correlatives; just as a son is the son of a father, so is a father the father of some son. In correlation some correlatives use the same grammatical cases as their relatives, some use different cases. For what I have said of a son, we can also say of a slave, since a slave is the slave of a master and a master is the master of a slave. These correlate in such a way that they retain the same grammatical cases in the reverse relationship. Similarly what is double is double with respect to something single, and the single is single with respect to something double; the greater is greater than the smaller, and the smaller is smaller than the greater. It is therefore obvious that those instances keep the same cases when the relationships are reversed. But, although knowledge is a relative (for knowledge is of some knowable thing), in the reverse relationship it changes its case. For because we say: *Knowledge is knowledge of some knowable thing* we cannot therefore say: *The knowable thing is knowable of knowledge.* Similarly, perception is perception of something perceptible, whereas the perceptible is perceptible by perception. These instances, therefore, when they reverse their relationships, do not like the previous instances retain the same cases, but change their cases. [376] Some things are coextensive in time with their correlates, and begin and cease to exist at the same time as they. For instance, there cannot be a slave until there is a master, and when there ceases to be a master there ceases to be a slave; and the master, when he has no slave, cannot be termed a master. But the knowable thing is prior in

[76] The Latin translates Aristotle's Greek literally, and fails to observe that the Greek genitive ("of") also covers the "than" of comparison. The first sentence of the following section makes an adaptation for Latin.

[77] The standard correlative of *double* is *half.* This unusual use of *single* as the correlative is found also in pseudo-Augustine *De decem categoriis* 11 (Migne, *PL,* Vol. XXXII, col. 1431), but with the simple genitive ("the double of the single") instead of with *ad* ("double in comparison with the single"). Cf. § 384.

nature to the knowledge of it; for if you remove knowable things there will be no knowledge; if, however, you remove the knowledge of it the knowable thing can still exist, although there is no one who knows it. [377] Relatives can have contraries, but not in every case. For knowledge is the contrary of ignorance, friendship of enmity, but there is no contrary to the double or the greater or the smaller. Anyone who thinks that those are contraries is compelled to admit that one and the same thing at one and the same time can be contrary to itself, for the greater is greater when compared to a smaller, and the same thing can be smaller when compared at the same time to a greater, which is quite impossible for contraries.[78] For a man cannot be both a fool and a wise man at the same time, nor both white and black at the same time. Since we have shown that this can[79] happen in the case of the greater and smaller, we must admit that greater and smaller are not contraries; similarly, double cannot be the contrary of single, since the same thing which is double can be single in relation to something else. Therefore not all relatives can be contraries. Similarly, some can accept the idea of more and less, but some cannot. For this man can be more a friend than that, but this double item cannot be more double than that; for if it is double it is implicit that if it were in any way more or less it would not be double.[80]

[378] It is argued whether any substance can be spoken of relatively. There is no question about a primary substance; for Cicero cannot be said to be *of* anything, nor can he be so called *in relation to* anything. Similarly, someone's horse—say Rhoebus[81]—is not

---

[78] Unlike Aristotle, Martianus repeats what has already been shown (§ 372).

[79] Dick reads *non posse* [cannot] although several good manuscripts omit the negative. Its omission or inclusion makes no difference to the final meaning, since the word corresponding to "this" in the original text may refer either to a subject's being able to be both *A* and *B* at once or to its being unable to be both *A* and *B*. See Willis, p. 31.

[80] The second half of this sentence is simple-minded commentary on Aristotle's text.

[81] Reading *alicuius* for the unintelligible *iam quis equus* rightly bracketed by Dick. Rhoebus (or Rhaebus) was the horse of Mezentius in Vergil *Aeneid* 10. 861. It is interesting to note Martianus' consistent use of Roman examples—such as Cicero, where the Greeks cited Socrates or Callias. In the passage corresponding to this one (*Categories* 8ª13 ff.), Aristotle speaks only of "some individual man" and "some individual ox." In Greek examples horses were often named

of anyone for the sole reason that he is Rhoebus, but it is because he is a beast of burden that he is someone's beast of burden.[82] Therefore a primary substance cannot be said to be relative; nor can any part of it, since without doubt that too is itself a primary substance. For in the same way as Cicero is a primary substance, so [is] his hand. [A hand—not as *his*, but in its general character as a hand; that is, as a secondary substance—][83] cannot be so termed relatively. For the terms do not reciprocate when they are interchanged; for instance, we can say *The hand is the hand of Cicero*, not *Cicero is the Cicero of the hand*. Nor is the hand itself a hand for the reason that it is Cicero's, but it is called a hand because it has such and such characteristics. Therefore, as we said, neither a primary substance nor its parts can be so called in relation to something else. Therefore the question arises, What of the parts of secondary substance? There is no question about a substance itself, for a man is not a man *of* anyone. But a hand in its general character as a hand is the hand of some man, and (so that the relationship can be

---

Xanthus, a name which belonged to horses of Hector and Achilles in the *Iliad*. See, for instance, pseudo-Augustine *De decem categoriis* 1 (Migne, *PL,* Vol. XXXII, cols. 1419-20).

[82] This opaque explanation largely misses Aristotle's point. Rhoebus, qua horse, is not necessarily someone's horse; but qua property he is necessarily someone's property. The substitution of "beast of burden" for Aristotle's "property" (*Categories* 8ª24) is less than helpful.

[83] This section is confused in the present state of the text. I believe that the words in square brackets cannot possibly belong where they are, since a reference to secondary substance disrupts the clear order of the passage: primary substances, parts of primary substances, secondary substances, parts of secondary substances. Moreover, the example of nonreciprocating terms which follows is still clearly concerned with the particular hand of Cicero, not with a hand in general (*manus specialiter*).

It seems best simply to omit the bracketed words, and to understand them as a gloss on *manus specialiter* later, thus: "Therefore the question arises, What of the parts of secondary substance? There is no question about a substance itself, for a man is not a man *of* anyone. But a hand in its general character as a hand (not *his* hand, but in its general character as a hand, so that it would be a secondary substance) is the hand of some man. . . ." Martianus is using the following classification: *Cicero* as a primary substance; Cicero's hand (*manus eius*) as a part of a primary substance; *man* as a secondary substance; a hand qua hand (*manus specialiter*) as a part of a secondary substance.

reversed) it is the hand of a handed person.[84] We can reverse the relationship in this way because something handed is handed with a hand. Similarly, a hoof is not a hoof of a primary substance but the hoof of something hoofed, because something hoofed is hoofed with a hoof, so that it can accept the reciprocating of relationships which I have said is proper to relatives. If, therefore, that definition of the relative stands—that the relative is that which can be said to be of something else—we can scarcely refrain from allowing that the parts of secondary substance are relative. But if the definition is changed, so that relatives are those things which are referred to something else when we except the fact that the items considered are already *in* the something else, then no substance comes under this definition.[85] For instance, consider servitude; when we except the fact that it is in the slave himself—that is, in some man—it is still related to a master. But a wing is the wing of something winged in such a way that if we except the fact that it is in something winged we cannot relate it to anything. [379] We must bear in mind not to be ashamed to coin new words where necessary to express correlations. For if correlation is not possible, we are not expressing a relative. For instance, when I say *wing*, wanting to show it as a relative, I should not be ashamed of saying something is *winged* to express the correlation; for *winged* is familiar enough not to offend our ears. If I am speaking of the foot, I should not be ashamed to form, by a similar derivation, a word suitable for expressing the correlation.

Again we should be aware that a man who does not know what some relative refers to cannot know whether the alleged relation

[84] The deficiencies of Martianus' arrangement as against Aristotle's are evident when one realizes that the content of § 379 is here assumed.

[85] This is a major departure from Aristotle, who does not allow that parts are *in* a whole, in his use of *in*. Martianus' revision of the definition of relatives equivocates between the uses of *in*, since servitude is not *in* a slave in the same way as his foot is in him. Aristotle's own revision (*Categories* 8ᵃ28 ff.) of the definition is not clear either, and has generated much discussion, both in antiquity and now. It seems, however, that Aristotle saw the possibility of forming reciprocating relationships (if necessary, by coining words) as a *necessary* but not *sufficient* condition for being a true *relative*. He then introduces an epistemological condition as well: can we definitely know, for example, that this is a hand without knowing what it is the hand of? If so, we are not compelled to see it as a relative in any important sense. See Ackrill, pp. 101-3.

can apply. For example, when you say, *This is double,* you know the single of it; that is, in comparison with what it is double—or if you do not know that, then you cannot know at all whether it is double.

[380] *Activity* and *passivity* can have contraries; for instance, 'to heat: to chill'; 'to be heated: to be chilled.' They also have more and less, as 'to burn more and less'; 'to be burned more and less.'

[381] The terms for *attitude* are all derivative; for example, 'to sit' from *sitting,* 'to stand' from *standing.* Although sometimes there are no words from which the names of postures may be derived, yet the corresponding notion exists in thought.

[382] Of the three categories that remain, the examples I have given above are sufficient. For we indicated *when* by, for example, *yesterday, tomorrow; where* by, for example, *in Rome, in Athens;* and *state* by *shod, armed.* Which of these will accept the idea of more or less is easily seen when an instance occurs in everyday speech.

[383] Those are the ten categories from which every individual thing we utter must come. For whatever we say which has some meaning but cannot yet be understood as true or false is within these ten categories, except only those words which are, in a sense, the joints of speech. For there are many words listed by the grammarians amongst the parts of speech which have no meaning at all by themselves, or else make no complete sense, but only become meaningful when they are joined to other words; such as conjunctions, prepositions, and such similar items as the grammarians lay down.

[384] It remains for me to speak about opposites. *Opposites* are what are seen to confront each other, as it were, face to face; for instance, contraries. Not all opposites are contraries, but all contraries are opposites. Opposites are opposed either as relatives, as large is opposed to small, or half to double; or as contraries, as foolishness is opposed to wisdom; or as possession to privation, as sight to sightlessness; or as affirmation to negation, as *Cicero discusses* to *Cicero does not discuss.* These forms of opposites differ greatly among themselves. A *relative* is opposed to another in such a way that it either is *of* that to which it is opposed or else is related to it in some way. Thus half is opposed to double, and the half is the half of the double. It is therefore opposed to it in such a way that it is *of* its opposite. And small is opposite to large [so as to be its contrary][86]

[86] The bracketed clause is an attempt to give a translation of the words *ut*

in such a way that the small item is small in relation to the large to which it is opposed. [385] *Contraries*, on the other hand, are opposites, but not in a way that makes them *of* their opposites or so that they are in any way related to their opposites; foolishness is opposed to wisdom without being the foolishness *of* wisdom or *in relation to* it. However, we should realize that some contraries have something intermediate between them, while others do not. Those contraries which are such that either one or the other *must* necessarily occur in a thing in which they *can* occur, have no intermediate; for instance, health and sickness. These two contraries are present by nature in the bodies of animals, and either one or the other must necessarily be present, as I have said. So where health is not present in the body of the animal there must be sickness, and where there is not sickness there must be health. But white and black, although contraries and naturally found in bodies, may nevertheless have an intermediate, since it is not necessary for a given body to be either white or black; it can lack whiteness without having blackness, and vice versa. Therefore some intermediate color can be found, like yellow or green. [386] *Possession* and *privation* are opposed to each other in such a way that, in instances where they can occur, one or the other of them must necessarily be present from the moment when nature allows it. For instance, we call 'toothed' that which has teeth, but we do not call 'toothless' that which does not have teeth, but only that which can have them in nature, and that from the time when nature allows it to have them. For we do not properly call[87] a stone 'toothless,' since it never has teeth; nor an infant—although it can at some stage have teeth, nature does not permit it to have them at that time. This third kind of opposites differs from the first,[88] the relatives, because sight is opposed to blindness in such a way that sight is not *of* blindness and is not referred to it in any way. It differs from the second kind, the contraries, between which there is

---

eius sit [so that it is of it]. Willis would delete these words, on the grounds that they are repeated from the preceding sentence, a simple and common form of corruption. The sense of the example requires an example of relationship *to* something, not *of* something, which would be the prima-facie meaning of the words. See Willis, p. 31.

[87] The examples which follow form a commentary on Aristotle's text.

[88] The rather fulsome distinctions between various kinds of opposites are abbreviated from Aristotle's own account (*Categories* 1ᵇ16 ff.).

something intermediate, because sight and blindness are understood with respect to eyes, so that either the one or the other of them must be present in them. They differ, then, from the contraries which have intermediates in that it is not necessary for one of the contraries which have an intermediate to be present in any substance, but it is necessary for one of these. But they differ from those contraries where there is nothing intermediate because one or the other of them must always be present in any substance in which they are naturally possible, like health or sickness in the body of an animal. One or the other of these is always present in the body of an animal. But these opposites can sometimes be present in a thing where they are naturally possible, and at another time they can both be absent. For instance, an infant for whom it is not yet time to have teeth is not said to be either toothed or toothless; and the eyes of some animal, before the time comes for them to have sight, are not said to be either sighted or blind, and at that time there is no intermediate condition either. [Therefore there are two kinds of contraries which have nothing intermediate between them: those of which either one or the other is present in any item in which it is possible for them to be present, and which allow nothing intermediate; as, for instance, health and sickness; and those which can both be absent at the same time from a substance in which they cannot both at once be present, and which, when they are so lacking, have no mean in their place; for instance, sight and blindness, or possession and privation.][89] [387] The fourth kind of opposites is affirmation and denial, such as *Cicero is discussing, Cicero is not discussing*. These differ from the former kinds because the members of those pairs are used as single terms but in this fourth kind the terms are used in combination.[90] They differ from relatives in that relatives are used rela-

[89] This sentence of summary is not found in the best manuscripts, and it confounds distinctions that have been made by the author. It should be deleted from the text. See Willis, p. 32.

[90] I.e., combined into complete utterances—in this case, propositions which are necessarily either true or false. In the standard exposition, found first in Aristotle (*Categories* 1ᵃ16 ff.) and later, for example, in pseudo-Augustine *De dialectica* I (Migne, *PL*, Vol. XXXII, col. 1409), the distinction between single and combined terms is explained earlier. In Martianus it is implied in the verse prologue of Book IV (§ 327, *associum*), but not made explicit until § 388. The final sentence of § 387 suggests some uneasiness on his part over the matter. Moreover, Martianus does not say explicitly that the proposition which results

tive to something, but these are not so used; for *discussing* is not relative to *not discussing*. They differ from contraries in that if contraries are used in combination, they are true or false for as long as that in which they can be present exists; but when it has ceased to exist, they are neither true nor false. For instance, of the statements *He is a fool* and *He is a wise man*[91] one is true as long as the 'he' is alive; when the 'he' has ceased to exist, both are false, since he who does not exist cannot be either a fool or a wise man. On the other hand, the statements *Cicero is discussing* and *Cicero is not discussing* are opposites of such a kind that as long as Cicero lives one of them is necessarily the case, and when he is dead the statement that he is discussing is false, but the statement that he is not discussing is true. Thus these opposites are distinguished from privation and possession;[92] for he who does not exist is neither blind nor sighted. Do not be concerned because we seem to have touched on the subject of propositions, which is a subject for later consideration; I have done so because it was appropriate to this discussion of opposites.

[388] A *noun*[93] is that which signifies a certain thing and which

---

when terms are combined is subject to truth or falsity, whereas single terms (whether relatives, contraries, or whatever) cannot be either true or false. The distinctions he goes on to make are based on Aristotle's further investigations into the differences between contradictory propositions, on the one hand, and the propositions resulting when relatives and contraries are combined with a subject, on the other. The doctrines which relate the truth value of propositions to the existence or nonexistence of the subject are found in Aristotle (*Categories* 13^{b}15 ff.), but are hardly satisfactory. Aristotle himself acknowledges (*De interpretatione* 21^{a}25 ff.) that *Homer is a poet* does not entail *Homer is*.

91 Reading: *ut 'stultus est ille' et 'sapiens est ille.'* See Willis, p. 34.

92 Again, Martianus should say "from propositions predicating privation and possession."

93 At this point Martianus turns from the Aristotelian *Categories*, after discussing only one of the miscellaneous topics which close that work: *opposites, priority, simultaneity, change,* and *having*—the so-called *postpraedicamenta*. The topics which follow in Martianus correspond in structure to the Aristotelian treatise *De interpretatione*, which deals with such things as name, verb, sentence, proposition, affirmation, and negation, as well as relationships between statements (Aristotle goes on to a discussion of modality, which has no counterpart in Martianus). In detail, however, the links with the *De interpretatione* are far weaker than those with the *Categories*. The connections with pseudo-Augustine's *De dialectica*, and so presumably with a lost work by Varro, are much stronger. In the systematic exposition adopted by both Augustine and Martianus, we now turn to the second part, *De eloquendo* [On complete utterance].

can be inflected in cases; a verb is that which signifies something and can be inflected in tenses; for instance, *Cicero* is a noun, *discusses* is a verb. Nouns or verbs in separation from each other can signify something, but cannot be said to be true or false. However, when used in combination they can be either affirmed or denied. For instance, just as we can say *Cicero discusses,* we can also say *Cicero does not discuss.* (What must be present are the nominative case of the noun and the third person of the verb). The first person[94] signifies something which can already be affirmed or denied and applies only to a man. In this person the noun is understood even if it is not expressed; for instance, *disputo* [I discuss] is complete, even if *ego* [I] is not expressed. The second person, too, is itself already subject to truth or falsity, and it also applies to a human being. We cannot correctly say *You discuss* to something which can neither hear nor understand what is said; when this is said without a noun expressed, again a noun is understood. We can, however, use the first and second persons in a different way, figuratively,[95] to introduce as speaking one who cannot speak, or to address speech to one who cannot hear or understand. [389] The third person, however, is used not only with a human being as subject but for other subjects also; and the subject is not understood as soon as the verb is used, unless we happen to be speaking about a god and saying something that could be used only of a god; when, for example, we say *It is raining,*[96] that can be true or false even when we do not add a name, since it is known who is sending rain. But when we say *disputat* [. . . is discussing], although this signifies something, it cannot be said to be true or false, unless a noun is added. And

[94] Martianus means the first-person form of the verb, which in Latin is usually a single word. The subject matter of this and the following section is fuller than that of the corresponding opening of the pseudo-Augustinian treatise, *De dialectica* I (Migne, *PL,* Vol. XXXII, col. 1409) but is clearly related to it.

[95] In figures of speech—personification and apostrophe.

[96] Martianus, like other Latin or Greek writers, assumes that what we call "impersonal" verbs of weather are really personal verbs with the appropriate god as subject. Cf. pseudo-Augustine *De dialectica* I: "An exception [to the rule that a Latin third-person verb form is not a complete utterance] is such verbs in which there necessarily inheres a signification of the person by custom of speech; for instance, when we say *It is raining* or *It is snowing,* even if there is not added *who* is raining or snowing. Nevertheless, because this is understood, these cannot be counted among simple utterances."

although *He is discussing* can be understood only of a man, it can be said of more than one man, and therefore it is necessary to add a noun as subject. And when we say *resistit* [. . . resists], this is the third person of the verb and requires as a subject a name, not necessarily of a man but of anything which is capable of resisting. So the first and second persons can be understood only of a human being as subject, and when used alone can be said to be either true or false, since with them the nouns are understood; but the third person cannot always stand alone, nor is it understood only of a human being. But the union of the third person of the verb and the nominative case of a noun [390] in such a way that it must be either true or false or doubtful[97] is called a *proposition.* For we all judge *Man is an animal* to be true; and *Every animal is a man,* we all judge to be false. *He is discussing* is doubtful; although 'he' must either be discussing or not discussing, the assertion is doubtful to us.[98] We understand that one or the other is necessarily true, but we do not know which one is true. When we use those verbs which are called impersonal, the sentence is not completed by the use of a nominative case; it accepts other cases, as when we say *disputatur* [it is being discussed][99] the sentence is complete when one adds an ablative such as *a Cicerone* [by Cicero]. When we say *paenitet* [it grieves] the sentence is complete if one adds the accusative *Ciceronem* [Cicero]. There are many such; [391] but the fact remains that personal verbs do not make up a complete sentence

[97] The allowance of some propositions as doubtful is a weakness, based on a failure to understand the difference between a proposition and the sentence which expresses it. *Ille disputat* [He is discussing] is not a proposition but a propositional function, equivalent to *X is discussing,* where *X* is a variable to be filled at will. *Ille* here stands for the Stoic *ekeinos,* which was precisely such a variable; see William and Martha Kneale, *The Development of Logic* (Oxford, 1962), p. 146. Martianus or his source would appear to have conflated the standard Aristotelian dichotomy of propositions into true and false with the Stoic classification of *axiomata* into definite and indefinite.

[98] This paragraph continues the confusions alluded to in the previous note, and adds a further, more serious one. The truth or falsity of a proposition does not depend on our judgment. The dubiety of *X is discussing* has to do with what is said, not with how it seems to us. The proposition *A sponge is an animal* may be "doubtful" to us and at the same time true.

[99] The "it" of this translation is to be understood without reference to some particular thing which is being discussed. This Latin impersonal passive is equivalent rather to "discussion is taking place."

unless the third person of the verb occurs with the nominative case. There are also sentences which consist indeed of a noun and a verb but cannot be affirmed or denied. Some have chosen to call these not *propositions* but *complete utterances;* an example is the imperative mood. When we say *Run!* the sentence is already complete; for what you say can not only be understood but even acted upon. It cannot, however, be denied, for it is no denial to say *Don't run!* This is not in opposition to the utterance *Run!* so that the question can arise which is true and which false. The question[100] certainly arises in affirmation and denial. For instance, in *He runs* and *He does not run* there is the question whether he runs. But *Run!* and *Don't run!* do not give rise to the question whether he runs. There cannot be understood here any question whether he ought to run.[101] That arises from affirmation and denial: for example, *He should run, He should not run.* The same applies to expressions of wishing.[102] For although the sentence is complete when we say *Would that I were writing!* or *Would that I were not writing!* no question can arise here of whether or not writing is being done. [392] There are many such sentences; these will suffice for illustration. The combination of a complete noun and a complete verb necessarily makes a sentence, but does not necessarily make a proposition, if there is nothing that can be affirmed or denied. I have said above that we can say in a complete sentence many things which cannot be affirmed or denied but that from a proposition the question does arise as to what can be affirmed or can be denied.[103] *Every man is an animal* is, therefore, a complete proposition. Although nature demands that the noun should be uttered

[100] Dick's text here mistakenly prints *quaesto* for *quaestio.*

[101] Dick proposes exclusion of this sentence. He ought to propose exclusion of the following one as well, or of neither. The two sentences together are a gloss, possibly Martianus' own, to guard against misunderstanding of the previous *utrum currat* [whether he runs], which can also mean "He is to run" or "He ought to run."

[102] Lit., "the optative mood." Mention of an optative mood seems curious in Latin, and suggests an ultimate Greek source. Some manuscripts of pseudo-Augustine (*De dialectica* 2), however, give an archaic Latin optative form, *di illum perduint,* in the corresponding example.

[103] Reading: *non necessaris facit proloquium si nihil est, quod iam et affirmari et negari protest. et supra diximus multa dici plena sententia quae tamen affirmari < et negari non possint, quaestionem vero nasci ex eo, quod affirmari > possit et negari possit.* See Willis, p. 35.

first and then the verb, as above, it does not cease to be a true proposition even if you say *An animal is every man.*[104]

[393] If anything is added to the sentence, one must consider carefully to which part it is added. For there are two parts of a proposition: one, which is the province of the noun, is called the *subject*; the other, which is the province of the verb, is called the *predicate (pars declarativa).* For what it is we are talking about is 'laid down' as subject; and what can be understood about it is 'declared' or predicated of it.[105] So when we say *Cicero is discussing,* if we add to this sentence *in the Tusculan Disputations,* these words are added to the predicate of the sentence; if we add *the Roman,* these words are added to the subject; if we add *wisely and fully,* it is to the predicate; again, if we say *with Cato,* it is added to the predicate. So whatever is added in the nominative case is added to the subject; whatever is added to the predicate is added in various cases and ways. For no other cases can be added to the subject, while to the predicate various cases can be added, with the exception of the nominative.

[394] It is to be noted that it is possible for a verb to be in the subject, and a noun in the predicate, but the verb then is in the subject in such a way that some pronoun is associated with it in place of a noun. And a noun is in the predicate in association with some verb through which it fulfils the function of a verb. Suppose, for example, we say *qui disputat Cicero est* [(He) who discusses is Cicero], then *qui disputat* [(He) who discusses] is subject, *Cicero est* [is Cicero] predicate. But it is the pronoun which makes the former the subject, and the verb which makes the latter the predicate.

[395] In this part, therefore, we have been discussing how the two are combined and nevertheless cannot form a complete sentence on their own; and if they do form one, how there are sentences which, though complete, are not subject to truth or falsity;[106]

---

104 This curious sentence should be understood as having "every man" as the subject. Despite Martianus' claim of what order is "natural," the inverted sentence is far more natural in Latin than in English.

105 This sentence, which cannot be adequately translated into English, explains the choice of terms *par subiectiva* [part laid down] and *pars declarativa* [part declared]. These terms are characteristic of Apuleius' *Peri hermeneias.*

106 The phrase *falsitati et veritati obnoxius* [subject to truth and falsity] is

and how we arrive at what is not merely a complete sentence but is also of necessity true or false. And this is the *proposition*.

[396] Now follows the third part,[107] in which I must discuss propositions themselves; we achieved an understanding of what they are in the preceding section. Propositions differ from one another in two ways, in *quantity* and in *quality*. The distinction of quantity is that some are *universal*, some *particular*, some *indefinite*. An instance of the universal is *Every man is an animal;* of the particular, *Some man is walking;* of the indefinite, *(A) man is walking.*[108] What we call an indefinite assertion we perforce take as particular, and not perforce as general and universal. Since the safe interpretation is the one to be counted by preference, an indefinite proposition is taken as a particular. There will be then a twofold distinction of quantity; namely, that between universal and particular propositions; and likewise a twofold distinction of quality, that between *affirmative* and *negative*[109] propositions. An example of the affirmative is *Every pleasure is good;* and of the negative, *All pleasure is not good.*[110]

[397] The converse of a universal affirmative proposition does

---

characteristic, with minor variations, of Apuleius and pseudo-Augustine, and may well be due ultimately to Varro's discussion of the *proloquium* [proposition].

[107] Martianus' discussion of the third part *De proloquendo* [On the proposition], while still corresponding in outline to part of Aristotle's *De interpretatione*, has very close affinities with the treatise *Peri hermeneias*, attributed to Apuleius. This is the probable source both for this section and also for the account of the categorical syllogism which follows.

[108] Latin syntax permits an ambiguity which is not possible in English. Martianus' example, *homo ambulat*, can mean either "Man walks" (a general proposition) or "A man is walking" (a particular proposition); hence it is called *indefinite*. He then goes on to give a rule of safe (i.e., minimal) interpretation, for if the general proposition is true so is the particular, but not necessarily conversely. Cf. Aristotle *De interpretatione* 17^{b}5-13; Apuleius *Peri hermeneias* 266 (ed. Thomas, p. 177, lines 14 ff.).

[109] *Dedicativa* and *abdicativa* are technical terms characteristic of Apuleius, and so are found also in Cassiodorus.

[110] *Omnis voluptas non est bonum.* This sentence is to be understood as asserting that all pleasure is other than good; that is, that no pleasure is good. But in normal English the form *All pleasure is not good* is equivalent to a negative particular rather than to a universal. For this reason expressions of this type are translated by the form *No pleasure is good* throughout this section, with an exception toward the end of § 397.

not necessarily follow. For it is not the case that if every man is an animal, every animal is a man. The converse of a universal negative proposition does, however, necessarily follow. For if no pleasure is a good thing, no good thing is a pleasure; and if no dumb animal is a man, then no man is a dumb animal. A particular affirmative proposition, however, is necessarily convertible. For if some man is an animal, then some animal is a man. The particular negative, on the other hand, is not necessarily convertible. For it is not the case that if some animal is not rational then some rational being is not an animal. Therefore the universal affirmative and the particular negative[111] are not necessarily reversible. But the universal negative and the particular affirmative propositions are necessarily convertible, in such a way, however, that when the conversion is made, the negation remains in the predicate. At any rate, the conversion is to be made in such a way that the former predicate term becomes the subject term. Therefore, when I say *Every pleasure is not good*, *Every pleasure* is the subject, *is not good* is the predicate. If I convert this to *Every good thing is not a pleasure*, what was the predicate has become the subject, but the negative remains with the predicate. If I wanted to express it as *No pleasure is good*, it should be converted as *No good thing is a pleasure*.

[398] But[112] because of the two kinds of propositions which, as I have said, are not necessarily convertible, we ought to look at[113] all the attributions made in propositions which enable them to be propounded correctly or incorrectly, in order to be able to indicate what is true or false. These five attributes have already been set out above: genus, difference, accident, definition, and property. Defi-

111 Martianus here, and in several other places, uses the feminine gender rather than his usual neuter. This suggests that *propositio* rather than *proloquium* is to be understood, and is thus a further link with Apuleius' *Peri hermeneias*. The use of the diminutive *particula* [term] in the next sentence is characteristic of the same work.

112 In reintroducing the five predicables here, Martianus follows Apuleius (*Peri hermeneias* 270-71; ed. Thomas, p. 182, lines 4-20), who gives the same examples as Martianus used in §§ 344-49. From the standpoint of formal logic this is irrelevant, since the question of what is a property, for example, of a given subject cannot be answered without empirical investigation. Martianus' account reads like an expanded explanatory paraphrase of Apuleius' account.

113 *intendere*. Willis suggests *intellegere;* the sense would then be "we ought to understand."

nition and property make those propositions convertible; the other three do not do so in any way. For just as every man is a rational mortal animal, so every rational mortal animal is a man; and just as every man is capable of laughter, so every being that is capable of laughter is a man. Again, in the particular negative proposition we must see what negative attribute is a property.[114] For just as it is a property of man to be capable of laughter, so it is a property of beings other than man not to be able to laugh. Therefore if we propound the particular negative proposition *Something capable of laughter is not other than man*,[115] it is without doubt convertible as *Something other than man is not capable of laughter.* Similarly, *Something inanimate, irrational, and immortal is not a man;* and *Some man is not inanimate, irrational, and immortal.*

[399] Again, there are other forms of conversion[116] which make the same terms of propositions indefinite while the sign of negation moves from its place. Indefinite terms are formed in this way: *man, nonman; animal, nonanimal.* It is indefinite, then, because you say only that this is not something and do not say what it is. Therefore, when I say *Every man is an animal*, if I want to convert that correctly, I add signs of negation so that the terms become indefinite. For if it is true that every man is an animal, it is also true that every nonanimal is nonman. Cicero used this conversion in his *Rhetoric:*[117] *Then if the issue itself or any part of it is in rebuttal*

---

[114] The last part of this paragraph is strange. It appears somehow related to Apuleius' cryptic conclusion to his account of the role of the five predicables in conversion: *igitur per haec agnoscetur particularis abdicativa non esse conversibilis* [Therefore it will be recognized through these (*sc.* five predicables) that the negative particular is not convertible]. Whatever the justification for Apuleius' curious demonstration may be, it seems that Martianus has misunderstood it—in particular, the words *non esse.* Could his text have had *abdicative*, giving the meaning "the nonbeing of a particular negative is convertible"?

[115] The Latin of this example (*quiddam risibile non est praeter hominem*) is far less strained than the translation given, which is intended to show how Martianus apparently construes a sentence which would normally mean: "Anything other than man which is capable of laughter does not exist."

[116] In more recent terminology this is known as *contraposition* (or, more precisely in the first example, an obverted form of contraposition).

[117] Cicero *De inventione* 1. 13. Martianus follows a common ancient practice in calling the *De inventione* the *Rhetorica.* The example has no counterpart in Apuleius.

of an accusation, anything that is not in rebuttal of the accusation is not the issue nor part of the issue.

[400] Likewise the particular negative proposition can be converted in this way. For if some animal is not a man, then some non-man is an animal. In this conversion we should note that in the place where there is no negative when we express the proposition directly[118] a negative occurs when we convert. The two forms of proposition which did not necessarily take the first kind can take this kind of conversion; only the universal negative does not take the other kind.[119] So for the sake of exposition let us call the former kind *primary conversion;* the latter, *secondary.*

The mutual relations of these propositions will be shown more clearly in the following way.[120]

[401] With four lines let us draw a square figure [see p. 142]. In the first corner of the upper line let us write *universal affirmative,* and in the other corner of the same line let us write *universal negative.* Below that, in the first corner of the lower line let us write *particular affirmative,* and in the remaining corner *particular negative.* Then let us draw diagonal lines from the universal affirmative to the particular negative and from the universal negative to the particular affirmative. The two upper propositions cannot both be asserted but can both be denied at the same time,[121] [402] for *Every pleasure is good* and *No pleasure is good* cannot both be true at the

118 I.e., before conversion. For the text: *ut ubi non est negatio . . . sit,* see Willis, p. 36.

119 The second part of this sentence is either very cryptic or else a simple mistake. The universal negative is the only proposition which will allow of both simple conversion and contraposition. Only the particular affirmative will not allow of contraposition. Apuleius has nothing corresponding to Martianus' statement.

120 Martianus: *Haec autem proloquia quemadmodum inter se affecta sint hoc modo manifestius apparebit. quattuor lineis quadrata formula exprimatur.* Cf. Apuleius *Peri hermeneias* 268. (ed. Thomas, p. 179, line 17): *Nunc dicendum est, quemadmodum quattuor illae propositiones inter se affectae sint, quas non ab re est in quadrata formula spectare.* Both the similarities and the differences of diction between Martianus and his probable source are characteristic of this whole section. Martianus does not give technical terms for the relations exhibited by the square. Apuleius' discussion of the square comes before his discussion of conversion.

121 In standard terminology these are "contraries" (Apuleius: *contrariae*).

same time. But it is possible for it not to be the case that[122] every pleasure is good, and at the same time for it not to be the case that no pleasure is good. The two lower propositions in their turn can both be asserted but cannot both be denied at the same time. For certainly it is not possible for *It is not the case that some pleasure is good,* and *It is not the case that some pleasure is not good* to be true at the same time,[123] but we can at the same time assert

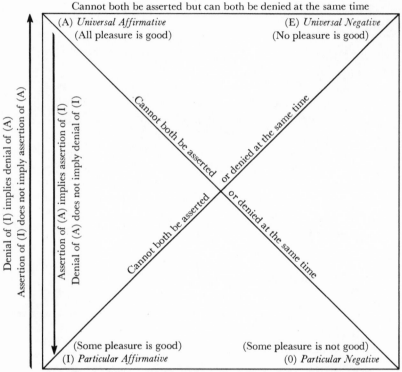

Cannot both be asserted but can both be denied at the same time

(A) *Universal Affirmative*
(All pleasure is good)

(E) *Universal Negative*
(No pleasure is good)

Denial of (I) implies denial of (A)
Assertion of (I) does not imply assertion of (A)

Assertion of (A) implies assertion of (I)
Denial of (A) does not imply denial of (I)

Cannot both be asserted

or denied at the same time

or denied at the same time

Cannot both be asserted

(Some pleasure is good)
(I) *Particular Affirmative*

(Some pleasure is not good)
(0) *Particular Negative*

Can both be asserted but cannot both be denied at the same time

[122] The form of statement used by Martianus, in which the initial *non* negatives the entire proposition and is translated as "it is not the case that . . . " is characteristic of Stoic logic; Apuleius *Peri hermeneias* 267 (ed. Thomas, p. 177, line 26); Benson Mates, *Stoic Logic* (Berkeley, 1961), p. 31.

[123] Reading: *nam utique non potest simul 'non quaedam voluptas bonum' et 'non quaedam voluptas non bonum' esse.* This reintroduces a double negative excluded by Willis (p. 37) following the better manuscripts, but accords better

both *Some pleasure is good* and *Some pleasure is not good*. Those propositions joined by the diagonals cannot both be asserted or denied at the same time.[124] For if *Every pleasure is good* is true, *Some pleasure is not good* is false. Again, if *Every pleasure is good* is false, *Some pleasure is not good* is true. This also happens if you mention the particular proposition first in each case.

Again, if *No pleasure is good* is true, *Some pleasure is good* is false; and if *No pleasure is good* is false, then *Some pleasure is good* is true. [403] Again, the assertion of a universal affirmative proposition necessarily implies the assertion of the corresponding particular; but its denial does not necessarily imply the denial of the corresponding particular. For if *All pleasure is good* is true, *Some pleasure is good* is necessarily true. But if we deny the first proposition and say it is not the case that all pleasure is good, it can still be true that some pleasure is good. Again, the assertion of a particular affirmative proposition does not necessarily imply the assertion of the corresponding universal, but its denial necessarily implies the denial of the universal. For if *Some pleasure is good* is true it does not follow that all pleasure is good; but if some pleasure is not good, then *Every pleasure is good* is false. You can observe this in the two remaining instances.

[404] When[125] we have propounded a complete sentence with the purpose of deducing something from it, after it has been granted[126] it is termed a *premise*. Another sentence should be joined to this sentence in a particular way, and of course this needs to be granted for the sake of what we want to infer; and when it has been granted, it is called a premise.

[405] From two premises rightly connected there results a *conclusion*. This conclusion cannot be called a premise, because you do not expect your opponent to concede it to you; rather, it follows despite his efforts, provided it has been inferred by keeping

---

with the context. The sense is clear, but the text demands further consideration. The propositions in question are *subcontraries* (Apuleius: *subpares*).

124 These are "contradictories" (Apuleius: *alterutrae*).

125 Here begins Martianus' fourth part, *De summa proloquiorum* [On the syllogism].

126 I.e., by an opponent. The subordination of logic as a pure science to practical debating, already seen in the naming and description of Dialectic, is here evident again.

the rules. To make this clear by an example, let us suppose that the question is whether pleasure is advantageous. If we begin by asserting *Every pleasure is good*, we have a complete sentence; if our opponent grants this, it becomes a premise. When this has been conceded, the further sentence must be joined to it, *Everything good is advantageous*. If that also is granted, it becomes a premise; from these two premises there follows, despite our opponent, the conclusion: *Therefore all pleasure is advantageous*.

[406] The whole which consists of two premises and a conclusion is termed by us *ratiocinatio* and by the Greeks *syllogismos*. A syllogism, then, is the necessary progression from two or more conceded positions to one not conceded. There can therefore be more than two premises but there cannot be fewer. For it is a complete syllogism if we wish to reach what we desire to show (that pleasure is advantageous) by means of even three premises, as in *Every pleasure is in accordance with nature; everything in accordance with nature is good; every good is advantageous; therefore every pleasure is advantageous*. From this it is clear that even more premises may be added if appropriate.

[407] Sometimes we reach a conclusion by inferring not what follows directly from the premises but what necessarily follows from what we ought to infer; for example, *Every virtue is good; everything good is advantageous; therefore every virtue is free from harm*. The proper inference would be *therefore all virtue is advantageous*; but from that it necessarily follows that it is free from harm, because what is advantageous is never harmful. This is called by the Greeks *symperasma* and by us it can be called *confinis conclusio* [related conclusion].[127]

The syllogism, then, whether it has its own proper conclusion or a related conclusion, is divided into two kinds: the categorical and the conditional syllogism.

[408] A *categorical syllogism* is one in which the premises are connected in such a way that they are completed by something else added from outside, as in the example given above: *Every pleasure is good; everything good is advantageous*. We see here that not all that was in the first premise has been mentioned [in the

[127] Martianus' term means literally "neighboring conclusion"; i.e., "conclusion one step removed."

second], but from the first premise one part, the predicate, has been taken and has become the subject in the second proposition. To form a complete sentence the second proposition has taken something from outside; namely, *is advantageous*. The conclusion is formed from the term which is added and the term which is not repeated; *therefore every pleasure is advantageous*.

This kind of syllogism has three figures.[128] The first is the one in which the predicate of the leading premise becomes the subject of the subsequent premise, or the subject of the leading premise becomes the predicate of the subsequent one.[129] The predicate of the leading premise becomes the subject of the subsequent one, for instance, in the example given above. The subject of the leading premise becomes the predicate of the subsequent one if you should wish to convert in the following way: *Everything good is advantageous; every pleasure is good; therefore every pleasure is advantageous*.

The second figure is that in which the predicate of the leading premise is also the predicate of the subsequent premise, as in *Every virtue is good; no pleasure is good; therefore no pleasure is a virtue*.

The third figure is that in which the subject of the first premise is also the subject of the subsequent one, as in *Some good is a pleasure; every good is advantageous; therefore something advantageous is a pleasure*.

[409] In the first figure a conclusion can be universal or particular, affirmative or negative; in the second figure no conclusion can be reached except negatively; in the third figure only a particular conclusion can be reached. There is, therefore, a point in keeping this order. For that figure is deservedly called first in which every

128 Modern textbooks recognize four figures. The recognition of the fourth is attributed to Galen, but was not usually indicated in textbooks until comparatively modern times. As Martianus does not distinguish between the major and minor premises, his characterization of the first figure is able to include the fourth. Of his nine valid moods of the first figure, only four are now usually classed as belonging to it; the other five belong to the fourth. For a full account, see Nicholas Rescher, *Galen and the Syllogism* (Pittsburgh, 1966), esp. pp. 13-15, 22-49.

129 The two possibilities arise because the order of the premises is immaterial to the validity of the conclusion. It has long been conventional, however, to state the major premise (that which contains the predicate term of the conclusion) first. In Martianus' examples the minor premise is often given first.

kind of conclusion can be reached; and that is rightly called second in which a universal conclusion can be reached, albeit negatively; and that is rightly called third, being lesser in range, in which only a particular conclusion can be reached.

[410] I must now discuss how many moods[130] each of these figures can have; these are restricted to a definite number and one should not lightly grant that any conclusion has been reached except in one of these moods. The first figure can have nine moods; the second, four; the third, six.

[411] In the first figure the *first mood*[131] is that in which a universal affirmative is concluded directly from two universal affirmatives; for example, *Everything just is honorable; everything honorable is good; therefore everything just is good.* If you make the inference conversely *therefore everything good is just,* it does not follow; but one can make the particular inference *therefore something good is just,* and that forms the *fifth mood.*[132] The *second mood*[133] is that in which a universal negative is concluded directly from a universal affirmative and a universal negative; for example, *Everything just is honorable; nothing honorable is base; therefore nothing just is base.* If you convert *therefore nothing base is just,* it forms the *sixth mood.*[134] We have said above that a universal negative can be converted. The *third mood*[135] is that in which a particular affirmative is concluded directly from a particular affirmative and a universal affirmative; for instance, *Something just is honorable; everything honorable is advantageous; therefore something just is advantageous.* But if you convert you form the *seventh mood,*[136] *therefore something advantageous is just,* since it has been said

---

[130] Martianus lists only the nineteen valid moods, not all the possible moods of the figures. In the Middle Ages these nineteen were given mnemonic names which are still used and are indicated in the notes. In these names the vowels indicate the kinds of propositions in the premises (i.e., the *A, E, I, O* propositions according to standard terminology; where, for instance, *A* = universal affirmative) when the major premise is placed first. Martianus gives the premises in the reverse order.

[131] *Barbara.*

[132] *Baralipton,* corresponding to *Bramantip* in the fourth figure.

[133] *Celarent.*

[134] *Celantes,* corresponding to *Camenes* in the fourth figure.

[135] *Darii.*

[136] *Dabitis,* corresponding to *Dimaris,* in the fourth figure.

above that the particular affirmative can be converted. The *fourth mood*[137] is that in which a particular negative is concluded directly from a particular affirmative and a universal negative; for example, *Something just is honorable; nothing honorable is base; therefore something just is not base.* It cannot be converted, for we have said above that the particular negative cannot be converted. The *eighth mood*[138] is that in which a particular negative is concluded conversely from a universal negative and a universal affirmative; for instance, *Nothing base is honorable; everything honorable is just; therefore something just is not base.* The *ninth mood*[139] is that in which a particular negative is concluded conversely from a universal negative and a particular affirmative; for instance, *Nothing base is honorable; something honorable is just; therefore something just is not base.*

[412] Of the second figure the *first mood*[140] is that in which a universal negative is concluded directly from a universal affirmative and a universal negative; for example, *Everything just is honorable; nothing base is honorable; therefore nothing just is base.* If you employ conversion here, the result is not another mood, since the conclusion is formed from the subjects of the two premises.[141] The *second mood*[142] is that in which a universal negative is concluded directly from a universal negative and a universal affirmative; for example, *Nothing base is honorable; everything just is honorable; therefore nothing base is just.* The *third mood*[143] is that in which a particular negative is concluded directly from a particular affirmative and a universal negative; for example, *Something just is honorable; nothing base is honorable; therefore something just is not base.* The *fourth mood*[144] is that in which a particular negative is concluded

---

137 *Ferio.*

138 *Fapesmo,* corresponding to *Fesapo* in the fourth figure.

139 *Frisesomorum,* corresponding to *Fresison* in the fourth figure.

140 *Cesare.*

141 The converse conclusion *Nothing base is just* is of course valid, and indeed results in a syllogism of the second mood (*Camestres*). Martianus' cryptic remark "the result is not another mood" must mean that no extra forms of syllogism are produced in this figure by conversion as are those forms corresponding to the fourth figure in the first figure.

142 *Camestres.*

143 *Festino.*

144 *Baroco.*

directly from a particular negative and a universal affirmative; for example, *Something just is not base; everything evil is base; therefore something just is not evil.*

[413] In the third figure the *first mood*[145] is that in which a particular affirmative is concluded directly from two universal affirmatives; for example, *Everything just is honorable; everything just is good; therefore something honorable is good.* The *second mood*[146] is that in which a particular affirmative is concluded directly from a particular affirmative and a universal affirmative; for example, *Something just is honorable; everything just is good; therefore something honorable is good.* The *third mood*[147] is that in which a particular affirmative is concluded directly from a universal affirmative and a particular affirmative; for example, *Everything honorable is just; something honorable is good; therefore something just is good.* The *fourth mood*[148] is that in which a particular negative is concluded directly from a universal affirmative and a universal negative; for example, *Everything just is honorable; nothing just is evil; therefore something honorable is not evil.* The *fifth mood*[149] is that in which a particular negative is concluded directly from a particular affirmative and a universal negative; for example, *Something just is honorable; nothing just is evil; therefore something honorable is not evil.* The *sixth mood*[150] is that in which a particular negative is concluded directly from a universal affirmative and a particular negative; for example, *Everything just is honorable; something just is not evil; therefore something honorable is not evil.* So all the moods keep to a fixed order, and the reason for the order is as has been shown in the figures themselves.[151]

[414] A *conditional syllogism*[152] is one in which the initial

[145] *Darapti.*
[146] *Datisi.*
[147] *Disamis.*
[148] *Felapton.*
[149] *Ferison.*
[150] *Bocardo.*

[151] Martianus means that the nineteen valid forms of syllogism can be classified, first by figure and then by ordering the kinds of conclusion that can be drawn in each figure, in the order A, E, I, O, according to standard terminology.

[152] Apuleius does not include an account of the conditional syllogisms, and Martianus' immediate source is unknown. His presentation has affinities with Cicero *Topica* 53-57; see Kneale, pp. 179-81.

premise contains both a full statement of the evidential proposition and a full statement of the demonstrandum,[153] in such a way that when the evidential proposition has been taken as an additional premise the demonstrandum can be inferred with certainty. For instance, let us suppose the demonstrandum to be whether rhetoric is advantageous. As we wish to show that it is advantageous, let us form an evidential proposition from its definition, "the science of speaking well." From this evidential proposition and the earlier demonstrandum a conditional syllogism is formed of which the first premise is *If rhetoric is the science of speaking well, it is advantageous;* as second premise we take the evidential proposition, *But rhetoric is the science of speaking well.* Whoever grants the truth of these two must grant, even against his will, that rhetoric is advantageous, which was in doubt before the first and second premises were granted. No term occurs in the second premise from outside the first, for that is a characteristic of the categorical syllogism. This is called by dialecticians the *first mode, from antecedents,*[154] for the reason that the evidential proposition forms the second premise just as it occurs in the first, with the difference only that it occurs conditionally in the first and categorically in the second.

[415] The *second mode,* which is called *from consequents,*[155] is one in which the evidential proposition follows the demonstrandum and not the other way round, for instance; *If rhetoric is not advantageous, it is not the science of speaking well.* The negation of the evidential proposition is taken as the additional premise, thus: *But rhetoric is the science of speaking well; therefore it is advantageous.*

---

[153] Martianus' use of *propositio* for "the leading premise of an argument" belongs to the same tradition as Cicero *De inventione* 1. 59 ff., and differs from the Apuleian use of the word, which Martianus has avoided (except by implication; see above, n. 111). The terminology which he adopts for the components of a complex premise seems unparalleled, based as it is on the relation of these components to the conclusion, instead of to the particle "if." For this reason, this unusual use of *argumentum* has been translated as the equally curious phrase "evidential proposition," rather than as "factual minor premise." The term "demonstrandum," by contrast, is used here to represent a Latin phrase *id de quo quaestio est* [the point at issue]. Again, the influence of disputation is clear.

[154] I.e., the *modus ponens,* or "affirming the antecedent."

[155] I.e., the *modus tollens,* or "denying the consequent."

[416] The *third mode* is called *from incompatibles*.[156] In this mode it is shown that it is not possible at the same time for one thing to be so and another not to be. When one of these two is asserted as an additional premise the other will necessarily be rejected, so that when the affirmative one is asserted the negative one is rejected. For example, *It is not the case both that rhetoric is the science of speaking well and that it is not advantageous; but in fact it is the science of speaking well; therefore it is advantageous.* Here the conclusion that it is advantageous is established by rejecting the negative disjunct in the first premise. These three modes can all be formed from one evidential proposition and they can all prove the one thing. In the first premise it makes no difference which part is put first, the evidential proposition or the demonstrandum, provided that the conditional form is preserved. When you say *If rhetoric is the science of speaking well, it is advantageous,* this can also be expressed as *Rhetoric is advantageous if it is the science of speaking well.* The same can be tried with the other two modes.

[417] The *fourth mode* is formed *by disjunction*[157] in such a way that when the truth of one disjunct is granted, the other is necessarily denied; for example, *Either he is healthy or he is sick; but he is healthy; therefore he is not sick.*

[418] The *fifth mode* is also formed by disjunction in such a way that when one disjunct is denied the other is necessarily the case. For example, *Either he is healthy or he is sick; but it is not the case that he is healthy; therefore he is sick.*

[419] There are two further modes which can be formed through the evidential proposition used in the fourth and fifth, though not by disjunction but *by negation.* There is then a *sixth mode*, in which it is shown that two things cannot both be the case at the same time. The second premise is formed by the assertion

[156] This mode and the following are classified under the heading of conditional syllogism although in their overt form they would be better classified as arguments with a composite premise.

[157] This mode requires exclusive disjunction, as shown by the Latin *aut*, and not the weaker disjunction (Latin *vel*) used by modern logicians. The weaker form allows either or both disjuncts to be true. The fifth mode, however, applies to both forms of disjunction. The use of exclusive disjunction is characteristically stoic; see Mates, p. 51.

of one, and the conclusion by the negation of the other; for example, *It is not the case both that he is healthy and that he is sick; but he is healthy; therefore he is not sick.* The *seventh mode*[158] has the same initial premise as the sixth, but the same second premise and conclusion as the fifth. [420] To enable the matter to be more easily understood, some formulas follow below, in such a way that their logical force may be appreciated through the facts themselves, not through stated examples. This is the formula for the first mode:[159] *If the first, then the second; but the first; therefore the second.* For the second mode: *If not the first, then not the second; but the second; therefore the first.* For the third mode: *Not both the first and not the second; but the first; therefore the second.* For the fourth mode: *Either the first or the second; but the first; therefore not the second.* For the fifth mode: *Either the first or the second; but not the first; therefore the second.* For the sixth mode: *Not both the first and the second; but the first; therefore not the second.* And for the seventh mode: *Not both the first and the second; but not the first; therefore the second.*[160]

[421] We must recognize that from one evidential proposition three of the above modes can be formed, and from a different one the other four. The reason for this order is so that the first mode may be the one called *from antecedents,* because what is antecedent comes first; and the one called *from consequents* is second, on the same principle, so that by its name it seems to show that it ought to follow the first in order. There remains the third one using the same evidential proposition, that *from incompatibles;* for we cannot leap across to *disjunction,* since it cannot be formed from the same evidential proposition. This will therefore be the fourth mode, but, as it were, the first of those using another evidential proposition, and in that class the one which asserts its second premise affirmatively ought to come first; for affirmation is prior to negation. The fifth mode ought to be through disjunction also, but after the fourth because in the fourth the second premise is formed by affirmation,

---

158 As stated, this is clearly invalid. See below, n. 160.

159 The use of ordinal numerals for propositional variables is characteristically Stoic; see Mates, p. 2, n. 4; and Apuleius *Peri hermeneias* 279 (ed. Thomas, p. 193, line 5).

160 A valid form, suggested by W. and M. Kneale (p. 180), would be *Not both not the first and not the second, but not the first; therefore the second.*

in the fifth by negation. This may be understood also in the two remaining modes.

[422] Syllogisms are combined in many ways, so that in one process of reasoning you may recognize the forms of both the categorical and conditional syllogisms. For example, if the question is whether dialectic itself is advantageous, the argument should be set out: *If it is advantageous to discuss well, the science of discussing well is advantageous; but to discuss well is advantageous; therefore dialectic is advantageous.* However, we must observe in the categorical syllogism what the second premise takes over from the first; for it is clear that it takes something from outside. But as I said, in what the second premise takes over from the first, we must note whether it takes it over correctly, in accordance with the patterns properly kept and remembered. For it happens that what was observed in the first premise to belong to the predicate, in the second premise clearly belongs to the subject; and again, if you form the second premise in a different way, the same phrase will belong to the predicate. For example, it is known that in the first figure the second premise is formed in such a way that either the predicate of the first premise is the same as the subject of the second, or else that the subject of the first is the predicate of the second; but in the second figure the predicates of the first premise and of the second are the same. So that if you were to advance an argument like this—*Every art is to be practiced by frequent exercise; but speech is the exercise of rhetoric; therefore rhetoric is to be practiced by frequent speech*—then in the first premise *exercise* was seen to belong to the predicate, and in the second premise again it belongs to the predicate. Then how has the form been preserved? Surely, because something has been left in the predicate of the first premise which has not come into the predicate of the second, from which a conclusion could be formed; and that is, *is to be practiced.* For if I wished to form the second premise thus—*Rhetoric is an art*—the whole[161] would be kept to form the conclusion: *Therefore rhetoric*

---

[161] I.e., the whole of either the subject or the predicate of the first premise (here, the subject, which forms the predicate of the second premise). By this time, even the serious student of logic is eagerly waiting for the end of Dialectic's speech. It would seem that a measure of unintelligibility is now in keeping with Martianus' purpose.

is to be practiced by frequent exercise. From this it is clear that there are many common elements which can be joined to either the subject or the predicate, according to the style of the second premise."

[423] While Dialectic was holding forth in this way and getting on to matters as complicated as they are obscure, Maia's son [Mercury] grew impatient and nodded to Pallas, who cut in:

"Madam, you speak with great skill; but now stop your exposition before you get entangled in the complexities of your subject, and its knotty problems exhaust the goodwill of Hymen. You have said in summary all that is fitting from that which learned discussion has contributed for the development of the subject in a large volume. A modest spring from deep learning is sufficient; it brings to light things hidden from sight, and avoids tedious discussion, without passing over anything and leaving it unrecognized. The matters that remain[162] are founded on great deceit, and false deception encompasses those who are caught by them, while you prepare sophisms fraught with guile, or seductively make sport with trickeries from which one cannot get free. And when you gradually build up a sorites, or fashion errors which truth condemns, then your sin, your wicked deed, resounds in the ears of the Thunderer, since the lofty denizens of heaven hate everything false in a woman of shame. If you ponder it, what is more cruel than making sport of people? You have had your say, and you will surely become a disreputable and itinerant charlatan if you go on to build up your snares. Away then with shifty profundity, and leave what time remains to your sisters."

[424] When Dialectic heard this she hesitated a little, but in obedience to the orders of the goddess she replied:

"I must respect your word, and in obedience to commands that I must honor I shall refrain and shall not say what I had commenced. But one indulgence should have been allowed me, that

---

162 Martianus' failure to include a discussion of fallacies is strange in the work of one supposedly teaching the science of disputation. Athena apparently does not recognize the value of being able to detect fallacious reasoning, whether in an opponent or oneself. Disproportions in the time allotted to various topics were, of course, evident from the time Dialectic began to speak.

as a matter of honor I should have been permitted to refute the story which Bromius invented;[163] he would then know that we daughters of Cecrops [i.e., women of Athens] know very well how to feel insulted; he would be able to see that I am more viperish than he had thought; his 'clumsy Marsian' would indeed become a magician; and he would not catch *me* asleep or drunk and babbling commonplaces when Jupiter's stars are rising. But I must wait upon you alone, lady; I shall be quiet."

With these words she fell silent, as if restrained, and many of the gods who had at first laughed at her trembled before her.

[163] See § 331.

BOOK V

Rhetoric

[425] Meantime the trumpets sounded,[1] their strident song pierced the sky and heaven reechoed with an unfamiliar din;[2] the gods were frightened and confused, the host of heaven's minor inhabitants quaked;[3] unaware of the reason, their hearts stood still, and they recalled the charges made about the battle of Phlegra long ago.[4] Then the Rivers and the fauns, the Pales, Ephialta,[5] and the Valley Nymphs looked at the chief gods and with astonishment saw no movement to rise amongst them; and each in turn uttered their wonderment at the peaceful calm in the hearts of the deities.[6] Then first Silvanus put down his cypress tree[7] and in a tremor of fear[8] held out his defenseless right hand,[9] begging for the bows of the Delians,[10] the arms of Hercules,

[1] Martianus: *Interea sonuere tubae;* cf. Silius Italicus *Punica* 12. 181: *Insonuere tubae.*

[2] Martianus: *raucusque per aethram/cantus, et ignoto caelum clangore remugit;* cf. Vergil *Aeneid* 8. 2: *rauco strepuerunt cornua cantu; ibid.,* 526: *tubae mugire per aethera clangor; ibid.,* 9. 504: *sequitur clamor caelumque remugit.*

[3] Martianus: *turbati expavere dii, vulgusque minorum/caelicolum trepidat;* cf. Vergil *Aeneid* 9. 538: *turbati trepidare intus frustraque malorum/velle fugat.*

[4] In ancient mythology, the giants tried to invade heaven and were defeated by the gods in a battle at Phlegra. Martianus refers to *crimina* [charges] almost as if the gods were guilty of war crimes in their treatment of the giants.

[5] Ephialtes, often regarded as Incubus, the nightmare-demon, though here he is presented amongst beneficent deities. See H. J. Rose, *A Handbook of Greek Mythology,* 6th ed. (London, 1958), pp. 57, 60-62.

[6] Martianus: *mirantur placidam per pectora sacra quietem;* cf. Vergil *Aeneid* 1. 691: *At Venus Ascanio placidam per membra quietem/inrigat;* cf. Vergil *Aeneid* 4. 5: *nec placidam membris dat cura quietem.*

[7] Vergil (*Georgics* 1. 20) represents Sylvanus uprooting a cypress.

[8] Martianus: *percitus ac trepidans;* cf. Apuleius *Metamorphoses* 3. 21: *percita . . . ac satis trepida;* also *ibid.,* 9. 2: *trepida facie percitus.*

[9] Martianus: *dextram tendebat inermem;* repeats the diction of Vergil *Aeneid* 12. 311.

[10] Apollo and Artemis (Diana), who were born on Delos.

crying with longing for Portunus' trident,[11] not daring to ask
for the spear of Gradivus [Mars]; being used to rustic warfare,
he was considering the scythe of Saturn and, distrusting his own
strength, was eying the missiles of the Thunderer.

[426] But while a great group of the earth-gods was disturbed
by such thoughts, in strode a woman of the tallest stature and
abounding self-confidence, a woman of outstanding beauty; she
wore a helmet, and her head was wreathed with royal grandeur;
in her hands the arms with which she used either to defend herself
or to wound her enemies, shone with the brightness of lightning.
The garment under her arms was covered by a robe wound about
her shoulders in the Latin fashion; this robe was adorned with the
light of all kinds of devices and showed the figures of them all, while
she had a belt under her breast adorned[12] with the rarest colors of
jewels.[13] [427] When she clashed her weapons on entering, you
would say that the broken booming of thunder was rolling forth
with the shattering clash of a lightning cloud; indeed it was thought
that she could hurl thunderbolts like Jove.[14] For like a queen with
power over everything, she could drive any host of people where
she wanted[15] and draw them back from where she wanted; she
could sway them to tears and whip them to a frenzy, and change
the countenance and senses not only of cities but of armies in
battle. She was said to have brought under her control, amongst
the people of Romulus, the senate, the public platforms, and the
law courts, and in Athens had at will swayed the legislative assembly, the schools, and the theaters, and had caused the utmost confusion throughout Greece.

[428] What countenance and voice she had as she spoke, what
excellence and exaltation of speech! It was worth even the gods'
effort to hear such genius of argument, so rich a wealth of diction,

[11] Martianus: *Portuni trifidam suspirans flagitat hastam;* cf. Valerius Flaccus
Argonautica I. 641: *trifida Neptunus in hasta.*

[12] Martianus: *omnium figurarum lumine variatum;* cf. Catullus 64. 50: *Variata
figuris.*

[13] Martianus is punning here, as *lumen* [light], *figurae* [devices], *schemata*
[figures], *colores* [colors], and *gemmae* [jewels] are all terms that may be applied to rhetorical ornament.

[14] Pericles was nicknamed "the Olympian" and had a reputation for oratory
with the force of a thunderbolt.

[15] The diction and thought echoes Cicero *De oratore* I. 30-32.

so vast a store of memory and recollection. What order in structure, what harmonious delivery, what movement of gesture, what profundity of concept! She was light in treating small topics, ready with middling topics, and with exalted ones a firebrand. In discussion she made her whole audience attentive, in persuasion amenable, full of conflict in disagreements, full of pride in speeches of praise. But when she had, through the testimony of some public figure, proclaimed some matter of dispute, everything seemed to be in turbulence,[16] confusion, and on fire.[17] [429] This golden-voiced woman, pouring out some of the jewels of crowns and kingdoms, was followed by a mighty army of famous men, amongst whom the two nearest her outshone the rest. These two were of different nationalities and styles of dress, one wearing the Greek pallium, the other the Roman trabea. Each spoke a different language, though one professed to have studied Greek culture at Athens and was considered quick in the studies of the Greek schools and in the constant disputes and discussions of the Academy.[18] Both were men from poor families, who rose to fame from humble beginnings.[19] And although a Roman *eques* fathered one, and a toiling workman the other,[20] both grew to such fame through their oratorical prowess that after their destinies in public life and their unmerited deaths they rose by their excellence to the stars and now outlast the ages through their eternal glory. [430] The one whom the people of Athens and the whole stream of Greeks followed had the reputation of being most forceful, more vigorous than the storms and raging of the angry ocean. He was described in verse such as this: "A man to fear, who might find fault even with the innocent."[21] [431] But the other,

---

16 The diction echoes Cicero's translation (*Orator* 29) of Aristophanes' description of Pericles.

17 The preceding two sections (427 and 428) are written with a wealth of rhetorical devices, figures of thought, and figures of speech unusual even for Martianus.

18 These two men are Demosthenes and Cicero; the latter was steeped in Greek literature and philosophy.

19 Martianus says "Both were new men", which in Latin means the first of a family to reach senatorial rank.

20 Demosthenes' father had been, in fact, quite wealthy; but the estate was embezzled by Demosthenes' guardian.

21 Homer *Iliad* 11. 654, where Patroclus is describing Achilles.

who wore the purple of a consul, and a laurel wreath[22] for suppressing a conspiracy, came into the senate of heaven, and, delighted to have come into Jove's presence, joyfully began to declaim: "How blessed we are, how fortunate the State, how brilliant the fame of my consulship!"[23] [432] After these two in different lines there came the great orators of the past: one could see Aeschines, Isocrates, and Lysias, bearing before them the highest honors and the rewards of their eloquence; and then, in the Roman ranks, the *Sosantii*, the Gracchi, Regulus, Pliny, and Fronto.[24] [433] But before them all, even before the woman who led the whole array, went an old man bearing the mark of office and the preceding rod, after the manner of a Roman lictor, and on the top of the rod there flew a golden-mouthed crow as a sign of the woman who was coming.[25] [434] But the man who was carrying the rod was called Tisias, and seemed older and more important than all of them; for with a glance at the crow perched above him, he called the others, his inferiors, their common bond, and the woman in the lead their daughter. [435] Stirred by this thought, very many of the gods believed that this

[22] This seems to be a misunderstanding of a line of verse by Cicero (*De officiis* 1. 77; *In Pisonem* 72). The verse ("Let arms yield to the toga, let the laurel wreath give way to the eulogy") praises civic over military achievement, and by implication Cicero's civic career over Pompey's military one. Although Cicero did regard the suppression of the Catilinarian conspiracy as a great, quasi-military victory, he was not awarded a laurel wreath (the prize of a military commander), and the whole context of the passage in *De officiis* makes it clear that he regards the wreath as a prize inferior to the words of praise and vote of honor which he did receive. Martianus seems to be alluding to the line of verse but misunderstanding its significance.

[23] Cicero *In Catilinam* 2. 10.

[24] All these are well-known Greek and Roman political figures, except for the so-called *Sosantii*, of whom nothing is known. The passage is regarded by all editors as corrupt. The more intelligible conjectures include *Crassos Antonios* [the Crassi, the Antonii]—Crassus and Antonius were celebrated orators of the Republic, but there seems to be no reason to refer to them in the plural—and *sonanti ore* [with resounding mouth].

[25] The two traditional inventors of rhetoric were the Sicilians Tisias and Corax; the latter's name is the Greek word for "crow." During the Roman Republic, the higher magistrates were preceded by six or twelve men, each bearing fasces (the symbol of authority of Roman magistrates, the fasces consisted of a bundle of rods and an ax bound together); these men were called lictors. The epithet "golden-mouthed" might perhaps apply to the woman and not to the crow.

woman of high nobility was, if a Greek, then the sister of Apollo, and if one of Romulus' people [i.e., a Roman], one of the Corvinian family.[26] Added to this mystery was the fact that fearlessly and with very ready self-confidence she kissed the breast of Pallas and of the Cyllenian himself, thus giving clear signs of her almost sisterly intimacy with them. Indeed some of the gods—who, in fear of the heralding trumpet and in wonder at her friendship with the heavenly beings, had long been uncertain, and wanted to learn from foresighted Phoebus, since great Jove was not yet making any inquiry —began with some perturbation to ask who she was.

[436] She then, looking at the whole assembly of gods, with some emotion[27] began to speak: "I call to witness great father Jove and the other dwellers in heaven, whom I have often invoked in a great many cases, and the very assembly of the celestial senate, that there is no more unsuitable or more inappropriate opinion of me than that I, who have constantly been the accuser in many political and legal disputes and who in many other instances have been the defender and have striven[28] with all my might for the glory of the contest and have obtained for myself from the hazardous fates the fame of a well-earned result, should now amongst you gods, to please whom seemed the price of immortality, be compelled against my will to recall the advice given to school children and the jejune rules of a timeworn subject.[29] Nor does poverty bring me to this, since I have thronging hordes of followers.[30] But apart from those who break the benches[31] and bring turmoil to the hearts and senses of all

[26] *Corvinus* is the adjective derived from *corvus*, the Roman word for "crow." Perhaps the sign of the crow suggests kinship with Apollo because the crow is traditionally a prophetic bird, and Apollo is par excellence the god of prophecy; cf. § 894.

[27] Martianus: *aliquanto commotior sic coepit;* cf. Apuleius *Metamorphoses* 2. 29: *aliquanto propheta commotior . . . ait.*

[28] It is not customary for *annixa* to govern a direct object, but it here appears to govern *gloriam.*

[29] This is a particularly long and elaborate sentence, like many first sentences in Cicero's speeches; this effect has been retained in the translation.

[30] Implicit is the contrast between the poor teacher of school children—an occupation of low status and small recompense in antiquity—and the rhetorician, who taught adolescents and young adults and could earn fame and wealth.

[31] A result of unrestrained enthusiasm and applause for a rhetorical performance (see Quintilian *Institutiones Oratoriae* 2. 9. 12).

those who know me, I have other devotees also, who have written detailed instructions and commentaries on the most esoteric points of the subject; under each category[32] of my followers my Cicero shines out, since he not only has thundered forth with the grandeur of impressive speech in forum, senate, and public assembly, but also in writing the rules of the subject has committed many books to use by future generations. [437] Since this is so, regard for the dignity I have earned and the fame of a reputation as widespread as I believe mine to be, would deter me from expounding these elementary first principles, were it not that you command me, and that command contributes to my reward of immortality, and the pledge of everlasting fame inspires me to set forth even the rudiments of my subject when Jove and the gods ordain it. So I prepare myself to traverse these arid topics, giving less pleasure, indeed, than I usually do in public performances; although if the approbation of His Gracious Majesty has allowed Pallas and the Arcadian to participate,[33] then in your assembly, mighty deities, shall I cause displeasure? [438] For I am Rhetoric herself, whom some term a science,[34] some a virtue, some a study; a science, because I am the object of teaching, although Plato disputes the title. Those who have discovered that I possess the knowledge of how to speak well call me a virtue. Those who are aware that the innermost secrets of speaking can be studied and learned, proclaim confidently that I am a study.[35]

[439] My duty is to speak appropriately in order to persuade; my object is through speech to persuade the hearer of the subject proposed.[36] I invoke the words of my Cicero, using whose examples

[32] That is, both as orator and as theorist or rhetorician.

[33] Lit., "has given the ears of Pallas and the reason of the Arcadian [Mercury] a share (*Pallados aures atque Arcadiam rationem . . . participarit*).

[34] The Latin word *ars* in this type of context means a body of teachable knowledge with internal consistency and its own intellectual methods; it is therefore better translated by our word "science" or "discipline" than by "art," which nowadays has connotations of virtuosity not in the Latin *ars* or the Greek τεχνή.

[35] *Disciplina.*

[36] Martianus: *Officium vero meum est dicere apposite ad persuadendum, finis persuadere id, quod est propositum, dictione;* cf. Cicero *De inventione* 1. 6: *Officium autem eius facultatis videtur esse dicere apposite ad persuasionem; finis persuadere dictione.*

I am going through all the branches of instruction in turn. [440] My material is twofold—namely, in what circumstances and from what resources a speech is made: in what circumstances, when I approach the elements of the *quaestio*[37] itself; from what resources, when the matter and words of a speech are put together.

[441] The *quaestio* is either limited or unlimited. It is limited when it arises from a particular action and concerns a given individual; for instance, in Cicero's speech for Roscius, the issue is whether Roscius killed his father. The *quaestio* is unlimited when it asks as a general question whether one ought to do something; for example, the *Hortensius*[38] discusses whether one ought to pursue philosophy. I am often vigorously engaged in the former, which the Greeks chose to call *hypothesis*. In the unlimited *quaestio*, which has the boldness to make a universal affirmation, I engage mainly when I have in prospect leisure and argument, although generally that aspect of it which is called *thesis* would have often furnished me with sturdy javelins and far-ranging spears[39] in the more exalted parts of my lawsuits. Is not this what happens in the speech for Scaurus,[40] when Cicero interpolates a discussion on 'the possible causes of sudden death,' or again in the speech for Milo,[41] 'whether the world is governed by providence'? And then, some of my followers, inspired by most keen and subtle reasoning, assert that no issue is a hypothesis, but that all that may be argued in defense of the accused or against them in prosecution can be reduced to general issues.[42]

[442] There is no doubt that my duty has five parts: matter,

[37] The *quaestio* is the particular question at issue in a given situation; identification of this formed a most important part of ancient rhetorical theory.

[38] The *Hortensius* is a dialogue by Cicero which urged the reader to interest himself in philosophy. It exists only in fragments.

[39] An image which Cicero twice applies to arguments (*De oratore* 1. 242; *Brutus* 271). Martianus is saying, in a roundabout way, that the "thesis," or unlimited *quaestio*, is mainly a pastime, rather than a serious rhetorical exercise, though it does have its uses. One might compare the attitude of a lawyer or a politician toward a debating society.

[40] The speech is extant only in fragments, which do not include the passage here described.

[41] *Pro Milone* 83-85.

[42] A view attributed by Augustine to Apollodorus, in opposition to Hermagoras; Carl Halm, ed., *Rhetores Latini Minores* (Leipzig, 1863), p. 140, lines 6-11.

arrangement, diction, memory, and delivery.[43] For judgment, which
some include,[44] is required in all the parts, and therefore cannot itself properly be considered a part, although it is the province of
judgment to weigh what should and what should not be said. Matter, or invention, is the prudent and searching collection of issues
and arguments.[45] Arrangement is that which puts the matter in
order.[46] Diction chooses words that are proper or figurative, in-
vents new usages, and arranges words of traditional usage.[47] Memory is the firm guardian of our matter and our diction.[48] Delivery
is the control of our voice, movement, and gesture according to
the importance of our matter and our words.[49] Of these, the most
powerful surely is invention, which has the task of discovering the
issues in a case and finding suitable arguments to prove it.

[443] There are two kinds of questions: principal and incidental.[50] Principal questions are those issues from which the case has
arisen; Cicero calls them 'constituting issues.'[51] Incidental questions

[43] Cf. Cicero *De inventione* 1. 9.

[44] Quintilian also refers to "some" rhetoricians who add judgment as a sixth
duty (*Institutiones Oratoriae* 3. 3. 5). Cicero emphasizes the need for judgment,
or discrimination, (*De oratore* 1. 142; 2. 308; *Partitiones oratoriae* 8), but includes it within the other five parts, Sulpitius Victor (*Institutio oratoria* 4; ed.
Halm, *Rhetores Latini Minores*, p. 315) sets out a radically different list of
three duties of rhetoric, a list which he asserts follows a Greek tradition different from that of Cicero, Quintilian, and the usual Latin rhetoricians; but
even he appears to include judgment under *inventio* [matter] (*Institutio oratoria*
13; Halm, p. 320).

[45] This definition of *inventio* is not found in the other Latin rhetoricians,
most of whom use the definition found in Cicero *De inventione* 1. 9; and the
Rhetorica ad Herennium 1. 3: "the discovery of true or plausible arguments to
make one's case seem probable."

[46] This definition of *dispositio* is not found in the other Latin rhetoricians.

[47] This definition of *elocutio* is not found in the other Latin rhetoricians.

[48] The phrasing of this definition is close to that of Cicero *De inventione* 1. 9,
and the *Rhetorica ad Herennium* 1. 3, but the image of the guardian probably
comes from Cicero *De oratore* 1. 18.

[49] This definition is a blend of those in Cicero *De inventione* 1. 9, and the
Rhetorica ad Herennium 1. 3.

[50] Although the distinction between principal and incidental questions is
implicit in Cicero *De inventione* 1. 18-19; the *Rhetorica ad Herennium* 1. 26;
and Quintilian *Institutiones Oratoriae* 3. 6. 7-9 and 3. 11. esp. 16 and 27 (citing
Theodorus), Fortunatianus (1. 28; Halm, p. 101) seems to be the first Latin
rhetorician to make it explicit and use this terminology.

[51] *De inventione* 1. 10.

are those which arise in the course of a case, when in refuting arguments or written submissions the case is led into further questions: for example, a principal question is, whether Milo was right to kill Clodius; an incidental question, which one set an ambush for the other.

[444] The principal issues are three in number:[52] whether a thing happened, what it was that happened, and what was the character of what happened. Whether a thing happened is a conjecture; as, for example, whether Roscius killed his father. What it was that happened is the definition of the action; for example, whether Cornelius did commit lese majesty. The character of a thing is its quality; for example, whether it was just for Saturninus to be killed. But in case someone should say that I am passing over a fourth type of issue which is the discovery of Hermagoras,[53] more refined reasoning calls it not an issue but a part of the qualitative issue, as I shall show in discussing this issue.

[445] Now I must say how the issues in a case are found. They are found by assertion and rebuttal. Assertion is the accusation of the deed which has come for judgment. Rebuttal is a rejection denying the assertion; for example, 'You killed your father' is assertion, 'I did not kill him' is rebuttal. From these two juxtaposed statements arises the question, which is called the *status* because in it stands, as it were, the battle line of the parties to the suit, drawn up for conflict.[54] But it is easy to see what reply to make when an accusation has been made. It is not easy to see what charge should be asserted, whether the deed (for example, 'You killed a man') or the name of the deed (for example, 'You committed homicide'). Although it seems to make no difference, yet if the former accusation is denied, the question will be one of conjecture when the accused has said: 'I did not kill him.'"[55] But if the accusation is not of a deed

---

52 The doctrine is as in Quintilian *Institutiones Oratoriae* 3. 6. 80.

53 The *Rhetorica ad Herennium* (1. 18) also holds that there are not four but three types of issues.

54 *Status* is derived from the Latin verb *stare* [to stand], but surely not because of any military connotation; rather, because the *status* of a case is the basis on which it stands or rests; *status* is the Latin equivalent of the Greek rhetorical term *stasis*, which has a similar etymology; cf. Quintilian *Institutiones Oratoriae* 3. 6. 4.

55 A sentence whose text is badly corrupt is omitted by Dick as a gloss here; Willis would restore it, with this meaning: "When the name of the deed is

but of the name of a charge, since one part or another may be
denied it will not be clear what is the issue at stake. For you do not
know what he is denying when a man says: 'I did not commit homicide'; is it that he did not kill a man, or that the assassination of
a tyrant is not called homicide? One should therefore make an
accusation of an action, so that, if your opponent denies the action,
you may have an issue of conjecture; but if he concedes the action and denies the title of the accusation, you may know that it is
the definition of the action that is at issue. [446] But if he concedes
both the action and the title of the accusation, yet says he was entitled or obliged to do it, then the issue of quality comes into the case;
the issue of quality arises either with regard to the deed or to the
lawsuit. For example, 'Milo[56] would have been entitled to do
what he did' concerns the deed. 'Whether a slave or bondman may
appeal to the tribunes'; 'whether a person of scandalous reputation
may hold a public assembly'—these questions concern the legal
processes, and this sort of qualitative issue is called *transference*.
But we need to take care that we do not impugn the function of
the person who hears the case and allow the issue of quality to become the only issue. For the person before whom the case comes
has to perform one duty: to either convict or acquit a man.

[447] There are three kinds of audience before whom cases
come: one who has decided some matter according to equity, and is
precisely a *judge;*[57] another who is in doubt over the propriety or

---

the charge here, its definition can be considered, so that if the accused says 'I
did not commit homicide' we must examine what homicide is—the killing of
any man, or the killing of an innocent man" (translation mine).

[56] *ut 'Miloni . . .'* Willis accepts Eyssenhardt's suggestion *utrum Miloni;* the
sense would then be "whether Milo . . ."

[57] In modern legal procedure of the British tradition, a judge is a trained
lawyer whose career is solely as a judge and whose duties are to guide the
conduct of a lawsuit and to deliver sentence. In Roman legal procedure, the
guidance of the more important lawsuits was in the hands of praetors, but determination of both the verdict and the sentence in such cases was in the hands
of the *iudices,* the jury; in less important lawsuits the parties agreed on a
iudex, who then acted like a modern arbitrator or magistrate, to determine
both the verdict and the sentence, or damages, or in other ways give judgment.
The difference between the *iudex* and the modern judge is that the *iudex* was
not necessarily a trained lawyer or a professional; hence, principles of rhetoric
designed to persuade a panel of jurymen applied equally well to a single *iudex.*

advantage of a course of action and looks for persuasion to another's opinion; he is a *deliberator* in perplexity.[58] The third kind is he who weighs with a free judgment the propriety or impropriety of an action, and it is customary to call him an *assessor*. These then are the three kinds of cases which are included in the hypothesis:[59] the judicial, the deliberative, and the demonstrative.

[448] But since all these people who listen to the cases as described are misled by uncertainty of their duties, it is necessary to examine the distinction between them and the particular function of each. The judge—whose function is to convict or acquit, to give possession of goods or remove them from possession—before a case comes to him, is in doubt how to discharge his duty. The deliberator is unsettled by the perplexity of his mind. The assessor of eulogy weighs with calculating thought whether a subject is being properly eulogized. But when these duties are being separated and distinguished, we concentrate on the differences between them caused by variations of time. For the duty of the deliberator is concerned only with a question in the future; for example, if Cato is deliberating whether he ought to commit suicide to avoid the spectacle of Caesar victorious. Sometimes the duty of the judge is exercised with regard to future time as well as to past time. The conjectural issue is found only in relation to a past action; the qualitative issue often arises from some future problem, as will be set out more clearly in due course.[60] The duty of the assessor of eulogy relates entirely to past actions, but it is distinguished from the duty of the judge by its purpose. For the judge's purpose is to acquit the innocent by the exercise of justice, while the purpose of the other is to adorn the famous man with praise by the contemplation of his outstanding merits. Furthermore, in the judicial type of case the judge weighs his decision concerning the affairs of others,[61] while in eulogy the assessor hears whether the things said are true and suitable, although

---

[58] *Inexplicabilis,* here translated as "in perplexity," is normally used in the sense of "inexplicable, incapable of being explained," but in this context that seems meaningless.

[59] See § 441 for a definition of "hypothesis."

[60] Cf. § 454.

[61] Here the words *in deliberativo vero quisque tam de suis quam etiam de rebus externis* [in the deliberative case each man considers his own affairs as well as those of others] have been deleted from the text by Dick.

the latest forms of flattery have brought a situation where the subject of the eulogy is often the judge of its eloquence. [449] Therefore we ought to be on our guard not to trespass on the functions of our audience's office. For example, if one were to declare to Verres that he ought to be punished, he would surely reply that he ought not to be punished, and the question whether he deserves punishment would appear to be merely a qualitative issue. Therefore the assertion arises from accusation of an action; for example, if in Verres' case one says: 'You plundered Sicily,' to which he replies: 'I did not,' a conjectural issue arises. It is indeed foolish not to make an accusation of the act itself and instead to charge something that remains in the hands of the judge, or to charge someone merely with the particular name of the deed. Equally one must be careful, when some law or writing is cited in a case, not to draw our assertion from the law—as, for example, to say: 'The law forbids you, an alien, to climb the wall.'[62] One should rather say: 'You climbed the wall,' so that if the defendant denies this, the dispute is not over the law, but over the action to which the law applies. If he admits the deed, then clearly he has acted against the law. But if the deed is denied, then no matter what law or document is cited it will seem to be a futile argument, since a dispute over truth, not over law, is what constitutes a legal question. This is a fault through which many have been misled.

[450] Besides the three kinds of issue which I have mentioned, there are said to be four or five others, which proceed from the quality of a document. Although they have their roles in a part of a case, they are never the central issue, since no one could cite for the purpose of proof a law or any kind of document unless there were something to be proved. The issue is the matter that has to be proved, and that always arises from the primary dispute; other questions in dispute are to be treated as incidental.

[451] Thus one will have an easy way of determining the issue, since neither the name of the action nor the function of the audience nor any law or document can be brought forward in place of the accusation. So an accusation is, for example: 'You killed a

---

[62] Since walls were an important part of a city's defenses, and it was undesirable that anyone—let alone an alien—should know a route by which a wall could be scaled, it would not be surprising if there were laws of this kind. The full case, which is an exercise for rhetorical practice, is set out in § 463.

man,' and the rebuttal: 'I did not'; from these statements arises the question, whether the accused did kill a man, and here the issue is one of conjecture. But when the defendant counters the accusation by alleging the righteousness of his action, the issue is one of quality, just as Milo did not deny his action, but argued the righteousness of his action; he admitted that he had killed Clodius, but claimed that he had been right to do it. For this kind of rebuttal there is a procedure, but it is not a single nor a simple one; for one and the same deed can seem justifiable for a variety of reasons. For instance, one argument is that Milo killed someone who lay in ambush for him; another is to say that he killed an enemy of the state who was inflamed with the ambition to become a dictator. In these assertions there is indeed a qualitative issue, but different kinds of qualitative issue emerge; for the first is revealed as a relative, the second as a comparative, qualitative issue. But if the accusation is opposed not by an assertion of the righteousness of the deed but by a denial of the name applied to it, although this is called denial rather than rebuttal, yet it does not make the issue one of conjecture, because it is not the deed but its name that is in dispute. For example, consider an action for adultery. A husband who has divorced his wife finds a rake with the divorced wife, and accuses him of adultery.[63] The defendant disputes the case, and does not deny the act but contests the name of adultery, and the question arises, what is adultery? This is a dispute over definition. [452] Therefore a conjectural issue is a denial of the fact, whereas an issue of definition is a denial not of an action but of its title; and therefore it is a rebuttal of the charge brought, since, when another name is put on a deed, the danger implicit in the charge made is denied, as in the charge:

[63] This sentence could also mean: "A husband who has married a divorced woman finds with his wife the rake who divorced her and accuses him of adultery." In the second translation the defense is presumably based on the rake's claim, as first husband, to retain some rights to the woman's favors; in the first translation the defense presumably is that since the woman is divorced there can be no case of adultery. The first translation seems more sensible, although the word order suggests the second. The words used for "divorce" (*repudiata, repudiaverat*, derived from *repudium*) imply that the divorce was not by mutual consent but on the first husband's initiative; the case (in either translation) seems to rest on the questions of whether a husband may revoke his initiative and retain his conjugal rights and whether the wife, having taken no legal initiative, remains bound by her earlier obligations.

'You stole goblets of the temple from the house of the priest: you have committed sacrilege.' The rebuttal is: 'I stole the goblets, but since I stole them from the priest's house and not the temple, it should be called theft, not sacrilege.' In this instance also there seems to be a certain denial of the deed, in another way; for the action admitted does not aim at injury to the gods but at cost to the priest, since the cups were stolen from his house. In this case each kind of action needs to be defined; that is, what is a sacrilege and what is theft.

[453] Now I must discuss the qualitative issue, the manifold nature of which first calls for division into parts, so that when one has run through the list the particular characteristics of each may be explained one by one. The qualitative issue, then, is concerned with either the action or the lawsuit. It is concerned with the action when it treats of the principle or the cause of the deed which has been brought to court, or when there is a dispute about what ought to be done; for example, whether Milo was entitled to kill Clodius, or whether Cicero should regain possession of his house. It is concerned with the lawsuit when there is a question whether a suit should be permitted and a judgment given. Since this part of the qualitative issue depends on the justice of the law, it is right and more accurate to include it under the heading of the qualitative issue; it is different from what Hermagoras preferred to distinguish from the qualitative issue as being a new point of dispute, and to call transferal, or limitation. [454] But this comes later. Just as the qualitative issue applies to past time, so it applies to the future. As applied to the past it is juridical, as applied to the future it is connected with one's business and public life. In either case there is an allegation about right. In juridical questions the allegations concern rights in nature; in connection with business they concern law or custom. The forensic qualitative issue is divided into an absolute and an extrinsic type. The absolute is that which defends the action itself by argument from its own nature and rightness. The extrinsic is that which, on finding nothing defensible in the act as such, has recourse to the motive, and claims that that was just; as, for instance, when Milo could not claim that homicide is right in itself, he claimed, as his motive for the killing, the ambush Clodius set for him. This type gets its name, 'extrinsic,' from the fact that

when an action cannot be defended absolutely the defense has recourse to the motives.

This extrinsic type has four parts: transferal, removal, comparison, concession. [455] Transferal occurs when a defendant, having admitted the action, transfers the responsibility for it to the victim of the action; as Milo transferred the responsibility to Clodius, or Orestes to his mother, or Horatius to his sister when he claimed that he had killed her because the provocation of her offense had compelled him to the deed.[64] [456] Removal occurs when responsibility for the alleged deed is transferred to some person or thing other than the accused. To another person: for example, when Tiberius Gracchus transferred the responsibility to Mancinus because Mancinus had been the author of the treaty which was repudiated by both the senate and the people.[65] Another example would be a case of this kind: 'Unless an ambassador sets out on his mission within thirty days, he faces capital punishment. The quaestor[66] does not give the ambassador his traveling expenses and allowance; the time has elapsed. The ambassador, when charged, argues against the charge, and transfers the charge to the quaestor.' The charge is removed to a thing if, having been delayed by illness, the ambassador transfers to his misfortune the charge of delay. The action itself can be transferred if it is alleged that it pertained to someone else's authority, or the cause of the deed can be transferred if it is alleged that something happened through someone else's fault. [457] Comparison is what I know is called compensation by some recent writers;

[64] Milo and Clodius were two political figures of Cicero's day. Each of the two had a gang of followers; in 52 B.C. Clodius was killed by Milo in a conflict between the two gangs. Cicero was to defend Milo, but suffered a complete failure of nerve; later, however, he published the speech he had intended to deliver, basing his argument on the grounds of self-defense and justifiable homicide of a public enemy.

In Greek legend Orestes, the son of Agamemnon and Clytemnestra, killed his mother in revenge for her murder of Agamemnon and her adultery.

In early Roman history Horatius killed his sister because she was betrothed to, and grieved for, one of the Alban enemy whom he had killed in battle; see Livy 1. 26.

[65] In 137 B.C., when trapped by the Numantines, Mancinus had come to terms with them to save himself and his army; Gracchus conducted the negotiations. The senate rejected the terms and resumed the war.

[66] A financial magistrate; a treasury official.

not when the good deed of some other time is invoked to mitigate a charge, but when an action is defended by the justification that some advantage follows from it. For if the merits of another time are recalled, as it were, for the sake of compensation, one ought rather move to the deprecative qualitative issue, which is contained in the type of case concerned with winning a pardon. But [in the qualitative issue of comparison] one contends that he has acted rightly, as in that reply of Verres: 'I sold the tax rights very dearly,' because the advantage gained compensates for the deed.[67] In this approach there is an admission of the deed, but the claim of benefit negates the enormity of the charge. In the other [the deprecative type] there is confession of the allegation and the deed, but it either is separated from the intention or, in the absence of justification, speaks with an eye to human feeling and compassion.[68] [458] But this kind of qualitative issue, which looks toward winning a pardon, is separated into two approaches: toward justification and deprecation. Justification is pleaded when we admit the misdeed and excuse our intention and will; without doubt there are three ways to do this; namely, through alleging carelessness, chance, or compulsion. Carelessness is pleaded when we deny that something happened with our intention or knowledge; for instance: "A man hunting throws his javelin at a beast and kills a man hiding under the hunting nets.' This is called error, and under this heading come ignorance, intoxication, forgetfulness, folly, insanity, and the other things which excuse an admitted error. Chance takes away the guilt of an event; as with the man with the animals for sacrifice on the religious feast day who encountered the rising river.[69] The man who murdered an

[67] The system of taxing the provinces under the Roman Republic was to auction the right to tax; the successful bidder then paid his bid to the Roman treasury and reimbursed himself with profit from the province, by taxing it on an agreed scale. Verres, the notorious Roman governor of Sicily successfully prosecuted by Cicero, defended himself on the charge of plundering the province by claiming that he got for the treasury a high price for the tax rights; Cicero alleged (In Verrem 3. 16. 40) that Verres got such a good price because he sold to the tax farmers the right to tax not 10 per cent but 50 per cent of the agricultural produce.

[68] For humanitatis Willis suggests humilitatis. The meaning would then be "to compassion for the defendant's abasement."

[69] This example is given in full in Cicero De inventione 2. 96. The Spartans had a law inflicting capital punishment on contractors who failed to provide animals for a particular religious ceremony of sacrifice. On one occasion a con-

innocent man on the order of his superior has committed a crime under compulsion. The difference between these three ways is that carelessness deceives, chance prevents, and compulsion compels. The deprecative type, however, makes no attempt to excuse, but expresses humble entreaty and supplication.

[459] Those who have studied these subjects note other questions, which they call incidental issues, as if the utterance of a first speech comprised essentially a defense.[70] Often the second speech [i.e., the defendant's] summons the force of a prosecution; for example, in this case: 'A brave man is given a free choice of reward. One man who has served bravely asks as his reward marriage to another man's wife.' In this case the man who has asked for the reward expects no opposition and accuses no one; but the husband opposes and accuses, although clearly he rises to speak second. The brave man will oppose him by rebuttal as if the husband were impeaching the request for reward which the brave man has asked; the brave man contends that the reward is just, as if he were defending an action that has been done according to law. [460] Moreover, the legal questions which, I have said, occur like issues in cases, are not reckoned by the same rule, in that they crop up in the secondary dispute; the primary one is assigned to the qualitative issue. Therefore the rule of assertion and rebuttal is confused in the aspect of the qualitative issue that I have mentioned.

[461] Now it is time for me to discuss what the Greeks call the judgment (*to krinomenon*). For when assertion and rebuttal have shown the issue and the status, then if that is a conjectural issue, it will offer equal scope for judgment; for there is nothing to be weighed by the court except the denial itself. But in the qualitative issue or the issue of definition the defense[71] through admission must

---

tractor who was driving the animals to their destination for sacrifice was prevented by a flooded river. Does he deserve punishment, or not?

[70] This passage is corrupt and its meaning obscure; I have attempted to combine Kopp's interpretation with a fairly literal translation. The first speech in a lawsuit was the prosecutor's; Martianus appears to be saying that sometimes it is in effect a defense. *Interius* can mean "more deeply," hence "essentially"; *demonstratio* does not normally mean "defense."

[71] The word used here (*depulsio*) is the one I have translated hitherto as "rebuttal"; but that translation seems inappropriate when speaking of an admitted misdeed. The sense of this difficult sentence may be elucidated by ref-

have an explanation of the misdeed on some point other than that where the issue appears; the prosecutor weakens this explanation, and a secondary question arises, as it were, through the argument for and against this explanation. In these circumstances that point can be liable to judgment, and can be what the assessor weighs by the standard of justice; it can occur in any case and can comprise the whole issue. And there are many arguments for and many against, and therefore many sources of judgment, since one action can be defended in many ways, as Cicero did on Milo's behalf because Milo killed a man who both laid an ambush for him and was a public enemy. In these cases, therefore, that issue will be stressed which the speaker has taken as most advantageous to the defense. That explanation is generally drawn from the orator's amassing of proof, and then other issues emerge, as it were, by logical consequence; [462] for instance, if a document is brought as proof, then there arises the legal judgment, of which there are five kinds. One is ambiguity, when more than one sense is contained in a document; the Greeks call this *amphibolia*, because the matter generally arises from common meanings in a noun;[72] for example: 'A man bequeathed *Taurus* in his will. He had a valuable slave of that name. But his principal heir gave to the beneficiary a bull (*taurus*), since the ambiguous name created this question.' Again, the question arises from the difference between nouns by one syllable; for example: 'A man had two kinsmen, one called Lesius and the other Milesius; in naming his heir he said *heresestomilesi*.'[73] The conflict arises from the doubt over the correct separation of the words; one heir, meaning Lesius, separates *esto mi*, while the other,

---

erence to Marius Victorinus' commentary on Cicero *De inventione* 1. 18: "The *question* is what arises from the basis of the case—was he justified in killing? The *explanation* is what causes the legal controversy: 'I killed Clodius because he meant to kill me.' The weakening of the explanation is: 'Even so, you were not justified in killing him.' The point for judgment is whether in those circumstances Milo seemed justified in killing Clodius." Martianus' "point where the issue appears" corresponds to Victorinus' "basis of the case."

[72] The Greek word basically means "a facing two ways," as of an army fighting on two fronts; the type of ambiguity Martianus brings as an example is of a noun which could be applied equally well to two different subjects.

[73] This is written continuously without spacing, as ancient Latin normally was written; it could comprise either of two sentences, *heres esto Milesi* [Milesius be my heir] or *heres esto mi Lesi* [My Lesius be my heir].

extending the noun to make the connection, makes Milesius the beneficiary. [463] There are also the ways included by dialectical proof. There is also the type of question relating to written documents which arises from the letter and the spirit of the document; for instance: 'A foreigner is forbidden to climb the city wall. In a city under siege, a foreigner goes onto the wall and repels one of the enemy; he is impeached.'[74] In this case the defendant relies on the spirit of the law, the accuser on the letter.

[464] The third type of question exists when laws contradict and conflict with each other; for example: 'Men are not allowed to enter the temple of Ceres. A man who does not assist his parents is liable to punishment. A man enters the temple of Ceres to assist his mother, who is being attacked there; he is impeached.' The difference between these laws, whose interpretations are contradictory, creates the problem as to which the man should rather have obeyed.

[465] The fourth question arises from a written document and is called the syllogism; in this we draw something that is not in writing by argument from what is in writing; for example: 'One is allowed to kill an exile if he is found within the territory from which he has been exiled. A man beats[75] an exile so found; he is impeached. It is argued by the defense that he was entitled to do what is less than the law allows.' This question has four modes: from similarity, from consequence, from greater to lesser, and from contrariety. From similarity: for instance, since the penalty for parricide is to be sewn up in a sack,[76] then this ought to be the penalty for matricide. From consequence: for example, there is a reward for tyrannicide; a man who has persuaded a tyrant to abdicate, claims the reward; he argues that he has equally deserved it, since he has restored liberty to the subjects. From greater to lesser: I have given an example above—if it is lawful to kill an exile then it is lawful to beat him. From contrariety: for example, if a brave man deserves a reward, then a deserter deserves a penalty.

[466] There remains the question of definition,[77] which follows from the ambiguity of a document, when some word in a law or a

[74] Cf. note on § 449.

[75] But does not kill.

[76] And drowned.

[77] Martianus also uses the adjective *finitivus* to mean "final"; cf. § 240. Either meaning suits this context.

will is doubtful and becomes clear by definition, for example: 'Let it be lawful to kill a man caught at night with a weapon; a man caught at night with a stick is killed by a magistrate, who is accused of murder. He defends himself by appeal to this law, but the question arises, What is a weapon?' This kind of legal question differs from the principal issues, since discussion centers not on the deed which gave rise to the lawsuit but on the definition of something in writing. The principal issues then are separate and distinguished from these legal questions, and these latter are termed incidental issues, while those which give rise to the lawsuit are more correctly called the issues, or fundamentals.

[467] Now that we have discussed these fundamentals, let us look at debates of the deliberative or demonstrative kind. For there is no doubt that there are three kinds of speech situation and in every one the issue should be treated, although some think that in the deliberative type of speech the issue is the qualitative issue concerned with business, because it considers future time. However, the qualitative issue is to be so regarded that other issues are not denied the possibility of occurring in this type of speech. Now we affirm that issues can be found in this type of speech as long as we do not take as our yardstick the rebuttal of an assertion, as was shown in the case of conflict. For what or who makes an assertion? Or do spokesmen, for and against, conflict in the usual way when we are allowed to choose one or another amongst an accumulation of arguments? However, the spokesman against a proposal seems to take the part of an accuser. For the person who shows that the case against which he is arguing is dishonorable or disadvantageous surely appears to be accusing the proposal itself. The proponent takes the part of the defender and seeks to acquit his treatment of the matter in hand by argument against his opponent. Therefore the opponent is to be spoken of as accusing, the proponent as rebutting. And thus, by the disagreement between them, the issue can be discerned, as in the case: 'When his army is continually retreating toward the walls, the commander debates whether to destroy the walls.' When he orders the walls to be destroyed, does he not seem to face prosecution if the order is carried out? Does it not seem that the army will be disturbed and mutinous at this action? Then there is a conjecture about the outcome of the disturbance. But then, if he says that one should not call it a victory if the city's defenses have been

destroyed, the definition comes into consideration; we must define what condition of the defenses permits the celebration of a victory. If our adversary then adds: 'That action ought not be taken without the senate's advice,' the question of limitation seems to come into it. Therefore it is certain that the role of accuser is correctly assigned to the opponent of a measure, and that in deliberative speeches all the issues readily appear. But we must be aware that the opponent is not to deliver judgment or restrain the proponent, in the manner of a judge; his duty is rather to prevent the proponent from persuading the audience to a course of action, by showing that it is dishonorable or disadvantageous.

[468] Now in the demonstrative type of speech it is not easy to say how the issue emerges, because blame is not the immediate alternative to praise—the man who is not praiseworthy is not thought blameworthy, nor on the contrary is the man who is free from blame exalted with praises, as if a man should be called praiseworthy because he has not committed murder. There is a term in between, which it is appropriate to call nonpossession, because the man who does not possess praise is not immediately consigned to censure, nor vice versa. The issue of the demonstrative type of speech appears when you set up one speaker to praise and one to censure and link the role of the accuser with the latter and that of the defender with the former. A subtler form of this exists when the listener, poised between praise and vituperation, is placed in the position of being an adversary, as it were. For not before you have shown that a person capable of being praised in fact ought to be praised is the listener free from a sort of accusing frame of mind, which does not yet believe the subject capable of being praised. The man speaking in praise or vituperation[78] must struggle against this preliminary frame of mind, although in the accumulation of argument mentioned above, a certain conflict[79] is evident, as when a man is praised by one speaker and accused by another (for example, Cato is praised

[78] One would think that the frame of mind described (suspicious of praise) would assist the vituperator. However, I believe that Martianus is being elliptical, so that in the previous sentence where he speaks of praise, its correlative, censure, is to be understood as well; when a speaker begins to praise or censure someone, the listener is predisposed to doubt whether the subject deserves the praise or censure forthcoming.

[79] I.e., between the speakers, not merely between speaker and audience.

by Cicero and accused in two works by Caesar); from which it is deduced that all types of cases are to be closely examined with regard to the issues.

[469] Having discovered the issue, you will discuss the nature of the case, which is comprised within either a simple or a double or a multiple question. It is simple when in a whole lawsuit we seek one single answer; for example, whether Milo was justified in killing Clodius. The question which, through investigation, arises later— the question, Who set an ambush for whom?—is not a question on its own, but a conjoint one from a double conjecture, which the Greeks call a counteraccusation (*antikategoria*); but a subsidiary question cannot determine the genus of the case. A double question arises from the matter, as in the speech for Caelius concerning gold and poison,[80] or by comparison, as in the speech for Roscius, asking whether the son or enemies killed the father. A multiple question arises when a case is made up of many questions, as all the speeches against Verres are made up of questions of extortion, and the speech for Scaurus inquires into the murder of Bostar, the wife of Aris, and the three tithes.[81]

[470] Now we must examine the direction of the case. The direction is a consistency in a particular approach, held throughout a case. There are five types of direction: the simple, the subtle, the figurative, the oblique, and the mixed. The simple exists when the speaker's words reflect what is in his mind directly; for example, if one praises the deserving and accuses the objectionable. The subtle exists when the words do not directly reflect the mind; for example, a man disowns his son because the son has no friends. The man is not really disowning his son but is frightening him into acquiring friends. The figurative exists when modesty forbids us to say something openly because of its obscenity and it is expressed under some

---

[80] Caelius was accused on five charges, one of which had to do with the property of a woman named Palla, and another with an alleged attempt to poison his former mistress Clodia.

[81] Only fragments of the speech of Cicero defending Scaurus have survived. As governor of Sardinia, Scaurus was accused of poisoning a Sardinian named Bostar, of displaying such incontinent passion for the wife of Aris that she hanged herself, and of extortion (hence the reference to the "three tithes"— presumably alluding to a tax rate of 30 per cent in place of the standard 10 per cent; cf. n. 67 on Verres, § 457).

other representation, dressed in clothing, as it were. The oblique exists when fear prevents us from saying something freely and we show that it must be presented in an underground[82] manner of speaking. For example: A tyrant who had moved to abolish his tyranny has performed valiantly, and asks as his reward the custody of the armory and the citadel. The magistrates oppose him.[83] The mixed kind is made up of both these two, when both shame and fear inhibit freedom of speech. For example: A tyrant had two sons; with the wife of one the father committed adultery; her husband hanged himself; the father ordered the other son to marry her. He refused. In this case one cannot speak freely either about the incest or the tyranny.[84] [471] These are the directions, which need to be worked out with care and should inconspicuously permeate the whole speech. They are distinguished from 'color' by the fact that color is observed in only one part of a speech, whereas direction is held throughout the case.[85]

[472] The direction is found from the matter in dispute; that is, from the cause of the controversy, which is either in past time—for

[82] *cuniculus;* lit. "rabbit burrow," or "tunnel."

[83] The Greek and Latin words *tyrannos* and *tyrannus* mean, basically, "one who has seized power unconstitutionally"—like our word "dictator"—they need not have any connotation of cruelty. In this example the tyrant has offered to restore constitutional government, on the condition that he not be punished. Then, presumably in warfare, he has shown signal courage, the reward for which (at least in rhetorical exercises) is the right to name one's own prize. He asks for the right to control the city's armaments, but is opposed, presumably on the grounds that this would immediately restore him to a position of tyranny. He could allege that refusal of this favor on the ground of his former tyranny constitutes punishment.

[84] I.e., if one assumed, for the purpose of the exercise, that one were defending the second son and were speaking in the city of the tyrant, where freedom of speech on both topics would be severely inhibited. In the conditions of the later Roman Empire this would by no means have been an unreal or irrelevant exercise.

[85] *Ductus* is translated as "direction," *color* as "color." These words are used by late Latin rhetoricians in a sense different from that found in the classical rhetoricians; see Johann Christian Ernesti; *Lexicon Technologiae Latinorum Rhetoricae* (Leipzig, 1797; repr. Hildesheim, 1962), pp. 63-66, 138-39; S. F. Bonner, *Roman Declamation* (Liverpool, 1949), pp. 55-56, and references therein. *Ductus* is, as Martianus describes, the general cast or tendency of a whole speech; *color* is a particular excuse or twist of argument, with special appreciation for ingenuity. Martianus' treatment of *ductus* is identical with that of Fortunatianus (Halm, pp. 84-86).

example, whether Ajax was killed by Ulysses, which keeps a simple direction—or, if the case concerns present or future time, it allows all the kinds of direction. So direction arises from one's purpose, and one's purpose arises from the matter in dispute. The matter in dispute is that which causes uncertainty; for example, in that story of the tyrant, the matter in dispute is the tyrant's request for the custody of the arms and the citadel. Cicero's *First Philippic* illustrates the use of the subtle direction, since with remarkable subtlety it covertly accuses Antony of tyranny, so that while it says everything, it appears to have said it all in good temper.

[473] Having covered all these points, we turn to look at arguments, by which credence can be brought to a disputed aspect of a question. Credence is formed in three ways: by winning goodwill, by instruction, and by emotional appeal. The first is called the ethical approach, the second the demonstrative, the third the emotional. Although one ought to win goodwill throughout the case, it should be pursued most of all at the commencement, while the end should be most vigorous with appeal to the emotions. Instruction should come particularly from the narrative section of the speech, although by resolving questions and putting forward accusations the argumentative section of a speech works in much the same way. Now I shall begin to discuss arguments.

An argument is a means of producing credence in a matter of doubt. [474] A matter of doubt is an accusation and a rebuttal, or a reason for action and a refutation of that reason. For when you make the accusation 'You killed a man,' in order to instruct your audience you will confirm what you say by proof, especially if the accusation is denied. The denial, too, requires proof, although to form credence in the audience one ought to bring forward what are called 'nonrhetorical proofs,' such as documents, witnesses, evidence obtained under torture[86]—matters which I shall keep for later discussion. At the moment I wish to treat the arguments which are inherent in the topic of discussion or those which are contingent to it. Arguments inherent in the topic are the topic as a whole, and some part of it, and its name, which the Greeks call 'etymology'; contingent to the topic are those matters connected to it in some relative way. These are thirteen in number: by conjugate relationship,

[86] Free men could not be tortured, but the evidence of slaves could be obtained only under torture.

by genus, by forms or species, by similarity, by difference, by contrariety, by adjuncts, by antecedents, by consequents, by contradictions, by causes, by effects, by comparison. The last has three parts: comparison of things greater, less, and equal. It is clear that a principle of relationship is inherent in all these; for a thing is called conjugate *to* something else,[87] and genus and species are interrelated. The similar, too, is similar to something, and all the sources of argument take their names from something other than themselves.

[475] So the matter which is in dispute and is therefore to be discussed should first be defined as a whole, and the arguments handled in the following way. Suppose the topic to be whether eloquence appears to be advantageous. Eloquence is the whole, and therefore should be defined as a whole, thus: 'Eloquence is the knowledge of how to speak well. But to speak well is advantageous; therefore eloquence is advantageous.' Dialectic, whom we have just heard, is of assistance in handling this source of argument; from her I believe we know what genus, species, difference, property, accident, and the rest are, which are included in her precepts. Nevertheless, I shall run through them as briefly and summarily as I can.

[476] Genus, then, is a concept common to many species and differences; for example, *animal,* which is applied to man, livestock, bird, fish, and other things which are different not only in number but also in species, in that some of them are aerial, some aquatic, some terrestrial, some rational, other irrational; when they are all included under one term, they are called by the name of the genus. [477] Species is a subsidiary of a genus containing elements which are divided from each other only as discrete units; for example, *man* includes both Cicero and Demosthenes, who share a common species but differ as discrete units.

[478] Difference is a distinction sufficient for the question; for example, if the question is, What is the difference between a man and a lion? the answer is that man is tame and lion is wild; this answer does not distinguish man from the other tame animals nor the lion from the other wild ones.

[479] Property is a thing's unique characteristic; for example, laughter, for laughter is unique to man.

[480] Accident is that which is in something but is not a part of it

[87] Dick postulates a lacuna here, but Willis points out that the passage seems to make sense as it stands.

and yet cannot be separated from it so as to exist independently; for example, color in the body, or learning in the mind. [481] Argument from the part is not directed to proving the whole, but to proving some part which includes a question. If the part be proved the whole is not thereby proved; for example, if the eye sees, the whole body does not therefore see, since it is not true that the whole body sees; but that is a discussion in dialectic. Now I shall show how argument is applied from one part to another: 'If we ought to protect our feet and arms, then all the more carefully should we protect our eyes.' Sometimes another argument, from greater to less, can be applied in place of this argument; but the force of the main argument is not upset by this, since nature allows some arguments to be duplicated. This also often happens in figures, which I shall have to discuss later. [482] Argument from the parts is sometimes constructed in this way also; when the idea of partition has been introduced, a number of parts have been put forward, and by rejecting the others we take as our conclusion a single part in which the question lies. For example: 'You have a horse. You either bought it or were given it or it was born on your property or you stole it. But you did not buy it, nor was it given to you nor born on your property; therefore you did steal it.' [483] We draw an argument from the name, or by etymology as the Greeks say. For example: 'If a consul is one who consults the interests of the state, what else did Cicero do when he punished the conspirators with death?'[88] In this situation one ought merely to attend to the origin of the word. [484] From those matters which appear to be contingent to the subject in dispute, arguments are drawn in the following manner: first, from conjugate words when some noun has been put forward as our starting point and we give our approval to something derived from that noun, in different circumstances or times.[89] For example: 'If piety is a virtue, we should praise a deed that is piously done,' for it is agreed that virtue

[88] During Cicero's term as consul (63 B.C.) he put down the conspiracy of Catiline and ordered the execution of the ringleaders; his action laid him open to severe criticism. This is a suggested line of defense.

[89] This phrase seems quite irrelevant. It could also be translated as "with alterations of case and tense," which would be not only irrelevant but meaningless in its application of tense to nouns. It seems as if Martianus is simply padding the passage with a stock phrase. The argument from conjugate words is mentioned by Cicero (*Topica* 12), but Quintilian calls it "ridiculous" (*Institutiones Oratoriae* 5. 10. 85).

is praiseworthy. This source of argument differs from the former in that it is one thing to examine how a name came to be given to something, another to get the force of an argument from the derivation of one word from another. [485] Arguments are drawn from the genus when what is true of the whole genus is applied to a species. For example: 'If "Woman is fickle and changeable,"[90] Dido also seems fickle and changeable and can turn from love to hatred.' This is the way Cicero has constructed his argument: 'Since you ought to take careful account of all your provinces and allies, gentlemen, then you should take particular account of Sicily.'[91] This source of argument seems to resemble argument from the whole to a part. The difference between them is that arguments from the whole to a part are drawn from a definition, whereas those from genus are drawn from the principle whereby the genus is a genus; and that a whole in a genus loses its wholeness by division, but the genus remains, even when distributed into parts. [486] Arguments are drawn from species or from form to create belief in the general question, as when Cicero says in the *Philippics*: 'What is so peculiarly an act of Caesar's as his law?' For act is the genus of law, as is shown by its species; that is, by the law enacted by Caesar.[92] The argument from similarity demonstrates the same thing: 'Look at the acts of Gracchus, produce the Sempronian laws, look at the laws of Sulla, of Cornelius.'[93] [487] There is the argument from similarity in itself. For instance: 'As Helen was to the Trojans, you are to your fellow-citizens the seed of war.'[94] Or again, 'Like men seriously ill, tossing in the grip of raging fever,'[95] and so on. The opposite of this

[90] Vergil *Aeneid* 4. 569.

[91] Martianus: '*Nam cum omnium provinciarum sociorumque rationem diligenter habere debeatis tum praecipue Siciliae, iudices*'; cf. Cicero *In Verrem* 2. 2. 2: *Nam cum omnium sociorum provinciarumque rationem diligenter habere debetis, tum praecipue Siciliae, iudices*.

[92] The quotations are from Cicero *Philippics* 1. 18. The *acta* of a Roman political leader—consul, tribune, or dictator—are the sum of his legislative and executive actions. After Caesar's assassination, the senate faced the crucial decision whether to repudiate his *acta* (as those of an unconstitutional ruler) or ratify them for the sake of peace and order. It is from this context that the quotations of Cicero come.

[93] *Ibid.*

[94] Cicero to Antony, *Philippics* 2. 55.

[95] The beginning of a simile applied to the Roman state; Cicero *In Catilinam* 1. 31.

is dissimilarity, which Cicero calls 'difference';[96] this sets forth matters different from each other, but not opposite. Cicero gives an example in the *Verrines:* 'You will have to be thought to have done the same thing if you acted for the same reason.'[97] This is demonstrated in persons and in things and in time and in places and in other details which it would now take too long to mention. [488] There is argument by contraries, as death is to life. For example, Terence's lines: 'If you blame a man who has helped to save life, what would you do to a man who caused harm and loss?'[98] Again, Cicero: 'If as consul he deserved the death penalty for desertion, what did the legions deserve which deserted him as consul?'[99] [489] There is an attempt to persuade by conjunction when arguments weak individually take on the force of truth when linked together. For example: 'What if it happened that you had been poor up to that time? Or greedy? Or foolhardy? Or the enemy of the murdered man?'[100] Since each of these arguments alone is not enough, they are heaped together.

[490] There is argument by antecedents, like Cicero's: 'Since he had no doubts about disclosing what he had in mind, can you have doubts about what he did?'[101] First he mentions the prediction, which supplies his argument; then he mentions the deed, from which the question at issue has arisen. [491] Arguments by consequents proceed conversely, so that the question at issue is mentioned in the antecedents, and the argument in the subsequents, in this way: if *A* has followed, *B* has preceded it. For instance, 'If she has had a baby, she has slept with a man.' There is an example from the *Verrines:* 'If the term of a praetor's edict ends on the calends of

[96] Cicero *Topica* 46.

[97] Cicero *In Verrem* 2. 3. 214; but Cicero uses the third person, rather than the second.

[98] Terence *Andria* 142-43.

[99] Martianus: '*Si ille consul fustuarium meruerit, legiones quid, quae consulem relinquerunt?*'; cf. Cicero *Philippics* 3. 14: *Si ille consul, fustuarium meruerunt legiones quae consulem reliquerunt.*

[100] Martianus: '*Quid si accedit, ut tenuis antea fueris? quid sit ut avarus? quid si ut audax? quid si ut eius, qui occisus est, inimicus?*'; cf. Cicero *Pro Sexto Roscio Amerino* 86: *Quid si accedit eodem ut tenuis antea fueris? quid si ut avarus? quid si ut audax? quid si ut illius qui occisus est inimicissimus?*

[101] Cicero *Pro Milone* 44; Clodius had predicted, three days before the battle between himself, Milo, and their gangs, that Milo would be dead in three days.

January, why does it not also begin from the calends of January?'[102]
[492] There is an argument by contradiction when it is shown that
two things cannot coexist; for instance, that a person should be a
parasite and yet not be ridiculous—the incompatibility of these two
conditions is expressed negatively in this way: 'It is not the case
that Gnatho is a parasite and not ridiculous.' One type of this source
of argument consists in the content rather than the form of words
used. For instance: 'A man who was not only freed from danger by
you but most magnificently honored by you is now accused of wanting to kill you in his own home.'[103] And in the first speech for Cornelius[104] he utters a contradiction: 'Would he want to trouble, by invoking the law against canvasing for office, the bribe brokers whom
he had wanted to be the agents of his elevation?'

[493] Argument from cause is extensive in scope, and is the subject of a great deal of discussion. For the present it will suffice to
show its form with this example: 'Since this money was handed over
in response to your decrees, your judgments, your orders, the question is not whose hand received and counted it but whose injustice
compelled its surrender.'[105] Again, there is Vergil's: 'Is it from me
you are fleeing?'[106] [494] Argument is drawn from effects when
there is uncertainty in a case, for example, the action of fate is proved
from the fact that men are kept alive even against their wills. For
fate is the cause of life or death; to be able to live or die is the
effect of fate. Cicero therefore commends the life of Aulus Hirtius,[107] which was cherished by the people, because the people praised
Hirtius. This is Vergil's 'Fear is the mark of a mean spirit'[108]—for
fear is the cause of the spirit's being mean; this is the result of fear.
[495] There is an argument from comparison with a greater. For

---

[102] Cicero *In Verrem* 2. 1. 109.
[103] Cicero *Pro rege Deiotaro* 15.
[104] This speech has not survived.
[105] Martianus: '*Sed cum ob tua decreta, ob iudicia, ob imperia dabantur, non
est ita quaerendum, cuius manu numerarentur, sed cuius iniuria cogerentur*'; cf.
Cicero *In Verrem* 2. 2. 26: *Sed cum ob tua decreta, ob edicta, ob imperia, ob
iudicia pecuniae dabantur, non erat quaerendum cuius manu numerarentur, sed
cuius iniuria cogerentur.*
[106] Vergil *Aeneid* 4. 314.
[107] In *Philippics* 1. 37.
[108] Vergil *Aeneid* 4. 13.

example: 'Can anyone doubt that Verres tried to get money from the Sicilians when he demanded it from Marcus Octavius Ligus?'[109] or Vergil's: 'You have the power to bring the closest of brothers into conflict.'[110] This argument proves also that strangers too can be brought into conflict, since this is a less difficult thing. Terence says: 'A man who decides or dares to lie and deceive his father will all the more dare to do it to others.'[111]

[496] There is argument from comparison with a lesser: For example: 'Publius Scipio, the *pontifex maximus*, as a private citizen killed Tiberius Gracchus, who was to some extent undermining the constitution.' Then follows the question, in which there is a change of scale: 'Shall we as consuls tolerate Catiline, who wants to lay waste the whole world with fire and slaughter?'[112] Terence also uses this argument in the passage: 'For a slight acquaintance with her, he is taking her death very much to heart.'[113] [497] There is argument from comparison with equals, like Cicero's: 'And if we find no less pleasant and bright those days on which we are rescued than those on which we are born';[114] and, in his speech against Piso: 'There is no difference whether the consul himself disturbs the state by holding disorderly meetings and making destructive laws or allows other people to do the same.'[115]

[498] Having now set out these arguments briefly, I turn to those which are not the result of the speaker's invention but are supplied by the case or by the accused; they are located, as I have said, in three areas: in documents, such as official records; in statements of authority, such as those of witnesses; and in statements arising from compulsion, such as those obtained under torture.

[109] This is not a quotation from the text of the *Verrines* as we have it; however, it does reproduce the situation and the style of Cicero *In Verrem* 2. 1. 127; and 2. 2. 119.

[110] Vergil *Aeneid* 7. 335.

[111] Terence *Adelphi* 55-56.

[112] Cicero *In Catilinam* 1. 3.

[113] Terence *Andria* 110-11.

[114] Cicero *In Catilinam* 3. 2.

[115] Martianus: '*Nihil interest, utrum ipse consul improbis contionibus, perniciosis legibus rem publicam vexet, an alios vexare patiatur*'; cf. Cicero *In Pisonem* 10: *Neque vero multum interest, praesertim in consule, utrum ipse perniciosis legibus, improbis contionibus rem publicam vexet, an alios vexare patiatur.*

[499] Argument is drawn from a document when to prove a doubtful point one cites an autographed surety or a will or contracts or other such documents which are so well known that they do not need examples from a speech. [500] There are statements of authority, such as: 'Africanus said that Tiberius Gracchus was killed justifiably'; or when a witness is called to lay bare the truth—for example: 'The speaker brings Gnaeus Pompeius to testify to us about the corn he sent with all speed'—the authority then is either that of the judge or that of the witness.[116] Oracles and other such statements come under this heading. [501] Statements arising from compulsion are credible because they come under torture, or in sleep, or in frenzy or drunkenness, conditions which extract a statement on a topic even against the speaker's will. When all these things are added to conjecture about the case or the person or the fact—that is, about the testimony or confession or document—then they produce or destroy credence. For the speaker's case is pondered, his personality is considered, and the quality of the document is compared with him or with the case. [502] Next, the speaker should turn his attention to those topics which either conciliate or arouse his audience, since I have said that this is also a part of winning credence. They are conciliated by regard for either a person or a matter—a person such as the man who is hearing the case or the accused or the speaker or his opponent. Regard for the person hearing the case—for example: 'That you should show yourself to us and to the Roman people at this time the man you were once before for the Roman people, when as judge you presided over this same court.'[117] Regard for the accused—for instance, in the speech for Deiotarus: 'Whom I and the whole Senate used formerly to extol because of his continuing service to our state.'[118]

[503] Regard for the speaker, when he speaks of himself modestly and without pride, as in that passage: 'When I had been quaestor in Sicily, gentlemen, and had left the province in a manner

116 The examples given are not quotations, though the first is probably based on Cicero De Oratore 2. 106.

117 Addressed to M. Fannius, the president of the court, in Pro Roscio Amerino 11. Martianus: 'Ut, qualem te antea populo Romano praebuisti, cum huic eidem quaestioni iudex praeesses, talem te nobis et populo Romano hoc tempore impertias'; cf. Cicero: Ut qualem te iam antea populo Romano praebuisti, cum huic eidem quaestioni iudex praeesses, talem te et nobis et reipublicae hoc tempore impertias.

118 Cicero Pro rege Deiotaro 2.

which left them a pleasant and lasting memory of my quaestorship and of my name, it happened that they considered me as one appointed to render at least some help to their welfare, just as they would receive the utmost help from many patrons long-established.'[119] However, I have discussed this more fully in the rules for the exordium. Conciliation arises from considering the person of one's opponent when, by showing his wickedness and arrogance, we win approval for our own modesty. But this is for later discussion. At the beginning of a speech (although I am not listing the sections of a speech but the forms of speech and the ways of winning belief) we give our attention to the power of emotional speech, though it employs its strength especially in commonplace and in epilogues. The beginnings of speeches amongst the early rhetoricians did not have this emotional appeal, as I shall show when I deal with the rules governing the structure of a speech; meantime, I shall outline in general terms and without subdivision into detail the means of moving our hearers by emotional appeal.

[504] The audience is aroused by pity or hatred or envy or fear or hope or anger and other such sentiments. By pity, when we treat with great grief someone's misfortunes, when we remind them of the decadence of the time or the greatness of the danger, as in the seventh *Verrine:* 'Gentlemen, the fathers whom you see here lay on the threshold, the mothers spent the night in misery before the entrance to the prison, denied a last look at their children, asking nothing but permission to receive the dying breath from their sons' mouths.'[120] By hatred, when the opponent's action is shown to be detestable to good men or to the jury, as when Verres is shown to be boasting of the corruption of the jurors; or again, 'since he thinks

---

[119] Cicero *Divinatio in Caecilium* 2.

[120] Cicero *In Verrem* 2. 5. 118. The speeches in the case against Verres number three: a preliminary speech against Caecilius, concerned with Cicero's right (as against Caecilius') to prosecute; the *actio prima,* or first speech, against Verres; and the *actio secunda,* or second speech. The first two of these are genuine speeches; but after the *actio prima* Verres realized the strength of Cicero's case and fled, so that there was no need to deliver the *actio secunda.* Cicero therefore wrote it up at great length and published it virtually as a political pamphlet against corruption in provincial government. Because of its length it is divided into five sections. When Martianus refers to "the seventh *Verrine*" he is counting the speech against Caecilius as the first, and the fifth part of the *actio secunda* as the seventh.

that you are like him in greed, crime, and perjury.'[121] By envy, which makes the audience spiteful; for example: 'the fact that his unrestrained criminal nature has readier access to your friendship and that of other men of high birth and distinction than do the honor and integrity of any of us';[122] and again, 'that this rogue should with impunity enjoy and wallow in the fruits of widespread plunder.'[123] It can also inflame the minds of your audience if you emphasize someone's tyrannical nature or his intolerable power. [505] Fear is excited by individual or communal perils—individual ones, for instance: 'This is a trial in which you will pass judgment on the accused, and the Roman people will pass judgment on you';[124] communal perils, for example: 'I imagine I see this city, the light of the whole world, the citadel of all nations, destroyed in one sudden conflagration.'[125] Minds are stirred by hope when advantages or services are promised, as when Milo's loyalty is pledged to Pompey; or again: 'You will have Caelius under an obligation of lifelong service to you and to your children.'[126] Anger also moves men forcibly, as when Cicero emphasizes that Catiline's partners are sitting in the senate, and exclaims: 'Immortal gods! What people are we amongst? What nation is this? What city do we inhabit? They are here, here in our midst, gentlemen.'[127] Other similar emotions will be incorporated into the speech, and have great persuasive power; however, they are not intrinsic to the case, and they ought not be too apparent in the orator, or he may seem to be beguiling the judge, not leading him by reason.

[506] To these devices, which have been cleverly worked out to create credibility, we must add the order in which our material is presented: this is called 'disposition.' By it we pay careful attention to what to say in which place in the speech; what should be left out altogether; and how and when and where something should be

---

121 Martianus: 'Cum in avaritia, scelere, periurio vos sui similes esse arbitratur'; cf. Cicero In Verrem 1. 42: Cum in avaritia, scelere, periurio vos sui similis esse arbitretur.

122 Cicero In Verrem 2. 3. 7.

123 Ibid., 9.

124 Cicero In Verrem 1. 47.

125 Cicero In Catilinam 4. 11.

126 Not so much a quotation as a paraphrase of part of the last sentence of Cicero's Pro Caelio.

127 Cicero In Catilinam 1. 9.

said. This part of rhetoric has two aspects, for the structure follows either a natural order or an artificial one devised by the skill of the orator. The natural order occurs when, after the introduction, there follow the narrative, the outline of main points, the presentation of one's thesis, the argument, the conclusion drawn, and the peroration. The skill of the orator is employed when we distribute the points to be made throughout the speech. Our arrangement, then, is not in chronological order but in the most advantageous order for our case, as was done in the speech for Milo, when Cicero, to dispel the hostile predispositions of the jury, brought in certain questions before his narrative; he made this change from the natural order because of the advantage it brought his case. In the first speech for Cornelius, Cicero rebutted the accusations concerning the period after Cornelius' tribunate, then went back to discuss the tribunate; this, as I have said, is called an artificial arrangement. [507] But in the speech against Verres he kept the natural, chronological order, so that he presented first Verres' quaestorship, then the legateship, then the two praetorships, keeping the chronological order which we inevitably follow unless the advantage of the case rejects this approach. But when great and heinous accusations require thorough refutation, the speech for the defense ought to begin with the accusations; for example, in the speech for Cluentius, he first gets the matters of fact out of the way and then comes to discuss the letter of the law, changing the usual order; if he failed to make an attack on the law in his defense of Cluentius, he might seem to be abandoning the case through lack of confidence.

[508] Having dealt with these two parts of my duties, I must turn my attention to expression. Since this consists in the consideration of individual words, it is distinguished from eloquence, because the latter is the caliber of the whole rhetorical work, while the former is one part of rhetoric, and, according to Cicero, has two foundations, as it were, and two summits.[128] The two fundamentals are, to speak Latin correctly and clearly; the first of these you learned from Grammar, when you absorbed her cleverness. The summits are, to speak with fluency and embellishment, which come not from natural abil-

---

[128] This is not a quotation nor even a direct reference to a passage of Cicero. Ideas similar to these are expressed in Cicero *De Oratore* 1. 144; and 3. 151-52, and in the pseudo-Ciceronian *Rhetorica ad Herennium* 4. 17.

ity but from the utmost effort and daily practice, which gives our style not only more richness but greater clarity and brilliance.

[509] There are two aspects of this subject: one adds luster to the individual words used, the other enhances the quality of the speech by the attractive combination of the words. In examining individual words, we consider whether they are proper, transferred, or borrowed. Proper words are especially the oldest ones, for our ancestors, either because they did not know the embellishments of speech or because they did not make so bold as to use them, customarily used words in their proper significances. But since old words have gone out of usage, we ought not too boldly employ those which have changed with age. So we pass over *alucinari* and *cerritum* and *caperratum* and similar words, and we use those which custom accepts, but not vulgar words, unless required by our topic and our sense; for example, when Cicero, wanting to arouse emotion against cruelty, says: 'They left them with their gullets slit,'[129] or 'to flog to bits ordinary Romans.'[130] And it is not inappropriate for Vergil to use *lychni* [the Greek word for 'lamps'] instead of *lucernae* [the Latin word], to avoid banality.[131] [510] But if a thing does not have words proper to itself, words must either be coined or be borrowed from other areas. Words are coined in two ways: either they are thought up by invention or derivation or they are formed by the combination of two words already in use. The commonest mode of invention is borrowing from other languages, as when 'qualities' are called *poeotetae*,[132] which never was a Latin noun; in this form of invention we must have regard to the ears of our audience and avoid the affectation of novelty. In avoidance of this, Cicero was unwilling to use the word *salvator* to translate the Greek word *soter* [savior], but said 'he who brought salvation,'[133] for *salvator* seemed unduly novel. [511] Words are formed by derivation—*paragoge*, as the grammarians call it—for example, '*flowery* countryside,'[134] and 'broad

129 Cicero *Pro Tullio* 21.

130 Cicero *In Verrem* 2. 1. 122.

131 Lit., "for snaring the avoidance of inelegance"—a particularly good example of Martianus' taste for circumlocution. The word *lychni* is used in *Aeneid* 1. 726.

132 A Greek philosophical term; this example occurs in Cicero *Academica* 1. 25.

133 Cicero *In Verrem* 2. 2. 154.

134 Vergil *Aeneid* 1. 430.

fields are *white* with bones.'[135] using *albeo*, while Horace, with an acceptable and elegant variation, uses *albico*.[136] These words are generally used in poetry, though Cicero speaks of 'grandiferous estates'[137] and 'grandiloquent orators.'[138]

[512] Related to this in our consideration is the question of transferred words,[139] when a subject either does not have terms appropriate to it or when we want to express something more elaborately than usual. Therefore words are transferred either because of poverty of vocabulary or for the sake of embellishment: for poverty, when we say that a vine 'is bejeweled'[140] or that the cornfields 'are prodigal'[141] or 'are in good heart.'[142] There are no words proper to these topics, and unfamiliar words are adapted. Words are transferred for embellishment, as when we say: 'War suddenly flared up,' when we could say that it 'came into existence.' Again, we can borrow from all our senses, as when we say (from the sense of sight) 'in the light of liberty and the scent of justice'[143] and (from hearing) 'the laws are silent in the midst of arms'[144] and (from taste) 'sweet name of liberty.'[145] But we should not try unrestrainedly to use these words borrowed from other areas. Nor should the words be transferred from very distant areas, as if one were to say: 'exuberant Charybdis' (*luxuriosam Charybdim*). Nor should one use an indecent similitude, as if one were to say: 'The state was emasculated by the death of Africanus'; or 'Clodius is the dung of the senate.' Into this kind of transfer the poets in particular have woven allegory; so does Cicero, when he says 'when you threw the senate from the

[135] Vergil *Aeneid* 12. 36.

[136] Horace *Odes* 1. 4. 4.

[137] Cicero *Philippics* 2. 101.

[138] Cicero *Orator* 20.

[139] The doctrine and many of the examples in this paragraph derive from Cicero *De Oratore* 3. 155-70.

[140] *Gemmare*, the usual Latin word for "to bud."

[141] *Luxuriare*. The literal meaning of this word is "to be luxuriant, to abound," and it is properly applied to crops. It was early transferred to people who lived lives of excess and prodigality; Martianus appears to be assuming that as its proper meaning, and the application to crops as figurative.

[142] *Laetas*, lit. "joyful."

[143] Cicero *In Verrem* 2. 5. 160.

[144] Cicero *Pro Milone* 11.

[145] Cicero *In Verrem* 2. 5. 163.

helm, tossed the Roman people overboard, and as chief privateer with a troop of scabrous pirates set full sail';[146] and, in the speech against Piso, 'that I, who sailed the ship of state through heavy seas and great storms, and brought it safe to harbor, that I should tremble at the little cloud on your countenance and the foul wind from your colleague?'[147] Using these similitudes he has said at some length what he would probably say more briefly or less elaborately in the words proper to the subject. Again, words are in a way transferred when they express the whole by the part or the part by the whole or a plurality by one or an individual by the plural. The whole is expressed by the part in 'it struck at the helm';[148] or 'that I can be safe within the same walls as you,'[149] when the meaning is 'in the same house.' The grammarians call this trope *metonymy;* the Greeks also cal it *catachresis,* or as we say, *abusio;*[150] as when we use 'the nature of the gods' for 'substance.' [513] In the sequence of words and the coherence of a speech we must ensure that the connection is firmly made, the conclusion comes smoothly, and the language is embellished by some figure.

[514] Now I shall run through the rules of proper arrangement; here the greatest fault is the failure to avoid hiatus and harshness, *dysprophoron, homoeoprophoron,*[151] polysigma, iotacism, labdacism, mytacism,[152] or the constant and irritating use of any other letter, as in *sale saxa sonabant*[153] and *casus Cassandra canebat.*[154]

---

[146] Cicero *De domo sua* 24.

[147] Cicero *In Pisonem* 20. Martianus uses *tempestatibus* where Cicero uses *turbinibus* for "storms."

[148] Vergil *Aeneid* 1. 115. The wave struck the stern of the ship, where the helm was.

[149] Cicero *In Catilinam* 1. 19.

[150] Quintilian (*Institutiones Oratoriae* 8. 6. 34-36) defines *catachresis* as the application of the closest available term to express something for which there is no proper term. This is not clear from Martianus.

[151] The terms *dysprophoron* and *homoeoprophoron* are clearly Greek, but they appear to be found only in Martianus. They mean "difficulty of pronunciation" and "similarity of pronunciation," respectively.

[152] Excessive use of *s, i, l,* or *m.* It is noteworthy that neither Martianus nor the other rhetoricians discuss alliteration in general, but only the repetition of one particular letter or another.

[153] Vergil *Aeneid* 5. 866. The full line is *tum rauca adsiduo longe sale saxa sonabant* [then with the surf unceasing the far rocks hoarsely boomed]. Servius

Mytacism is the interruption of the sequence of words by the constant use of *m;* for example, *mammam ipsam amo quasi meam animam.* Labdacism is the excessive use of *l;* for example, *sol et luna luce lucent alba leni lactea.* It is iotacism if you say: *Iunio Iuno Iovis iure irascitur.* Polysigma is excessive repetition of *s;* for example, *Sosia in solario soleas sarciebat suas.* Homoeoprophoron is, for example, *o Tite tute Tati tibi tanta tyranne tulisti.*[155] Dysprophoron is, for example, *persuasitrices praestigiatrices atque inductrices striges.*

[515] Harshness is especially to be avoided between the last and penultimate words; for example, *phaleras ablatas gratis,*[156] or if a charioteer were to swear *per lora, per flagella, per frena.* [516] Hiatuses occur when, as we speak, vowels similar in sound and in length cause disharmony and interruption in the rhythm of the sentence; for example, *suscepisse se liberos secundo omine,* and when Cicero said in his speech for Milo *auctoritate publica armare;*[157] Cicero frequently does this deliberately, to conceal his rhetorical skill.[158] [517] Similarly, we should avoid placing three or four long syllables or short syllables in one place, consecutively; nor should the rhythm of the sentence be based on well-known verse rhythms, particularly heroic or iambic rhythms,[159] although Cicero does not avoid them when he says *senatus haec intellegit consul videt,*[160] nor does he abstain from using the beginning or ending of a heroic line when he says *o miserum, cui peccare licebat;*[161] or, in the *Academics, latent ista omnia, Varro, magnis obscurata et circumfusa*

(*ad loc.*) says of it: "This pleased earlier generations but nowadays we condemn it."

154 Vergil *Aeneid* 3. 183. The full line is *sola mihi talis casus Cassandra canebat* [Cassandra alone foretold this fate to me].

155 Ennius *Annals* 108 (fragment 53).

156 Cicero *In Verrem* 4. 29.

157 Cicero *Pro Milone* 2.

158 Cf. § 505, last sentence. It was a cardinal principle of Cicero's oratory to avoid giving the audience the impression that he was trying to overwhelm and mislead them with rhetoric; such an impression, if allowed to develop, would lead them to suspect him and defeat his case.

159 Dick's text says "dithyrambic"; but some manuscripts support "iambic," and the example is an iambic trimeter line.

160 Cicero *In Catilinam* 1. 2.

161 This is not part of any surviving speech of Cicero.

tenebris;[162] and in the *Verrines* he has uttered a line of verse complete except for one syllable, when he says *cum loquerer, tanti fletus gemitusque fiebant.*[163] He has not avoided the ending of an elegiac line, as when he says *oderat ille bonos.*[164] He even ventures into the frivolity of the Phalaecean hendecasyllable when he says *successit tibi Lucius Metellus.*[165] Cicero, however, may be defended both by the volume of his output and by his own reputation. This fault is at its worst at the ends of sentences. Nevertheless, we should be careful not to forgo a good sentence ending to escape the appearance of using verse, as if one were afraid to say *strepitumque plagarum*[166] because the *pla-* is long and would make a good sentence-ending.

[518] We should also avoid ill-sounding expressions caused by the intrusion or alteration of words. There are undignified examples like 'stick up your ears, Pamphilus'[167] or 'with resentment of the rescued girl';[168] in these instances, the language is coarse. We should also avoid 'tongue twisters,'[169] which are formed by very harsh letters running together, like the passage in Terence's *Hecyra: per pol quam paucos reperias meretricibus fidelis evenire amatores, Syra.*[170] The same fault is thought to be in things beginning with the same letter; for instance, *Non fuit istud iudicium iudicii simile, iudices;*[171] or ending

---

162 Cicero *Academica* 2. 122. Martianus' text differs markedly from Cicero's: *Latent ista omnia, Luculle, crassis occultata et circumfusa tenebris.*

163 Cicero *In Verrem* 2. 4. 110. This would be a complete dactylic hexameter, except that the *i* of *fiebant* is long, and will not fit the pattern.

164 This is not part of any surviving speech of Cicero.

165 Cicero *In Verrem* 2. 3. 43. The hendecasyllable is a metre of light and humorous verse.

166 Cicero (*In Verrem* 2. 5. 162) uses the phrase *crepitumque plagarum*, and it is not the end of the sentence.

167 Terence *Andria* 933. Kopp points out that the verb can be interpreted in an obscene sense.

168 Vergil *Aeneid* 2. 413: an elliptical way of saying "with resentment at the rescue of the girl." Servius notes nothing in it except the figure of thought, but Kopp suggests that the participle meaning "rescued" can also mean "raped."

169 The word used by Martianus, *freni*, means "bridles" or "bits," and translates *chalinoi*, the Greek term for such difficult turns of speech; see Quintilian *Institutiones Oratoriae* 1. 1. 37. No other Latin writer appears to use *freni* in this sense.

170 Terence *Hecyra* 58-59.

171 Cf. Cicero *Pro Cluentio* 96: *Non fuit illud igitur iudicium iudici simile, iudices.*

with the same sound, as in *fortissimorum, proximorum fidelissimo-rumque sociorum*.[172] We should also avoid a long sequence of short syllables, like that line of Serenus: *perit, abit avipedis animula leporis*.[173]

[519] After this brief explanation, I must now discuss the rhythms with which sentences may appropriately be ended. Cicero[174] has thrown these into a certain amount of confusion by saying at one time that they should end with a double trochee;[175] at another time commending the first paeon[176] for the beginning of sentences, and the fourth paeon[177] for the ending; at another time the doch-miac, which consists of a short, two longs, a short, and a long (he gives the example *amicos tenes*); and again he commends the am-phimacrian[178] rhythm; or again, the dactylic;[179] now the anapaest,[180] now the dithyramb;[181] whereas there is no certainty. I shall go through them rather briefly to appear to lead along some paths in this maze.

[520] When a sentence ends with a monosyllable, one ought to see whether the final syllable is long or short. If it is long, a trochee ought to precede it, as in Cicero's *non scripta, sed nata lex*,[182] or *debet esse legum in re publica prima vox*,[183] which is a neat ending, how-ever, with the meaning kept in suspense until the end. But if the

---

[172] This does not appear to be a quotation.

[173] Septimius Serenus, a minor poet of the late second century A.D., of whose poems only fragments survive; see M. Schanz and C. Hosius, *Geschichte der römische Literatür*, Vol. III (Munich, 1922; repr. 1959), pp. 23-24.

[174] Cicero *Orator* 212-33, *De oratore* 3. 184-86; cf. Quintilian *Institutiones Oratoriae* 9. 4. 145-46.

[175] $-\cup-\cup$

[176] $-\cup\cup\cup$

[177] $\cup\cup\cup-$

[178] $-\cup-$, also called the cretic.

[179] $-\cup\cup$

[180] $\cup\cup-$

[181] "Dithyramb" is not the name of a foot, but of a poetic genre characterized in the post-classical Greek period by very free rhythmical arrangements. Cicero (*De oratore* 3. 185) refers to it in that way; and insofar as he commends it, he does so in the sense in which Quintilian understands him (*Institutiones Oratoriae* 9. 4. 56): that prose should have some rhythm, rather than that it should adhere to rigid rhythmical rules. However, it is conceivable that for "dithyramb" here we should read "iamb" (see § 517, n. 159); Cicero *Orator* 217 mentions the iamb (and not the dithyramb) in exactly the context Martianus is quoting here.

[182] Cicero *Pro Milone* 10.

[183] This is not from any surviving speech of Cicero.

final syllable is short, an iamb[184] or an anapaest should precede it, as in Sallust's *tota autem insula modica et cultibus variis est*.[185] For a short syllable to follow a short one, or a long syllable a long, is not commendable, as if one were to say *ista res mea est* or the opposite, as in Cicero's speech for Ligarius, *non tu eum patria privare, qua caret, sed vita vis*.[186] He wrote this on purpose, not by mistake. But this rule about monosyllabic ending is better applied earlier in the sentence, before a colon or a comma, and not at the ending of a sentence.

[521] If the last word is of two syllables the sentence should not end with an iamb, but if the penultimate word is a spondee[187] an iamb should follow it; for example, *tenui servos meos*; or a pyrrhic[188] instead of an iamb; for example, *consul videt*. But an iamb followed by a spondee or a trochee makes a good ending; for example, *patria continet bonos cives* or *caput legis*. However, we must take care not to put two iambs or an iamb and a pyrrhic at the end; for example, *pugnare iuvenes pro parentibus suis*. We must also take care that a pyrrhic does not follow a pyrrhic and make four short syllables; for example, *perdidi bona mea;* or that a pyrrhic is not followed by a trochee or a spondee; for example, *conqueritur sua fata* or *imputat sibi demens*. But a trochee and an iamb or a trochee and a pyrrhic (instead of an iamb) make a poor sentence ending; for this gives the ending of an elegiac pentameter, which is inappropriate. What is the difference whether you say *omnia nempe vides* or *aspice facta mea?* But two trochees or a trochee and spondee go well at the end of a sentence; for example, *haec est bonorum civium magna cura* or *haec sunt, quae maximi principes sola curant*.

[522] If the last word is of three syllables, the rule is that if you want the ending to flow smoothly the penultimate word should be a trochee and the last a molossus,[189] whether the last syllable is long,

184 ᴜ —

185 According to Dick, a fragment of Sallust *Histories* 3; I am unable to find it amongst the extant fragments.

186 Cicero *Pro Ligario* 11.

187 — —

188 ᴜ ᴜ. The example is from Cicero *In Catilinam* 1. 2.

189 — — —. If the last syllable is short the foot is not a molossus but what Quintilian (*Institutiones Oratoriae* 9. 4. 82) calls a *palimbacchius*. Martianus' rule here, giving the rhythm — ᴜ — — ᴜ, conflicts with Quintilian's recommendation (*ibid.*, 102) when the sentence ends with a palimbacchius to precede that

or short as in *Cicero's* phrase *mare fluctuantibus litus eiectis.* If you put a spondee in place of the penultimate trochee, it makes a dreadful ending; for example, *mare fluctuantibus rupes eiectis;* so it does if you put a pyrrhic[190] in place of the trochee; for example, *mare fluctuantibus apex eiectis.* Again, the ending is faulty if the first syllable of the molossus is short, even if it is preceded by a trochee; for that gives a clausula of heroic verse; for example, *litus amicis. . . .*[191] Again, it makes a good ending if after a trochee a minor ionic foot[192] is put in place of a molossus; for example, *mare fluctuantibus litus agitanti.* But in this type of ending we must take care not to put a spondee in place of a trochee in the penultimate word; for then, if you resolve the third syllable of the molossus, you fall into the fault Cicero shows when he says: *si te semel ad meas capsas admisero.*[193] But if you have a trochee preceding a molossus and resolve the middle syllable of the molossus, you make a fine ending, such as *litus Aemiliae.* Again, when a trochee precedes it, the third foot of a molossus can also be resolved to good effect; for example, *litus aequabile.* Again, if we resolve the long syllable of the preceding trochee and the first syllable of the final molossus, it makes an elegant ending; for example, *curas regere animorum.*

[523] Irony (*eironeia*)[194] is a pretense, commonly used by Cicero, and a striking figure, in which we say one thing but mean another, as in the beginning of the *Pro Ligario:* 'A new charge, Gaius

---

with at least two long syllables ($- - - - \cup$). Martianus may be echoing Cicero's idea that "the final syllable is irrelevant" (*Orator* 218); Quintilian strongly disagrees with this view (*Institutiones Oratoriae* 9. 4. 93-94). The example is from Cicero *Pro Roscio Amerino* 72.

190 $\cup \cup$. However, *apex* ($\cup -$) is not a pyrrhic.

191 Dick presumes a lacuna here introducing sentences which end with four-syllable words; §§ 520, 521, and 522 began with reference to words of one, two, and three syllables, and the examples henceforward are of four-syllable words. Willis, however, considers that Martianus is merely discussing resolution of the molossus; i.e., the use of two short syllables as the metric equivalent of one long syllable; Willis therefore denies the lacuna.

192 $\cup \cup - -$.

193 *Divinatio in Caecilium* 51.

194 Willis, following Halm, presumes a lacuna at this point, partly because of the abrupt transition from a discussion of meters to definitions of figures, and partly because the first six figures mentioned by Aquila Romanus—whom Martianus follows closely from this section to § 537—are not mentioned.

Caesar. . . .' *Paraleipsis* is the act of passing over something, when in 'passing over' certain points we nevertheless express them. *Apostrophe* is a diversion of attention to someone else, when we turn our address to another party in such a way that we thereby inform the jurors. *Diaporesis*, or hesitation, is a figure we use when, as if hesitating, we ask of the jurors themselves advice on how to begin, as in the *Pro Cluentio*[195] 'Gentlemen, I do not know where to turn'; or in the *Pro Cornelio:*[196] 'Am I to fight against the wishes of our leading men? Am I to reveal their interests, their plans, their thoughts?' and so on. [524] *Erotema* is a figure we use when by repeated questioning we accumulate points on a topic and enlarge upon its unattractive elements. *Pysma* is a form of question which differs from the preceding figure in that erotema postulates only one answer, whereas to *pysma* there cannot fail to be several answers; for example: 'What are our resources for waging war? What assistance shall we have? Who will be willing to come to our aid, when we have treated our allies so harshly'?[197] *Diatyposis* is description or representation in which we express the very look and appearance of the people or things under discussion, as Cicero does in the *Pro Milone:* 'If you were not hearing an account of this but watching a representation,'[198]—and he describes Milo sitting in his chariot, wearing his cloak, accompanied by his wife; and Clodius on horseback leaving his villa with a hand-picked troop of supporters, and so on. *Anteisagoge* is a counterbalancing admission; this is the figure when something is difficult and we bring forward a counterbalancing idea,[199] as Cicero does concerning King Ptolemy: 'It is a difficult way to fight, but utterly honest and loyal,'[200] and so on. [525] *Diasyrmos* is disparagement or ridicule; in this figure we destroy our adversary's argument by ridicule, as in the speech for Murena in that whole

---

[195] Cicero *Pro Cluentio* 4.

[196] This speech has not survived.

[197] The source of this quotation is not known.

[198] Cicero *Pro Milone* 54; these words introduce a vivid verbal representation of the scene.

[199] Translating the Dick text. Willis reads *difficile et contrarium confitemur.* The sense would then be: "We admit something difficult and against our interest." This is the sense of the corresponding passage in Aquila Romanus (14; Halm, p. 26).

[200] This speech has not survived.

section concerning the civil law,[201] directed against Sulpicius. *Metasta-sis* is a kind of transference, when we transfer some detail from our-selves to someone else, but not in such a way as to settle the whole case on the other person; for then it becomes a problem of status, not a figure.

[526] So much for figures of thought; now let us get on to figures of speech. However, I want to recall briefly how many kinds of style there are and the number of modes that they use. There is the type which the Greeks call *lexis eiromene,* which is suited to every kind of narrative; in this, clause follows clause in the normal sequence of ideas. This is suitable for historical and narrative writing and does not require an inverted or periodic style of expression, but one which flows continuously, as in the speech for Milo: 'I have killed, I have killed not Spurius Maelius, who. . . .'[202] and so on. [527] There is another style, which the Greeks call the period (*periodos*), which puts, as it were, a terminus and limit to the sentence, as in the Caecina speech:[203] 'If shamelessness had as much power in the forum and the lawcourts as boldness has in the uninhabited countryside, Aulus Caecina would now yield to the shamelessness of Sextus Aebu-tius, just as he then yielded to his bold violence.' This type of sen-tence is made up of many members,[204] which the Greeks call *cola;* and of sections, which they call *commata.* [528] A member is part of a speech, comprising several words with a complete meaning; for instance: 'Although, gentlemen, I fear it is disgraceful to be afraid when beginning to speak on behalf of a very brave man. . . .'[205] A section[206] is a part of a speech comprising two or more words and not complete in its meaning. However, we call speech 'cut up'[207] when it includes single words complete in meaning; for instance: 'Who is this Lollius who is not unarmed when with you, even now?

---

[201] Cicero *Pro Murena* 19-29, where Cicero ridicules Murena's opponent Sulpicius, an eminent jurist.

[202] Cicero *Pro Milone* 72.

[203] Cicero *Pro Caecina* 1.

[204] Translating Dick's *quae multis.* Willis suggests *qui ambitus* (from Aquila Romanus 18: *sed hic ambitus*); the sense would then be "this period is made up of clauses."

[205] Cicero *Pro Milone* 1.

[206] *Caesum,* lit. "a cut part."

[207] *Caesam.*

Who is this Lollius, Catiline's armor-bearer, your bodyguard, the irritant of shopkeepers, a bandit, who throws stones at the senate?'[208] And in the *Verrines:* 'Those were your chosen comrades, lackeys, quacks, soothsayers, clerks, those were of your company.'[209] [529] But the period I have mentioned above[210] consists of two or three or four members, sometimes even of six,[211] although there are some people who think it can be achieved in one, and call that a 'monocolar period (*monocolos periodos*),' although it is rather just a member. The best type of speech is one made up now of a rounded period, now of a continuous flow, sometimes broken in sections, another time built up in members. [530] The difference between a figure of thought and a figure of speech is that the figure of thought remains even if the order of the words is changed, whereas a figure of speech cannot remain if the word order is changed, although it can often happen that a figure of thought is in conjunction with a figure of speech, as when the figure of speech epanaphora is combined with irony, which is a figure of thought.

[531] There are other figures of speech,[212] suitable only for embellishment and decoration of a speech; I shall now deal with these. Antithesis (*antitheton*) is the association of opposites, when words with conflicting meanings are used as parallels, or matching words are used in opposition; for example, Cicero's 'You owned no home,

---

[208] Martianus: '*Quis est iste Lollius, qui sine ferro ne nunc quidem te cum est? quis est iste Lollius, armiger Catilinae, stipator tui corporis, concitator tabernariorum, percussor, lapidator curiae?*'; cf. Cicero *De domo sua* 13: *Quis est iste Lollius? qui sine ferro ne nunc quidem te cum est, qui te tribuno plebis, nihil de me dicam, sed qui Cn. Pompeium interficiendum depoposcit. Quis est Sergius? armiger Catilinae, stipator tui corporis, signifer seditionis, concitator tabernariorum, damnatus iniuriarum, percussor, lapidator, fori depopulator, obsessor curiae.*

[209] Cicero *In Verrem* 2. 2. 27.

[210] Translating Dick's *superior;* Willis, following Barwick, would delete it, as a doublet of *verum periodos*. The sense would then be: "But the period consists . . . ."

[211] Willis would delete this phrase. The anonymous *Carmen de Figuris* explicitly denies that the period can have more than four cola (lines 10-12; Halm, pp. 63-64). Quintilian equally explicitly affirms that it can (*Institutiones Oratoriae* 9. 4. 125).

[212] Dick supposes a lacuna here, but there seems to be no need for it. The text is a simple transcription of Aquila Romanus 21.

but you had one; there was money, but you were in want';[213] or if you were to say: 'In time of peace he was full of hostile energy against his fellow-citizens, in time of war he was full of lethargy toward the enemy.'[214] *Isocolon*, a matching of members, is formed not by the conflict of words but by the correspondence of similar words; for example: 'He built a most sturdy and sightly fleet, raised a most courageous and impressive army, and acquired a most plentiful and reliable body of allies.'[215] *Parison* is almost the same; it differs from isocolon in that in isocolon there is an equal number of words in each clause, whereas in parison the other details occur, but with an extra word in one clause or another. [532] *Homoeoptoton* is a correspondence of case endings; it gets its name from the fact that all the clauses end with the same cases: for example, *huic socios vestros criminanti et ad bellum vos cohortanti et omnibus modis ut in tumultu essetis molienti.* *Homoeoteleuton* is defined in a similar way; the difference is that in the former the final words end in the same case as well as in the same sound, whereas in the latter there is only the similarity of sound, regardless of the form of the word.[216] *Paronomasia* is a slight change of a verb or a noun when the alteration of a letter or a syllable changes the meaning; for example: 'Is he a praetor or a predator?' *Ploké* is juxtaposition, when a verb or a noun is repeated in use in different senses; for example: 'For that day

[213] Cicero *Pro Scauro* 45m. Dick punctuates Martianus' text as statements, but in Cicero the first and third clauses are questions, as Quintilian makes clear (*Institutiones Oratoriae* 9. 2. 15).

[214] This speech has not survived.

[215] "Isocolon" strictly refers to equality of length of the members (*ibid.*, 3. 80), but in Martianus' example the equality is rather of the adjectives in the pair within each member; however, each member has an equal number of words, if not of syllables, and the adjectives are all similar, being superlatives in form.

[216] This is Aquila Romanus' definition (26; Halm, p. 30). Quintilian is fuller and clearer (*Institutiones Oratoriae* 9. 3. 77-80). Homoeoteleuton is similarity of sound in the endings of phrases or clauses, whether the matching words are verbs, adverbs, nouns, adjectives, or any part of speech. Homoeoptoton is similarity of cases, and can therefore apply only to nouns, pronouns, or adjectives; nor need it result in similarity of sound, since the same case in different declensions will have different endings. Martianus and Aquila Romanus claim that homoeoptoton requires similarity of sound in the final words of phrases, but Quintilian is explicit that the matching words need not have the same terminations (hence the same sound) and may occur at any point of the sentence.

Memmius, Memmius for that time!'[217] [533] Palilogy (*palillogia*) is a reiteration; this figure uses repetition of a verb or a noun without alteration of meaning but with added force because of the repetition; for example: 'It is we, we I say, we the consuls, who are at fault.'[218] *Epanalepsis* is a repetition: this differs from palilogy in that the preceding figure is formed by the repetition of the same part of speech, either juxtaposed or with perhaps one word or another in between, whereas epanalepsis is formed not by a single part of speech but by the association of whatever words one likes,[219] such as: 'It is not possible, it is not possible for this state to be free.' *Anadiplosis* is another form of repetition; it is at its best when what was at the end of one clause is repeated at the beginning of the next clause, as in Terence's: 'Does Demipho deny he is related to this girl? This girl—does Demipho deny he is related to her?'[220] *Prosapodosis* is the recurrence of a word; that is, when a noun with which a clause (or any other single section of a speech) began, recurs at the end of the section; for example: 'The commonwealth ought to lay on you the blame for the common ruin.' [534] *Epanaphora* is another form of reiteration, when the same part of speech is repeated clause by clause, thus: 'Verres fixed the accusers, Verres heard the case, Verres gave judgment.'[221] *Antistrophe* is a rearrangement, and differs from the preceding figure in that that one usually begins clauses with the same part of speech, whereas this usually ends with them, as in the speech for Fonteius: 'The most corn comes from Gaul, the most infantry comes from Gaul, the most cavalry comes from Gaul.'[222]

217 Translating Dick's text. Willis would read (following Aquila Romanus 28; Halm, p. 31): *ad illum diem Memmius erat Memmius.* The sense would then be: "For that day Memmius was Memmius indeed"—that is, he lived up to his reputation. This would be a more meaningful example to illustrate *ploké*.

218 The example, which is taken from Cicero (*In Catilinam* 1. 3) and not from Aquila Romanus, has one more "we" than the text of Cicero. The repetition here is of a pronoun, which in Latin is included under the term *nomen* (which I have translated as "noun" in this passage).

219 That is, palillogia is the repetition of a single word (e.g., "we"), while epanalepsis is the repetition of a group of words (e.g., "it is not possible").

220 Terence *Phormio* 352-53.

221 Martianus: '*Verres calumniatores apponebat, Verres de causa cognoscebat, Verres pronuntiabat*'; cf. Cicero *In Verrem* 2. 2. 26: *Verres calumniatorem adponebat, Verres adesse iubebat, Verres cognoscebat, Verres iudicabat.*

222 This speech survives only in fragments. Martianus and Aquila Romanus are the only sources for this fragment.

Symploké is an interweaving; it usually begins with one part of speech and as often ends with one and the same; for example: 'Who passed the law? Rullus. Who created the ten magistrates he wanted? This same Rullus.'[223] [535] *Polyptoton* means 'from many cases'; this occurs usually when a part of speech begins a sentence, and the same part undergoes changes of case and number; for example: 'The senate ordered it: it was pleasing to the senate. It is sure that the senate commanded it: it was chosen by the senate.' Synonymy (*synonymia*) is the participation of a noun when one word is not adequate to express the importance or greatness of a subject and so we use more than one word with the same meaning. Tautology (*tautologia*) is the same meaning expressed in many words: it differs from the preceding figure in that the preceding expresses one idea in single words,[224] whereas this uses many words.[225] [536] *Climax* is an ascending scale; for example, in Cicero's speech for Milo: 'He entrusted himself not only to the people but to the senate; not only to the senate but to the public guards and the armed forces; not only to these but to that one power to whom the senate had entrusted the whole charge of the state.'[226] *Asyndeton* is disconnection, when we dispense with the conjunction with which verbs or nouns are linked together and utter each word individually; for example: 'I look to the enforcing of the edict, the strictness of the praetor, I support the farmer, I want Apronius to suffer the eightfold penalty.'[227] *Diezeugmenon* we call disjunction, since we separate two or more clauses by the recurrence of different verbs, thus: 'They will take over Capua and remove the colonists, they will garrison Atella, they will take Nuceria and Cumae with their numbers, they will make fast the other towns with garrisons.'[228] [537] *Antezeugmenon* is injunction; this differs from the preceding figure in that in the preceding each sepa-

---

[223] Cicero *De lege agraria* 2. 22. In Cicero there are a total of six questions, and four times the answer is "Rullus."

[224] I.e., synonymous single words.

[225] I.e., tautologous clauses.

[226] Cicero *Pro Milone* 61.

[227] Cicero *In Verrem* 2. 3. 28. Cicero is referring to Verres' edicts that a tax collector may name the amount of corn due in tax from a farmer, and that if the farmer considers this excessive he may sue the collector, who, if convicted, must make restitution of eight times the sum in dispute.

[228] The form of this passage resembles Cicero *De lege agraria* 2. 86; but it is in no sense a quotation.

rate section of the sentence has its own different verb, but in this many phrases are joined to one verb. For example: 'Their rank shuns a lowly, their fortune a mean, their nature a base consideration;' the word 'shuns' joins all the words before it.[229] Pleonasm (*pleonasmos*) is saying more than is necessary, when we add words which are not necessary to explain the subject but are to heighten its importance; for example, 'That man Cato,' when it would be enough to have said the name, but we add 'that man' to emphasize it. *Elleipsis* is removal, a figure contrary to the previous one, when we rather pass over what is to be expressed with somewhat fewer words, winning approval by our brevity. These are the figures of speech; however, they should not be studiously crowded together in any single sentence.

[538] Next to be considered are the precepts of memorization. Although it is accepted that memory is a natural faculty, there is no doubt that it can be assisted by training. This training comprises some brief rules but a lot of practice, the goal of which is that words and ideas should be grasped not only surely but also quickly. We must remember not only what we have found to say but also what our opponent has discussed in his treatment of the case. Simonides, who was both poet and philosopher, is said to have discovered the rules of this subject; for when a banquet hall suddenly collapsed, and the next of kin could not identify those buried, he supplied the seating order and names from memory. From this experience he learned that it is order which makes possible the rules of memory. This order must be exercised on distinct topics, to which should be attributed material forms and representations of ideas;[230] for example, you might remember a wedding by the bride veiled in saffron or a homicide by a sword and arms—images, as it were, put down in, and given back by, the appropriate section of our memory. For just as what is written is contained in wax and letters, so what is committed to memory is written into areas as if in wax and on the written page;

---

229 In the Latin the verb is at the end of the clause.

230 *Is vero in locis illustribus meditandus est, in quibus species rerum sententiarumque imagines collocandae sunt.* My translation differs markedly from that of Frances Yates: "These [precepts] are to be pondered upon in well-lighted places in which the images of things are to be placed"; *The Art of Memory* (Chicago, 1966), p. 51. The problem is whether to take *locus* literally ("a place") or as a rhetorical term ("a topic").

but the memory of things is contained in images as if in letters.
[539] But, as I have said, much practice and effort are required for
memorization, in which has been discovered the practice of writing
for ourselves what we want to remember easily; and if what we must
learn is rather long it stays in the mind more readily if it is divided
into sections; then it will be of advantage to make symbols individually at those points which we particularly want to remember;[231] they should not be read out loud, but rather memorized under
our breath; and it is clear that memory is better aroused at night than
during the day, since the silence of night is a great help and our concentration is not distracted by our senses. Memory is applied to
things and to words, but words do not always have to be memorized;
unless there is time for this, it will be enough for anyone to hold the
matter itself in the mind, especially if nothing comes naturally from
the memory.[232]

[540] I am not unaware that we nowadays commonly call 'enunciation' what in former times was called 'delivery.' The purpose of
delivery is to win the goodwill of the listener, to persuade him to
believe, and to inflame and move his spirit. Delivery has three parts:
voice, countenance, gesture—many would add to these the mouth, its
conformation and training. The voice is present by nature and is kept
under control by studied skill. Nature supplies the quality and amount
of voice we have; study comprehends how you use it and what principles to observe. [541] The excellence of the voice consists in
clearness, firmness, and its agreeable sound, and all these are fostered
by attention to food, drink, and sexual intercourse,[233] and especially
to physical exercise by walking for a short time and returning
quickly. Just as this exercise aids the digestion, so it certainly purifies
the voice; an excessively long walk or journey strains and tires it.

[231] Quintilian (*Institutiones Oratoriae* 11. 2. 28) is clearer. The difficulty is to
remember a long written speech; it will be of advantage to mark with symbols
the more important or more difficult sections, so that the mark itself may
stimulate the memory.

[232] This vague clause is elucidated by comparison with Quintilian *Institutiones
Oratoriae* 11. 2. 48-49; and Fortunatianus *Ars rhetorica* 3. 14 (Halm, pp. 129-30):
if one cannot remember a whole passage word-perfect and with ease, then it is
better simply to remember the substance and to extemporize, for groping after
half-forgotten words destroys the natural effect desirable in a speech. Martianus
may also be referring to those persons whose memory is naturally weak.

[233] Cf. Celsus *De medicina* 1. 1. 4; 4. 5. 2-3.

After this walk, let us go straight to our studies and give some color to our voice by reading[234] before we speak. [542] You ought not shout at the beginning, but start speaking softly so as to be able to raise your voice in turn.[235] Many people have said that in looking after the voice it is useful to sit and recite a few verses in a slow and solemn voice, then to raise the level of sound gradually step by step and to bring the speech back in the same steps, so that it comes back again to a murmur without any loss. [543] The expression should be varied according to the weight of what one is saying; but it should not be varied according to the extent customary with actors, who twist their faces about in ridiculous movements for the audience. For it is meaning, and not spectacle, which delivery and expression are meant to enhance. Control of the eyes is important in this field; they move in mirth, in concentration, in an expression of threat. They ought not be too much closed by frowning eyebrows nor too much exposed by raised eyebrows, which Cicero bitterly criticizes in Piso.[236] Gestures should not be made too delicately nor should one wiggle the torso effeminately; nor should one toss one's neck about in an ugly way nor twist it in the blandishments Hortensius used, which, for all their charm, seemed unmanly.[237] In sum, the orator should not use gesture to the extent that actors use it to please their audience. In argument the hand is stretched right out, in discussion or narrative it is drawn in; in this area especially is it important that everything should be seemly, which is achieved more by good sense than by any knowledge of this rule.

[544] Now in the order of the things I promised I must survey the parts of a speech; some people, rather cleverly, have claimed that there are two, others five, some say more. Those who say that there are two specify one as the instruction of the jurors and the other as the moving of their emotions: in instruction they include both the narrative and the proof of it; they combine the introduction and the peroration as 'moving the emotions' because in the beginning of a speech the listener who is to give the judgment must be prepared and swayed. However, those who say that there are five parts of a speech

[234] I.e., aloud.

[235] Translating Dick's *invicem*. Willis suggests *in summum* [high] or Grotius' *sensim* [gradually].

[236] Cicero *In Pisonem* 14; cf. *Pro Sestio* 19.

[237] Cf. Cicero *Brutus* 303.

follow the rational order: for there are the introduction, the narrative, the statement of the case, the proof and argument, and the peroration.

[545] The exordium is the part of the speech which prepares the listener to get acquainted with the case. Its qualities are three: to make the listener attentive, well-disposed, and receptive. We make him attentive if we say that the subject is important or new or a public issue or one that concerns many people; we make him receptive if we briefly mention something in the case of a kind to give him instruction. We make him well-disposed through either a person or a thing; through a person, either ourselves or the jurors or our adversaries; through ourselves, by mentioning some action of ours likely to win favor, or by nullifying or minimizing some aspect of ourselves likely to alienate sympathy; through the jurors, if we win them over to us either by attractive elements in the case itself or by means external to the case; through our adversaries, in three ways—by bringing them into hatred or unpopularity or contempt; into hatred, by portraying them as wicked and cruel; into unpopularity, by showing that they are unrestrained; into contempt, by showing that they are of no importance. [546] There are two kinds of introduction: the fundamental and the insinuatory. In the fundamental we simply and openly win the audience over to ourselves; in the insinuatory we get around the judge by a guileful introduction. There are four occasions[238] to do this: first, when our case is a bad one; second, when the judge has a prejudice against us; or, when he is tired; or, when acclamation or laughter has caused some interruption.

[547] Before anything else, we must consider what is the character of our subject matter. There are five possibilities: honorable, base, doubtful, unimportant, and obscure. If it is honorable, we should either not use the fundamental type of introduction or we should conclude it with amplification; if it is base, we should use the insinuatory introduction; if doubtful, we should make the listener well-disposed; if unimportant, we should make him attentive; if obscure, we should make him receptive to instruction.

[548] The insinuatory introduction is explained in four ways: when we substitute consideration of a topic for that of a person, or a person for a topic, or one topic for another, or one person for another. For

[238] *Modi,* lit. "ways."

if in a case we must discuss a prostitute, we tell the jury that they must concentrate their attention on the topic rather than the person; or if someone's client or freedman goes before the law, we urge the audience to consider the person of the patron, not of the dependent, and so on.

[549] These are the faults of introductions: to be general, to say what can come into any case; to utter ideas common to your opponent, which he also can use; to display affectation by the use of unexpected language and irrelevant topics; to utter redundancies, which make the listener neither attentive nor receptive nor well-disposed; we should also avoid being too long-winded or obscure.

[550] There are four kinds of narrative: history, fable, fiction, and the statement of law or business. History is, for example, Livy's. Fable is neither true nor credible; for example, the tale of Daphne turned into a tree. Fiction is what tells not of what was done but of what could have been done; for example, in comedies, as where a young man fears his father and falls in love with a prostitute. The legal statement is a description of things which were done or which are credible.

[551] Narrative has three good characteristics: that it be clear, credible, and brief. Its vices are the contraries of these. It will be clear if we set out our subject truthfully, without confusion, in familiar terms, without circumlocution;[239] it will be credible if we appear to set out everything naturally and without affectation; it will be brief if the narrative is not poured out with prolixity or beyond what the situation requires.

Some narratives arise from the case itself and the matter in hand; some are incidental to it. Those from the case itself are those without which the subject under discussion cannot be understood; the incidental are those which are brought forward from outside the case for the sake of support or example or amplification or to arouse ill will.

[552] Some have said that there are five types of narrative: for instance, Theodore of Byzantium[240] distinguishes in Greek terms *prodiegesis, hypodiegesis, paradiegesis, anadiegesis, katadiegesis.* Narrative has seven elements: the person, the cause, the manner, the

---

239 *Longo circuitu* might mean "lengthy circumlocution."
240 A rhetorician contemporary with Plato; see Plato *Phaedrus* 226E.

place, the time, the material, and the action. Some narratives are
called continuous, some segmented. The continuous are those which
are delivered in a continuing context without any interruption; the
segmented are those interrupted by some argument or digression. We
narrate in six ways: exaggerating something, or minimizing it, or
exceeding it, or advising, or instructing, or creating favor or ill will.

After narrative one ought to discuss digression, which the Greeks
call *parecbasis;* by this we inflame or mollify the jurors. However,
since it is not an integral part of the speech and does not always have
to be used, I have decided to pass over it.

[553] The statement of the case is either our own or our opponents' or is common to both: our own, for instance 'I accuse of murder'; our opponents', for instance 'He says that I committed murder';
and in common, for instance 'The question is, Which of us has committed murder?' [554] Statements of the case are either of fundamental questions or of incidental ones, and are either simple or
compound. A simple statement is: 'You love a prostitute'; a compound: 'You are lustful and love a prostitute.' Compound statements
are mostly expressed divided into sections, which is done in two
ways: either we simply set out what we are going to say or we first
explain what is agreed between us and our opponent and what is
in dispute.

[555] Statements of the case either are bare statements or are
accompanied by a reason; a bare statement is: 'You aimed at becoming a tyrant'; when accompanied by a reason it is: 'You aimed at
becoming a tyrant; for you have arms in your house.' Statements of
the case are introduced either simply or by induction: simply, for
example 'I shall show that he is a traitor'; by induction, for example—
if we recall what we said earlier and introduce what follows—as you
might say: 'Having shown that the law is unjust, I shall now show
that it is not advantageous.' We state a case either by concession or by
omission: by concession, when we make a concession of something
we said first, but introduce something new, for example 'I admit for
the moment that the man was killed, but I deny that he was killed by
this man'; by omission, when we make the transition to another statement in such a way as not to concede the earlier one, for example 'I
have shown that only in the case of his own private affairs is permission for a lawsuit denied to a man of bad reputation; I shall show
that in a charge of treason it is not denied.'

[556] The division is that part which comprises a brief outline of all the sections in the speech; for example, in the speech for Quintius:[241] 'We deny that you have taken possession of Publius Quintius' property in accordance with the praetor's edict.' The first point is: 'There was no reason to ask for a proscription of property';[242] the second point: 'And you could not take possession of them by an edict'; and finally: 'Nor did they pass into your possession.' 'When I have shown these three things,' he said, 'I shall conclude.' You notice that the body of the whole speech is set out in order in this outline. The division ought to be such that each single point contains a number of issues in itself; for if the division is carried into each little incidental issue, it will be overloaded, and as a result the jurors will be put off by the matter to be absorbed. That is why Cicero, in this same speech for Quintius, made the division in such a way that each single heading contained more details of the issues. Look at the first point—'There was no reason to ask for a proscription of property'—see how much it contains: 'Because there was no money owed to Sextus Naevius, and the matter should have been handled in another way since Quintius did not forfeit his surety';[243] second, 'because the accuser could not have gained possession of Quintius' property by edict, because Quintius had an administrator and was defended in his absence and did not hide away and the other creditors were not pressing,' and 'because the message expelling him from the estate he shared was sent before the proscription of the estate was ordered,' and 'because he was dispossessed of his land by force, against the praetor's orders.' From this it is clear that we must include within the division questions which are to be brought forward later in the speech, so that the judge may give us his attention and not be depressed by the quantity of what we are promising to say. We should also note what is agreed between us and the opposite party, and what is to be called into dispute; the items in agreement should be enumerated if they suit our case, as Cicero said in his

241 *Pro Quinctio* 36. Publius Quinctius (Martianus uses the spelling Quintius) had inherited the property of his brother Gaius, who had been in partnership with the plaintiff, Naevius; Naevius is laying claim to Publius Quinctius' property.

242 For debt. Neither Publius nor Gaius Quinctius was in debt to Naevius.

243 Naevius alleged that he had made an appointment with Quinctius, subject to certain financial sureties, to settle by legal processes the dispute between them, but that Quinctius failed to appear and forfeited his sureties.

speech for Marcus Tullius: 'My opponent and I agree that Marcus Tullius has suffered a loss; they do not deny that this was caused by armed men using violence; they do not dare to deny that it was done by the household of Publius Fabius; the dispute is whether it was done by treacherous stealth.'[244] You see that here he has introduced in the division from conceded points the details which favor his case.

[557] The section of proof is that section of a speech in which we express in words the arguments themselves—the arguments, that is, with which the case is proved. This section is divided into two parts: proof and refutation. There are two kinds of arguments: artificial and inartificial. The artificial kind has four chief sources of argument: before the act, in the act, around the act, after the act. 'Before the act' is divided into seven sources of argument: from the person, from the act, from the cause, the time, the place, the manner, the matter. 'In the act' there are twelve sources of argument: from the whole; the part; the genus; the species; from difference, using the seven circumstances (this source of argument contains those from greater to lesser and from lesser to greater); from property; from definition; from name; from synonymy; from the beginning; from the development, or advancement; from the conclusion, or consummation. [558] 'Around the act' there are ten sources of argument:[245] from likeness—of which there are five kinds: example, similitude, tale, image, and vignette, which is taken from comedy. Some also add allegories, like those of Aesop—to resume: around the act there are sources of argument from the dissimilar; the equal; the contrary by affirmation and negation; and with respect to something, which is represented by four cases, the genitive, the dative, the accusative, and the ablative; by conflicts through possession and loss; from greater to lesser, from lesser to greater; from what precedes; from what is simultaneous, or conjoint; from what follows. There are two

---

[244] Only mutilated sections of this speech have survived. This section is not found in manuscripts but is cited as an example by the rhetoricians Victorinus (Halm, p. 209) and Julius Victor (*ibid.*, p. 419).

[245] It is not easy to discern the ten sources in the way Martianus has expressed them. They are: (1) from the like; (2) from the dissimilar; (3) from the equal; (4) from the contrary; (5) with respect to something; (6) by conflict; (7) from greater to lesser, and vice versa, (8) from what precedes; (9) from the simultaneous; (10) from what follows.

sources of argument after the act: from the result and from the decision. [559] There are other sources of argument from syzygy (*apo tes syzygias*)—that is, from conjunction or from union—which is, as it were, joined to a quality of a person; for example, if we call one who feels hostile sentiments 'an enemy.' Again, from quality; for example: 'If he acted in anger, he acted without reason.' From quantity; for example: 'If he is a serious man, the action was the same.'[246] From conjunct matters; that is, from forms and covenants (*apo typoseos kai syntheton*)—as the rods and chair of office are the insignia of magistrates.[247] Again, from partition: that is, from division (*apo tes diareseos*), through all the circumstances; that is, when we subdivide by persons, times, and the other things which are distinguished and acceptable by diversity.[248]

[560] Inartificial arguments are divided into precedents, hearsay, torture, public records, an oath, witnesses, which the orator handles in the same way as the artificial arguments. In arguments we must beware not to damage ourselves in any part, not to be inconsistent, not to be banal, not to use arguments open to our opponent, nor farfetched arguments beyond or beneath what the case calls for.

I have spoken briefly about affirmation; now let us look at the rules of refutation. Our opponent's plea is refuted either by turning it back on him, when we show that either his whole argument or parts of it apply against his case; or by rebutting it, when we show that his premises are false or that no conclusion follows from them; or by

---

246 The example (which comes from Fortunatianus; Halm, p. 116) seems to have more to do with quality than quantity. The explanation may perhaps be found in Quintilian *Institutiones Oratoriae* 7. 4. 41-44, where he points out that assessing the measure of guilt or benefit involves assessing the quality of an action. Martianus' example (thus interpreted) might mean: "If he is a frivolous man, this was a frivolous act, not deserving great blame or praise; but if he is a serious man, the act should be taken seriously, and the blame or praise should be in large quantity."

247 This example (like the preceding, from Fortunatianus) seems to mean that one may base argument on details which by custom accompany certain persons or actions; e.g., if a man has the rods and chair of office they are, as the customary insignia of the office, proof that he is a magistrate.

248 This last clause (*quae varietas grata discriminat*) seems meaningless. It is not found in Fortunatianus (Halm, p. 116). Two explanations are possible: first, that it is a gloss; second, as Willis suggests, that for *grata* we read *Graia*, changing the meaning of the clause to "which are distinguished by the subdivisions of the Greeks."

counterbalancing, when we bring another argument to match the one used against us.

[561] Of questions there are two kinds: one is called introduced (*proegoumene*), which we ourselves bring forward to prove; the one brought forward by our opponents, which we have to rebut, is called necessary (*anagkaia*). The first kind, which we introduce, is handled in two ways: the questions either are raised separately, one by one; or more than one, interconnected. We raise them in different ways: putting them forward either simply or by subdivision or in figures, which they call *dianoiai*. This source of argument has many forms; there are almost as many occasions to raise a question of this kind as there are figures of thought. [562] It is done by resolution (that is, by analysis [*kat' analysin*]) or by addition or by omission or by concession or by refutation (that is, by distinguishing [*aphorismos*]) or by separation or by correction or by concealed assertion or by supported assertion or by subdivided assertion or by affinity with an earlier question or reply or by inversion (that is, when we take first the question which is really second, and then the first).

[563] The question which is raised by our opponents can be rebutted in the same ways, and we usually add to it, when our opponent has put forward something either obscurely or with an eye to amplification rather than proof or when by way of objection to him we make a transition to our own case or when we turn our opponent's assertion to our advantage, which we call *peristrophe*, or when we handle first the proposition he put second. This must be done either to achieve an effect of elegant variation or when the first assertion is one which is forcefully against our case and should not be put first. In raising an objection we should be careful not to be too full and prolix; although sometimes, to ridicule our opponent if he dwells on his point where there is no point at issue, we should exaggerate this, or show that he is inconsistent. Objections are minimized in three ways: by the addition of words, the altering of words, or the removal of words. An objection is the assertion of an opponent; a counterobjection, the reply to this.

[564] Recapitulation is a brief repetition of the issues by listing the headings of a case. We should not always use it, but when we have made a subdivision or when a case has developed into a large number of issues, we should recapitulate in such a way that we review the essence of each, not every last detail. We shall use it also in an-

other part of the speech, when the memory of the judge is perhaps getting overtaxed, and we then call it a digest (*epimerismos*). Recapitulation is not one of the basic parts of the speech, but is one section of the conclusion.

[565] The conclusion has three parts: the recapitulation, just mentioned; the exciting of indignation, which we call exacerbation; and the arousing of pity, which we call commiseration and compassion.[249] Exacerbation comes from the sources of the arguments; for by these we not only prove things but enhance them. But the arousing of pity (that is, commiseration) is taken from the same sources of argument as exacerbation. Peroration should be used not only at the end of a speech but wherever the subject permits it; that is, by way of digression from the opening remarks or from constant narrative, and even sometimes from the discussion of the basic issues. In the conclusion, on the whole, we should take care that it is brief, if the judge is to be sent straight away with his emotions stirred to cast his verdict, while he is either angry with our adversary or in sympathy with your tears or moved by compassion for the accused."

But as Rhetoric reached this point, the Cyllenian nodded to her to move across into the company of her sisters and the service of the bride. Seeing his signal, she concluded her address and with ready confidence went to Philology's throne, kissed her forehead noisily—for she did nothing quietly, even if she wanted to—and mingled with the company and fellowship of her sisters.

[566] At last there was a rapid conclusion to the statements of the eloquent work which, fat and swollen, wrapped up the scroll's red staff,[250] almost hidden by its many folds.[251] If it meets with ap-

---

[249] Martianus uses the Greek words *deinosis* [exacerbation], *oiktos* [commiseration], and *eleos* [compassion].

[250] Ancient bookrolls were wound around a central wooden staff. Martianus' phrase suggests that it was a custom to color the staff red. Kopp refers to Persius *Satires* 5. 90, but Persius may be referring to red script, not a staff.

[251] This sentence means simply that at last Rhetoric has finished her long exposition. Martianus goes on to say that if the audience attends to the work of Rhetoric, they may learn some new points overlooked by previous writers; however, if like Silvanus (cf. § 425) they are fearful or contemptuous of Rhetoric, they will suffer for it, and Saturn's scythe will not defend them; but now the clarion call of Rhetoric gathers orators to become followers of Cicero, whereby their power and fame are assured. The Latin poem which closes this book is circumlocutory and difficult to a degree remarkable even in Martianus.

proval and not repugnance, it will bring forth some new things which it has fashioned, things which former ages overlooked and which will now be handed on. But if, Silvanus, in mockery you turn up your nose with pride, then the inhabitants of heaven will be sorry to have been afraid of Rhetoric's arms, and the source of their fear will be changed when you look for the scythe of Saturn. But you, O trumpet, summoning the crowd of rhetoricians with altered note, are withdrawing into the Tullian camp, where neither hateful enmity nor black envy may follow your fame.

BOOK VI

Geometry

[567] "Virgin goddess Pallas, comely in your panoply, bearer of all knowledge, quickener of the heavens, intelligence and perspicacity of Fate, guiding genius of the universe, revered mentor of the Thunderer, ardent flame and founder of learning, zealous worker on our behalf; with anxious foresight you form the wise man's judgment; you are the pinnacle of reason, the holy Mind of gods and men; ranging beyond the vault of the swift and glittering heavens, you alone are loftier than Jove;[1] you are the circle of flaming ether; you are the Heptad[2] among numbers; you are prior to fire; you are the third moon.[3] [568] Sculptors represent you in a habit and attitude of learning; from your crown three ruddy crests radiate, because you are a leader and flashing patron of bloody warfare, or because it is for you that the tricuspid flame[4] catches fire and gleams. [569] The sculptors provide you with a shield because wisdom rules the world, or because the frenzy of battle looks to reason for succor; your brandishing spear displays a piercing point, your shield is yet more bright and encircled by a ring. [570] Your attributes are branches of verdant olive, because through you the disciplines of learning are acquired in studious vigils by the oil lamps. [571] Sculptors associate the swift owl with you because your eyes have the color of fire; you are the apex of flame, and you are addressed as Athena Glaucopis.[5] Or rather is the night-seeing bird associated with you because the

---

[1] Macrobius (*Saturnalia* 3. 4. 8) says that Jove is the middle ether, Juno the lowest air, and Minerva (Athena) the uppermost reaches of ether.

[2] See § 738 and the notes thereon.

[3] I.e., the moon on the third day of its cycle. See the note in the Kopp edition.

[4] Plato *Timaeus* 56b states that the corpuscles of fire are pyramidal. See also Paul Friedländer, *Plato*, Vol. I: *An Introduction* (New York, 1958), chap. XIV.

[5] A Homeric epithet of Athena, meaning "with gleaming eyes." The Greek word *glaux* (gen. *glaukos*) means "owl," because of that bird's glaring eyes; the adjective *glaukós* means "gleaming, glaring."

vigils of learning are attended by sleepless cares? [572] They say
that the petrifying head of Medusa, which turns observers to stone,
glares from your breast,[6] because sagacity and learning confound
the timorous crowd. [573] To you the ancients consecreated
temples upon their city heights,[7] because reason enhances and is
more exalted than cities. Men say that you were begotten from a
father without union of a mother,[8] because the prudent senate heeds
not the advice of women. You preside over the councils of men;
hence you are called the masculine goddess. [574] O holy Wisdom of the learned Muses, you the one inspiration of the Nine,
one Mind for all the Muses, I beseech: deign to draw near and assume your appropriate function, inspiring us as we present the
Greek arts in Latin tongue.

[575] "I am grateful to you, O Goddess, and shall ever be
obliged to render thanksgiving to you for deigning to nod your
eminent[9] head in approval of our desires. I acknowledge and respect
what I have witnessed. Even now a select coterie of ladies are appear-
ing, ready to offer service to the discipline. They are bearing a beautiful little board colored with a sprinkling of greenish powder; and
they take their place, with obvious self-assurance, in the midst of the
celestial senate. But who those ladies are, and what they are bearing,
I do not perceive, unacquainted as I am with what is going to
transpire."

[576] At this point Satire, in her usual charming manner, an attentive listener to my entire story from the very beginning, playfully
remarked: 'Unless I am mistaken, my Felix, you have needlessly used
up more than enough oil to anoint whole palaestras,[10] or at least the
school of the groom himself; and Mulcifer [Vulcan] has burned up
your allotment of wick—to no avail, since you do not recognize
Philosophy, mother of so many scholars and men so illustrious.[11]

[6] The Gorgon Medusa's head was represented upon the aegis of Athena.

[7] Pallas Athene was regarded as the protector of acropolises. See Vergil
Eclogues 2. 61-62, *Aeneid* 2. 615-16; Catullus 64. 8.

[8] According to the myth, Athena sprang full-grown from the head of Zeus.

[9] Souter's meaning for *fulgidus*.

[10] The term *palaestra*, originally meaning a wrestling school, came to be used
for schools in general, since the palaestra was a favorite place for teachers to
offer lessons. Wrestlers and other athletes anointed themselves with oil to make
it easier to clean themselves after exercise.

[11] Cf. §§ 94-96.

When, not long ago, Jupiter called upon her to promulgate a decree of the celestial senate and, in seeking a marriage partner for Philology, dispatched her to address the suitor [Mercury] on the subject of matrimony, even then were you unable to recognize her?

[577] "But because now you are wise as an Arcadian or a Midas,[12] particularly since the time when your feverish exertions and devotions to the wrangling and pettifoggery of the courts[13] tied you down and blunted your edge for better occupations, you seem to have forgotten all about this lady, and wish to take no notice of her sister. [578] Now the lady over there, prepared to perform equally important functions, as you observe, is called Paedia [Learning],[14] a very well-to-do woman, who regards the wealth and treasures of a Croesus or a Darius as contemptible alongside her own. Philosophy, as one fully aware of her own endowments and rarely in attendance at plenary gatherings, proudly refusing to present glimpses of herself to anyone—at least amongst the leaders—nevertheless has frequently tarried behind, and smiled at the starveling philosophers, particularly the ones she sees barefoot, or those shaggy with uncut hair, or [those with] bodies half covered with filthy mantles.[15] In fact, if you except Marcus Terentius [Varro] and a few other Romans of consular rank, there is no one else whose threshold she has crossed. [579] You notice the haughty and austere look on the faces of both ladies; even so, both of them, attendants of Mercury's bride, shortly to arrive, are being readied for their duties.

"That object which the women brought in is called an abacus board,[16] a device designed for delineating figures; upon it the straightness of lines, the curves of circles, and the angles of triangles

---

[12] Midas was given donkey ears by Apollo because he chose Pan the winner over Apollo in a musical contest. "Arcadian ass" was a proverbial term for a stupid person.

[13] H. Parker, "The Seven Liberal Arts," *English Historical Review*, V (1890), 443, argues that *forensis rabulationis* merely refers to wrangling in the market place, and that Martianus was a farmer, not a lawyer. The latter occupation is the one usually ascribed to him. Cf. Vol. I, pp. 16-20.

[14] Lucian *The Dream* (or *Life of Lucian*) 9 also introduces a female figure, named *Paideia*, personifying learning.

[15] Remigius of Auxerre (*Commentum in Martianum Capellam, ad loc.*) identifies the three groups described by Martianus as Sophists, Stoics, and Cynics.

[16] See William Smith's *Dictionary of Greek and Roman Antiquities* (London, 1890), s.v. "Abacus," V.

are drawn. This board can represent the entire circumference and the circles of the universe, the shapes of the elements, and the very depths of the earth; you will see there represented anything you could not explain in words."

I replied: "The woman soon to appear doubtless surpasses Apelles and Polyclitus;[17] indeed, she is so highly reputed to be able to represent any object that we must conclude that she is the offspring of Daedalus, of Labyrinth fame."

[580] Immediately there came into view a distinguished-looking lady,[18] holding a geometer's rod in her right hand and a solid globe in her left. From her left shoulder a peplos was draped, on which were visible the magnitudes and orbits of the heavenly bodies, the dimensions, intersections, and outlines of the celestial circles, and even the shadow of the earth, reaching into the sky and giving a dark purplish hue to the golden orbs of the sun and the moon amidst the stars. [581] The peplos itself glistened with the sheen of the vernal sky;[19] it was marked with many figures—to serve the purposes of her sister Astronomy as well—numbers of various kinds, gnomons of sundials, figures and designs showing intervals, weights, and measures, depicted in many colors.[20] This tireless traveler was wearing walking shoes, to journey through the world, and she had worn the same shoes to shreds in traversing the entire globe. [582] She entered the senate of the gods. Though she could have told at once how many stadia and fathoms, down to the inch, she had measured in the distance between the earth and the celestial sphere,[21] instead, moved by the majestic appearance of Jove and the heavenly company, she hastily made her way to the uncovered abacus board, glancing about at the adornment of the outer canopy and the palace studded with constellations.

[17] The painter Apelles (4th cent. B.C.) and the sculptor Polyclitus (5th cent. B.C.; Martianus uses the spelling Polycletus) were among the most renowned artists of Greek antiquity.

[18] Geometry.

[19] Pliny (*Natural History* 2. 136) remarks that in Italy the air is always somewhat vernal or autumnal.

[20] The peplos worn by Geometry seems to anticipate the gowns of learning worn by medieval sorceresses and fortunetellers. On Geometry's association with weights, see R. E. F. Klibansky, E. Panofsky, and F. Saxl, *Saturn and Melancholy* (New York, 1964), p. 330.

[21] Cf. § 198.

[583] Geometry came to a halt, struck with amazement at the glittering sky. Her hair was beautifully groomed, but her feet were covered with dust. The fulgent globe, a likeness of the starry heavens, adorned her left hand. For the intricate patterns of the celestial sphere, its circles, zones, and flashing constellations, were skillfully set in place. [584] The stationary earth, no larger than a point, sustained the revolving heavens, clinging to the middle and lowest position.[22] About it a soft atmosphere floated, hemming it in with limpid breezes and drenching it with rains. The earth was riven by an immense and deep ocean, which girded it about. A brightly shining outer sphere of ether covered over the planets with a starry mantle. [585] The gleaming Titan [the sun] next inflamed his fiery orb; and then, beneath, the milky Moon imitated goodly day. Thus you could see the orbs gleam forth in the dusk of night, as a sacred flame sparkles forth from gold.[23] Similarly the Cyprian [Venus] bestowed her full light upon her morning star, when the orb was still submerged in the waters of Ocean.[24] A like ordinance keeps all the celestial bodies under control, and the globe itself is no less awesome than the lofty dwellings of the gods. The land of Sicily marveled at this replica of the universe, wrought by the hand of Archimedes fashioning the stars.[25] Indeed a remarkable handiwork and ingenuity not found in men, to have wrought a universe like Jove's with matter from our realm!

[586] Geometry finally broke the spell of her rapt admiration of the glittering heavens and turned her eyes to regarding the gods about her, with a reserve becoming a dignified lady who enjoyed the respect of all and was considered mistress of the other arts which

[22] The doctrine of the earth as comparable to a point located in the middle and at the bottom of the universe, is one of the most frequent commonplaces in the popular geographical and astronomical literature of antiquity; it is the first theorem in Euclid's *Phaenomena*.

[23] This sentence, which intrudes upon the order of the description of the planetary orbs, is deleted from the text by some editors.

[24] An echo of Vergil *Aeneid* 8. 589-91.

[25] References to the celestial globe constructed by Archimedes are frequently found in the popular literature on astronomy. See E. J. Dijksterhuis, *Archimedes* (Copenhagen, 1956), p. 23. References to globes are common in ancient literature: Cicero *De Natura Deorum* 2. 35, *Tusculanae Disputationes* 1. 25; Ovid *Fasti* 3. 277-80; Plutarch *Marcellus* 20; Sextus Empiricus *Adversus Mathematicos* 9. 15; Claudian *In Sphaeram Archimedis*; Archimedes, ed. Heiberg, II, 467. Geminus (5. 63) notes that the stand that holds the globe marks the horizon.

are known to the gods. A request was made that she begin disclosing the secrets of her knowledge, from the very beginning. As she brushed aside a lock of hair, her face shone with distinction and majesty. [587] She began drawing diagrams on the powdery surface of her abacus and spoke thus: "I see my Archimedes and the most learned Euclid among the philosophers present. I could call upon them to expound my doctrines to you at length, to ensure that every matter is expertly explained and no veil of obscurity is interposed. However, I deem it more appropriate, on this occasion which calls for[26] rhetorical skill, to disclose these matters to you myself, as best I can, in the Latin tongue, something that rarely happens in this field. Those men, in fact, speak no Latin, and expound what I have taught them only in Greek.

[588] "First, I must explain my name, to counteract any impression of a grimy itinerant coming into this gilded senate chamber of the gods and soiling this gem-bedecked floor with dirt collected on earth. I am called Geometry because I have often traversed and measured out the earth, and I could offer calculations and proofs for its shape, size, position, regions, and dimensions. There is no portion of the earth's surface that I could not describe from memory."

[589] Now inasmuch as many present in the celestial senate had not been born on earth and said that they had never trodden upon the earth, and since Jupiter as well was eager to investigate all the hiding places on earth—for the reason, I suppose, that no beautiful girl of that epoch, either, might escape that lecher of many transformations—Geometry therefore was bidden to expound this first, and then to reveal the other precepts of her discipline. She began her discourse as follows:

[590] "The shape of the earth is not flat, as some suppose who imagine it to be like an expanded disc; nor is it concave, as others suppose who have spoken of the rains 'descending into the lap of Mother Earth.'[27] Rather it is rounded—even spherical—as Dicaear-

---

[26] Following Remigius' reading: *excudit*. (The reading followed by Dick, *excludit*, would mean "excludes" or "precludes," which seems to make little sense in this context.)

[27] Cf. Vergil *Georgics* 2. 325-26; Lucretius *De rerum natura* 1. 251. See also Friedländer, *Plato*, I, 272-73, and notes thereon. On the supposed concavity of the earth, see Democritus apud pseudo Plutarch *Placita Philosophorum* 3. 10, refuted by Ptolemy *Almagest* 1. 4.

chus[28] maintained. [591] For the rising and setting times of the stars would not vary according to the elevation or sloping of the earth if the operations of the heavenly firmament were spread out above a flat surface and the stars shone forth over earth and seas at one and the same time; or, again, if the rising of the sun were concealed from the hollowed cavities of the more depressed parts of the earth.

[592] Since the latter supposition may be disregarded as a worthless opinion, it behooves us to examine the former opinion, to which even the natural philosopher Anaxagoras gave his approval,[29] even though he is believed to have supported it with some arguments. Indeed, he says that the flatness of the earth is clearly proved by the risings and settings of the sun and the moon: as soon as the first flash of radiance has appeared above the horizon, the beams are immediately directed to our eyes in straight lines; the proof of this phenomenon becomes more evident when we get clear of the obstacles of mountains and take a position on a seashore beach. Now if Anaxagoras' opinion were true, celestial bodies, on rising above the horizon, would become visible to inhabitants of all lands at the same time and, on being hidden beneath the horizon, would be able to cover all lands with darkness in one setting. In that case the observation of the Roman bard would be controverted when he says: 'While rising Sun first breathes on us with panting steeds, / Down there the evening Sun is red with waning light.'[30] [593] Besides, all nights and days would correspond, their intervals and hours always being equal, and in no portion of the earth would some stars be visible and others be obscured.

But when the constellation of the Great Bear wheels overhead in Italy it is completely buried from view and unknown to the Troglodytes and to adjacent inhabitants in Egypt. The brilliant stars Canopus and Crinis Berenices [Berenice's Hair] are not seen in Scythia, Gaul, and, in fact, in Italy; yet in antarctic regions they

28 Dick here deletes *sicut Secundus* as a gloss. Martianus' statement appears to have been derived from Pliny (C. Plinius Secundus) *Natural History* 2. 162.

29 Cf. Aristotle *De caelo* 294B. See also J. Burnet, *Early Greek Philosophy*, 4th ed. (London, 1930), pp. 270-71. Manilius (1. 228) uses the same arguments as Martianus against the flat-earth theory.

30 Vergil *Georgics* 1. 250-51. On Vergil's confused notion in this passage, and on the confusion of other ancient writers on this subject, see J. O. Thomson, *History of Ancient Geography* (Cambridge, 1948), p. 219.

are conspicuous stars and are seen almost directly overhead. ..c Alexandria, Canopus is elevated above the horizon by a quarter of one interval,[31] but the Triones [Ursa Major and Ursa Minor] are not visible because of the slope. In Arabia, in the month of November, Helix [Ursa Major] is not visible at nightfall, but becomes visible during the second watch;[32] in Meroë, at the summer solstice, it is barely visible for a brief space of time, when it rises at dawn about the time of the rising of Arcturus.[33] Likewise, in India, it is seen in the port of Patavitano[34] only in the early evening, and on Mount Maleus it is visible for only fifteen days each year. Who, then, would doubt that the obstruction of the curving slopes of the spherical earth causes some constellations to be hidden from view while others emerge clearly above the slopes?

[594] For those who doubt the sphericity of the earth, additional evidence is found in the fact that eclipses of the sun and the moon occurring in the west are not seen by inhabitants of the east, and, similarly, inhabitants of Britain and of western lands are not aware of eclipses that occur in the east. In regions in between, the times of eclipses vary by hours. Servius Nobilis[35] reported that, at the victory of Alexander the Great in Arabia, the moon was eclipsed at the second hour of the night, whereas in Sicily this eclipse was observed as the moon was first rising. An eclipse of the sun that took place during the consulship of Vipstanus and Fonteius, on April 21,[36]

---

[31] Pliny (2. 178) says "a quarter part of one sign." Pliny's statement coincides with a commonly accepted figure of 7½ degrees for the elevation of Canopus at Alexandria. See Thomson, *op. cit.*, p. 212. The rest of Martianus' discussion here of the changes in celestial phenomena at different latitudes also comes from Pliny 2. 178.

[32] The Loeb translator of the Pliny passage erroneously supposes that Canopus is being referred to here.

[33] Pliny (2. 178) has two appearances of Ursa Major at Meroë: in the early evening at the summer solstice, and at daybreak a few days before the rising of Arcturus. Not infrequently Martianus shortens passages and consolidates data without concern for the nonsense that results. For a list of such conflations, see my *Roman Science* (Madison, Wis., 1962), pp. 279-80.

[34] Probably Patala. Pliny (2. 184) calls the port *Patalis;* the Martianus manuscripts read *Patavitano*.

[35] This fictitious name results from a misreading by Martianus (or an intermediary) of the text of Pliny 2. 180: *serius nobis illi*.

[36] Pliny (2. 180) dates the eclipse April 30 and gives the names of the consuls as Vipstanus and Fonteius (*ibid.* and 7. 84). The Martianus manuscripts read

was seen in Campania in the seventh hour and was verified as occurring in Armenia during the eleventh hour of the same day. These discrepancies are the result of the sloping surface of the spherical earth.[37]

[595] Finally, hemispherical bowls which are called *horologia*, or sundials, are adjusted according to variations in latitude. Gnomons are replaced at distances beyond five hundred stadia,[38] as the shadows are depressed or elevated according to the location of the dials. Consequently, the longest day of the year at Meroë lasts twelve and two thirds hours, at Alexandria fourteen, in Italy fifteen, and in Britain seventeen. At the summer solstice, when the sun is borne toward the celestial pole, it bathes the regions that lie beneath in continuous daylight; but when it makes its wintry descent, it causes northern regions to shiver in darkness that lasts six months. Pytheas of Massilia reported that he found such a condition on the isle of Thule. Those discrepancies of the seasons, unless I am mistaken, compel us to admit that the earth is round.

[596] We must now reveal the size of the earth and what position it holds in the universe. Eratosthenes, a most learned man, used a gnomon in calculating the earth's circumference as 252,000 stadia. [597] There are bronze hemispherical bowls called scaphia, which mark the passage of the hours by means of a tall, upright stylus, located at the center of the bottom of the bowl. This stylus is called a gnomon. The length of its shadow, measured at the equinox by a determination of its distance from the center, when multiplied twenty-four times, gives the measure of a double circle.[39] [598]

Alpiano, or variants thereof, which Dick emends to Vipstano on the basis of Pliny. Pliny credits the general Corbulo with the Armenian observation and says that the eclipse occurred in Italy between the seventh and eighth hours and in Armenia between the tenth and eleventh hours. There is roughly a two-hour time difference between Italy and Armenia. Martianus, as is his wont, stretches Pliny's statements.

[37] J. Beaujeu, in his edition of *Pline l'Ancien, Histoire naturelle* (Paris, 1950), II, p. 233[n], points out that Bede used this discussion of Martianus in two of his works.

[38] Geminus (5. 58) says that sensible differences occur over 400 stadia.

[39] Martianus obviously did not understand the geometrical procedures used by Eratosthenes. These are correctly reported in Cleomedes *De motu circulari corporum caelestium* 1. 10. Nor do we know of any Roman who understood the simple geometrical demonstration involved in Eratosthenes' measurement of the

Eratosthenes, upon being informed by official surveyors in the employ of King Ptolemy as to the number of stadia between Syene and Meroë,[40] noted what portion of the earth's surface that distance represented; and multiplying according to the proportionate amount, he straightway determined how many thousands of stadia there were in the earth's circumference.

[599] So much for a brief account of the determination of the earth's dimensions. Now let us reveal its position. That the earth stands stationary at the middle and bottom of the universe is demonstrated by several arguments. First, it was in the very same position, from which it could not be moved, before the universe was founded. Hence, when the elements of the primal mixture were separated from each other, the vast and voluble expanse of waters and the diffusion of the atmosphere spread all about the stationary earth and hemmed it in, making that which was enclosed within the rounded and voluble substance the middle portion. Or again, everything that is the middle in a sphere becomes the bottom, since whatever supports lines that are equidistant from the surface of a sphere is compressed by them.[41] [600] That which is lowest must come to a halt by the very extremity of its position, for there is no place below where it can fall. All weights fall downward upon the earth—rain, hail, snow, lightning—the ocean, too, which sinks into the nethermost parts of the earth, and the darkling streams that 'welter in the bottommost abyss.'[42] The earth, which supports the floods and all

---

earth's circumference. Is Martianus' puzzling statement to be explained by supposing that his source was referring to the twelve demarcations of the daylight hours in the hemispherical bowl and that by multiplying by twenty-four, one accounts for a full circle? Eratosthenes actually made his measurements at the summer solstice. Pliny twice (2. 247; 6. 171) refers to Eratosthenes' accomplishment and gives his estimate, but does not attempt to explain his method. On errors in Martianus' account, see Assunto Mori, "La misurazione eratostenica del grado ed altre notizie geographiche della 'Geometria' di Marciano Capella," *Rivista geographica italiana*, XVIII (1911), 586f.

[40] Eratosthenes actually used the distance between Syene and Alexandria for his calculations.

[41] Compare this discussion of the distribution of the elements, and the proof of the earth's location at the middle of the universe, with the discussion found in Pliny 2. 162 and in Macrobius *Commentary on the Dream of Scipio* 1. 22. 1-7.

[42] A quotation from Vergil *Aeneid* 6. 581.

other weights, you see, is compressed on all sides and has nothing beneath it, to which it may retire. It must be assumed to be at the middle, since it holds the last position.

The intervals of time at the equinox are a clear proof of this truth: water clocks show that the hours of the forenoon and the afternoon and of the day and the night are of equal duration.[43] [601] Another proof that the heavens are equidistant on all sides from the earth is found in the two solstitial circles: the length of the day, when the sun reaches its highest point in the heavens, is equal to the length of the night, when the sun descends to the winter solstice. Similarly, the length of daylight allotted under each of the signs of the zodiac corresponds to the length of darkness occurring when the sun is in the opposite quarter. This goes to prove that the celestial circles and the constellations are equidistant from us in all directions, and that the earth is at the middle. If this topic seems to have been adequately discussed, I shall now proceed to name the zones of the earth, all of which I myself have traversed.

[602] The earth's surface is divided into five zones, or belts, marked by differences in their conditions. Intemperate conditions of excessive heat or cold render three of the belts uninhabitable.[44] The two zones that border upon the north and south poles have reason to be deserted, with their enormous chill and cold, and severe snowfalls; the belt in the middle is scorched by fires and stifling heat, and burns all living things that draw near. The two belts between, tempered by the exhalations of life-giving breezes, are conducive to human and animal habitation. These belts, of course, curve entirely about the spherical earth and gird the lower as well as the upper hemisphere.

[603] You must know that the earth is divided into two distinct parts, or hemispheres: there is an upper hemisphere, which we inhabit and which Oceanus encircles; and there is a lower hemisphere. The upper one begins at the place of the sun's rising, the lower one at the place of its setting. The Greeks have given the name *horizon*

43 Cf. Pliny 2. 176.
44 This is another example of the stale, stereotyped data of the compilers: centuries after exploration had proved the torrid zone to be habitable, they perpetuated the view of Crates of Mallos (*fl.* 165 B.C.), and other popular writers, that it was uninhabitable.

to the circle of demarcation. [604] Now, inasmuch as the five zones encompass both parts, upper and lower, they actually form ten regions. The one inhabited by us extends northward. Another, tending southward, is believed to be inhabited by men called antecians (*antoikoi*). [605] Correspondingly, there are two habitable regions in the lower hemisphere. Those diametrically opposite us are called antipodes and those who are diametrically opposite our antecians are called antichthones.

Our condition is distinct from theirs in the oppositeness of our seasons. When we are scorched with summer's heat, they are numbed with cold; when spring here bedecks the meadows with flowers, the heat of summer there is yielding to the gentle warmth of autumn; when we have our shortest day, they have their longest; we get a clear view of Arctos [the Bear], which is wholly invisible to them.[45] [606] Our antipodes experience with us a common period of winter and the heat of summer, but we have our days and nights at opposite times from them: that is, long days in summer and long nights in winter for us, and long nights in summer and long days in winter for them. Septentrio [the Great Bear] is visible to us, but always lies hidden from them. The same is true of the earth's inhabitants who are called antecians: they and their antipodes experience the four seasons of the year in common, and they alone have a view of the south pole, which is ever invisible to their antipodes and to us.[46]

[607] Those who inhabit the middle belt observe daily variations in risings and settings. For those who have the sun overhead, its rising is swifter and its setting slower. At the time of the equinox, risings and settings are alike, and there are no stars that are not visible to them; stars that rise at the same time also set together. Inhabitants here have their days equal to their nights, and objects cast no shadows at noon. Their antipodes also have days and nights of equal length. Since the sun, in its haste to reach its northern solstice, draws its path across these inhabitants, and again passes them by as it moves to its winter solstice, receding far from them on either side, it is

---

[45] The discussion of the earth's habitations and the variations of seasons experienced by them is stock handbook material.

[46] Martianus appears to be confusing antipodes and antecians when he twice remarks that antipodeans have common seasons.

undoubtedly true that they experience two summers[47] and two winters each year. When the sun is rising for them, it is setting for their antipodes.

[608] But the two regions, or belts, referred to above—one of which is covered with ice because of its proximity to the chill of Plaustrum [the Wain], the other deserted because of antarctic winds —do not have antipodes of their own.[48] However, because of their diametrically opposite locations, they become antipodal to each other. Inhabitants here observe no risings of the celestial bodies, except the planets, which do not course over their heads but have risings near the middle of one side.[49] Fixed stars are visible for six months, and for six months they are out of sight. The equator is the circle that marks risings for them, and only six signs of the zodiac are visible. Days and nights are of six months' duration, and the poles are visible directly overhead.[50] But the one region, adorned with the luster of Septentrio, and the other, with the star Canopus, have no acquaintance with the remaining portions of the sky. [609] That most learned man Pytheas has disclosed what conditions are like in those regions; but I myself have traversed them: there is no portion of the earth's surface that is not known to me.[51]

The full measurement of the earth's circumference—to convert into Roman miles the figure in stadia which I recorded in the calculation above—is thirty-one thousand five hundred miles.[52] At this point it would be well to include the opinion which Ptolemy records in his *Geography*.[53] [610] He cuts the circumference of the zodiac

---

[47] Pliny (6. 58) says this about India. A compiler could get from mathematical compilers the statement that the torrid zone is uninhabitable, and from geographical compilers, like Pliny, statements regarding the inhabitants of the torrid zone. Such discrepancies apparently caused Martianus no concern.

[48] Once again Martianus appears confused about the nature and true meaning of antipodes. He seems to conceive of antipodes as dwellers in the lower hemisphere, the upper being the hemisphere of the known world.

[49] I.e., on the south or the north, not the east.

[50] Geminus 5. 31-34.

[51] The handmaiden Geometry is still speaking.

[52] I.e., by multiplying Eratosthenes' estimate of 252,000 stadia by Pliny's figure of 125 paces in one stadium, and by dividing by 1,000 (1,000 paces in a Roman mile). See Pliny 2. 85, 247.

[53] 1. 3. 7, 11.

into three hundred and sixty segments of the sky. Each segment, when brought down toward the earth's center, according to him, stretches across the earth's surface a distance of five hundred stadia. Each stadium is equal to one hundred and twenty-five paces. Multiplying by the five hundred stadia that are measured in each segment, we obtain a figure of sixty-two thousand five hundred paces. The same five hundred stadia, multiplied by three hundred and sixty, give a figure of one hundred and eighty thousand stadia for the entire circumference. Next, multiplying by the number of paces in one stadium, as recorded above, we get a figure of twenty-two thousand five hundred miles for the earth's circumference.[54] So much for our disclosures about the globe of the entire earth.

[611] Now the length of the earth from east to west—that is, from the farthest part of India itself to the pillars consecrated to Hercules at Cádiz—is eight thousand five hundred and seventy-seven miles, according to one authority, Artemidorus.[55] Isidore,[56] in fact, says that the distance is nine thousand eight hundred and eighteen miles. But then again Artemidorus adds to his aforementioned figure the territory beyond Cádiz. He notes that that land extends along the perimeter of Spain, around the 'sacred promontory,'[57] as far as the last of the capes, called the Artabrian promontory,[58] a distance of nine hundred and ninety-one miles.

[612] The total dimensions can be shortened by traveling over the seas. From the Ganges River and its mouth, where it flows into the eastern Ocean, across India and Parthia to the Syrian city of Myriandrus, on the Gulf of Issus [Iskenderun Körfezi], the distance is five thousand two hundred and fifteen miles. From there, by the shortest sea route, to Cyprus, then to Patara in Lycia, Rhodes, the island of Astypalaea in the Carpathian [Aegean] Sea, then to Taenarum in Laconia, and on to Lilybaeum in Sicily and Caralis

[54] Martianus correctly records the estimates of Eratosthenes (252,000 stadia) and Ptolemy (180,000 stadia) for the earth's circumference. The conversion of Ptolemy's estimate given here goes back to some Roman intermediary. It is not to be supposed that Martianus consulted Ptolemy's work directly.

[55] Artemidorus' figure comes from Pliny 2. 242, where, according to the reading adopted by J. Beaujeu, the figure is 8,578 miles.

[56] Isidore of Charax. See p. 141, n. 52, of the first-volume introduction to this translation.

[57] Cape Saint Vincent.

[58] Cape Finisterre.

[Cagliari] in Sardinia is three thousand four hundred and fifty miles; from there to Cádiz is four thousand two hundred and fifty miles. The total distance from the eastern Ocean is eight thousand five hundred and seventy-eight miles.[59]

[613] Another route can be taken over land and sea: along the Ganges and Euphrates rivers, across Cappadocia and Phrygia, over the Aegean and Laconian seas and the other gulfs to the Peloponnesus, on to Leucas, Corcyra, Acroceraunia, Brundisium, and Rome, across the Alps and Gaul, over the Pyrenees to the western Ocean, down the coast of Spain to Cádiz—a total distance of eight thousand six hundred and eighty-five miles. My estimate is corroborated by Artemidorus. Thus you have the length of the earth calculated by various methods.[60]

[614] The breadth of the lands from the southernmost region to the northern limits is very much smaller, inasmuch as it is contracted on either side by the excessiveness of the intemperate climates. What is more, on the northern side the rude and uncivilized nation of the Sarmatae prevents explorers from determining dimensions there. Nevertheless, all the regions that intrepid explorers have been able to penetrate have been adequately measured, and the breadth of the inhabited earth has been found to be almost one half smaller than the reckoning of its length. [615] It has been determined that the breadth is five thousand four hundred and sixty-two miles. This measurement is taken from the shores of the Ethiopian Ocean, which is the farthest limit of habitation, to Meroë, thence to Alexandria, Rhodes, Cnidus, Cos, Samos, Chios, Mytilene, Tenedos, the cape of Sigeum [Kumkale], the entrance to the Pontus [Black Sea], the cape of Carambis [Kerempe], the entrance to the Maeotis [Sea of Azov], and the mouth of the Tanais [Don River]. This measurement, if it is taken across the open seas, is reduced by six hundred and seventy-eight miles. [616] Artemidorus maintained that this was the farthest extent of geographical knowledge; but Isidore added one

[59] The figures for the first segment of the journey over the seas (5,215 miles) and for the total distance from India to Cádiz (8,578 miles) coincide with Pliny's figures, as given in the Beaujeu edition, pp. 108-9. Pliny's figures for the second segment (2,113 miles) and the third segment (1,250 miles) combine with the first to produce a correct total. On some of the difficulties involved in reconciling discrepant figures in the manuscripts, see Beaujeu, pp. 264-66.

[60] Artemidorus' figure, as given in the Beaujeu edition of Pliny, p. 109, is 8,945 miles.

thousand two hundred and fifty miles, as the distance to Ultima Thule, which seems to me to be an unreliable opinion. For I assert that the earth has as much breadth as it has length. We offered above a demonstration and proof that the orb of the earth is round, and it is impossible for a globe to have unequal sides. The authorities mentioned above have declared the earth's surface to be habitable.[61]

[617] Voyages in all directions prove that a circumambient ocean girds the shores of the globe.[62] The entire western coast, winding around Spain and Gaul from Cádiz, is navigated these days. [618] During the time that the late emperor Augustus was sailing around Germany with his fleet, he traversed the entire northern Ocean. First he reached the Cimbrian promontory [Denmark], and from there he crossed a great sea and got as far as Scythia and its frozen waters. [619] Similarly, with regard to the distant eastern borders and the Indian Ocean, Macedonian fleets, during the reigns of Seleucus and Antiochus, cruised along the shores that verge into the Caspian Sea. Lake Maeotis is considered a bay of the same ocean. Of a like kind are the reports of the seas flowing around the left-hand side[63] of the earth's habitations. [620] From the pillars consecrated to Hercules at Cádiz all the way around to the Arabian Gulf, the southern Ocean is navigable, as has been attested in many instances. [621] The victories of Alexander carried his fleet over the greater part of this sea. When Gaius Caesar, the son of Augustus,[64] was

[61] Martianus' discussion of the earth's breadth is a somewhat abridged version of Pliny 2. 245-46. The figure for the shortening of the distance over the seas (Martianus gives 678 miles) is, according to Beaujeu's text of Pliny, 79 miles. The absurd closing remark here may be original.

[62] Regional descriptions of the known world were regularly constructed on a periplus framework, a sort of coastal pilot's guide, beginning at the Strait of Gibraltar and circumnavigating first the upper (Europe and West Asia) and then the lower half (Africa and South Asia) of the world. Such maritime accounts were satisfactory to the Greeks, who were not greatly interested in the interior; but the Romans, whose interests lay mainly in the interior, would have done better to abandon this framework. Instead they cramped and confounded their geographical data of the interior regions and regularly apologized for using the periplus pattern by prefacing their accounts with reports of fabulous circumnavigations such as those given here.

[63] I.e., the southern continent of the known world. As one sails toward Cádiz, this continent would be on the left-hand side.

[64] Actually the son of Marcus Agrippa and Augustus' daughter Julia, Gaius Caesar was adopted by Augustus.

stationed in this same Arabian Gulf, the shipwrecked hulls of Spanish ships were discovered here, together with other fragments that had been cast ashore. Hanno, at a time when the Carthaginian Empire was at its height, sailed around Mauretania [Morocco] and from there turning south, in a very long voyage, reached the borders of Arabia.[65] Cornelius [Nepos] is our authority for the report that a certain Eudoxus, escaping from the evil designs of his king, fled from Arabia to gain asylum at Cádiz. Caelius Antipater reports that he saw a man who, in his eagerness for trade, had sailed from Spain to Ethiopia. The same Cornelius, after taking some Indians captive, sailed past Germany.[66] [622] I consider the fact that the seas have been navigated on all sides to be proof that the lands of the upper hemisphere are girded by a sea that stretches over a circular course.

I shall now discuss the divisions of the earth, insofar as this brief account allows. The entire expanse of habitable land in the upper hemisphere is divided, according to most authorities, into three continents: Europe, Asia, and Africa. The first and last of these continents are separated by an irruption of the Ocean; [623] for the mighty flood of the Atlantic, cutting through the depths of land from the Strait of Cádiz [Gibraltar], cleaves the African from the Iberian shore and pours itself rapidly into the waters of the adjacent sea. Lengthwise the strait extends scarcely fifteen miles, from the opening toward Cádiz to the entrance of the inner sea. The breadth at the narrows is five miles, at a wider point seven miles, and at the widest point ten miles. Through the strait poured a deluge of crashing waters swollen by different seas, engulfing the various bays and subsiding plains.

[624] This onrush of the invading Ocean created the European continent on the left hand and the African continent on the right, and terminated them with mountains on either side. For the sea is kept from Europe by Mount Calpe [Gibraltar] and from Africa by

[65] Hanno probably got no farther than Sierra Leone, on the west coast of Africa.

[66] These confirmations of a circumambient ocean were ultimately derived from Pliny 2. 167-70. How badly Martianus garbles the Plinian account may be seen in the last report about Cornelius Nepos. In Pliny's account, Nepos was only the reporter, and Quintus Metellus Celer, proconsul of Gaul, received as a gift from the king of the Swabians some Indian sailors who had been blown off their course and had been swept to Germany.

Mount Abinna [Ceuta]⁶⁷ which, looming on either side, deserve to be called the pillars of Hercules because in the testimony of antiquity the bounds of his labors were immortalized by them, since the impassable limits of the world prevented him from advancing further. [625] Here, too, is evidence of the power of his divine strength: whereas, heretofore, nature used to keep the seas and the lands apart and to confirm that fact by the great encircling belt of Ocean, Hercules, sundering the above-named mountains by their roots and breaching the barrier, admitted the sudden flood to the low-lying fields and the hollows of the earth's surface, providing a challenge to the energies of mankind, changing the earth's features and the decrees of nature.

[626] To the left of this strait, Europe stretches, as far as the waters of the river Tanais. Here Asia begins, and in turn is bounded by the Nile River. This Nile severs Asia and Africa and divides the land around itself with numerous tributaries. However, very many authorities have said that the European continent terminates at the entrance to the Propontis, and that the Propontis, flowing down through narrows, extends to Lake Maeotis.⁶⁸

[627] The starting point and commencement of Europe is assigned to Spain, a fruitful and rich province, famous for its production of metals and gold, red lead, marble, and gems. Because the river Hiberus [Ebro] flows through it, this land has acquired the name of its river [Iberia]. The part of Spain that borders on the Atlantic and extends along the shores of the Strait of Cádiz [Strait of Gibraltar] is called Baetica, also taking its name from that of a river; the region extending closer [to Italy], from the territory of the Oretani,⁶⁹ is called Tarraconensis from the city of Tarraco,

---

⁶⁷ *Abinna* here and in Solinus *Collectanea rerum memorabilium* 23. 13 is better known by the name used in Pliny 3. 4: *Abyla*.

⁶⁸ Martianus' brief preceding statement about the Nile River is a scanty vestige of Pliny's impressive disquisition (5. 51-59) on that river's course. Martianus' "very many authorities" actually number but one, Solinus 23. 15. Here Martianus is beginning to draw upon Solinus, his second most important source on geography, as well as upon a Plinian intermediary. Martianus' discussion of the divisions of the earth is to be compared with Pliny 3. 3-5.

⁶⁹ Martianus uses the phrase *ab Urcitano*, but atlases of ancient and modern Spain do not include such a name. The Oretani and their town Oretum were on the border between Baetica and Tarraconensis.

which the Scipios founded. The Carthaginians established Cartagena, calling towns, wherever they founded them, by names familiar to them. [628] But the area alongside that aforementioned is constituted as another province from the Pyrenees Mountains, in that Lusitania adjoins Baetica along its northern border. Legend has it that Lusitania got its name from the sport (*lusus*) of Liber [Bacchus] or of those who reveled with him.[70] This province is also penetrated by a river which has its own name, although the Tagus also brings fame to the province because of its auriferous sands. [629] They say that Ulysses founded the town of Olisipo [Lisbon][71] there, which gave its name to the promontory that separates the seas from the land. The Gallic sea and the northern ocean have their beginning as they bend around this projection, and the Atlantic and western oceans come to an end here, delimited by the extrusion of Spain. In that territory, mares are impregnated by the winds, Favonius himself endowing their offspring with swift flight.[72]

[630] Baetica surpasses the other provinces in fertility. It has two jurisdictions, that of Cádiz and that of Córdoba, and has one hundred and seventy-five well-inhabited towns.[73] [631] In length it stretches from the confines of the town of Castulo to the town of Cádiz, a distance estimated at more than two hundred and fifty miles; its breadth is two hundred and twenty-four miles.[74]

[632] The entire province has seven jurisdictions: those of Cartagena, Tarragona, Caesaraugusta [Saragossa], Clunia, Asturia [Astorga,] Lucus Augusti [Lugo,] and Bracara Augusta [Braga]. In addition to islands and communities dependent on others, numbering two-hundred and ninety-four, it contains one hundred and

[70] The Greek word *lussa* [frenzy] was applied to Bacchic rites.

[71] Olisipo (*Ulysippo* in Mela *De situ orbis* 3. 1. 6) was believed to have derived its name from Ulysses. Cf. Solinus 23. 6. Martianus here spells it *Olisipone*.

[72] Cf. Pliny 4. 113-16; and, on the Lisbon mares, cf. Pliny 8. 166; Varro *De agricultura* 2. 1. 19.

[73] Pliny (3. 7) names four jurisdictions and classifies the towns according to administrative status.

The translation here departs from the Dick edition. For the number of jurisdictions, some Martianus manuscripts read *duo,* some read *quattuor* (but give the names of only two). Dick follows the *quattuor* reading and adds the names of the two other jurisdictions mentioned by Pliny.

[74] Cf. Pliny 3. 17.

seventy-nine towns.[75] It extends, according to Marcus Agrippa's calculations, four hundred and seventy-five miles in length and two
hundred and twenty-four miles in breadth, when the boundary is
carried as far as Cartagena.[76] This figure of Agrippa constitutes
no small error, [633] for all of Hispania Citerior [Hither Spain]
from the Pyrenees to the confines of Castulo stretches six hundred
and seven miles in length; and the figure is a little more along the
coast. The breadth is estimated to be three hundred and seven miles
from Tarraco to the shore at Oasso [San Sebastian], at the foot of
the Pyrenees, where the land is hemmed in by the sea on either side.
As the land gradually extends outward, it adds appreciably to the
breadth.[77]

[634] This same Pyrenees range on the other side forms a boundary of the territories of the Gauls. The land extending from the foot-
hills of the Pyrenees to the Rhine River and from the Ocean to the
Cevennes and the Jura has been allotted to the Gauls. Besides, there
is a province called Narbonensis, formerly called Bracata, which is
washed by the Mediterranean. It is separated from Italy by the
ranges of the Alps[78] and by the Var River. The length of this province, according to Agrippa's measurements, is three hundred and
seventy miles and its breadth two hundred and forty-eight miles.
[635] The Rhone River flows in this province, rising in the Alps
and passing through Lake Leman [Lake Geneva]. It bring fertility
in crops and livestock to the lands. Its mouths have different names:
one is called the Spanish, another the Metapinic; and the third, which
has a fuller flow, is called the Massiliotic. The province is famed[79]

[75] Martianus confuses his readers by inserting into his section on Baetica the
preceding two sentences, which pertain to Tarraconensis. Pliny 3. 16-18, the
ultimate source for this passage, keeps them separate.

[76] Martianus is once more speaking of Baetica.

Marcus Agrippa, second in command to his father-in-law Augustus, at the
latter's direction conducted a professional survey and mapping of the entire
known world from the British Isles to China. Particular attention was given to
dimensions of provinces and distances along highways. Agrippa died in 12 B.C.,
before the project was completed. Pliny made extensive use of the data compiled
by Agrippa's surveyors. See Thomson, pp. 332-34, 374.

[77] Martianus' description of Spain is to be compared with Pliny's account in
3. 6-8, 16-18, 21, 29-30; 4. 113-16; and with Solinus 23. 1-9.

[78] Alpes Graiae, Alpes Cottiae, and Alpes Maritimae.

[79] A favorite expression of Martianus when he is reducing paragraphs of
Pliny to a single statement.

for its manhood, towns, and produce, and it has only one shame to
be mentioned, the fact that formerly it was considered right to perform human sacrifice there.[80]

[636] On the other side of the Alps, where the slope stretches
out and is bathed in the rays of the rising sun, Italy begins its descent
—a country extolled by the ancients far more than all others for the
beauty of its city of Rome. [637] The Ligurians are the first nation
across the border; next the sacred region of Etruria occupies a fertile soil, a land famed for its compact with the hero Aeneas,[81] as
well as for its discovery of remedies and for the unearthing of
Tages.[82] Next come the Umbrians and Latium and the mouth of the
Tiber, and then the capital of the nations, Rome herself, as long as
she was in her prime,[83] a city to be extolled to the skies for her military prowess, men, and religious worship. Rome is situated sixteen
miles from the coast. [638] The next stretch of coast is held by the
Volscians and named after them; then, in succession, Campania, the
Picentes, the coast of Lucania, and Bruttium. The peninsula of Bruttium faces the sun and wind of the south and juts out into the sea,
and with an arm going out to the left [Calabria] it embraces the
waters of an enclosed bay [the Gulf of Taranto]. So, if from the
edge of the Alps you look down to the right and the arm of long
mountain [the Apennine range], putting out spurs on either side,
you seem to see a kind of theater of water [the Tyrrhenian Sea].[84]
Italy, indeed, is crescent-shaped,[85] and extends in a half-circle down

[80] Martianus' discussion of Gaul is to be compared with Pliny 3. 31, 33, 37;
4. 105; and Solinus 21. 1.

[81] Martianus is referring to Latinus' betrothal of his daughter Lavinia to
Aeneas.

[82] An important mythological figure among the Etruscans, Tages was unearthed, according to the legend, by a peasant plowman. He was said to be a
grandson of Jupiter, and to have the features of a boy but the wisdom of a
sage. His utterances, upon his being unearthed, were later taken down to form
the books of Tages. He was regarded as a founder of Etruscan divination. Cf.
above, §§ 8, 157; and Cicero (*De divinatione* 2. 50), who reports the story with
amusement.

[83] A statement which has been regarded as of crucial importance in determining Martianus' date. See Vol. I, p. 14.

[84] Martianus' account here is obscure, and Dick's edition confuses the passage
by using a comma, rather than a full stop, after *complectitur*. Pliny's description
is very clear.

[85] Italy, on Ptolemy's somewhat distorted map, takes on a crescent shape.

to the aforementioned promontory. To sum up, starting at Cádiz, where the jaws of the strait open, to the Bruttian gulf, the first in Europe, the inflowing seas are quiet.

[639] On the interior side the land extends northward, into the Upper [Adriatic] sea, along the coast of [Magna] Graecia, and is inhabited by the Sallentini, Pediculi, Apuli, Peligni, Istri, Liburni, and other less well-known peoples.[86] The land bends to the left and, with two promontories, assumes the shape of an Amazon's shield,[87] having Leucopetra on the right projection and Lacinium on the left. Although its lengthwise measurement, from the Alps at Augusta Praetoria[88] through Rome and Capua, down to the town of Rhegium, and not including the curvature backward, is one thousand and twenty miles; nowhere does its breadth exceed three hundred miles.[89] The distance from Italian soil to Istria and Liburnia is one hundred miles; from Epirus and Illyricum fifty miles; from Africa, according to Varro,[90] less than two hundred miles; from Sardinia one hundred and twenty; from Sicily one and a half miles; from Corcyra less than eighty miles; and from Issa fifty. [640] The entire circuit of Italy is two thousand and forty-nine miles.[91] Its central point is said to be in the district of Reate.[92] Its narrowest point is at the port that is called Castra Hannibalis [Hannibal's Camp]; here it is scarcely 40 miles wide.[93]

Italy is also famous for the Padus [Po] River, known to the Greeks as the Eridanus. This stream originates in a remarkable spring on Mount Vesulus [Viso], one of the loftier peaks of the Alps; it becomes a river in the territory of the Ligurians; then

---

The "Bruttian gulf" is the northwestern portion of the Mediterranean from Gibraltar to the toe of Italy; see Pliny 3. 5.

[86] Martianus uses expressions like this when he tires of repeating place names from Pliny's tedious lists. Cf. Pliny 3. 38.

[87] Crescent-shaped, with a projection from the middle of the curve. Pliny (3. 43) observes that the Cocynthum Promontory forms that middle projection.

[88] Aosta.

[89] Pliny (3. 44), copied by Solinus (2. 23), says that the breadth varies from 410 to 136 miles, but that across the middle of the peninsula it nowhere exceeds 200 miles.

[90] The attribution here, as well as the figures, comes from Pliny 3. 45.

[91] Cf. Solinus 2. 23; Pliny 3. 44.

[92] A statement which Pliny (3. 109) attributes to Varro, who was born there.

[93] Pliny (3. 95) says 20 miles.

the river submerges deep under the ground and emerges again in the
vicinity of Forum Vibi. Its volume increases at the rising of the
Dog Star; for when the snows on the Alps have melted in the heat
of the summer sun, the river overflows its banks and, surpassed
by none of the famous streams, it picks up thirty streams in its course
and, swelling to an immense size, pours into the Adriatic Sea.[94]

[641] There are other memorable features of Italy, lauded by the
poets: the town of Scyllaeum[95] and the Crateis River,[96] which
was the mother of Scylla; the writhing whirlpool of Charybdis; the
rose gardens of Paestum;[97] the cliffs of the Sirens; and the lovely
glades of Campania, long famous; then the Phlegraean Fields and
Tarracina, the dwelling place of Circe, formerly an island, now
joined to the mainland. Rhegium is separated from Sicily, which has
been detached into an island to compensate for the annexation of the
island at Tarracina; then there is also Formiae, famed as the abode
of the Laestrygonians.[98]

[642] At this point I could run through the names of the found-
ers of cities: for example, Janiculum, named from Janus; Latium
from Saturn,[99] Ardea from Danaë,[100] Pompeii from Hercules, when
he was leading a procession of Spanish oxen.[101] Also connected
with Hercules' labors are the fields in Liguria known as the Campi
Lapidarii [Lapidei; 'Stony plain'] because, according to legend, the
sky rained rocks when Hercules was fighting there.[102] He also gave

[94] Cf. Pliny 3. 117.
[95] Cf. Homer *Odyssey* 12. 235.
[96] Cf. *ibid.*, 124; Ovid *Metamorphoses* 13. 749; Pliny 3. 73.
[97] Famous for its twice-blooming roses. Cf. Vergil *Georgics* 4. 119; Propertius
4. 5. 39; Martial *Epigrams* 12. 31. 3.
[98] Martianus' list of place names familiar to the poets seems to have been
drawn from Solinus (2. 22), who gathered the references from scattered passages
in Pliny 3. 57, 59, 73, 86, 87.
[99] *Latium*, popularly derived from *latere* [to lie hidden], because, according
to the myth, Saturn lay hiding there after being driven from the heavens by
Jupiter. Cf. Vergil *Aeneid* 8. 319-23; Ovid *Fasti* 1. 235-38.
[100] Cf. Vergil *Aeneid* 7. 372, 409-11; and Servius *Commentary, ad loc.*
[101] The oxen of Geryon. The etymology of *Pompeii* is uncertain. The ancients
derived it from *pompa* [Gr. *pompē;* a procession], but modern authorities derive
it from the Oscan word *pompa* [five].
[102] Cf. Pliny 3. 34; Solinus 2. 6.
In the next sentence Martianus confuses further legends about Hercules. The
Ionian Sea was supposedly named after Io, daughter of Inachus. Autoclus is not

the Ionian Sea its name, because he slew Io, the daughter of Autoclus, while she was engaging in highway brigandage. Iapyx, the son of
Daedalus, founded Iapygia; Dardanus founded Cora; the Pelasgians,
Agyllina;[103] and Catillus, commander of Evander's army, founded
Tibur.[104] Parthenope got its name from the tomb of a Siren by that
name. It is now called Naples. Praeneste was founded by Praeneste,
the grandson of Odysseus. Some authorities prefer to consider Caeculus as the founder, who, they say, was an offspring of the flames.[105]
Diomedes founded Arpi and Beneventum; Antenor, Patavium; and
the Pylians, Metapontum. However, I am not really interested in
investigating the origins of cities.[106]

[643] Now, since the boundary of a continent is determined by
the limitations imposed by intervening seas and straits, it is not inappropriate here to call attention to the lands, particularly the memorable ones, that emerge from the waters; these, because they are in
the salt water, are called islands.[107] A concise survey ought not to be
tedious.[108] So, in passing, I will mention the Pityussae, so called from
their pine forests,[109] and now called Ebusus, in the vicinity of Cartagena; two Balearic Islands, Colubraria, and the islands which the
Greeks call Gymnasiae;[110] there is also Capraria, treacherous to
ships. Off the coast of Gaul, near the mouth of the Rhone, is the
isle of Metina; then comes an island called Blascon; next are three
islands which are called Stoechades [lit., Islands in a Row]: they are

---

known to legend, but Autolycus—a cattle-stealer like Hercules—is; Autolycus
was the son of Hermes and Chione, and had a daughter Anticlea.

[103] Pliny (3. 51) calls it Agylla.

[104] Cf. Vergil *Aeneid* 7. 670-72.

[105] Vergil (*ibid.*, 680-81) says that Vulcan found Caeculus on his hearth.
Servius (on *Aeneid* 7. 678) says that a sister of two *dii indigites,* sitting at a
hearth in Praeneste, had a spark fall into her lap and thus conceived Caeculus.

[106] Martianus would not have included the preceeding list if Solinus (2. 5-10),
or his source, had not culled the information from Pliny.

[107] Martianus here derives the word *insula* from *in salo* [in the salt]. Festus
(*De significatu verborum* 9. 82) and Isidore (*Etymologiae* 14. 6. 1) give the
same etymology.

[108] Avoiding tedium is the regular excuse of compilers for digesting or omitting the technical details of earlier writers.

[109] Cf. Pliny 3. 76. The Greek word for "pine" is *pitus.*

[110] Pliny (3. 77) gives the Greek name *Gymnasiae* to the Balearic Islands.

known as First Island, Middle or Pomponiana Island, and Hypaea; then there are other small islands opposite Antipolis. [644] In the Ligurian Sea is the island of Corsica, which the Greeks call Cyrnos. It is one hundred and fifty miles long and fifty miles wide. Its circumference extends three hundred and twenty-five miles. It has thirty-three states. The island of Elba is on the mainland side, and Oglasa below it. Sixty miles from Corsica is Planasia, treacherous to sailors, who are deceived in approaching it.[111] Then there are Urgo and Capraria, the Greek name for which is Aegilion; then Egilium, Dianium, Columbaria, and Veneria. Then beyond the Tiber mouth, in the vicinity of Antium, are Palmaria and Sinonia; and off the shore of Formiae are Pontiae, Pandataria, Prochyta, Abaeneria, called by the Greeks Inarime;[112] and, in the vicinity of Naples, Pithecusa and Megaris. Eight miles from Sorrento is Capri; then comes Leucothea.[113]

[645] Sardinia, facing the African Sea, is eight miles from Corsica. In the narrow strait there are small islands, which are called the Cuniculariae [Rabbit Islands];[114] besides these there are Phinton and Fossa. Sardinia, named after Sardus, the son of Hercules, has the shape of a human foot. Indeed, it was called Sandaliotis and Ichnusa, both words suggesting the shape of a footprint. On the east coast the island extends one hundred and eighty-eight miles; on the west one hundred and seventy-five; on the south seventy-seven; and on the north one hundred and twenty-five. Off the Gorditanum promontory there are two islands, called the Islands of Hercules; off Sulci[115] the island of Enusis; and off the Caralis promontory the islands of Ficaria and Galata. Some authorities say that the Balaridae Islands, Gallode,[116] and the Islands of the Baths of Hera are not far distant. Across from Paestum is Leucasia, which gets its name from

---

[111] Pliny (3. 80) says that the island gets its name from its shape, level with the sea, and that for this reason it is treacherous.

[112] Cf. Homer *Iliad* 2. 783. Pliny (3. 81) locates Pontiae off Formiae, the other three islands off Puteoli.

[113] Martianus' survey of the islands of the northern Mediterranean is to be compared with Pliny 3. 76-83.

[114] See E. H. Bunbury's remarks in William Smith's *Dictionary of Greek and Roman Geography* (Boston, 1865), s.v. "Cuniculariae Insulae."

[115] See the article s.v. "sulci" in Smith's *Classical Dictionary*.

[116] Pliny (3. 85) calls them *Berelis* and *Callode*.

a Siren buried there. Across from Velia are the Oenotrides Islands, and opposite Vibo are the Ithacan Islands, which got their name from the watchtower of Odysseus.[117]

[646] Next we must mention Sicily, which is called Sicania by Thucydides, and by many writers Trinacria. King Sicanus gave his name to the islands; he came there with a band of Spaniards before the Trojan War.[118] Next came Siculus, the son of Neptune, who changed the name of the island to his. It is called Trinacria for the reason that, with its three projections, it is regarded as triangular: the Pachynus promontory faces south, toward the Peloponnesus, and is four hundred and forty miles from Greece; the Pelorus promontory faces westward[119] and Italy, which is separated from it by a strait one and a half miles wide. Lilybaeum faces Africa and is one hundred and eighty miles distant from it. The distances between these capes, by overland measurement, are as follows: from Pelorus to Pachynus one hundred and seventy-six miles; from Pachynus to Lilybaeum two hundred miles; and from Lilybaeum to Pelorus one hundred and forty-three miles. [647] There are five colonies in Sicily and sixty-three cities, many rivers and springs, and the awe-inspiring sight of Mount Aetna, spewing forth flames every night. Its crater measures twenty stadia;[120] it showers Tauromenium and Catana with hot ash, bellowing in loud uproar and thunderous crashings as the flames toss about.

[648] There are islands in the Sicilian Sea, too, to be sure. On the African side, Gaulos and Malta, lying at a distance of eighty-eight miles from Camarina and one hundred and thirteen miles from Lilybaeum; Cossyra, Hieronnesos, Caene, Lampadusa, Astusa (called by some writers Aegusa), and still other islands. On the Italian side there are the following islands: opposite the Metaurus River, at a distance of 25 miles from Italy, are the seven Aeolian Islands, called the Hephaestiades by the Greeks and Vulcan's Islands by us. These islands have separate names: the first Lipara, the second Therasia, the third Strongyle, where Aeolus is said to have reigned and where he

---

[117] Bunbury, in his article s.v. "Ithacesiae Insulae" in Smith's *Dictionary*, says that the islands are mere rocks, too small to be marked on ordinary maps.

[118] Cf. Solinus 5. 7.

[119] Martianus' error here follows Solinus (5. 2), whose mistake seems to have arisen from a misreading of Pliny's *vergens* (3. 87) as *vespero*.

[120] Pliny (3. 88) says "in circumference."

knew, from the flames and their smoke erupting in the vicinity, from which direction the wind was going to blow; as a matter of fact, the inhabitants of this locality today have the same premonition. The fourth island is Didyme, the fifth Erephusa, and the sixth Phoenicusa, and the last Euonymus.

[649] The first European gulf of the Ausonian Sea[121] extends ninety-six miles, and has three bays. The fore part of Italy, which is called Magna Graecia, begins here; it has an abundance of streams and towns. Then there is the port called Castra Hannibalis, at which point the breadth of Italy is a mere forty miles.

[650] The second gulf of Europe begins at the Lacinian promontory and, with a deep fold of coastline, terminates in the Acroceraunian promontory in Epirus; this point is eighty-five miles distant from the town of Crotona.[122] From here Italy extends past many towns and bays, far into the sea, and reaches the city of Hydruntum, where the Upper and Lower Seas are separated by nineteen miles;[123] at this point is found the shortest crossing into Greece. From here Italy continues past many peoples, bays, cities, rivers, mountains, and barbarian nations[124] to the territory of Illyricum, which extends, from the river Arsia to the Drina River, a distance of five hundred and five miles; and from the Drina to the Acroceraunian promontory, a distance of one hundred and seventy-five miles. The Illyrian coast has more than a thousand islands.

[651] The third gulf of Europe begins at the Acroceraunian Mountains and terminates at the Hellespont. It has nineteen bays[125]

121 Martianus once again confounds the geographical data of Pliny (3. 94-95) in his omission of some of Pliny's statements. In summing up what went before, Pliny says: "So much for the first gulf of Europe"; then he goes on to describe the three bays of the Ausonian Sea in the following paragraph.

122 Again Martianus is garbling Pliny (3. 97), who gives 85 miles as the distance between the Lacinian and Acroceraunian promontories. Crotona belongs with the following sentence. Furthermore, 85 miles is merely the distance across the Gulf of Taranto, and not nearly the distance across the Adriatic to Epirus.

123 Another misreading of Pliny (3. 100), where 19 miles is the distance from the Iapygian Point to Hydruntum.

124 This is Martianus' way of skipping over fifty sections in Pliny (3. 101-50). Like Pliny, who admits that he prefers to list names that are easy to pronounce (3. 7, 139), Martianus may have felt that barbarian names would repel his readers.

125 Pliny (4. 1) says that the coastline extends 1,925 miles, not counting smaller bays.

and many provinces. For there are Epirus, Acarnania, Aetolia, Phocis, Locris, Achaea, Messenia, Laconia, Argolis, Megaris, Attica, and Boeotia. Also, on the other side, on another sea, Phocis and Locris, Doris, Phthiotis, Thessaly, Magnesia, Macedonia, and Thrace—all of Greece.[126] Epirus begins at the Ceraunian Mountains. Here the first people are the Chaones, from whom Chaonia gets its name. Next comes Mount Pindus, the Dryopians, Molossians, and Dodoneans, famous for their celebrated oracle of Jupiter. Behind them, among other peoples, Moesia and Media border upon the Pontus; the Thracians extend to the Pontus. Presently the lofty peaks of Rhodope and Haemus are seen. Then come the colony of Buthrotum, and the Gulf of Ambracia, admitting the sea through narrow jaws; into it flows the Acheron River, famed in the legends of the underworld. Omitting several peoples, there is the colony of Actium, with its temple of Apollo, who has received an epithet from this place;[127] also the city of Nicopolis. Going from the Gulf of Ambracia into the Ionian Sea, we are confronted by various peoples, and then the Aetolians, within whose borders, among other cities, is found close by the sea the city of Calydon, famous as the ancestral home of Diomedes and Tydeus.[128] Here an intervening gulf separates Aetolia and the Peloponnesus. In Acarnania there is Aracynthus; in Aetolia . . . .[129] Then the Ozolae, with their town of Oeanthe, where the harbor of Apollo is located.[130] Next, in the plains of Phocis, are the town of Cirra, the harbor of Chaleon, from which, seven miles inland, is the town of Delphi, beneath Mount Parnassus, famous for the oracle of Apollo; the Castalian spring is located there. Then, in the deepest recess of the gulf, is the angle of Boeotia, near Mount Helicon.

[652] The Peloponnesus is a peninsula between the Aegean and

---

[126] In Pliny (4. 1) this phrase is the beginning of the following sentence: "All the legendary lore of Greece and its brilliant literature first shone forth from this gulf" (Loeb ed.).

[127] Strabo (325) refers to the temple of the Actian Apollo.

[128] Calydon was the birthplace of Oeneus, father of Tydeus and grandfather of Diomedes.

[129] Martianus' digest does not indicate that Pliny (4. 6) is listing mountains here. There is a lacuna where the names of Aetolian mountains should appear.

[130] Pliny (4. 7) regards Oeanthe and the harbor as separate. According to Smith's Classical Dictionary (s.v. "Phaestus") the harbor belonged to the adjacent interior town of Phaestus.

Ionian seas, having deep inlets, with a perimeter of five hundred and sixty-three miles and, if the bays are measured, almost as much again. The narrow neck from which it protrudes is called the Isthmus. The opposing seas dash against it on either side, only five miles apart, and bite into the sides of the passageway. In the land between, which I have called the Isthmus, is the city of Corinth, sixty stadia from either shore, looking down upon both seas from a high elevation which is called Acrocorinthos. At the Isthmus begins a province called Achaia, formerly called Aegialos because of the cities located in a row along the coast.[131] In this province are many bays, harbors, mountains, towns, and peoples.[132]

[653] Hellas begins at the narrows of the Isthmus—the land which we call Greece. The first state in Greece is Attica, called Acte in antiquity. The part of it that borders on the Isthmus is called Megaris. On the coast is a harbor called 'Scironian Rocks,'[133] six miles in length, with Athens set back from the sea by a wall five miles long.[134] There are many springs in Attica, of which a famous one is Callirhoe; and the springs of Boeotia are no less famous than those of Athens: they include Epicrene, Arethusa, Hippocrene, Aganippe, and Gargaphie.

[654] After many towns, mountains, and peoples we come to Haemonia, behind which is Mount Oeta.[135] This country is also known by the name Thessaly. Here was born a king by the name Graecus, who gave his name to the land of Greece; here also Hellen was born, from whom the Hellenes got their name. In Thessaly the most famous mountains are Pierian Olympus and Ossa, facing which are Pindus and Othrys, the abode of the Lapiths; these peaks

[131] The Greek word *Aegialos* means "seashore."

[132] An uninformative statement to cover the omission of twelve sections of Pliny (4. 12-23). Here Martianus has been copying Pliny's summary statements almost verbatim and omitting hundreds of place names and the occasional tidbits of information associated with them.

[133] See Smith's *Dictionary*, s.v. "Scironia Saxa."

[134] Another example of the confusion that arises from Martianus' condensations. Pliny (4. 23-24) lists a harbor and some towns along the coast, including a precipitous mountain pass called Scironia Saxa, six miles in length. He then proceeds to name the harbors of Piraeus and Phalerum, connected to Athens by a wall. (Dick adds *iuncta*, which would make the sentence mean that the Scironian Rocks were joined by a five-mile wall to Athens.)

[135] Pliny (4. 28) says, in a sentence immediately preceding a paragraph on Haemonia, that Oeta is behind Doris.

look to the west; Mount Pelion looks to the east. All these mountains curve around, like a theater; before them lie seventy-five cities. Next to Thessaly is Magnesia, with its fountain Libethra, famed for its poetic inspiration.[136] The length of Thessaly is four hundred and ninety miles, and its breadth two hundred and ninety-seven miles.[137]

[655] Next comes Macedonia, a country of one hundred and fifty different peoples, and famous for outstanding kings; in particular Alexander; though it was believed that he was the son of Philip, his mother, Olympias, said that she had conceived him by a serpent. He was the conqueror of the world, for he had the same limits in his explorations and conquests as Bacchus and Hercules.[138] This country of Macedonia gave its name to the people who were formerly called Edonii, and to all of Mygdonia, Pieria, and Emathia. It extends as far as the borders of Thrace.[139] The southern part is inhabited by the Epirotes, the western by the Dardanians and the Illyrians; on the northern side is Paphlagonia and Paeonia.[140] The boundary between Macedonia and Thrace is the Strymon River, flowing down the crest of Mount Haemus. In this range is Mount Rhodope, which they say is a Mygdonian mountain; then comes Athos, cut off from the mainland by Xerxes, who availed himself of his mighty Persian forces; and then the land of Orestis, undoubtedly getting its name from the son of Orestes and Hermione. Then comes Phlegra, now a town, famous for the reckless and monstrous battles of the giants. . . . This peak alone is said not to have been covered over in the deluge—to be sure, because of its preeminent elevation.[141]

[136] Pliny (4. 32) and Solinus (8. 7) merely mention the spring of Libethra. This is a rare, if not unique, instance of Martianus' adding information not drawn from those two sources. Did Martianus have in mind the story told in Pausanias' *Description of Greece* (9. 30. 9-11) about an oracle relating to the bones of Orpheus, whose tomb was located there?

[137] Pliny (4. 32) gives these figures for the dimensions of Epirus, Achaia, Attica, and Thessaly, taken together.

[138] Cf. Solinus 9. 18-19; Pliny 4. 39.

[139] Cf. Solinus 9. 2.

[140] Cf. *ibid.*; Pliny 4. 33. These authors write *Pelagonia*, not *Paphlagonia*.

[141] Martianus is referring to the Greek legend of Pyrrha and Deucalion, who constructed a boat and were the sole survivors of a flood sent by Zeus. Various peaks have been named as the one on which their boat came to rest. Solinus (9. 8) does not name the peak. (Dick postulates the lacuna.)

[656] Then comes Thrace, whose dull-witted inhabitants have the greatest yearning for death; the Bessi and the Denseletae live on the right bank of the Strymon,[142] up to the Mesta River, which flows around the base of Mount Pangaeus. The snows of Odrysia fill the Hebrus River, which flows among various barbarian nations and also waters the lands of the Cicones, within whose borders is Mount Haemus, whose peak rises six miles[143] and is buffeted by winds because of its proximity to the stars. Behind it are found various nations, among them the Getae, the Sarmatians, and the Scythians. Next, the Sithonian people inhabit the area around the Pontus; their fame is derived from the genius of their poet Orpheus, who was born there; for his life on the Spertican promontory was devoted to either religious activity or the lyre.[144]

[657] Next comes the Maronian region and the town of Tyrida, in which the horses of Diomedes were stabled. Nearby is Abdera, to which the sister of Diomedes gave her name when it was built; this city is more celebrated as the birthplace of the natural philosopher Democritus. The poets have not overlooked the fact that Thrace is the burial place of Polydorus. There, too, is the promontory of the Golden Horn, famous for the city of Byzantium,[145] which is seven hundred and eleven miles distant from Dyrrhachium; that is the distance between the two seas, the Adriatic and the Propontis. At this point the Hellespont, narrowing to seven stadia, separates Europe from Asia. [658] Here, too, are located two towns: one, Sestos, belonging to Europe; the other, Abydos, to Asia. Then there are facing promontories: Mastusia, on the Chersonesus, which marks the end of the third gulf of Europe; and Sigeum, in Asia, which is said to be the location of Cynossema, the tomb of Hec-

---

[142] Pliny (4. 40) says that the Bessi live on the left bank, the Denseletae on the right bank.

[143] Pliny (4. 41) says that the journey to the peak is six miles. By this time readers will have noted Martianus' characteristically tortuous style in Book VI— a style resulting partly from his frequent condensing of several Plinian statements into a single sentence.

[144] Cf. Solinus (10. 8).

[145] Martianus' calling the city Byzantium and not Constantinople is used by some scholars as evidence that the work was compiled before the name of this city was changed, A.D. 330, to honor Constantine. Such an argument ignores the fact that Martianus was a mere compiler and that he was drawing his information here from Solinus (10. 17) and Pliny (4. 46.)

uba.[146] Not far off is the island of Tenedos, from which point the sea that lies between, as far as Chios, broadens out. On the right is Antandros. The smallness of the islands was frequently remarked upon by sailors, who compared them to a goat. Hence the Aegean got its name.[147] And on the Phalarian[148] promontory of Corcyra a rock resembles the form of a ship, into which [rock], according to ancient legend, the ship of Odysseus was changed.

[659] Crete, splendid with her hundred cities, stretches east and west. It got its name from a nymph, a beautiful daughter of Hesperis, or from Cretes, king of the Curetes. At first it was called Aeria; subsequently Curetis; then it was called Isle of the Blessed because of its bland climate. In length it stretches two hundred and seventy miles; its breadth does not exceed fifty miles; its circumference extends five hundred and eighty-eight miles. Its highest peaks are Mounts Ida and Dictynna.

Euboea is separated from the mainland of Boeotia by so slight and narrow a current that it is linked in several places by bridges.[149] It is enhanced by two promontories: Geraestus, facing Attica; and Caphareus, facing the Hellespont. Its breadth ranges from two to forty miles. The length of the whole of Boeotia, from Attica to Thessaly, amounts to one hundred and fifty miles; its circumference is three hundred and sixty-five miles.[150] On this island are the cities of Chalcis, opposite Aulis, and Carystus, producing marble that is the color of the sea.

[660] In the Myrtoan Sea the Cyclades Islands get their name from their circular arrangement; of these the better-known are Delos and Antandros.[151] Then, too, the Sporades Islands, of which Naxos

---

[146] The name Cynossema means "Bitch's Tomb." According to legend, Hecuba was changed into a bitch near the end of her life.

[147] From the Greek word *aix* (gen. *aigos*), meaning "goat." Martianus follows Solinus (11. 1-2) here, whose statement is a garbled reduction of Pliny (4. 51).

[148] Phalacrum promontory, according to Strabo 324 and Ptolemy *Geography* 3. 14. 11.

[149] Pliny (4. 63) mentions only one bridge over the strait separating Euboea from the mainland.

[150] Martianus is here misreading Pliny (*ibid.*), who says that Euboea stretches lengthwise along the entire length of Boeotia from Attica to Thessaly; Pliny gives these figures for Euboea.

[151] Antandros was mentioned shortly before (§ 658). This probably accounts for the misreading here of *Antandros* for *Andros*. Pliny (4. 65-67) names Delos and Andros among the many Cyclades Islands that he enumerates and describes.

is remembered for the tomb of Homer, and many other islands extend across seven hundred miles of longitude and two hundred miles of latitude. Between the Chersonesus and Samothrace are certain large and now barbaric[152] habitats.

[661] The fourth of the great gulfs of Europe begins at the Hellespont and ends at the mouth of the Maeotis [Sea of Azov]. The sea between Europe and Asia is constricted and flows through narrows, seven stadia in width, called the Hellespont. Xerxes, king of Persia, collected his fleet, constructed a bridge, and led his army across here. These narrows extend along a channel for eighty-six miles;[153] then the sea becomes very broad and, soon again, it becomes constricted. The broadening of the sea is known as the Propontis, and the second narrows are called the Bosporus, one half mile in width. At this point Darius, the father of Xerxes, led his troops across by means of a bridge. The distance from the Hellespont is two hundred and thirty-nine miles.

[662] Next the Scythian bay of the broad sea[154] stretches out, at the middle of which is the Maeotis, joined by a narrow entrance; this inlet is called the Cimmerian Bosporus; it is two and a half miles wide. Between the two straits, the Cimmerian Bosporus and the Thracian Bosporus, is a distance of five hundred miles. The circumference of the entire Black Sea is two thousand one hundred and fifty miles, according to Varro, who says that the entire length of Europe is six thousand three hundred thirty-seven and a half miles. The Ister River rises in Germany, on the slopes of Mount Abnoba,[155] picking up sixty streams; it is also called the Danube. [663] Beyond here extend the Scythian shores, a region densely populated with various barbarian races. Here are the Getae, the Dacians, Sarmatians, Amaxobians [Wagon-Dwellers], Troglodytes,

---

[152] This adjective may have originated in a misreading of a Pliny manuscript at 4. 74: *ferae* [wild] in the place of *fere* [almost]. Pliny says: "Between the Chersonesus and Samothrace, about (*fere*) fifteen miles from each, is Halonesus . . ." and then goes on to mention many other islands. Martianus, reading *fere* as *ferae* and seeing the numerous proper names, has erroneously condensed the passage.

[153] Pliny (4. 75) gives this figure as the distance from the Hellespont to the town of Priapus, on the south shore of the Propontis.

[154] The Black Sea. The "Scythian bay" is the northern half.

[155] The Black Forest. Tacitus (*Germania* 1) also gives this as the source of the Danube.

Alani, and Germans. The entire stretch, from the Danube to the ocean,[156] is two thousand one hundred miles long, and in breadth four hundred miles, up to the wastes of Armenia.[157] Not far away are a river, a lake, and a town called by the same name, Borysthenes.[158] Nearby is the Isle of Achilles, famous for his tomb. Inland live the Auchetae, in whose territories the Hypanis [Bug] River originates; and the Neuri, in whose territories the Borysthenes [Dnieper] begins. There are the Geloni, the Agathyrsi, the Man-Eaters, and behind them the Arimaspi, then the Rhipaean Mountains and a region covered over in darkling shadows.

[664] Behind these mountains and beyond the north wind are the Hyperboreans,[159] in whose vicinity the axis of the world continually rotates—a people remarkable for their customs, length of life, manner of worship, benignity of climate, six-month-long day, and their abode at the limit of human habitation. The region of Sarmatia, Scythia, and Taurica extends in length nine hundred eighty-eight miles, and in breadth 710.[160] I am of the opinion that there is nothing to mention beyond here in Europe, since Asia has claimed even the Hyperboreans for itself.

[665] If, after crossing the Rhipaean Mountains, you go to the left, along the stretch of the northern Ocean, you will come a second time to the peoples of Germany, Gaul, Spain, and back to the Strait of Gibraltar. The Ariphaei, located in Asia, lead a life comparable to that of the Hyperboreans, and are admired by all races, so much so that people who are living in fear flee to their country to seek asylum.[161] Beyond them are the Cimmerians and the Amazons, reaching as far as the Caspian Sea; this sea bursts into the Scythian

156 Presumably the eastern Ocean. Pliny (4. 81) gives the distance as 1,200 miles.

157 Probably a misreading of *Sarmatia*.

158 As noted subsequently, the river is probably the Dnieper.

159 The myths about the Rhipaean Mountains and the happy Hyperboreans can be traced back to Herodotus' day. For classical references and recent scholarship on the myths, see Thomson, pp. 21-22, 61-62.

160 Cf. Pliny 4. 89-91.

161 Here is another instance of Martianus' drawing upon Solinus in preference to Pliny. Pliny (6. 34-35) deals with the Arimphaei on his southern periplus. Solinus, who was adept at rearranging the Plinian materials, deals with them (17.2) next after the Hyperboreans.

Ocean near the place of the summer rising of the sun.[162] After a long stretch of land we come upon Hyrcania.

[666] Then, returning to the shore of the Atlantic Ocean,[163] along the farther borders of Aquitania and Europe, we come to Britain. This island lies to the north and the west, in length eight hundred miles, in breadth three hundred; the circumference is three thousand eight hundred and twenty-five miles. Nearby is the Caledonian Forest and very many islands, among which are the forty Orcades [Orkneys], almost joined together; then there are the Electrides [Frisian Islands], on which amber is found. The last of all the islands is Thule,[164] on which, at the summer solstice, there is continual daylight, and, at the winter solstice, continual night. At one day's sailing beyond this island the sea is frozen over. Below Britain is the territory of Gaul and Spain. Were it not for the incursion of the Atlantic Ocean, Spain would be joined to Africa. For the town of Belon in Baetica is only thirty-three miles distant from Tingi,[165] which is a colony in Mauretania. Antaeus is said to have been the founder of this town.

[667] Africa and Libya got their names from Afrus, the son of the Libyan Hercules. In this region is the colony of Lissos. This is the site of the palace of Antaeus and of his famous wrestling match with Hercules; here are located the Gardens of the Hesperides. Here also is the winding estuary which the ancients sportively referred to as a guardian serpent. Not far away is Mount Atlas, raising its peak from the bosom of the sands. The natives call it Mount Addiris.[166] It rises up to the vicinity of the moon's orbit, above and

---

[162] Ancient geographers were uncertain whether the Caspian was an inland lake or a gulf of the eastern Ocean. See Thomson, index, s.v. "Caspian Sea."

[163] Martianus above (§ 629) had said that the Atlantic Ocean ended, and the northern Ocean began, at the peninsula of Lisbon.

[164] The location of Ultima Thule—identified, among other suggestions, as Iceland, Norway, the Faroes, the Shetland Islands, or the Orkneys—is one of the most controversial subjects of ancient geography. Accounts of Thule were circulated by Pytheas of Massilia (Marseilles), who made a voyage around Britain and along the North Sea coast. For a full discussion of Pytheas' voyage, see Rhys Carpenter, *Beyond the Pillars of Heracles*, pp. 143-99. Carpenter prefers to date the voyage in the middle, rather than the first decade, of the third century B.C. For a bibliography of recent scholarship, see Thomson, pp. 147-51.

[165] Tangiers.

[166] Solinus (24. 15) was responsible for this mistake. Pliny (5. 13) was speaking

beyond the forces of the clouds. The western side faces the shores of Oceanus; it is thickly wooded, teeming with springs, but infertile because of its rocks. But the side that faces the province of Africa is all luxuriant. It grows trees that look like cypresses but have an oppressive odor; these produce a precious fleece, like that of silk. By day the mountain is silent, but at night there is a flashing of fires and a commotion of flutes and pipes, cymbals and drums, and of frenzied Satyrs and Goat-Pans.[167] [668] Beyond it, toward the west, for a distance of four hundred and ninety-six miles, stretches a forest filled with wild African animals. Not far distant are seven mountains which, because of their equal height, are called 'The Brothers'; they are teeming with elephants, and lie beyond the province of Tingitana, whose length is one hundred and seventy miles.[168] Then there is the town of Siga, the royal residence of Syphax, facing the city of Málaga in Spain. Along the coast is Cartenna, and the larger town of Caesarea; then Icosium, with no less favorable political status; then Rusguniae and Rusuccurru, Saldae, and other towns, Igilgili and Tubusuptu. The river Ampsaga is three hundred and twenty-two miles distant from Caesarea. [669] The length of the two Mauretanias is one thousand and thirty-eight miles, the breadth four hundred and sixty-seven miles.

Numidia, famous for its association with Masinissa, begins at the Ampsaga River. Its name is derived from the Nomads. Inland is the colony of Cirta, and further inland are Sicca and Bulla Regia. Along the coast are Hippo Regius and Thabraca; inland is the district of Zeugitana, properly called Africa. It has three promontories: Candidum; Apollo, facing Sardinia; and Mercury, facing Sicily. Projecting into the sea, they form two bays, beginning at Hippo Diarrhytus. Then comes the promontory of Apollo; and, on the next bay, Utica, remembered as the place of Cato's death; the river Bagradas; and, nearby, Carthage, once famous in war, now awesome

---

about the distance to Mount Diris (*ad Dirim*). Solinus included the preposition in the name. Strabo (825) informs us that Dyria was the native name for Atlas.

[167] Most of these reports about Atlas go back to Pliny, some to Herodotus. See the article s.v. "Atlas" in Smith's *Dictionary of Greek and Roman Geography*. See also Thomson, p. 261

[168] The bits of information in this sentence are derived from scattered sentences in Pliny (5. 17-18).

in her prosperity.[169] Finally there are Maxula, Carpis, Missua, and Clupea, on the promontory of Mercury; then Curubis and Neapolis.[170] [670] Then come those, called Libyphoenicians, who inhabit Byzacium, a region whose circumference measures two hundred and fifty miles and whose sowings are repaid by hundredfold harvests. Here are the towns of Putput, Hadrumetum, Leptis, Ruspae, Thapsus, Thaenae, Aves, Macomades, Tacape, and Sabrata, on the fringe of the Syrtis Minor. To this point from the Ampsaga River the length of Numidia and Africa is five hundred and eighty miles, the breadth two hundred miles.

[671] The third gulf is divided into the two bays of the two Syrtes with shallow tidal waters. Syrtis Minor is three hundred miles distant from Carthage. The journey to the Syrtis Major is through deserted regions that are infested with various kinds of serpents and wild beasts. Next come the Garamantes; beyond them the Psylli once lived. Along the recessed coast are the municipalities of Oea and Leptis Magna; then comes Syrtis Major, which measures six hundred and twenty-five miles around.

[672] Next is Cyrenaica, also called Pentapolis, famous for the oracle of Jupiter Ammon, which is four hundred miles from Cyrene. There are five leading cities here: Berenice, Arsinoë, Ptolemeïs, Apollonia, and Cyrene. Berenice [Benghazi] is on one end of the horn of the Syrtis; here are the Gardens of the Hesperides,[171] the river Leton, and a sacred grove; the distance from Berenice to Leptis is three hundred and seventy-five miles. Arsinoë is forty-three miles away from Leptis; and next comes Ptolemaïs [Barce], twenty-two miles farther on. Far distant are Catabathmos and the Marmaridae and, along the shore of Syrtis, the Nasamones; then Mareotis; then a locality in Egypt, Apis, which is sixty-two miles from Paraetonium; from there to Alexandria is two hundred miles. The length of all

---

[169] This statement about Carthage—Martianus' presumed birthplace—would seem to place the *terminus ad quem* for his book at A.D. 439, when Carthage was captured by Gaiseric.

[170] Martianus is better informed and makes fewer mistakes in excerpting from Pliny here, because he is describing a familiar region.

[171] Pliny gives two different locations for the gardens: in Mauretania (5. 5) and in Cyrenaica (5. 31), and explains that in Greek myths the locale often varies. Martianus pays no attention to the discrepancy in excerpting Pliny here and in § 667.

Africa from the Atlantic Ocean, including Lower Egypt, is three thousand and forty miles; from the ocean to Greater Carthage is one thousand one hundred miles; from it [Greater Carthage] to Canopus, the nearest mouth of the Nile is one thousand six hundred and eighty-eight miles.

[673] The interior of Africa faces south, with deserts intervening, and is the abode of the White Ethiopians, the Nigritae, and other peoples of monstrous strangeness. After these, to the east, are appalling wastelands. The river of this region is the Niger, of the same nature as the Nile. The Atlantes dwell amidst these wastes; they possess no names and curse the sun because it scorches them and their crops relentlessly. These people seem never to have dreams. [674] The Troglodytes live in caves, and feed upon serpents, and hiss instead of speaking. The Garamantes generally consort with women without marrying them. The Augilae worship the powers of the underworld. The Gamphasantes are naked and unwarlike, and never mingle with outside peoples. The Blemmyae have no heads and have their mouth and eyes in the chest. The Satyrs have nothing human except their faces. The Goat-Pans are as they are represented in paintings. The Strap-Feet, because of a disability of their feet, crawl rather than walk.[172] The Pharusi were companions of Hercules. These people mark the end of Africa.

[675] After this comes Egypt, which is the beginning of Asia. This land measures two thousand six hundred and thirty-eight miles from the Canopic mouth of the Nile to the entrance to the Black Sea; and from the entrance to the Black Sea to the entrance to the Maeotis, one thousand six hundred and seventy-five miles. The interior of Egypt stretches southward as far as the Ethiopians, who border it in the rear. Lower Egypt is embraced by the Nile, which divides on the left and the right, so that you might refer to Egypt as an island of the Nile; for the circumambient river is thought to mark off the delta, too, in the shape of the letter *delta*. From the point of its division, to the Canopic mouth, is a distance of one hundred and forty-six miles.

---

[172] Pliny and Solinus were responsible for the credence given to this list of monsters as late as the seventeenth century. See Lloyd A. Browne, *The Story of Maps* (Boston, 1949), pp. 85-88. See also Thomson, pp. 361-62. Martianus' description of Cyrenaica and the interior of Africa was derived from Pliny (5. 31-48) and Solinus (31. 2-6).

[676] The upper part of Egypt, bordering upon Ethiopia, has many prefectures of towns, called nomes: among them are Menelaite, the district of Alexandria, and Mareotis of Libya. Heracleopolis is an island of the Nile, on which are the towns of Hercules, Arsinoite, and Memphite,[173] which extend to the apex of the delta. The sources of the Nile itself are believed to be undetermined, although King Juba[174] points out that it rises on a mountain of lower Mauretania, on a lake of the Nile—a theory that is substantiated by the animals there, and their method of reproduction, resembling those of other parts of the Nile. The entire delta area once contained two hundred fifty towns, according to Artemidorus. On the seacoast of Egypt lies Alexandria, one of the more illustrious cities, founded by Alexander the Great—twelve miles from the Canopic mouth, and bordering upon Lake Mareotis, which has many islands and four hundred crossings.[175] Its length, as well as its breadth, is one hundred and fifty miles.

[677] Beyond the Pelusiac mouth is Arabia, stretching to the Red Sea, which is also called the Erythraean Sea, from King Erythras, the son of Perseus and Andromeda; the name Red Sea comes from its color.[176] There is a spring along the shore which causes sheep, where they drink of it, to begin to change the color of their wool to a reddish hue. Arsinoë is a town on this sea. [678] Arabia extends as far as the perfume-bearing and opulent land.[177]

The country next to it is Syria, delimited under many names. For it is Palestine where it borders upon Arabia; and Judaea and Phoenicia; the part inland is called Damascene; extending to the south, Babylonia and also Mesopotamia, between the Tigris and Euphrates rivers; where it crosses the Taurus Mountains, Sophene; on this side of Sophene it is called Commagene; and, on the other side of Armenia, Adiabene, which was formerly called Assyria; and where it borders upon Cilicia, Antiochia. The length between

173 Martianus confuses names of towns and nomes. Cf. Pliny (5. 49).

174 King of Mauretania, restored to his throne in 29 B.C.; he was one of Pliny's most important sources on geography. On King Juba and the fabulous sources of the Nile, see Thomson, pp. 70-71, 267-69.

175 Martianus (*traiectusque quadringentos*) is misreading or misinterpreting Pliny, who says (5. 63) that the lake is "30 miles across" ($\overline{xxx}$ *traiectu*).

176 Martianus is copying Solinus (33.1) here, who drew his statements from Pliny (5. 65; 6. 107).

177 A reference to Arabia Felix. Cf. Pliny 5. 65.

Cilicia and[178] Arabia is four hundred miles, and the breadth, from Seleucia to the town of Zeugma on the Euphrates, is one hundred and seventy-five miles.

[679] Arabia begins at Ostracina, sixty-six miles from Pelusium. Next comes Apollonia, advancing along one hundred and eighty-eight miles of Palestine.[179] Across from Idumaea and Samaria, Judaea extends far and wide. The part of it that borders upon Syria is called Galilee, separated from the rest by the river Jordan,[180] which originates in the spring of Paneas. . . .[181] the second elevation of Judaea from Jerusalem; on the same side is the spring of Callirrhoe. On the west are the Essenes, who live without indulging in intercourse or any other pleasures. Somewhat farther inland is the fort of Masada, marking the border of Judaea. Decapolis is just across the border, getting its name from the number of its towns. [680] As we return along the shore of Phoenicia, there is the colony of Ptolemais. Behind Phoenicia are the Libanus and Antilibanus mountains, and in the intervening plains Mount Bargylus is situated. As Syria comes to an end, amidst the towns of Phoenicia,[182] there is Antioch, which is split by the Orontes River. Above it rises Mount Casius, from whose heights the sun is visible through the darkness at the fourth watch of the night.[183]

[681] The Euphrates River rises in Syria on a mountain called Capotes. There is also another stream, called the Marsyas. Between Syria and Parthia is the city of Palmyra,[184] and presently the Euphrates River. By a ten days' sail along this river, one reaches Seleucia, the chief city of the Parthians. The Euphrates River splits, flowing to the left into Mesopotamia and pouring into the Tigris; the right-

---

[178] The words *attingit Antiochia. Longitudo eius inter Ciliciam et,* missing in a lacuna in the archetype of the Martianus manuscripts, are supplied here from Pliny's text (5. 66-67).

[179] Pliny (5. 69) says that Apollonia marks the boundary of Palestine, 189 miles from the Arabian border.

[180] Pliny (5. 70) says that Peraea is separated from the other parts of Judaea by the Jordan River.

[181] At this point Martianus again omits some of the information given by Pliny. This information can be supplied from Pliny 5. 71-72.

[182] Pliny (5. 79) says that Syria begins again where Phoenicia comes to an end.

[183] The last watch before dawn.

[184] A flourishing city and kingdom under Queen Zenobia—destroyed in A.D. 273 by the Romans. Again, this incident has no bearing upon the date of Martianus' work, since his ultimate source was Pliny (5. 88).

hand course makes its way to Babylonia, which is the capital of Chaldea.[185]

[682] We must now return to the coast of Syria, bordering upon which is Cilicia; here are located the town of Venus, the island of Cyprus, and the river Paradisus.[186] Cilicia is joined to Pamphylia, the last town of which is Phaselis. Next comes Lycaonia, assigned to the jurisdiction of Asia; on that side where it borders on Galatia, it has fourteen towns. [683] Lycia borders upon Pamphylia. Here the Taurus range begins, looking down upon almost half of the world, which it would run through continuously if the seas did not stand against it.[187] Swerving somewhat, it passes alongside, and under various names it makes its way to the peaks of the Rhipaean Mountains; for, among other names, it is called the Niphates, the Caucasus, or the Sarpedon; it is also known as The Gates, in one place the Armenian Gates, in another the Caspian Gates . . . ; still other names of the mountains are the Hyrcanian,[188] the Coraxian, the Scythian, and the Ceraunian.

[684] In Lycia there is another mountain, Chimaera, which flashes with fires at night. Lycia once had seventy towns; now it has thirty-six. It comes to an end at a town called Telmesus. Here begins the Asiatic or Carpathian Sea and the province which is properly called Asia. To the east of it are Phrygia and Lycaonia, to the north Paphlagonia. The length of this province is four hundred and seventy miles, and the breadth three hundred miles. The other part[189] is bounded by Armenia on the east and Pontus on the north.

[685] Nearby is Caria; then comes Ionia and beyond it Aeolis. In Phrygia is the town formerly called Celaenae, the name now

185 Pliny (5. 90) says: " . . . to Babylon, which was once the capital of Chaldea."

186 No Christian influence is involved here. The name of the river comes from Pliny 5. 93. The Greek word means "park."

187 This conception of the Taurus range, as extending from the Mediterranean to the eastern Ocean and bisecting the eastern half of the world, goes back to Eratosthenes, according to Strabo (2. 5. 31). The conception was perpetuated by Strabo (68. 519); Mela 3. 7; and Pliny 5. 97-99.

188 The name *Myreanus* in the manuscripts is presumably a misreading of Pliny 5. 97: *Hyrcanius*. Pliny also supplies the name Cilician Gates, missing in Martianus' lacunary account.

189 Martianus again confuses his readers by omitting Pliny's remark (5. 102) that Agrippa divided the province of Asia into two parts. The dimensions given in the preceding sentence apply only to the first part.

changed to Apamea. Marsyas was born and died there; he gave his name to the river and competed with Apollo. That part of the river is called the Aulocrene,[190] from which the Maeander River originates. [686] Phrygia looms above the Troad; on the north is Galatia; on the south it borders upon Lycaonia,[191] Pisidia, and Mygdonia; on the east it borders upon Lycia; on the north Mysia and Caria. Then comes Mount Tmolus, abounding in saffron, and the Pactolus River. Miletos is the capital of Ionia; there is also located Colophon, famous for the oracle of Apollo Clarius. The chief city of Maeonia is Sipylus;[192] then Smyrna, best remembered for Homer;[193] around it the Meles River flows. The Hermus River cuts through the Smyrnaean plains, rising at Dorylaus, and dividing Phrygia from Caria. Near Ilium is the tomb of Memnon. Inland, above the Troad, is Teuthrania, which once was the district of the Moesi;[194] the town of Teuthrana is washed by the Caicus River. Among all the cities of Asia, Pergamum is the most famous.

[687] Bithynia marks the beginning of Pontus, and on the east, facing Thrace, it has its first inhabitants at the Sagaris River.[195] This river joins with another river, called the Gallus, from which the Galli, the priests of the Great Mother,[196] get their name. Bithynia, named after its king Bithynus, was also called Bebrycia and Mygdonia. In it is the city of Prusias, which Lake Hylas inundates; here the boy by the same name is said to have been overtaken.[197]

---

[190] "Flute Spring," so called because the contest was on the flute. Xenophon also saw fit to remark upon this legend when he came to Celaenae (*Anabasis* 1. 2). He went on to relate that Apollo flayed Marsyas and hung up his skin in a cave there, from which the springs of the river emanated.

[191] Martianus mistakenly makes Lycaonia nominative. Grotius corrected the passage from Solinus 40. 9. Kopp, in the note on this passage in his edition, wryly asks whether the intention is to correct Martianus or the manuscript readings. Furthermore, Lycia is south of Phrygia, not east; and Mysia and Caria are to the west rather than the north.

[192] Pliny (5. 117) included Sipylus among a group of cities that no longer existed in his time.

[193] Smyrna was one of seven cities that claimed to be Homer's birthplace.

[194] Pliny (5. 125) correctly names the inhabitants Mysi.

[195] Pliny (6. 4) gives the name as Sangarius and Sagiarius. Solinus (43. 1) calls it Sagaris, and Martianus adopts his spelling.

[196] Cybele. The cult of the Magna Mater became popular in the Roman world, particularly in Gaul and Africa.

[197] Hylas, a beautiful youth beloved of Hercules, was caught up by naiads

Here also is the place Libyssa, near Nicomedia, where the tomb of Hannibal is said to be located. [688] Next comes the shore of Pontus. After the mouth of the Bosporus and the Rhesus and Sagaris rivers comes the bay of Mariandynus,[198] on which are found the town of Heraclea and the harbor of Aconae, where the poisonous herb aconite grows; and the Acherusian cavern, which plunges into the depths of the earth.

[689] Next comes Paphlagonia, and behind it is Galatia. Here also is the town of Enetosa,[199] from whose citizens it is asserted that the Veneti in Italy were descended. There is the cape of Carambis, two hundred and twenty miles from the mouth of the Black Sea, and the same distance from the entrance of the Sea of Azov. There are also Mount Cytorus and the town of Eupatoria, founded by Mithridates; but after his defeat, its name was changed to Pompeiopolis.[200]

[690] Cappadocia recedes into the interior, running past both [Greater and Lesser] Armenias and Commagene on the left, and past many peoples of Asia on the right. It rises in the east toward the ridges of the Taurus Mountains, passes Lycaonia, Pisidia, and Cilicia, and going beyond the expanse of Syria Antiochia, it extends partly into Scythia.[201] Cappadocia is separated from Greater Armenia by the Euphrates River. Armenia begins at the Panedri Mountains. In Cappadocia there are many notable cities, among them Melita, founded by Semiramis, and Mazaca, called the mother of cities. It is located beneath Mount Argaeus, on whose white peak the snow does not melt even in the summer heat. On this side of Cappadocia the length of Asia is one thousand one hundred and forty miles.

---

when he went to fetch water at a spring. The story is told by Apollonius Rhodius *Argonautica* 1. 1207-72; Theocritus *Idyll* 13; Propertius *Elegies* 1. 20.

198 Martianus follows Solinus (43. 1) here. Solinus misreads Pliny (6. 4), who gives the name Mariandyni to the people and the name Heraclea to the bay and the town.

199 Both Martianus and Solinus (44. 1) misread Pliny (6. 5), who is naming the people (Eneti) here.

200 Appian (*Bella Mithridatica* 115) says that Mithridates Eupator built the city and later destroyed it, and that Pompey the Great restored it and renamed it Magnopolis.

201 Martianus follows Solinus (45. 1-2), who is loosely paraphrasing Pliny's statements (6. 24) about the territories bordering on Cappadocia.

[691] Assyria begins at Adiabene;[202] Media comes next, facing the Caspian Sea, which is girt by the Caucasus Mountains. The Caucasus has gates, which are called the Caspian Gates—abrupt cliffs further barred by iron beams to prevent outside peoples from passing through; in addition, the passage is blocked in the springtime by serpents.[203] The distance from the Gates to the Black Sea is known to be two hundred miles. The Symplegades Islands are in the Black Sea; next comes Margiana, the only vine-bearing region in that area, shut in by mountains of one thousand five hundred stadia, hard to reach because of the sandy wastelands which extend one hundred and twenty miles. Alexander the Great was attracted by the delightfulness of this region, and founded there the first city named after himself. Subsequently destroyed, it was later rebuilt by Antiochus, son of Seleucus, and given the name of his father.[204] The city is seventy-five stadia in circumference. [692] Then comes the Oxus [Amu Darya] River, which flows around Bactra, with a town and a river of this name.[205] Beyond that is Panda, a town of the Sogdiani, where Alexander founded his third Alexandria, as a memorial to the long extent of his journey; indeed, altars were set up there by Dionysus, then by Hercules, to bear witness to their immense labors in traversing those regions. The Laxates [Iaxartes, Syr Darya] River cuts through that part of the world, a river which formerly was presumed to be the Tanais [Don]. But the general Demodamas crossed the river and pointed out that the two were not the same; and beyond he set up an altar to Didymaean Apollo.

[693] The Persians and the Scythians have a common border. At the Scythian Ocean and the Caspian Sea, as our course goes toward the eastern Ocean, there are deep snows at first and then a long desert, beyond which the Man-Eaters make passage impossible. Still

---

[202] Martianus above (§ 678) said that Adiabene was formerly called Assyria. This apparent discrepancy may be traced to Pliny's reference (5. 66) to "Armenia Adiabene, formerly called Assyria" and (6. 41) "Adiabene, the beginning of the land of the Assyrians."

[203] Cf. Pliny 6. 28,30; Solinus 47. 1-2.

[204] This city was known to classical geographers as Antiocheia Margiana. Pliny (6. 47) says that Antiochus preferred to name the city after himself.

[205] Pliny (6. 52) says that the Bactrus River is a tributary of the Oxus. Solinus (49. 1) mentions both a town and a river by the name of Bactrus. The region is Bactria (now Afghan Turkestan), spanning the border of Afghanistan and Turkmenistan.

farther in are the Chinese, who drench their trees with water, so that the fleece which produces silk can be gathered. The Chinese shun contacts with other nations, but they delight in negotiating a transaction by laying out their wares without exchange of words.[206] Then comes Attacenus Bay, rivaling the land of the Hyperboreans in its blissfulness; here the inhabitants take great joy in the fact that because of the curving of their valleys they suffer from no pestilential winds.[207]

[694] Next comes India. A mistaken notion[208] has placed the Cicones in between. India begins with the Medi Mountains.[209] Stretching southward to the eastern Ocean, it is a healthy land because of the invigorating breezes of Favonius; its soil is enlivened by a second summer each year, and it produces two crops; instead of winter it suffers from etesian winds. India had five thousand towns[210] and was believed to be a third part of the world. Dionysus was the first to make his way into India and celebrate a triumph. The largest rivers in it are the Indus and the Ganges. The Ganges comes down from the Scythian Mountains. The Hypanis River is there, a raging stream which brought the march of Alexander to a halt, as the altars on its banks bear witness. The breadth of the Ganges at its widest extent is twenty miles, at its narrow point eight miles; its depth is one hundred feet. Kings rule in India, and there is a great diversity of nations and an abundance of armies and elephants. Beyond the city of Palibothra is Mount Maleus, where the shadows in winter fall to the north and in summer to the south, alternating every six months. In this locality Ursa Major is visible for only fifteen days a year. [695] The men are dark-skinned. Pygmies live in the mountainous regions; those who border on the ocean get along without kings. Women hold sway over the Pandaean race;

---

[206] On methods of producing silk and on dumb barter ascribed to the ancient Chinese, see Thomson, p. 307.

[207] An ancient Shangri-la, apparently in the region of Burma (see Pliny 6. 55).

[208] Solinus (51. 1) says that expert authorities (*gnarissimi*) locate the Cicones between the Attaci and India. Did Martianus' text of Solinus perhaps read *ignarissimi?*

[209] Solinus (52. 1) is responsible for this corruption of Pliny (6. 56): *Emodi montes.*

[210] Pliny (6. 59) says that the reporters who accompanied Alexander recorded that the area of India conquered by him (a comparatively small part) contained five thousand towns.

their former queen was a daughter of Hercules. In this region is also found the city of Nysa, sacred to Dionysus, and Mount Merus, sacred to Jupiter; whence the story originated that Dionysus sprang from the thigh of Jupiter.[211] There are also two islands remarkable for their mineral deposits and production of silver and gold; this is borne out by their names, for one is called 'Golden Island,' the other 'Silver island.' [696] All Indians beautify themselves by dyeing their hair; some with bluish, others with yellowish, dyes; they adorn themselves with jewels; they give little thought to funerals, and consider it a distinction to ride on elephants.[212]

On the island of Ceylon the elephants are larger than the Indian elephants; and the pearls are larger. This island extends seven thousand stadia in length and five thousand in breadth. It is divided by a river, and it stretches along the side of India; the journey takes seven days, as has been proved by Roman sailors. The sea there, apart from deep channels, is six paces in depth.[213] Ursa Major is not visible there, nor are the Pleiades ever seen; the moon is visible only from the eighth to the sixteenth day of each month. [697] The brightest star there is Canopus; the sun rises on the left-hand side.[214] Sailors do not observe the stars in sailing, and instead follow the flight of birds, which they carry on board. They navigate during only four months of the year. The men there are larger than any humans, have reddish hair, blue eyes, and harsh-sounding voices; they have no oral dealings with other people. They come to a river bank with foreign tradesmen and lay down their wares and make an exchange as soon as it is agreeable.[215] Their span of life is ab-

[211] *Meros* is the Greek word for "thigh."

[212] Martianus depends upon Solinus (52. 1, 4-8, 10-20) for his information about India.

[213] Pliny (6. 82) says that the sea between India and Ceylon is shallow, only six paces deep, but that in some channels the depth is so great that anchors do not reach the bottom.

[214] Martianus' digesting here destroys the point of an observation Pliny had been making. Pliny had been telling (6. 84-88) about a visit of Ceylonese ambassadors to Rome and of their surprise in finding that in northern latitudes the sun rises on the left (i.e., as the observer faces the midday sun). Martianus omits the story and has the sun rising on the left in Ceylon, which in fact occurs only during autumn and winter, since Ceylon lies near the equator.

[215] In Pliny (6. 88) these remarks are attributed to the Ceylonese ambassadors to Rome.

normally long, so that a man who dies at the age of one hundred, is not long-lived. They do not sleep in the daytime. The cost of grain does not fluctuate. Their buildings are small and insignificant. They have no knowledge of the vine, but they have plenty of fruits. [698] They worship Hercules. They select as their king a man who is gentle, elderly, and childless; if he has offspring during his reign, they depose him, because of their fear of hereditary rule. Thirty others hear a court case with him, and if there is an appeal seventy judges are appointed.[216] The king is dressed in the manner of Dionysus; and if he commits a sin he is cut off from all communication and conversation, and has his throat cut. They love to till the soil and to go hunting—that is, on tiger- and elephant-hunts. They delight in fishing, especially for turtles, whose shells they use to cover their large houses.[217]

[699] Next come the Fish-Eaters, whom Alexander forbade to eat fish. Not far away is the Island of the Sun, so called, and the red 'Couch of the Nymphs,' where all animals die because of the intensity of the heat.[218] Then the Hypanis River[219] of Carmania, where Ursa Major first becomes visible. Then there are three islands where sea serpents are found twenty cubits long. Along these shores the Red Sea is parted in two gulfs; the eastern one is called the Persian Gulf, after the inhabitants there; this gulf measures two thousand and sixty miles in circuit; the other gulf, across from it, is called the Arabian Gulf.

[700] Persia borders upon Carmania, beginning at the island of Aphrodisias; it changed its name to Parthia. The shore, which faces west, is five hundred and fifty miles long. A famous city there is Susa, in which is located the temple of Diana of Susa. Carbyle or Barbita is one hundred and thirty miles away; there are men there who bury gold deep in the ground, to keep anyone from using it. The Parthian kingdom extends nine hundred and forty-four miles.

216 Martianus, generally supposed by scholars to have been a lawyer (see above, Vol. I, pp. 16-20), is here using the technical terms for "hearing" (*cognoscere*) and "appealing" (*provocare*) a case. Pliny (6. 90) and Solinus (53. 16) do not use *cognoscere*.

217 Pliny (6. 91) was referring to the large size of the shells.

218 Martianus here ventures his own reason; Pliny (6. 97) says that they die of undetermined causes.

Martianus has jumped from Ceylon (§ 698) to Pakistan and Iran (§ 699).

219 The Hyctanis River, according to Pliny 6. 98.

Media, Parthia, and Persia, taken together, are bounded on the east by the Indus River, on the west by the Tigris, on the north by the Caucasian Taurus range, and on the south by the Red Sea. Together they extend one thousand three hundred and twenty miles in length and eight hundred and thirty miles in breadth.

[701] Babylonia[220] is the capital of the Chaldaean people; in fact, Assyria and Mesopotamia, because of the fame of that city, are known as Babylonia. The city itself is surrounded by walls sixty miles in extent, two hundred feet high, and fifty feet wide, or even more; for the Babylonian foot is three inches longer than our measure. The city is washed by the Euphrates River. The temple of Jupiter Belus, who was the discoverer of the science of the stars, is here. This city has now gone back to desert waste, its population drained by nearby Seleucia. For this very purpose the Parthians founded Ctesiphon, three miles from it; and Ctesiphon is now the capital of the kingdoms.

[702] The remote and scorched portions of Ethiopia are inhabited by Troglodytes and Fish-Eaters; the former surpass wild beasts in speed of foot, the latter swim faster than the creatures of the sea.[221] The Gorgades Islands are opposite a promontory which is called the Horn of Hesperus. It is reported that the Gorgons lived there, two days' sail from the mainland. Beyond these are the Isles of the Hesperides, which are far out to sea. There is no doubt that the Isles of the Blessed are situated to the left of Mauretania, toward the southwest. The first of these is called Membronia,[222] the second Junonia, the third Theode,[223] the fourth Capraria; and still another, Nivaria,[224] with a cloudy and frosty sky. Next come the Canary Islands, full of dogs of an immense size. All the islands are filled with birds and are heavily wooded with palms and conifers, abounding in honey, streams, and sheatfish.

[703] In my brief survey of the regions of the world, I could

[220] Pliny (6. 121) says Babylon.

[221] Pliny (6. 176) merely says that the former have remarkable speed and the latter swim like creatures of the sea.

[222] Pliny (6. 203) calls it Ombrios; Solinus (56. 15), Embrios. Martianus has moved from East to Northwest Africa.

[223] Probably a corruption of *eodem nomine* in the text of Pliny 6. 204.

[224] The name given by Solinus (56. 17). Pliny calls it Ninguaria.

not tarry, and I skipped over those areas that are insignificant; never-theless, so that it will be appreciated that I have traversed the entire sweep of lands and seas, I shall briefly indicate the total dimensions. The longitudinal distance, by direct route, from the Strait of Gibraltar to the mouth of the Sea of Azov, is 3,437 miles. The entire circuit, starting at the same point and measured along the bays that have been listed above, is 15,700 miles, and, with the addition of the Sea of Azov, 18,290 miles. The measurement of Eu-rope alone is 8,294 miles. The length of Africa is 3,794 miles; the breadth, going into the Cyrenaic region, is 910 miles. The length of Asia is 6,375 miles; the breadth, from the Ethiopian Ocean to Alex-andria on the Nile, measured through Meroë and Syene, is 1,825 miles.[225] I have set forth the dimensions of the lands and the seas which I have traversed. Now, in accordance with your request, I shall come to the subject matter of the discipline of geometry."

[704] Thus Geometry discoursed. As for the Paphian [Venus], she sat there frowning, vexed by the complicated diatribe; and, resting for support upon her attendants, she reclined wearily, the more becoming because of her languorous posture. At this point Pleasure, for some time relaxed among her beautiful girls, spoke up anxiously: "For what reason has this pitiless boor with coarse limbs completed her circuit of the earth and, after traipsing over so many mountains, rivers, seas, and crossroads, has come to relieve[226] boredom? I could believe that her limbs prickle with thorns and with shaggy hair. She is so covered with dust and so tough and peasant-like that one would naturally suppose her to be a man."

[705] At these words Mirth was aroused by the maidservants of Venus, and joked with Venus herself (who was close by), but in soft and restrained tones. Mercury, with the good-humored nod with which he usually regarded Venus, cautiously checked her, for fear

---

[225] Martianus earlier (§ 611-16) gave a different set of figures, derived from Book II of Pliny, for the over-all dimensions of the known world. The estimates here are also derived from Pliny (6. 206-7), though the figures of Pliny and Martianus differ because of manuscript corruptions.

[226] Dick considers the reading (*delere*) of the manuscripts to be corrupt, and suggests *deferre* or *ciere* as expressing the author's thought. Remigius *ad. loc.* offers *prolongare* as a gloss to *delere*.

of rebuke from the gods. But Juno Pronuba,[227] seated near, said: "It is not at all strange that Venus is readily inclined to play the wanton with such a jovial company of favorites and attendants; for she is always gay at weddings and charming when Mercury smiles at her."

At this point Geometry was ordered to get on with the subject she had promised, but to touch lightly on the main points of the discipline, so as not to vex her audience with her protracted discourse.[228] [706] She then spoke out:

"Every affirmation that I make which extends to infinity is distinguished by numbers or lines, which are acknowledged to be either corporeal or incorporeal. For the one we apprehend solely by our intellects, and the other we apprehend by sight. The first class, whch arises from the rules and reckonings of numbers, is assigned to my sister Arithmetic. The second class is the linear and demonstrable knowledge drawn from this dust;[229] begotten indeed from incorporealities, and fashioned into manifold perceptible shapes from a slight and scarcely comprehensible beginning, it is elevated even into the heavens.[230]

[707] That which is incorporeal and an invisible first beginning is shared in common by me and my sister Arithmetic. Her indivisible monad is the begetter of numbers; with me it is referred to as a mark or point because, being that it is not apprehensible, it is not divided into parts; with her the dyad produces a line; for me a line is that which is produced in length, but takes on nothing of breadth. Moreover, a surface with me extends in length and breadth but is thought of as having no depth; with her, number, which is able to refer to all figures, in groups or singly, is found to be incorporeal, unless it is applied to objects. And so the beginnings that belong to both of us are incorporeal.[231]

---

[227] An epithet of Juno as patroness of marriages. The *pronuba* in a Roman wedding protected the bride and presided over the preparations for the ceremony and in escorting the bride to her husband.

[228] A plausible pretext. Actually very little was known about Euclidean geometry in the Latin West in the first Christian millennium.

[229] I.e., the dust on the surface of the abacus.

[230] Geometry, the mathematical specialty of the Greeks, was peculiarly adapted to representing the phenomena of the observable universe.

[231] Macrobius (*Commentary on the Dream of Scipio* 1. 5. 5-7) gives a clearer explanation of the relationship between incorporeal lines and surfaces and cor-

[708] In my discipline there are two primary categories of figures: one, which is called plane, *epipedon* in Greek; the other solid, in Greek *stereon*. The beginning of the first type is called *semeion* in Greek; we call it a point (*punctum*) or mark (*signum*) in Latin; the beginning of the second type is a surface, called *epiphaneia* in Greek. A point is that whose part is nothing.[232] If there be two points, they are joined by a connecting line.[233] The line (as we call the Greek *grammē*) is length without breadth.[234] [709] Some lines are straight, *eutheiai* in Greek; others are curved into circles, *kyklikai;* others I classify according to their deviation as spiral, *helikoedeis* in Greek, and still others as curved, *kampulai* in Greek.[235] These lines terminate in points at either extremity, just as the lines themselves bound surfaces. A surface has only length

---

poreal bodies: "All physical bodies are bounded by surfaces, in which their extremities terminate. Moreover, although these termini are always around the bodies whose termini they are, they are nevertheless considered incorporeal. For wherever body is said to exist, terminus is not yet understood; the concept of terminus is distinct from that of body. Consequently the first transition from the corporeal to the incorporeal brings us to the termini of bodies; and these are the first incorporeality after corporeality, not pure nor entirely free from corporeality, for although they are naturally outside of bodies, they are not found except around bodies. Indeed, when you designate a whole body, the surface is also included in the name. But even if surfaces are not kept separate from bodies in the material realm, the intellect does distinguish between them. As the terminus of a body is the surface, so the termini of the surface are lines . . . ; and lines terminate in points. Now these are what are known as mathematical bodies, about which geometricians dispute with skill and zeal."

232 A mistranslation of Euclid's first definition: "A point is that which has no part." T. L. Heath (*The Thirteen Books of Euclid's Elements* [New York, 1956], I, 155) thinks that Martianus may have been the only one to make this mistranslation. It is evident, however, that Martianus here is digesting some Latin Euclidean primer and that the faulty definition was not originated by him. The same mistranslation is found in Cassiodorus *Expositio in psalterium* (ed. Migne, Vol. 70, col. 684).

233 Cf. Euclid's *Elements* I. Def. 3.

234 Euclid's second definition. Martianus offers a fairly close translation of most of the definitions of Book I.

235 Euclid does not classify lines, and mentions only one species, the straight line. Heron of Alexandria divides lines into straight and not straight, the latter class being subdivided into circular, spiral, and curved. Pseudo Boethius *Ars geometriae*, ed. Friedlein, 394. 1 has three species: straight, circular, and curved. On the classical divisions of lines, see Euclid *Elements*, ed. Heath, I, 159-60.

and breadth,[236] and lacks depth, as is the case with color on a body. The Greek name for surface is *epiphaneia* and, as I have said, the extremities of a surface, whether it be plane or curved, are lines.[237]

[710] A plane angle is formed on a surface by two lines meeting one another and making not one inclination to each other.[238] When the lines that contain an angle are straight, the angle is called rectilineal,[239] or in Greek *euthygrammos*. When a straight line stands upon another straight line and forms equal angles to the right and left, each of the angles is called a right angle, and the line that stands above is called a perpendicular, or in Greek *kathetos*.[240] An angle greater than a right angle is called an obtuse angle,[241] and one less than a right angle, an acute angle.[242] A boundary is that which is an extremity of anything.[243] A figure is that which is contained by any boundary or boundaries.[244] [711] A circle is a plane figure which is contained by one line; the line is called a periphery, to which, from one point lying within the circle, all straight lines are drawn equal.[245] The middle point of the circle is the center.[246] A diameter is any straight line, drawn through the center, which divides the circle into equal parts.[247] A semicircle is the figure which is contained by the diameter and the half-cir-

---

[236] Cf. Euclid *Elements* I. Def. 5.

[237] Cf. *ibid.*, 6.

[238] Cf. *ibid.*, 8. Something is omitted from Martianus' definition, the fault of Martianus or the scribe who wrote the archetype. Martianus meant to say: "A plane angle is formed on a surface by two lines meeting one another and making not one line but an inclination to each other." I indicate in brackets the words that may have been omitted from his definition: *Planus autem fit angulus in planitie duabus lineis se invicem tangentibus et non unam [lineam] facientibus [sed] ad alterutram inclinationem.* Cf. the definition of pseudo Euclid *Ars geometriae* 374. 10: *Planus angulus est duorum linearum in plano invicem sese tangentium et non in directo iacentium ad alterutram conclusio.*

[239] Cf. Euclid *Elements* I. Def. 9.

[240] Cf. *ibid.*, 10.

[241] Cf. *ibid.*, 11.

[242] Cf. *ibid.*, 12.

[243] Cf. *ibid.*, 13.

[244] Cf. *ibid.*, 14.

[245] Cf. *ibid.*, 15.

[246] Cf. *ibid.*, 16.

[247] Cf. *ibid.*, 17.

cumference which that same diameter cuts off.[248] Three straight lines lying in different directions form a triangle, four, a tetragon; and many, a polygon.

These are called plane figures, of which there are three kinds: the first is contained by straight lines, and is called by the Greeks *euthygrammos;* the second is contained by curved lines, and they call it *kampulogrammos;* the third, which is fashioned from both straight and curved lines, they call a mixed (*mixton*) figure.[249]

[712] Rectilinear figures are called trilateral, quadrilateral, or multilateral.[250] A trilateral figure has three forms: a triangle is either equilateral, having three sides of equal length; or isosceles, having two of its three sides of equal length—two equal legs, as it were, and hence it is called 'equal-legged'; or scalene, having three sides of unequal length.[251] Quadrilateral figures have five different forms: first, the square is contained by four straight lines of equal length and is right-angled; the second is right-angled but not equilateral, and is called oblong; the third is equilateral but not right-angled, and is called a rhombus; a figure that has its opposite sides and angles equal to one another and yet does not have equal sides nor right angles is called a rhomboid; and any other quadrilateral figure not having one of these forms is called a trapezium.[252] Parallel lines are straight lines which lie in the same plane and, if produced to infinity, never meet.[253] Our discussion has been concerned with quadrilateral figures whose resemblance to multilateral figures can teach us about the latter. These include pentagons, hexagons, and others of a rectilineal nature.

[713] Next comes the second kind of figures, those that are formed by curved lines; the Greek name for these figures is *kampulogrammos*. They are of two types: the first deals with propositions involving perfect circles. Now a circle is 'perfect' if all lines produced to its circumference from a central point, in all directions, are of equal length. The second type shows the different kinds of

[248] Cf. *ibid.,* 18.

[249] On "mixed" lines see Euclid *Elements,* ed. Heath, I, 159, 162.

[250] Cf. Euclid *Elements* I. Def. 19. In this translation the Greek words which Martianus uses are rendered by their Latin-based English equivalents.

[251] Cf. *ibid.,* 20.

[252] Cf. *ibid.,* 22.

[253] Cf. *ibid.,* 23.

elliptical figures. [714] Then there is a third kind of plane figures, which is called 'mixed': these figures are contained partly by curved lines and partly by straight lines, as in the case of a semicircle, whose curved line forms the circular part and whose straight line, as I have said, is called the diameter, or *distermina* in Latin. If the diameter is found in a complete circle, it extends through its center to the circumference on either side.

[715] Of demonstrations involving these kinds of plane figures, some have to do with problems (*ergastica*), others with theorems (*apodictica*).[254] Those that apply to problems contain instructions for constructing any sort of figure; those that apply to theorems present proofs of what the theorems state. The former class have Greek designations: first, *tmēmatikos;* second, *sustatikos;* third, *anagraphos;* fourth, *engraphos;* fifth, *perigraphos;* sixth, *parembolikos;* seventh, *proseuretikos. Tmēmatikos* deals with the steps involved in cutting off lines in the required manner. *Sustatikos* demonstrates the steps involved in joining given lines. *Anagraphos* is the term applying to the steps in describing a prescribed figure. *Engraphos* shows the steps by which we enclose a prescribed triangle or other figure within a given circle. *Perigraphos* is the term applying to the demonstration of circumscribing a given circle with a square or other figure. *Parembolikos* has to do with inscribing a given triangle within, for example, a given quadrilateral so that the spaces[255] of the quadrilateral may increase without changing the figure. *Proseuretikos* is the term for finding, for instance—given two lines of unequal length—a third line which is as much smaller than one of the two lines as it is larger than the other. These are the general terms for figures applying to problems.[256]

[716] We may now touch lightly upon the terminology of figures applying to theorems, inasmuch as I have those in common with my sister, Dialectic, whom you have already heard. All these figures involve five steps, which are known by their Greek names: first, *protasis;* second, *diorismos;* third, *kataskeuē;* fourth, *apodeixis;* fifth

---

[254] On the two types of enunciation, see Euclid *Elements,* ed. Heath, I, 126-27.
[255] Martianus' term *spatia* is glossed as *latera* [sides] by Remigius *ad loc.*
[256] Martianus' list of terms and their definitions does not appear elsewhere in the extant ancient mathematical literature.

sumperasma.[257] We can explain these in Latin as follows: the first is the enunciation of the proposition (*schematis propositum*); the second is the definition (*determinatio*) of what is sought (*questionis*); the third is the construction (*dispositio argumentorum*); the fourth is the demonstration and proof (*demonstratio, comprobatio*); and the last is the conclusion (*conclusio*). So much for the classifications of plane figures. Now let us return to the components of theorems; to be sure, these components are lines and angles.

[717] Angles are of three different kinds: an angle is either upright, narrow, or broad. An upright angle is a right angle and is always the same; a narrow angle is an acute angle, and is always variable; a broad angle is an obtuse angle, and is likewise variable. For if an angle is broader than a right angle, whether much or slightly broader, it will still be obtuse; and when you change the degree of the angle, it remains in the same category, because its variability comes from the lines, when they form larger or smaller obtuse angles.

There are four terms that are used in proportions: first, *isotēs* [equal]; second, *homologos* [corresponding]; third, *analogos* [analogous]; fourth, *alogos* [disproprotional]. The ratio is equal when two lines of equal length bear a double[258] or equal[259] relationship to a third line; a corresponding ratio, when the lines compared are in agreement; an analogous ratio, when the line that is half as long as another is twice as long as a third; and lines are disproportional when they are neither equal nor bear any other ratio—half, third, double, triple—to each other.[260]

[718] All magnitudes are said to be commensurable or incommensurable. A magnitude is commensurable if it is the first to be considered or is commensurable with another line when they are

[257] The formal divisions of a proposition. These terms are listed and defined by Proclus in his *Commentary on Euclid*, ed. Friedlein, pp. 221-22, Defs. 13 and 14. Proclus includes after *protasis* another term, *ekthesis*, meaning "setting out," or "marking off what is given." On these formal divisions, see Euclid *Elements*, ed. Heath, I, 129-31.

[258] Taken separately.

[259] Taken together.

[260] The theory of proportions is set forth in Book V of Euclid's *Elements*. On proportional magnitudes in Euclid and other classical writers, see Euclid *Elements*, ed. Heath, II, 112-13, 134.

measured by a common measure.[261] Whatever is proportional is said
to be commensurable. A given line, though it has not been compared, nevertheless because it is still not incommensurable when
compared with another and has something which, in itself and by
itself, performs rationally, is called commensurable. A line becomes
incommensurable if it does not have any common measure when
compared with another line. [719] Lines which are proportional
to each other we call commensurable; and those that are not proportional, incommensurable. Measure is not alone responsible for
commensurability; power also causes lines to be commensurable, and
they are said to be 'commensurable in power.'[262] Lines commensurable in measure are called commensurable. All lines that are
commensurable neither in measure nor in power are called incommensurable.

[720] Of these there are thirteen irrational straight lines: the
first is called medial; the second, binomial (which is divided into
six species: first binomial, second binomial, third binomial, and so
on); the third kind is called the first bimedial, and corresponding
to the one above; the fourth is called the second bimedial; the fifth
is called the major; the sixth is called 'the side of a rational plus
a medial area'; the seventh is called 'the side of the sum of two medial
areas'; the eighth is called the apotome, and there are six species
of this (they are called first, second, third, and so on, as above);
the ninth is called the first apotome of a medial straight line; the
tenth, the second apotome of a medial straight line; the eleventh
is called the minor; the twelfth is called 'producing with a rational
area a medial whole'; and the thirteenth is called 'producing with
a medial area a medial whole.'[263] All these irrational lines, mingled
with other lines, either bear their own virtues or receive those of
others, and by various relationships demonstrate definite measures
of space, which the Greeks call *chōria* [areas]. Let this suffice
about plane figures.

[721] Now let us consider solid figures, which are called *sterea*.

[261] Cf. Euclid *Elements* 10. Def. 1.

[262] Martianus uses the Greek expression *dynamei symmetroi*, which Heath, in
his edition of Euclid's *Elements*, III, 11, prefers to translate as "commensurable
in square," stating his reasons.

[263] On the thirteen irrational lines, see Euclid *Elements* 10. Prop. 3 (ed. Heath,
III, 243).

A solid is a figure which has length, breadth, and depth.[264] Its extremities consist of surfaces,[265] just as the extremities of surfaces consist of lines. Solid figures are based upon surfaces which are plane figures: a pyramid is imposed upon a triangle lying beneath; a cone or a cylinder upon a circle; a cube upon a square, and so on. [722] The sphere, containing all other figures within itself, consists of circles into which it is resolved. Solidity brings into being the basic figures: those which the Greeks call pyramids; also the prism, the sections of which are similar; also, likewise, the cube, the cone, the cylinder, and the sphere. To these are added the 'noble' figures fashioned from them: the octahedron, the dodecahedron, and the icosahedron.[266]

To enable us to demonstrate these matters as a whole in proper order in the dust of our abacus, the following must be postulated at the start: from any point to any point to draw a straight line; to produce a finite straight line continuously in a straight line; to describe a circle with any center and any distance; that all right angles are equal to each other; to produce any finite straight line of any length; if a straight line falling on two straight lines should make the two interior angles on the same side less than two right angles, then the two straight lines meet on that side on which the angles are less than two right angles.[267] [723] There are three common notions: things which are equal to the same thing are equal to each other; if equals be added to equals, the wholes are equal; if equals be subtracted from equals, the remainders are equal."[268]

[724] When Geometry saw that these matters were accepted,

---

[264] Cf. Euclid *Elements* 11. Def. 1.

[265] Cf. *ibid.*, 2.

[266] Primary bodies, according to Plato *Timaeus* 55b-c. See the notes in the F. M. Cornford edition, and the extended discussion of Plato's physics in Friedländer, *Plato*, Vol. I, chap. XIV.

[267] These are, basically, the five postulates of Book I of Euclid's *Elements*. However, Martianus expresses them as six postulates; his fifth appears to be a restatement of his (and Euclid's) second postulate; his final postulate differs from Euclid's fifth in the omission of the important phrase "if produced indefinitely" between the words "line" and "meet."

[268] These are the first three axioms of Book I of Euclid's *Elements*. Euclid has five axioms here. The first three are accepted as genuine, the other two ("congruent figures are equal" and "the whole is greater than a part") are omitted by Heron of Alexandria, as well as by Martianus, and are regarded as of doubtful authenticity. See Euclid *Elements*, ed. Heath, I, 62.

she drew a straight line upon the abacus and asked: "How does one go about constructing an equilateral triangle upon a given finite straight line?" When the learned company,[269] who were standing around in a close crowd, realized that she was intending to construct the first proposition of Euclid, they immediately began to break out in acclaim and applause of Euclid. Geometry herself was greatly pleased by this ovation, realizing that she too was being extolled and elevated by the recognition accorded to one of her followers; and she quickly snatched from his hands his books, which she by chance observed him carrying, and she offered them to Jove and the heavenly company as texts for further teaching and instruction. Through this performance of hers she was acknowledged to be the most learned and generous of all the bridesmaids.

[269] Martianus calls them *philosophi*, a term which was used in relation to all kinds of wisdom, including poetry; see Ernst Robert Curtius, *European Literature and the Latin Middle Ages*, trans. from the German by Willard R. Trask (New York, 1953), chap. XI, esp. pp. 209-10.

BOOK VII

Arithmetic

[725] At the completion of this expert survey of the earth in its full dimensions, Innuba [Pallas]—she who instills in men's hearts a love for the learned arts—requested that the abacus be kept in place and that its greenish powdery surface be kept ready for the drawing of figures. One of the handmaidens[1] was ordered to summon the sister[2] of the learned lady who had determined the measurements of the world. She went off without delay. Thereupon, heavenly Pleasure[3] once again whispered in the Cyllenian's [Mercury's] ethereal ear: "While these erudite bridesmaids are impressing the celestial company, and winning the approval of Pallas Athene, will you in your languorous mood put off the pleasures of love you yearned for, and let the prize slip from you when it is in your grasp? Do serious discourses dull the senses of a listless groom? The attractive maiden observes your indifferent manner. Have you no thought for the nuptial couch; does Venus' son Cupid not entice you; will you not seize my pleasures? Are these the rules of Hymen? Pallas is usurping[4] a rite that belongs to Venus. Far more appropriate for sweet Wantonness to glow in the marriage chamber! The celibate Tritonian [Minerva] depresses the nuptial spirits; she comes to a marriage ill-disposed to the bride. Call for Dione![5] Far better for you to pay homage to Priapus!"[6]

[726] Mercury could scarcely contain his amusement at these remarks. Yet, in order not to appear ill-mannered or ill-matched in wit, he replied in a genial whisper:

[1] Of the two attendants of the bride, Philosophy and Paedia, described above (§§ 578-79), Paedia (Learning) is the one referred to here.

[2] Arithmetic.

[3] Handmaiden of Venus, according to Remigius.

[4] Martianus: *sibi vindicat;* cf. Lucan *Pharsalia* 6. 73: *sibi vindicat.*

[5] Mother of Venus by union with Jupiter.

[6] Priapus was a minor fertility god.

"Pleasure, in spite of your chiding and importuning me to consummate my marriage, these bridesmaids shall display their learning in their brief discourses. At the end I will not in embarrassment dawdle or delay the approach to the marriage bed. And whatever Venus' Pleasure will bring to our love, I will not deny to you. Let Philology take pleasure in violent passion and let her give me the lilies and roses of her little breasts; and let not desire of marital passion gnaw at us and, convulsed with black bile, tear at our hair."[7]

[727] Pleasure beamed, on hearing these words, and with a lighter step than usual returned to Venus' side and told her everything. And Venus, with a wanton charm, a blush stealing over her cheeks, almost disclosed to the gods the whisperings of Pleasure. Then, glancing at Maia's son [Mercury], with a coy twinkle in her languid eyes, she gave him a seductive nod. But Saturnia [Juno], standing near, reprimanded Venus with a stare of reproof.[8]

[728] Meanwhile Paedia, who had stepped out a moment earlier, returned, accompanied by a lady of striking appearance.[9] She had a stateliness of bearing that reflected her pristine origin, antedating the birth of the Thunderer himself,[10] and shone in the light of her countenance. Certain strange manifestations on her head gave her an awesome appearance. For from her brow a single, scarcely perceptible, whitish ray appeared, and from it emanated[11] another ray, the projection of a line, as it were, from its original source.[12] Then came a third and a fourth ray, and on to a ninth and a

[7] The drift of thought in these lines must be conjectured. The text is badly corrupted.

[8] Remigius observes that Hermaphroditus was the offspring of an earlier affair between Venus and Mercury, and Juno did not want a second monster to be produced.

[9] Arithmetic.

[10] Jupiter, as we shall see in § 731, is represented by the monad, the beginning of all numbers.

[11] *defluebat*. See § 732, and the note thereon, on the use of this verb to denote the extension of a line from a point.

[12] The first ray is intended to represent the monad, perceptible to the intellect but not the senses, itself not a number but the beginning of numbers. The second ray represents the dyad, or a line, which is the first extension of the indivisible monad or point.

tenth, the first decad[13]—all radiating from her glorious and majestic brow in double and triple combinations.[14] But even as the rays emanated in boundless profusion, so they gradually diminished again in a remarkable way, and she reduced them to one.[15] [729] A robe concealing the operations of universal Nature covered her manifold and intricate undergarment.[16] The maiden's fingers vibrated with a speed that blurred the vision. Shortly after entering the room, Arithmetic, by way of greeting Jove, made a finger calculation and expressed the numbers seven hundred, ten, and seven. Philosophy, who was standing next to the Tritonian [Pallas], asked her what Arithmetic intended by such a sum; and Pallas replied that she had greeted Jove by his very own name.[17]

Then the ray that first protruded from her forehead, jutting straight outward, bathed the head of Jove in its luster. At this strange apparition of countless rays suddenly proliferating, some of the earthly and sylvan deities, fancying that Arithmetic was sprouting heads like the Hydra, glanced at Hercules.[18] And as the earthborn deities began whispering to each other, the swarthy boy[19] was directed to enjoin them to silence. Pythagoras, who was standing among the philosophers, followed after the lady as far as the abacus, and when she was ready to expound her discipline,

[13] Sacred, according to the Pythagoreans, because it embraces all numbers.

[14] This would not apply to the number seven, which is not divisible; nor, when doubled, does it produce a number under ten.

[15] Remigius explains: "As numbers increase to infinity, so they decrease again to unity."

[16] The robe perhaps symbolizes pure numbers; and the undergarment, numbers applied to corporeal objects.

[17] There have been several efforts, medieval and modern, to explain the connection between the number and the name. Perhaps the best explanation is offered by Remigius, who points out that according to the Greeks, the name of Jupiter, was H $APXH$ [The Beginning]. The numerical values of the Greek letters are: $H = 8$; $A = 1$; $P = 100$; $X = 600$; $H = 8$; a total of 717.

[18] Hercules was foiled in his first efforts to slay the Hydra of Lerna, because, as he cut off each of her heads, two sprang up in its place. He succeeded in destroying her by burning her tentacle heads and burying her main, immortal head.

[19] Introduced above (see § 90, and the note thereon) and here without mention of his name. The boy is Harpocrates, the Egyptian sun god Horus as a youth, generally represented with a finger pressed to his lips. The Greeks and Romans regarded him as a god of silence.

he stood by her side and graciously held a bright torch before her. Then Arithmetic, before she was ordered to reveal what she was bringing, began to speak as follows:

[730] "Heaven knows me, and I am recognized in the mundane realms, which I have produced.[20] I do not consider it beneath my dignity to come to your assembly, though I reckon every one of you as sprouting from my branches. And I ask you in particular, Jupiter, the first of all to spring forth, to acknowledge me as the source of your unique and primordial nature. And the service that I perform for Mercury will not cause you to despise me, the mother of all of you, for I am eager to prove to you the original stock of your mysterious lineage. While I am engaged in such matters on earth, let the host of heavenly bodies recognize the venerable author of their multitude.

[731] Before all things, let the monad be called sacred; numbers coming after it and associated with it have taught that before everything the monad is the original quickener. For if form is an accident of anything that exists, and if that which numbers is prior to that which is to be numbered, it is fitting to venerate the monad before that which has been called 'the beginning.' Then too, I shall not neglect to point out to those who examine the matter that because the monad is unity, it alone is self-sufficient: from it other things are generated; it alone is the seminal force[21] of all numbers; it alone is the measure and cause of increases and the extent of losses. The monad is everywhere a part, and everywhere the whole; it endures through all things. For that which is prior to things existing and which does not disappear when they pass away, must be eternal. Rightly is the monad called Father of All, and Jove—a conclusion corroborated by the causative force of its ideal and intelligible

[20] According to Pythagorean concepts, numbers are the key to the universe; they underlie physical objects on earth, and the motions of the celestial bodies conform to mathematical laws.

[21] On the possible connection between the monad as seed principle and the Stoic doctrine of divine fire, see Nicomachus of Gerasa *Introduction to Arithmetic*, tr. into English by M. L. D'Ooge, with studies in Greek arithmetic by F. E. Robbins and L. C. Karpinski (Ann Arbor, 1938), p. 96. Nicomachus' *Introduction* and Euclid's *Elements* 7-60 were the two ultimate sources for Martianus' arithmetic. Readers seeking background information on Greek arithmetic are referred to Nicomachus, tr. D'Ooge, and Euclid *Elements*, ed. Heath.

form.[22] To cite examples: there is one God, one universe, one sun, a single moon; even the elements are regarded as individual. Aristotle, one of my disciples, from the fact that the monad alone is itself and always wishes itself to be sought after, declares that it has been called Desire; for it desires itself, if indeed it has nothing beyond; it is not subject to elevation or union; it directs its yearnings toward itself. Some have called the monad Concord, others Piety or Friendship, because it is so compact that it is not cut into parts. But more properly it is called Jupiter, because it is the head and father of the gods.[23]

[732] When the monad has extended itself[24] in any direction, although an indivisible[25] line is produced without any suggestion of breadth, it forms the dyad. The dyad, because it is the first offspring, is called Genesis by some. Because between it and the monad the first union and partnership occurs, it is called Juno or Wife or Sister of the monad. The dyad is also capable of mediacy, for it has a share in good and evil. Discord and adversity originate from it, inasmuch as it is the first to be able to be separated from that which clings to it. Among the good things, it is Justice, since it rejoices in two equals, of equal weight; and it is Union,

---

[22] On the identification of the monad with the mind of God and on the ideal world as a pattern of God's thought, see Nicomachus, tr. D'Ooge, pp. 96-97.

[23] The discussion here of the attributes and epithets of the monad is followed by a similar treatment of each of the numbers of the sacred Pythagorean decad. Pythagoreans, from the time of the master, were absorbed in the mystic properties and associations of the numbers of the first decad, inasmuch as all numbers were a repetition of these and numbers were believed to be the key to creation. Greek treatises on arithmetic have two divisions: the mystical treatment of numbers, as in Martianus' opening discussion (§§ 731-42); and the scientific treatment of number theory, as in the remainder of Martianus' discussion (§§ 743-801). It is to Martianus' credit that he gives far greater attention to the properties than to the mysteries of number. The mystical treatment of numbers is called "arithmology." See F. E. Robbins in Nicomachus, tr. D'Ooge, pp. 90-92, *et passim*. On the attributes and epithets of each of the numbers of the Pythagorean decad, see *ibid.*, chap. VII.

[24] The Latin verb Martianus uses here is *defluxerit*. Macrobius *Commentary on the Dream of Scipio* 1. 6. 18 uses *defluxit* in this very sense. Favonius Eulogius *Disputatio de Somnio Scipionis* 15.3, referring to the dyad, says: *defluere in lineam*.

[25] I.e., one-dimensional.

since the two extremes, which contain the means, take their position on either side. Number takes its beginning from the dyad;[26] and it is conceptual embodiment and the evidence of first motion.[27] It is also the mother of the elements; for from the dyad the number of the four elements springs; and it is the first manifestation of equality.

[733] The triad is the first odd number, and must be regarded as perfect. It is the first to admit of a beginning, a middle, and an end,[28] and it associates a central mean with the initial and final extremes, with equal intervals of separation. The number three represents the Fates and the sisterly Graces; and a certain Virgin who, as they say, 'is the ruler of heaven and hell,'[29] is identified with this number. Further indication of its perfection is that the number begets the perfect numbers six and nine.[30] Another token of its respect is that prayers and libations are offered three times. Harmony comprises three concords: the octave, the fifth, and the fourth.[31] Concepts of time have three aspects; consequently, divinations are expressed in threes. The number three also represents the perfection of the universe: the monad refers to the Divine Creator; the dyad to generating matter; and the triad to ideal forms. The soul has a threefold division into reason, emotion, and appetite.[32]

[734] What shall I say about the tetrad? In it is found the sure perfection of a solid body; for it comprises length, [breadth],[33]

[26] On the monad as the beginning of numbers but not itself a number, and the dyad as the first number, see Nicomachus, tr. D'Ooge, p. 116.

[27] The line, represented by the dyad, is the extension of the moving point, represented by the monad.

[28] Cf. § 105.

[29] The *dea triformis* [threefold goddess]: Diana (earth), Luna (heavens), and Hecate (underworld). The quotation is from Vergil *Aeneid* 6. 247.

[30] Six is a "perfect" number in the Euclidean sense, because it is equal to the sum of its parts. See below, n. 42, and Nicomachus, tr. D'Ooge, pp. 52, 209-12. Martianus' calling three, eight, and nine perfect numbers is an indication of the reverence in which they were held.

[31] The octave consists of a fourth and a fifth.

[32] Martianus' discussion of the triad resembles that of Macrobius *Commentary* 1. 6. 42-43.

[33] The number four represents the most elemental solid body, the tetrahedron. The inadvertent omission of the word *latitudine* from the Martianus manuscripts is revealed when we compare the text of the passage borrowed by Isidore in his *Liber de numeris* 183a. See C. Leonardi, "Intorno al 'Liber de numeris' di Isidore di Siviglia," *Bullettino dell' Istituto storico italiano per il medio evo e Archivio muratoriano*, LXVIII (1956), 225, 228.

and depth. The full decad is the sum of four numbers, arranged in order: namely, one, two, three, and four. Likewise, the hecatontad is the sum of four decads: namely, ten, twenty, thirty, and forty— which make a hundred. Also four centenary numbers produce a thousand: namely, one hundred, two hundred, three hundred, and four hundred. Ten thousand and other multiples are completed in a similar manner. Moreover, it is plain to see that there are four seasons of the year, four principal regions of the sky, and four primary elements. Then, too, are there not four ages of man, four vices, and four virtues?[34] The number four is assigned to the Cyllenian himself, for he alone is regarded as the fourfold god.[35]

[735] The pentad comes next, the number assigned to the universe. This identification is reasonable, for after the four elements, the universe is a fifth body of a different nature.[36] The number represents natural union, for it is the sum of numbers of each sex, for three is considered a male number, and two a female number.[37] The number five is also called a recurrent number: whether it is joined with other odd numbers or with its own kind, it is always cropping up. For the product of five times five is twenty-five; five times three is fifteen; five times seven is thirty-five, and five times nine is forty-five.[38] Then, too, there are five zones of the earth. In man there are five senses; the same number of classes of creatures inhabit the earth:[39] humans, quadrupeds, reptiles, fish,

[34] Remigius lists the regions of the sky as north, east, south, and west; and the four ages of man as infancy, boyhood, adolescence, and young manhood, or, according to some authorities, old age. He lists the four cardinal virtues as prudence, temperance, fortitude, and justice, and says that the four vices are the contraries of the four virtues.

[35] Cf. Plutarch *Quaestionum convivialium* 9. 3. 738; Macrobius *Saturnalia* 1. 19. 15.

[36] To the four Empedoclean elements (earth, air, fire, and water), Aristotle added a fifth, confined to the celestial regions.

[37] Pythagoreans called the pentad the "marriage number" for this reason. See Nicomachus, tr. D'Ooge, p. 106.

[38] On the treatment of five as a recurrent number by ancient writers on arithmetic, see *ibid.*, p. 257 and note 1. See also Martianus, § 742.

[39] The reading of the extant text does not make sense: *totidemque habitatores mundi generibus*. The text of the passage in Isidore of Seville *De numeris* 184b, copied by him from his manuscript of Martianus, reads: *totidem habitatorum mundi genera*. See Leonardi, p. 219.

and birds.[40] Does anyone deny that the number five is also the diameter? For the perfection and circle of the decad is bisected by the semicircle of this number.[41]

[736] Who would doubt that the number six is perfect and proportional, since it is the sum of its parts?[42] For six contains within itself a sixth of itself, which is one; a third, which is two; and a half, which is three. There are six natural properties without which bodies cannot exist: magnitude, color, shape, space,[43] rest, and motion. There are also six different kinds of motion: forward, backward, to the right and the left, upward, and downward. There is also that eternal motion of the circle.[44] The number six is assigned to Venus,[45] for it is formed of a union of the sexes: that is, of the triad, which is male because it is an odd number, and the dyad, which is female because it is even; and twice three makes six. Moreover, a solid quadrate figure [cube] has six surfaces.[46] There are six tones in a complete octave; that is, five full tones and two semitones.[47]

[737] The number six, in combination with the first motion—that is, the dyad—produces the number twelve. Between six and twelve are found two means; namely, eight and nine. One of these, nine, has

[40] The association of the pentad with terrestrial and celestial zones and with the senses is regular in arithmological treatises. I do not recall any other writer's associating the number with the classes of creatures.

[41] Martianus and Remigius (in his comment on this passage he notes: "a diameter is half of ten or half of a circle") are both confused in supposing the circumference of a circle to be twice the diameter. Martianus' blunder misled John Scot Eriugena into supposing the earth's circumference to be twice its diameter when he attempted to explain Eratosthenes' method of measuring the globe in *De divisione naturae* 3. 33 (Migne, *PL*, Vol. CXXII, cols. 716-18). See also above, Vol. I, p. 135.

[42] Euclid (*Elements* 7. Def. 22) defines a perfect number as one that is equal to the sum of its own parts. Cf. Nicomachus 1. 16. 2; Theon, ed. Hiller, p. 45, lines 10-11; Macrobius *Commentary* 1. 6. 12-13. And see Heath, *History*, I, 74-75. The next perfect number is 28.

[43] Martianus: *intervallum;* cf. Remigius: *spatium corporis in longitudine, latitudine, altitudine.*

[44] Plato himself was probably responsible for the confusion in assigning the number of motions to both six and seven. He refers in the *Timaeus* 43 b to six motions, and in 34a to seven motions.

[45] Venus, representing the combination of two and three, was assigned to both six and five.

[46] The cube often is regarded as the perfect rectilinear figure.

[47] Two tetrachords of 2½ tones each plus one tone between them.

the distinction of my name and my rule;[48] for it is known as the arithmetic mean. This number is exceeded by twelve by the same amount that it exceeds the number six—that is, by three. The other number, eight, is a harmonic mean.[49] For twelve exceeds eight by the same part that eight exceeds six; that is, by a third; for a third of six is two, and a third of twelve is four. These numbers are also arranged in a geometric proportion.[50] The means—that is, eight and nine —can be combined; also the extremes, six and twelve; in both cases the product is seventy-two. Similarly, with larger numbers the means and the extremes produce identical products when they are multiplied by the number six. For six times 72 makes 432; eight times 72 makes 576; nine times 72 makes 648; and twelve times 72 makes 864. Multiplying the means produces numbers that are equal to the product of the extremes. It has been demonstrated that the number six is the source and origin of the musical concords: the ratio of six to twelve represents the interval of the octave; six to nine is the interval of the fifth; and six to eight is the interval of the fourth. For this reason Venus is said to be the mother of Harmony.[51] The number six, coupled with the square number, or solid quaternary,[52] marks the number of hours of the day and night; for four times six is 24.

[738] What reasons should I recount for your veneration, O Heptad?[53] Since you fashion the works of nature without the

[48] The "rule of nine," referred to in § 103.

[49] The numbers 6, 9, 12 are in arithmetic progression; and 6, 8, 12 are in harmonic progression. On the three proportions—arithmetic, geometric, and harmonic—see Heath, *History*, I, 85-86; and Nicomachus, tr. D'Ooge, pp. 62 f.

[50] I.e., the series 12, 9, 8, 6, where the first term is to the third term as the second is to the fourth. See *ibid.*, pp. 285-86.

[51] Venus' daughter by Mars.

[52] That is, there are four angles in the first square (plane) number, and four faces and four vertices in the first solid number—a pyramid with a triangular base. On Pythagorean doctrines on figurate numbers, see Nicomachus, tr. D'Ooge, pp. 54-60; and Heath, *History*, I, 76-84.

[53] The number seven usually receives the greatest attention of all the numbers in the Pythagorean decad. Macrobius, in his arithmological excursus (*Commentary* 1. 5-6), devotes more attention to seven (1. 6. 6-81) than to all the other numbers of the decad combined. F. E. Robbins (Nicomachus, tr. D'Ooge, p. 106) feels that the reason for this veneration was the supposed connection with lunar periods and with periodicity in gestation and the ages of man. W. H. Roscher has made exhaustive studies on this number in ancient arithmological

contacts of procreation, you have been given among the deities the name of Minerva. For all [other] numbers found within the decad either beget other numbers or are begotten and produced by other numbers:[54] the number six and the number eight are merely begotten; the number four both begets and is begotten; but because the heptad begets no number it is called virgin. Because it springs from no number, it is called Minerva, and because it is the sum of masculine and feminine numbers, it is named for the mannish goddess Pallas; for seven consists of three and four. It is the number that marks the phases of the moon: first there is the crescent moon, in Greek *menoeide;* then the half-moon, or *dichotomon;* then the gibbous, in Greek *amphikurtos,* greater than the half-moon; then the full moon, called *panselenos.* Then the three phases of the waning moon are repeated.[55] This number also marks the orbit of the moon; for one, two, three, four, five, six, and seven total 28.[56] Moreover, there are seven circles,[57] seven planets, seven days,[58] and seven transmutations of the elements. For out of shapeless matter fire comes first; then from fire, air; from air, water; and from water, earth; likewise, in ascending order, from earth comes water; from water, air; and from air, fire; there is no going beyond fire into imperceptible matter.

[739] Is it not demonstrable that man's nature is governed by the number seven? Seven-month parturitions are the first to produce

---

and medical literature; see his *Hebdomadenlehren der griechischen Philosophie und Ärzte* (Leipzig, 1906).

[54] Seven is the only number that is both prime and has no factor in common with other numbers within the decad; hence its identification with Athena (Minerva)—who, according to Greek mythology, sprang fully armed from the brow of Jupiter (was not begotten) and remained a virgin (did not beget).

[55] Cf. § 864.

[56] By approximate reckoning a lunar month is 28 days. Martianus later notes (§ 865) that a sidereal month is 27⅓ days and a synodic month 29½ days.

[57] The celestial circles are usually associated with the number five: two arctic and two tropic circles, and the equator. Aulus Gellius (*Attic Nights* 3. 10. 3) informs us that Varro counted seven celestial circles, including two polar circles that touch the extremities of the celestial axis and are too minute to be represented on an armillary sphere. Since Varro appears to have had the dominant influence upon Martianus' astronomical doctrines, it is reasonable to suppose that Martianus is following a Varronian tradition here.

[58] In the week. The Emperor Constantine, in A.D. 321, made the observance of the Judaeo-Christian seven-day week official throughout the Empire.

fully developed offspring. Further proof is that man has seven apertures in the head, which provide him with his senses: two eyes, two
ears, two nostrils, and one mouth.[59] Then teeth appear in infants in
the seventh month, and the second teeth come in the seventh year.
The second hebdomad of years brings puberty and the faculty of
producing offspring; the third brings a beard to the cheeks;[60] the
fourth hebdomad marks the end of increase in stature; the fifth
marks the full flowering of the young manhood.[61] Nature has concealed seven vital organs within the body: the tongue, the heart, the
lung, the spleen, the liver, and the two kidneys. Likewise there are
seven parts of the body over-all: the head (including the neck), the
chest, the belly, two hands, and two feet. And there are seven stars
at the top of the celestial axis.[62]

[740] The number eight is the first cube and is a perfect number,
assigned to Vulcan.[63] It originates in the first motion—that is, the
dyad, which is Juno. For the dyad multiplied by the dyad makes the
tetrad, and twice the tetrad makes the octad. A perfect number is
one that is covered by the number six; for every cube has six
sides.[64] Moreover, the sum of eight is completed by consecutive odd
numbers; for the first odd number is three; the second, five; together

---

[59] Martianus' associations of the number seven with the universe and the human body often correspond to those of Macrobius *Commentary* 1. 6. 55-80; but
there is no reason to suppose that either read the other's work. The great store
of close parallels, often verbatim copying, found in Pythagorean writings on the
number seven, have been carefully studied by Roscher (see § 738 and n. 53) and
by Robbins, "The Tradition of Greek Arithmology," *Classical Philology*, XVI
(1921), 97-123. Varro may have had a great deal to do with the prominence
given to this number in late Latin literature. According to Aulus Gellius *Attic
Nights* 3. 10. 3, he wrote a long work on this number.

[60] How contrived this scheme was, is indicated by the fact that some Pythagorean writers assign the beard to the second hebdomad.

[61] Isidore of Seville, who is copying from this passage in *De numeris* 188c-d,
includes a sixth hebdomad, marking deterioration, and a seventh, marking the
beginning of old age. Leonardi, p. 227, believes that there was a lacuna in the
archetype of the Martianus manuscripts.

[62] Martianus is probably referring to the seven bright stars of Ursa Major, the
dimmest of which is of the third magnitude.

[63] Nine was more commonly associated with the god of fire. See Nicomachus,
tr. D'Ooge, p. 106.

[64] The number eight refers to a cube because it has eight vertices. A cube also
has six surfaces and twelve edges, and thus was venerated because it manifested
the harmonic proportion 6:8:12. See *ibid.*, p. 277.

they make eight. Likewise the [three] odd numbers that follow three and five produce the cubic number which originates in the triad; namely, 27: add seven, nine, and eleven, and they make 27. Likewise the third cubic number, which originates in the tetrad, namely, 64; for four times four is sixteen, and four times this is 64. And the four odd numbers which follow those mentioned above—namely, 13, 15, 17, and 19—together amount to sixty-four. Thus a cube of a number is found through the addition of that very num• ber of odd numbers.[65] Indeed the cubic number eight, being the first of all cubes, is the monad of all numbers. Every cube is to be assigned to the Mother of the gods; for that is the origin of the name Cybebe.[66]

[741] The ennead is also perfect and is called more than perfect, since it is perfected from the multiplication of the perfect triad. Then, because it marks the end of the first numerical series, it is called Mars,[67] by whom all things are brought to an end. The square number also marks the limit of terms in a proportion.[68] The number nine is also the last element of harmony: a tone is produced according to the ratio of eight to nine.[69] No less noteworthy is the fact that the Muses are nine in number. In the universe there are nine zones: the celestial sphere, the seven belonging to the gods, and the terrestrial sphere.[70]

[65] A discovery usually credited to Nicomachus. See *ibid.*, pp. 57-58.

[66] The Great Mother of the gods, called Cybele or Cybebe. The etymological association of the name with the Greek word *kubos* stems from a coincidental resemblance of words.

[67] Richard Bentley, in an emendation which he penned in the margin of a copy of the Grotius edition in the British Museum, suggested the reading *Mors* [Death]; Remigius derives *Mars* from *mors*. Mars was one of the gods generally assigned to the ennead. See Nicomachus, tr. D'Ooge, p. 106.

[68] I.e., four terms. Nine is referred to as a square number here because it is the product of three times three. The other square number within the decad is four (two times two). See *ibid.*, p. 242.

[69] The superoctave ratio. Cf. § 953; Macrobius *Commentary* 2. 1. 20.

[70] The text is correct and clear, if punctuated according to our practice: *In mundo etiam novem sunt zonae: id est, sphaerae, et deorum septem, et terrae.* Eyssenhardt misunderstood the passage and added *duae* after *terrae*. Dick retains the reading of the manuscripts, but his punctuation indicates confusion. For the correct interpretation of the sentence, see Paul Tannery, "Ad M. Capellae librum VII," *Revue de philologie*, XVI (1892), 137.

[742] The decad must be respected above all other numbers.[71] It contains within itself all numbers with their varied attributes and degrees of perfection. Though it is the end of the first series, ten serves as a helpmate of the second series. The decad comprehends the rules, ratios, classes, types, differences, perfections, and imperfections of the numbers of the first series. It is assigned to Janus;[72] many authorities have referred to the number as 'recurrent.'[73]

[743] We have briefly discussed the numbers comprising the first series, the deities assigned to them, and the virtues of each number. I shall now briefly indicate the nature of number itself, what relations numbers bear to each other, and what forms they represent. A number is a collection of monads or a multitude proceeding from a monad and returning to a monad.[74] There are four classes of integers: the first is called 'even times even'; the second 'odd times even'; the third 'even times odd'; and the fourth 'odd times odd';[75] these I shall discuss later.

[744] Numbers are called prime which can be divided by no num-

---

[71] On the sacredness of the decad among the Pythagoreans, see Nicomachus, tr. D'Ooge, pp. 106-7, 267; John Burnet, *Early Greek Philosophy* (4th ed., London, 1930; reprinted, New York, 1957), pp. 102-3.

[72] This epithet is not among the many listed for the number by Robbins in Nicomachus, tr. D'Ooge, p. 107. The appropriateness of calling the decad "Janus" is obvious, for, like the two-faced god, the decad looks backward to the first series and forward to the second.

[73] Martianus uses the Greek term *apokatastasis*. Nicomachus (2. 17. 7) regards five and six as "recurrent" numbers and defines the term as applying to those numbers that have "the property of ending at every multiplication in the same number as that from which they began" (D'Ooge translation). Martianus above (§ 735) also regards five as a recurrent number.

[74] The definition of Theon of Smyrna, ed. Hiller, p. 18, lines 3-5, comes closest to that of Martianus. On the definitions of number given by Euclid, Nicomachus, and others, see Euclid *Elements*, tr. Heath, II, 280; Heath, *History*, I, 69-70; Nicomachus, tr. D'Ooge, pp. 48, 114-15. At this point Martianus begins his treatment of arithmetic proper, which continues through to the setting portion at the close of this book (802). For a conspectus of the topics dealt with by Martianus, and a brief comparison of his treatment with those of Nicomachus, Euclid, Isidore of Seville, and Cassiodorus, see *ibid.*, pp. 138-42. It should be pointed out that Robbins used Isidore's *Etymologiae* for comparisons here, and was apparently unaware of the existence of his *De numeris*.

[75] Euclid *Elements* 7. Defs. 8-10 omits odd times even; Nicomachus 1. 8. 3. omits odd times odd. See Nicomachus, tr. D'Ooge, p. 49.

ber; they are seen to be not 'divisible' by the monad but 'composed'[76] of it: take, for example, the numbers five, seven, eleven, thirteen, seventeen, and others like them.[77] No number can divide these numbers into integers. So they are called 'prime,' since they arise from no number[78] and are not divisible into equal portions. Arising in themselves, they beget other numbers from themselves, since even numbers are begotten from odd numbers, but an odd number cannot be begotten from even numbers. Therefore prime numbers must of necessity be regarded as beautiful.[79]

[745] Let us consider all numbers of the first series according to the above classifications: the monad is not a number;[80] the dyad is an even number; the triad is a prime number, both in order and in properties; the tetrad belongs in the even times even class; the pentad is prime; the hexad belongs to the odd[81] times even or even times odd (hence it is called perfect);[82] the heptad is prime; the octad belongs to even times even; the ennead belongs to odd times odd; and the decad, even times odd. These classifications apply equally to higher series. The first series runs from the monad to the ennead; the second from the decad to ninety; the third from one hundred to nine hundred; the fourth and last from one thousand to nine thousand; although some Greek writers appear to have included the myriad [ten thousand].[83]

---

[76] Remigius *ad loc.* (ed. Lutz, II, 196) explains that *divisio* is division into equal parts, and that *compositio* "is lacking in measure, as in the case of seven, which is composed of three and four."

[77] Martianus calls three a prime number in the next paragraph. Cf. Nicomachus 1. 11. 2 and Theon, ed. Hiller, p. 23, line 11.

[78] The monad is not a number, as we learn in the next paragraph.

[79] Dick regards this sentence as an "inept gloss," and brackets it in his text. I have not found the epithet "beautiful" given to prime numbers by any other writer on arithmetic.

[80] The monad is potential number, "not a number but the beginning of numbers." Cf. Theon, ed. Hiller, p. 24, line 23; and Macrobius 1. 6. 7; and see Nicomachus, tr. D'Ooge, pp. 116-17.

[81] Dick ineptly brackets the word thus: [*im*]*par*, making six an even times even number.

[82] See § 736.

[83] Martianus means that some writers included a fifth series or course, beginning with the myriad. Nicomachus 1. 16. 3 enumerates the perfect numbers found only in the first four series. On the Greek use of series, see Heath, *History*, I, 114; Nicomachus, tr. D'Ooge, pp. 119-20.

[746] The only numbers that find favor with me are those that are counted on the fingers of both hands: in other cases we must resort to contorted movements of the arms in order to make numbers correspond to the figures and lines dealt with by my sister who discoursed before me.[84] According to my discipline, the beginning, the indivisible, in the first series, is the monad; according to hers, this beginning is in the point, which has no parts.[85] In the second series, numbers from ten are extended like a line. In the third series, quadrate figures are produced from the number one hundred and those that follow: these numbers represent the combining of latitude with the first longitude. In the fourth series are found the cubes; and thus, from one thousand and other numbers in the series, solidity is derived. In my discipline, therefore, the limits are the monad, the decad, the hecatontad, and the milliad; but for my sister Geometry, these limits are found in the point, the line, the plane, and the solid figure. For the monad is indivisible, as is the point; the decad in numbers represents the line, which has length only; the hecatontad represents the quadrate figure, a plane surface, which extends in length and width.[86]

[747] Every odd number advancing from the monad in single steps of necessity produces a square number. Take first the monad itself and add the triad; that makes four, the first square number. Then add five, and you get the second quadrate number, 9. Add seven, and the next quadrate number will be 16. Again add 9, and you get the quadrate number 25. The same procedure may be extended to infinity.[87]

But I shall return to the classifications above. Every number is even or odd, and each is bounded by the other; whatever is added to a finite number is a finite addition, for a finite cannot be produced from infinites.

[748] All numbers are either even or odd. A number is even

[84] On finger reckoning and manuscript illustrations depicting movements of the hands and arms in reckoning, see Vol. I, p. 158, n. 49.

[85] Nicomachus 2. 7. 1, 3 also notes the analogy between the indivisible point and the monad.

[86] Martianus' representation here of the first number in each series as referring to the genesis of geometric figures is highly unorthodox. Earlier (§ 707) he referred the monad to the point; the dyad, the first extension, to a line.

[87] This method of forming square numbers was known to Pythagoras, according to Heath, *History*, I, 77.

which is divisible into two equal parts;[88] for example, 2, 4, or 6. A number is odd which cannot be divided into two equal parts;[89] for example, 3, 5, and 7. Of the odd numbers, some are merely uneven, as 3, 5, and 7; others are multiples as well—as 9, 15, and 21, which the Greeks classify as odd times odd.

But among those that are even there are many types . . .[90] or they are even and can be divided. Others are even from evens, even from odds, or odd from evens. The Greeks call the first *artiakis artioi* [even times even]; the second *perissakis artioi* [odd times even]; and the third *artiakis perissoi* [even times odd].[91]

[749] There are even numbers from evens—like four, which consists of twice two; and eight, which consists of twice four. And there are types of evens from odds: both those which are made even by multiplication by odds, as three times two makes six, or five times four makes 20 (a type which the Greeks designate as odd times even); or those in which odd numbers are multiplied by evens, as twice three makes 6, or four times five makes 20 (a type which the Greeks call even times odd). Although the products are the same, the manner of their multiplication is different. Of these numbers some, when divided in half, immediately revert to odd numbers; others may be evenly divided one or more times before being reduced to odd numbers above the unit. For twelve and twenty are divisible into evens only once; but forty-eight, indeed, is twice twenty-four, then twice twelve, then twice six, all factors still being evens; and finally it is reduced to three. No number can go through the multiplication stages without having its steps of multiplication correspond conversely to its steps of division. For twenty is twice ten, and five times four, and four times five, and ten times two.

[750] There are four classes of numbers: some are incomposite [prime]; others are composite in relation to themselves; some are incomposite to one another [relatively prime]; others are composite to one another.[92] The first two classes are prime, the second two are called secondary. To clarify this matter, we must speak more plainly.

---

[88] Euclid's definition (*Elements* 7. Def. 6).

[89] Cf. *ibid.*, 7.

[90] There is a lacuna in the text here.

[91] See § 743.

[92] This classification is Euclidean, not Nicomachian. Cf. Euclid *Elements* 7. Defs. 11-14; Nicomachus, tr. D'Ooge, p. 38.

The first and least measure of all numbers is the unit; for there is no number that cannot be divided into units. Numbers are susceptible of other measures, such as duplications, which increase a number by doubling it, or triplications, which increase it by tripling it. Consequently, the sole measure for some numbers is in the unit—numbers that cannot be divided except into units, as is the case with the number three. Three is merely odd. Other numbers can be divided into still other numbers, as in the case of four and nine; for twice two is four, and thrice three is nine. We measure the former by duplication, the latter by triplication. Often there is not a single such measure for a number but several; for example, eight is readily measured by qradruplication and duplication, since four times two and twice four are 8. It is likewise evident that whatever number we measure by some multiplication, we can also measure by units; but conversely, wherever there is a measure by units, there is not always one of multiplication. The unit is the common measure for all numbers, but for some it is the unique measure.[93] [751] Consequently, numbers that have no measure but units are called prime and incomposite; those that are measured not only by units but also by some other factor are called composite in relation to themselves. So much for numbers considered by themselves.

Two or more numbers together that have no common measure except units are called prime to one another, as in the case of 3 and 4. It does not matter that 4 has a measure by duplication, since that measure is not in three. Numbers are composite to one another that have some other common measure besides the unit, as in the case of 9 and 12; both of these are measured by triplication, since three times three makes 9, or three times four makes 12. [752] Since some numbers are divisible only into units, and others are divisible also into other whole numbers, a distinction that exists in fact, I too shall distinguish them by terms, lest any confusion arise in the minds of my readers. The whole numbers into which a number may be divided I shall call members (*membra*) of the number, as in the case of 12; but the units or any whole numbers that are combined with the units I shall refer to as parts (*partes*), as in the case of 7, made up either of as many units or of twice the number three, with a unit added.[94]

---

[93] Cf. Nicomachus I. 11. 3; and Euclid, tr. Heath, II, 284-85.
[94] Members and parts are discussed in §§ 757-67.

[753] Some numbers are perfect, some are superabundant, and some are deficient; the Greeks call them perfect (*teleioi*), over-perfect (*hyperteleioi*), and underperfect (*hypoteleioi*).[95] Perfect numbers are those that are equal to the sum of their parts; super-abundant, those that have more in their parts than in themselves; and deficient, those that have less in their parts than in themselves. For example, let us take six. It can be divided into units, two, or three, since six times one, three times two, or two times three makes six; thus its parts are 1, 2, and 3; let these parts be added together and the sum is 6. This number is equal to its parts, and this type of number derives virtue from that fact; the other types are faulty, because of superabundance or deficiency, as, for example, the number 12. Twelve times one, six times two, four times three, three times four, or two times six makes 12. The parts are 1, 2, 3, 4, and 6, which, when added together, make 16. The number twelve is therefore super-abundant.[96] Now take the number 16; it is made of sixteen times one, two times eight, four times four, or eight times two, and these are the only factors of the number. Add the numbers together and you get only 15, less than the number from which they sprang. This number is deficient.[97]

[754] Some numbers are plane, others are solid. The Greeks call a number plane which is the product of two numbers.[98] That is to say, in the reckoning of measures, they consider that as much is contained by the *norma*[99] as by the entire rectangle of which the *norma* is a part. Thus those numbers are regarded as plane numbers that are arranged along two sides so that they form a right angle and present the appearance of a *norma*. For example, if one side is extended to a length of 4, another side to 3, the product of these two numbers is 12; and they call this a plane number.[100]

[95] Cf. Nicomachus 1. 14-16; Theon, ed. Hiller, pp. 45-46; and see Euclid, tr. Heath, II, 293-95.

[96] Cf. Nicomachus 1. 14. 3.

[97] Cf. *ibid.*, 15. 1-2.

[98] Cf. Euclid *Elements* 7. Def. 16; Theon, ed. Hiller, p. 26; Nicomachus 2. 8-11.

[99] The basic meaning of the Latin word is a carpenter's square. The Greek word used by writers on arithmetic is *gnomon*, which also originally meant a carpenter's square. See Heath, *History*, I, 77-78.

[100] Following the practice of Nicomachus and other Greek writers, Euclid represents numbers as lines corresponding in length to the units in those num-

According to the Greeks, solidity arises from three numbers. Let one side be four, another three; then let four be added above.[101] They say that altitude is filled out by these numbers placed above the underlying *norma*, and that twenty-four is represented. There is no point in being obscure in this matter: it is very clear that a plane number comes from single numbers joined together in such a way that one is not above another; and that solidity is produced from numbers placed above other numbers.

[755] Surfaces have various forms, with numbers arranged in the likeness of different figures. These begin with a line, then they become triangles;[102] those that have four angles either are square or have sides that are longer than the smaller sides by a part. The Greeks call the latter heteromecic.[103] Moreover, a greater number of angles are at times also able to represent sides of unequal lengths, so that when their numbers increase to represent solidity, and many figures are produced, the cube is seen to be the most perfect among them.[104] The smallest number represented in a triangle is three; in a quadrate,

---

bers. A plane number is the product of two linear numbers used as sides. Nicomachus and other writers on arithmetic represent numbers by dots or points arranged in geometric forms. Thus, whereas Euclid limited himself to square and oblong numbers, his successors recognized triangular numbers (the first of which was three) and polygonal numbers (beginning with five) as well. On the difference between their conception of plane and solid numbers, see Euclid, tr. Heath, II, 287-90.

[101] A literal translation of Martianus' statement, this points to his limited comprehension of the subject of solid numbers. He conceives of a solid number as a plane number multiplied by 2; or, represented geometrically, as two identical plane surfaces, one superimposed on the other, the altitude being two. Remigius has a clearer understanding of the subject and offers (*ad loc.*) as his example $3 \times 3 \times 3 = 27$. The figure that Martianus uses is called a "brick" by Greek arithmeticians. Cf. Nicomachus 2. 17. 6; and the D'Ooge translation, p. 256.

[102] Three points, in a nonlinear arrangement, represent the first surface.

[103] Cf. Nicomachus 2. 17. 1; Theon, ed. Hiller, p. 26; Boethius *Institutiones arithmeticae* 2. 26 (ed. Friedlein, p. 115, line 9) and Martianus both use the expression "longer by a part." See also Euclid, tr. Heath, II, 288-89.

[104] The cube, having six faces, eight vertices, and twelve edges, represents the harmonic ratio (6:8:12) and was called "geometric harmony" and venerated by early Pythagoreans as a perfect figure. See §§ 736-37, above; also Heath, *History*, I, 85; Nicomachus, tr. D'Ooge, p. 274. Martianus uses the word *tessera* for "cube." Remigius (*ad loc.*) rightly points out its derivation from the Greek word for "four."

4. The smallest in a figure with an uneven number of sides is 5.[105] The smallest number in an oblong with sides of unequal length is six. The smallest solid number, representing a cube, is eight.

The number two represents a simple row; three can be arranged so that it has the same number of angles; four, arranged to form a quadrate, has two on each side; five is arranged so that on one side there are two, on the other three;[106] six, to represent an oblong, has two on two sides and three on two sides; but when four is represented so that solidity arises from it, and all sides on the plane surface and the altitude are of equal length, each side consists of two.[107]

[756] Plane numbers are similar whose sides have the same ratio, as with 6 and 600: for the former, one side is 2, the other 3; and for the latter, one side is 20, and the other 30.[108] Correspondingly, solid numbers are similar whose sides have the same ratio, as twenty-four and ninety-six. With the first, one side is 4, another 3, making a plane surface of 12, and a solid of 24; with the second, one side is 8, the other six, making a plane surface of 48, and a solid of 96.[109] The ratio between two and three is the same as that between 200 and 300; and the same is true of the ratio of 3 to 4 as of 6 to 8. This will become clear when I discuss the ratios that exist between numbers.

[757] Every number is a part of some larger number; the greater number is produced either through multiplication or from a ratio of

[105] Five is the first pentagonal number. I follow here the reading of the texts of Eyssenhardt and Kopp. Dick, perhaps not understanding the passage, deleted this sentence as a gloss, pointing out that no previous mention was made of this type of figure. But a moment later Martianus does include five as a figurate number; moreover, a discussion of pentagonal numbers was a regular feature in the discussion of figurate numbers in Greek arithmetical treatises. Cf. Nicomachus, tr. D'Ooge, pp. 243-44; Euclid, tr. Heath, II, 289.

[106] I.e., points representing units, thus: ∴∴

[107] The cube, with eight vertices, and a unit represented at each vertex.

[108] The manuscripts actually read CC and CCC here, which Dick corrects to XX and XXX. It appears that Martianus, and not the scribe who copied the archetype, was responsible for the blunder. In a moment Martianus speaks of 2 and 3 as having the same ratio as 200 and 300; and later (§ 761), in using 300 and 200 as an example of the superdimidius ratio, he refers to this passage. If the scribe had been responsible for the error, he would have had to misread the figures in three places.

[109] Once again (cf. § 755) Martianus displays his limited comprehension of solid numbers by using examples in which one plane surface is superimposed upon another plane surface; as Remigius observes (ed. Lutz, II, 206), his solid figure "has nothing within and is merely surfaces."

members or of parts,[110] or at one and the same time, from both multiplication and a ratio of members or of parts. A ratio of members is in one or more members; a ratio of parts, in one or more parts. The smaller number is reduced by division or by a ratio of members or parts; sometimes by both division and a ratio of members or of parts. There is no ratio of number to number that is not contained within these relationships. The Greeks call numbers multiplied *pollaplasioi* [multiples]; numbers divided *hypopollaplasioi* [submultiples]; numbers exceeding other numbers by a member or members *epimorioi* [superparticulars]; and numbers smaller than other numbers by a member or members *hyperepimorioi* [subsuperparticulars]. . . .[111] They also use compound names where the ratios are twofold.

[758] Accordingly, one number may bear a relation to another number of equality, which the Greeks call *isotēs*, as in the case of two to two, three to three.[112] This is the relation of a perfect number to its parts, and the number is therefore considered superior to others. For what better relationship can there be than that of equality? But when one number is greater, the other is smaller; and immediately there is a discrepancy between them. This happens in all numbers which either exceed or are exceeded by others in a ratio of members or parts. Therefore those numbers are inferior which have some discrepancy between themselves and their parts. But though the difference between two numbers, greater and smaller, is the same, yet the ratio between the same numbers is contrary. There is the same difference between three and four as between four and three, but the ratio between these numbers is different, and what it is will be discussed below.

[759] I pointed out earlier that the first ratios are in multiplication. The number six has the relation of multiple to the number

---

110 Cf. § 752.

111 There seems to be a lacuna in the Latin text here, and various editors have conjectured that the following should be added: "numbers exceeding other numbers by a part or parts *epimereis* [superpartients], and numbers smaller than other numbers by a part or parts *hypepimereis* [subsuperpartients]."

The Latin terms *superparticularis* and *subsuperparticularis*, in common use among historians of mathematics, got their currency from Boethius' Latin translation of Nicomachus. See *Institutiones arithmeticae* 1. 24, 28. Robbins (Nicomachus, tr. D'Ooge, pp. 140-41) briefly discusses Martianus' treatment of ratios and draws some comparisons with Nicomachus' treatment.

112 Cf. Theon, ed. Hiller, p. 74.

three; or eight, to four. Conversely, the number three has a relation of submultiple to the number six, as has four to eight. One number surpasses another by a ratio of members if it exceeds it by a solid member or members, as nine exceeds six; for it surpasses it by three, which is found twice in the number six. Conversely, the number six is exceeded by nine by a ratio of members. But one number surpasses another number by a ratio of parts if the larger number contains within itself both the smaller number and some part or parts of it, as in a comparison of the number 7 with 4, the number seven contains the number 4 and 3 parts of it; conversely, 4 is exceeded by 7 by a ratio of parts.

The same number exceeds another by multiplication and by a ratio of members if, for example, two numbers like 8 and 3 are compared; 8 contains three twice and also has a member in two. And one number surpasses another by multiplication and by a ratio of parts if, for example, the numbers 5 and two are compared; in the number five there are twice two and a remainder of one, which is a part of two. Conversely, in the case of these numbers the smaller is exceeded by the larger, at one and the same time, by division and by either a ratio of members or a ratio of parts.[113]

[760] Now these are the classes of ratios existing among numbers; there are also several types in each class. Let us take up multiplication and division first: between numbers there is a ratio of double, triple, or quadruple; multiplication can also go beyond that. And the same number is divided through the very same steps, in reverse order. Thus two is larger than one by the double ratio, and 4 than two, and 8 than 4; one is smaller than two by the double ratio, and two than 4, and 4 than 8. Likewise, 3 is larger than 1 by the triple ratio, and 9 than 3; 1 is smaller than 3 by the triple ratio, and 3 than 9; 4 is larger than 1 by the quadruple ratio, and 16 than 4; 1 is smaller than 4 by the quadruple ratio, and 4 than 16. The same ratios of increase and decrease exist in multiplications beyond those numbers.

[761] When a ratio of members exists between larger and smaller numbers, the larger exceeds the smaller either by a half (*superdimidius;* in Greek *hēmiolios*) or by a third (*supertertius;* in Greek *epitritos*) or by a quarter (*superquartus;* in Greek *epitetartos*); and in like manner the ratio proceeds to an excess of a fifth (*super-*

---

[113] Cf. Nicomachus 1. 18; Theon, ed. Hiller, p. 16.

quintus), sixth (*supersextus*), and beyond. A superdimidius contains a number and a half part of it; a supertertius, a number and a third part of it; a superquartus, a number and a fourth part of it; and similar ratios exist beyond. Conversely, taking the same numbers, the smaller bears the *subdimidius* (*hyphēmiolios*), *subtertius* (*hypotritos*), or *subquartus* (*hypotetartos*) relation to the larger. Three has the ratio of superdimidius to two; and 300 to 200, as we mentioned above. Conversely, two has the ratio of subdimidius to three; and 200 to 300. But 4 has the ratio of supertertius to 3; and 8, to 6, which was also mentioned above; and 3 has the ratio of subtertius to 4; and 6, to 8; 5 has the superquartus ratio to 4; and 10, to 8; and 4 has the subquartus ratio to 5; and 8, to 10.[114]

[762] The ratio of parts is closest to the supertertius in certain numbers, in certain others to the superquartus; and the ratio can proceed beyond this. A ratio is like the supertertius when the larger number contains the smaller number and some third parts of it; and like the superquartus, when it contains the smaller number and some quarter parts of it. Let us pair 5 and 3, and 10 and 6. Five exceeds three in that it contains three and two third parts of it. Likewise, in 10 there are 6 and two third parts of six. The ratio is closest to the superquartus in the case of 7 and 4, or 14 and 8. Seven contains 4 and three quarter parts of it. In these combinations, just as the larger numbers exceed by a ratio which is closest to the supertertius and the superquartus, so the smaller numbers have a ratio with the larger that comes closest to the subtertius and subquartus.[115] Let no one suppose that there is some ratio of parts that is *like* the superdimidius; for if one number contains another number and a half part of it, it *is* a superdimidius; and if it has that number and two half parts of it, it bears the double ratio.[116]

And whereas two thirds bear the closest ratio to the supertertius, two quarters do not assume the closest ratio to the superquartus. For if a number contains another number and two quarter parts of it, it is a superdimidius, as in the case of 6 and 4; in six there are four and two quarter parts of it. Conversely, in these combinations, just as the larger numbers exceed by a ratio which is closest to the supertertius

114 Cf. Nicomachus I. 20-21; Theon, ed. Hiller, pp. 76-77.
115 Dick agrees with Petau that this sentence should be deleted because it is repeated immediately below.
116 Cf. Nicomachus I. 20. 2.

and the superquartus, so the smaller numbers have a ratio with the larger that comes closest to the subtertius and subquartus. The same ratio obtains where it is like the superquintus and those beyond.

[763] Several types arise from combinations of these ratios, as when one number can be generated from the double and the super-dimidius, or the supertertius, or the superquartus, or ratios beyond; or by ratios of multiplications and of members. Let us take as an example 4 and 10: of these 10 is produced by the double and the super-dimidius; for twice four is 8, and then half of 4 is two. Or take 4 and 14: 14 is produced by the triple ratio and the superdimidius; for three times four is 12, and a half of four is two. Proceeding beyond to 4 and 18, 18 is produced by the quadruple and the superdimidius, for four times four is 16 and in addition half of four is two.

In the case of 3 and 7, the latter is produced by the double and the supertertius; for two times three is 6, and a third part of three is one. Or take 3 and 10: 10 is produced by the triple and the supertertius; for three times three is 9, and a third part of three is one. Take 3 and 13: 13 is produced by the quadruple and the supertertius; for three times four is 12, and a third part of three is one. Let us next take the case of 4 and 9: 9 grows from the double and the superquartus, for twice four is 8, and a fourth part of 4 is one. In the case of 4 and 13, the ratio is the triple and the superquartus. Likewise 4 and 17 have the ratio of the quadruple and the superquartus. And the same is true of numbers beyond. And conversely, the smaller numbers in the above combinations have ratios with the larger numbers of division and the subdimidius, the subtertius, the subquartus, or a ratio beyond.[117]

[764] From these examples it becomes clear that multiplication begins with the smallest ratio and proceeds to larger and larger ones by ratios of members or of parts. Division begins with the largest ratio and proceeds to smaller and smaller ones. A ratio is said to be 'larger' that becomes greater, and 'smaller' that becomes smaller. The ratio of the triple is greater than that of the double; and the ratio of the quadruple is greater than that of the triple; conversely, the ratio of the double is smaller than that of the triple; and the ratio of the triple is smaller than that of the quadruple.

[765] Multiplication begins with the double and proceeds to the

117 Cf. Nicomachus 1. 21.

triple, the quadruple, and ever greater ratios. But the ratio of members begins with the superdimidius and goes to the supertertius, the superquartus, and to ever smaller and smaller ratios. All the above ratios are between two terms; for example, the ratio of the double is between two and one; of the triple, between three and one; of the quadruple, between four and one. Under these ratios the terms are minimal and are much smaller than their analogous ratios; the minimal terms for the double are two and one; for the triple, three and one; and for the quadruple, four and one. Beyond these you can go as far as you please with analogous ratios. The terms are increased for these numbers.[118] The Pythagorean Thymarides gave the name *pythmenes* [root ratios] to minimal couples;[119] for, as in the case of a container superimposed above its bottom, so numbers of the same ratio are superimposed above others; and the same is true of the ratio of members.

[766] The minimal terms of the superdimidius are two and three, of the supertertius three and four, of the superquartus four and five; and then larger numbers are coupled under the same ratios. The same holds true for the ratio of parts, which begins with a third part, and for the ratio of members, which begins with the hemiolius, then first comprises the minimal terms, then proceeds to the larger ones.

[767] It is reasonable to suppose that the first [of the ratios] to be discovered was multiplication, next came ratios of members, and then of parts.[120] For no complication appeared in the ratios of the double, the triple, and the quadruple. Then from the double the relation of the superdimidius arose, from the triple the supertertius, and from the quadruple the superquartus, and similarly with the ratios beyond. For when anyone was able to comprehend the double, he was at the same time beginning to understand the

[118] Dick supposes a lacuna in the text here, with two words omitted. On his supposition, the full translation would be: "However, the terms are not increased for these numbers."

[119] The reading of the extant text is corrupt. I have followed the emended reading of Paul Tannery, pp. 137-38: *Pythmenes pythagoricus Thymarides* [sic] *nominabat*. Dick was unaware of Tannery's emendation. On root ratios, cf. Nicomachus 1. 20. 1; 1. 21. 1; 2. 19. 3; and see Nicomachus, tr. D'Ooge, p. 141.

[120] Nicomachus (1. 19. 8) considers the multiple a more elementary and older form, and proceeds to indicate diagrammatically the development of ratios of members and parts.

dimidius; for just as four is the double of two, so two is the half
(dimidius) of four. And just as four was created by adding two to
two, so, by adding two again to four, the superdimidius was created.
And just as the number six was produced by the tripling of two,
so the supertertius was discovered by adding two more to the number six; and so on with ratios beyond. Then when numbers not fitting into the regular ratios were confronted, the question arose of
how many times one number, or how many parts of it, were found
in another number, for the purpose of establishing some definite
relationship of one number to another. After this no great difficulty
arose in dealing with numbers in a twofold ratio.[121]

[768] Since I have discussed the classes of numbers and of the
ratios found between numbers, I shall now return to the individual
properties of numbers. I shall begin with evens and odds. An even
number, in every multiplication of itself, remains even. By doubling,
the steps of increase are 2, 4, 8, and 16; by tripling, 2, 6, and 18;
by quadrupling, 4, 16, 64, 256 and so on. An odd number, when
multiplied by an even number, disappears, and the product is an
even number.[122] The product of an odd number multiplied by an
odd number remains odd.[123] For example, twice three becomes
six, twice four becomes 8; similarly, four times three becomes 12,
four times five, 20; but three times three becomes 9; and three times
9 becomes 27; in like manner, five times three becomes 15, and
five times five becomes 25.

This holds true in all multiplications. The consequence is that,
whether there is an even or an odd set of even numbers to be
added, the sum is even:[124] in the case of 2, 4, 6, and 8, which
is an even number of numbers, the sum is 20; or with 2, 4, and 6,
which is an odd number of numbers, the sum is 12. Both sums are
even numbers. [769] Similarly, an even number of odd numbers to
be added gives a sum that is even:[125] 3 and 5 are 8, which is an even
number. But an odd number of odd numbers to be added gives

[121] Remigius *ad loc.* (ed. Lutz, II, 219) says that this refers to ratios combining multiplication and a ratio of members or of parts.
[122] Cf. Euclid *Elements* 9. 28.
[123] Cf. *ibid.*, 29.
[124] Cf. *ibid.*, 21.
[125] Cf. *ibid.*, 22.

only a sum that is an odd number:[126] for 3, 5, and 7 are 15, which is an odd number. For this reason, as often as an even number multiplies either an even number or an odd number, the product is even. In the duplication of a number, whether two doubled makes 4, or 3 doubled makes 6, the result is an even number in either case; and if an odd number is multiplied an even number of times, the product is even. But if it is multiplied an odd number of times, the product is odd. If the number two is tripled, the product is 6, which is even. But if the number is 3, the product is 9, which is an odd number.

[770] If an even number is added to an even number, the sum is even,[127] as when 4 is added to two, the sum is 6. If an odd is added to an odd, the sum is even;[128] as when three is added to 5, the sum is 8. An odd number, if another number not of the same class is added to it, always acts in the same way: whether an even number is added to an odd or an odd to an even, the sum will be odd; whether three is added to 4 or 4 to 3, the sum is 7, which is an odd number.

If a number of either class is subtracted from an even number, a number of that class remains. The contrary is the case with an odd number, so that a number of the class of the number that is taken away does not remain. Thus, if evens are taken from evens, evens remain: if two is taken from 8, 6 remains. If an odd number is taken from an even number, that which remains is odd: if 3 is taken from 6, 3 is the remainder. But if an even number is taken from an odd number, that which remains is odd: if two is taken from 7, the remainder is 5. If an odd number is taken from an odd, the remainder is even: 3 taken from 7 leaves 4.[129]

[771] Any number that has an even half is an even times even number; as in the case of 12, whose half is the number 6, itself an even number. Likewise, any number that increases by duplication, beginning with 2—for example, 4, 8, or 16—or any number that increases from other numbers in such a way that reciprocally it can return to an even number, which happens in quadruples, octuples,

126 Cf. *ibid.*, 23.
127 Cf. *ibid.*, 21.
128 Cf. *ibid.*, 22.
129 Cf. *ibid.*, 24-27.

and similar increases, belongs to the class of even times even.[130] But any number that has an odd half is even times odd; as half of six is three.[131] And if any number neither increases from 2 by doubling nor has a half that is odd, it belongs to the even times even class; however it originates from the class of even times odd;[132] as in the case of 12. Neither does this number originate by duplication from 2 nor does it have an odd-numbered half; but it increases from the number 6 by duplication; and that number belongs to the even times odd class, for the odd number is three.

[772] Let us pass on to the incomposite and composite numbers —which, as I indicated above,[133] are classified as prime and secondary. No prime and incomposite numbers are even, with the number two excepted, as I explained above.[134] Whatever others are prime and incomposite are all odd; for example, 3, 5, 7, 11, 13, 17, 19, and similar numbers. All numbers that are composite in relation to themselves are even, whether they come from evens or odds.[135] For we measure 4 and 8 by duplication, one of them being divided into two, the other into four; and it is easy to do the same in the case of 6 or 10, since the former is divided into three, the latter into five. In addition many odd numbers are composite in relation to themselves; that is, those which are multiplied by an odd number. For if the number three or five, or any other odd number multiplies odd numbers, the resulting product is odd and is composite in relation to itself. Let three multiply itself; the product is 9. Let five multiply itself; the product is 25. Or let three multiply five, or five multiply three, and the product is 15. All these numbers, 9, 25, and 15, are composite in relation to themselves, and any other odd numbers belong to the same class.[136]

[773] But no two even numbers are prime to one another, whether they come from evens or odds, because they all have some common measure. Let us take two even numbers, 4 and 6, the one coming from an even, the other from an odd number; they are

130 Cf. *ibid.*, 32.
131 Cf. *ibid.*, 33.
132 Cf. *ibid.*, 34.
133 § 750.
134 Cf. § 751, and § 773 (end).
135 By "odds" he means "evens from odds." See § 749.
136 Cf. Euclid *Elements* 9. 29.

nevertheless composite to one another, because their common measure is duplication, twice two making 4, and twice three making 6.

All numbers that are prime and incomposite are odd; for numbers
which do not even have any measure of their own cannot have any
common measure except the unit.[137] Thus 3, 5, 7, and all such
numbers, as they are prime by themselves, are also prime with respect to one another; and in the same category is that number which,
though even, falls under the same rule—namely, two; for two is not
composite with three, five, or any similar number.[138]

[774] Then, if any number that is prime and incomposite is
taken with another number that is composite in relation to itself, the
two numbers are found to be prime with respect to one another,
as when 3 and 4 are combined.[139] What does it matter if one
number is measured by some other part than the unit if this is not
true of the other?

Or take two or more numbers that are not only composite in
relation to themselves but also composite with respect to each
other; the inclusion of an incomposite number causes all of them
to become prime with respect to one another, because, although
some measure is common to several, no measure is common to all,
except the unit. This happens in the case of 4, 6, 8, or similar numbers, as many as you please to consider; then let 3 be added to those.
Although the first three numbers are composite to each other, the
four taken together are incomposite.

[775] Not only does the addition of a number that is prime and
incomposite bring it to pass that the several numbers become prime
to one another, but a concomitant result is that numbers which are
composite in relation to themselves, when brought together, become
prime in relation to each other; then, although they have some
measures, nevertheless they take on different ones. This happens
between two odd numbers and also between an even and an odd.

---

[137] Cf. *ibid.*, 7. Def. 11; Nicomachus 1. 11. 2.

[138] On the dyad as the only even number that is prime, see Heath, *History*,
I, 73.

[139] This statement is not true, as is seen in the example of 3 and 9, or 7 and
14. Martianus is not following a known source here. In § 781 he makes the
correct statement about a prime and incomposite number that is taken with a
number that is composite in relation to itself.

Let us take 9 and 25; each of these is composite in relation to itself; for the number nine has its measure in three; and 25, in five. Nevertheless, they are not composite to each other, because 9 does not admit a measure in five, nor does 25 in three. The same is true of 8 and 9, an even and an odd number; for we are not able to measure 9 by duplication or quadruplication, nor 8 by three. And so numbers that are composite in relation to themselves are not immediately able to become composite to one another as well.

[776] All even numbers are composite to one another, as was indicated above,[140] whether they come from evens or odds; then certain odd numbers are composite to each other, too—for example, 9 and 15, since each number is divisible by three; then in some cases odds and evens, like 9 and 12, since tripling is common to both: thrice three is 9 and thrice four is 12. This fact is worthy of note: that never is an even number that comes from evens, but only one that originates from odds, able to be composite with an odd number. Some affinity persists even though the category changes. Thus 9 cannot be composite with 4, 8, or 16, nor with any other similar number; but it is composite with 12 and 24, which take their beginning from three.

[777] Not every odd number that is composite in relation to itself can be composite with all even numbers that come from odds, because the odd numbers may not be divisible by the same measure. Thus 9 and 50 cannot be composite, because 50 cannot be produced by triplication, which is the only measure, besides the unit, that exists for nine. This happens because not even 25—which, when doubled, produces 50—can be produced by triplication.

If an odd number from which an even number is made has the same measure as another odd number, then at last the even number which is made from it can be composite with that odd number. But where that prior condition does not exist, this result does not follow. Thus 9 and 50 are prime to each other, but 9 and 30 are composite to each other; for 30 arises from the doubling of 15; and 9 and 15 can be composite to each other, since their common measure is the number three. And other numbers that belong to this class of numbers originate from these.

---

[140] § 773.

[778] If one or the other of two numbers that are prime to each other is composite in relation to itself, the measure of the one is not composite with respect to the other.[141] Take the numbers 4 and 9: these are composite in relation to themselves but are prime to each other. The measure of four is in two, of nine in three; but two is not composite with respect to 9, nor 3 with 4. In the case of 5 and 4, the one is prime and incomposite; the other, four, has a measure in two; but two and 5 are not composite.

If two numbers are prime to each other, and one of these multiplies itself, the product is not composite with that other number.[142] Take 3 and 4. These numbers are prime to each other; if three multiplies itself, 9 and 4—or if four does the same, 16 and 3—are prime to each other.

If two numbers that are prime to each other multiply themselves, the resulting products will be prime to each other.[143] Take the numbers 3 and 4, and let each multiply itself. The products 9 and 16 will also be prime to each other.

[779] If two numbers are prime to each other, and one of these multiplies itself, and if that number multiplies the product again, the number resulting will not be composite with the other number.[144] Take 2 and 3; let either multiply itself: twice two becomes 4, or thrice three becomes 9; again let the same numbers multiply these numbers; twice four becomes 8, and thrice 9 becomes 27 Now take 2 and 27, or 2 and 9: in either case they are prime to each other.

If two numbers are prime to each other and each multiplies itself, and multiplies the product again, the resulting numbers are also prime to each other, as in the case of the numbers just used. From two we get 8, and from three, 27; these numbers are prime to each other.

If two numbers that are prime to each other are added, the sum of the two numbers cannot be composite with either of the former numbers.[145] Let the numbers 3 and 5 be added together, the sum is 8; 8 is not composite with either 5 or three.

141 Cf. Euclid *Elements* 7. 23.
142 Cf. *ibid.* 25.
143 Cf. *ibid.* 27.
144 Cf. *ibid.*, 27.
145 Cf. *ibid.*, 28.

[780] If a number is separated into two numbers that are prime to each other, it cannot be composite with either of them. Let 9 be separated into 4 and 5; 9 cannot be composite with either 4 or 5.

If two numbers are taken together with a third, and all are prime to one another, and if either of the two numbers is multiplied by the other, their product cannot be composite with that third number.[146] Take the numbers 4 and 8, and join 3 to them; they are prime to one another. Multiply either of the first two numbers by the other, four times 8, or eight times four, and the product is 32. This number and 3 will be prime to each other.

[781] Any number that is prime and incomposite cannot be composite with another number unless it measures that number.[147] The number 3 is composite with 9, and 5 with 15, because three times three is 9, and five times three is 15. If a number does not contain some measure of a number, it will not be able to be composite with that number.

If two numbers are set out and the lesser is continually being subtracted from the greater, and if the number which is left is not the measure of the one before it, these numbers are prime to one another.[148] Take the numbers 3 and 8; let three be subtracted from eight as often as possible, and two is the remainder; but two is not the measure of 3; therefore 3 and 8 are prime to each other.

If three numbers joined together[149] are the least[150] of those which have the same ratio with them, any two of these added together are not composite with the third. Take the numbers 9, 12, and 16. The following number in this series is always the super-tertius of the preceding, and the two smaller numbers added together will not be found composite with the third. Let 9 and 12 be added; the sum, 21, is not composite with 16.

[782] If an odd number cannot be composite with another num-

---

[146] Cf. *ibid.*, 24.

[147] Cf. *ibid.*, 29.

[148] Cf. *ibid.*, 1.

[149] I.e., in continued proportion, as seen from Martianus' example. Cf. Euclid 9. 15.

[150] To the reading of the text—*si tres iuncti sunt*—Petau added the words *numeri minimi*, assuming, according to Dick, that the words were missing from the Latin translation of the Euclidean proposition. Tannery, p. 128, reads *minimi* in place of *iuncti*.

ber, it is not composite with respect to the double of that number.[151]
Take 5 and 8; these are prime to each other. Let 8 be doubled;
the product is 16. The number five cannot be composite with
respect to it.

If two numbers are set with two other numbers so that neither
of the first pair can be composite with respect to either of the
second pair, then the sum of the numbers of the first pair cannot
be composite with respect to either of the numbers of the second
pair.[152] Take the numbers 4 and 8, and a second pair of numbers,
5 and 7; neither of the former pair can be composite with respect to either of the latter pair. Let 4 and 8 be added together,
the sum is 12; this number is not composite with respect to either
5 or 7.

[783] The least numbers of those which have the same ratio
with them are prime to each other.[153] For example, in the double
ratio, the least are 2 and 4; in the triple, 2 and 6; these are prime to
each other. And however large the numbers are that are taken, numbers that are prime to each other are the least of all those that have
the same ratio with them.[154] Take the numbers 200 and 101; these
are prime to each other. There is, moreover, a ratio of parts between them, because 200 exceeds 101 by 99 parts, and this cannot
be the case between any smaller numbers.

[784] Since, in a reckoning of measures, some numbers are found
to be prime and incomposite or composite in relation to themselves,
and some to be prime to one another or composite to one another,
it does not seem inappropriate at this point to add some observations
about measures.

Any number is either prime and incomposite or, if it is composite
in relation to itself, is measured by some prime number,[155] as in
the case of those numbers which have their increase by triplication,
9 in three, or 15 in 5. Of those numbers that are evens from
evens, the least measure is in two; of those that are evens from

[151] Cf. Euclid *Elements* 9. 31.
[152] Cf. Euclid *Elements* 7. 26. Martianus adds the first pair and compares the
sum with either number of the second pair. Euclid states that the products of
the pairs will be prime to each other.
[153] Cf. Euclid *Elements* 7. 22.
[154] Cf. *ibid.*, 21.
[155] Cf. Euclid *Elements*, 7. 32,31.

odds or are odds, the least measure can be in larger numbers, but they must all be odds.

The smallest and largest measures of a composite number are easily found. When a number is divided, the measure closest to the number is the largest measure, the one farthest from it is the least measure. Take the number fifty, and let it be divided. A half part of it is 25; this is the greatest measure of the number. Again, let us consider what smaller measures the number has: there are ten times five in 50, or five times ten; or two times twenty-five; there is not any smaller measure among these numbers than two; this is therefore the smallest measure of the number fifty.

[785] If two numbers are composite to one another, a greater and a smaller, how can their largest and their smallest common measure be found?[156] From the larger number let the smaller be subtracted as often as possible; then let whatever amount is left from the former [larger] number be subtracted from the smaller number as often as possible. The amount of the difference will be the greatest measure of these numbers. Take the numbers 350 and 100. Let one hundred be subtracted as often as possible from 350, which is three times. The remainder is 50. From the other number of the pair, one hundred, let 50 be subtracted; the remainder is 50. This number is the greatest common measure of 350 and 100; for fifty times two is one hundred, and fifty times seven is 350. From this calculation it becomes clear how one finds, of all the numbers which measure two numbers, their greatest common measure.

The smallest measure of the same numbers is found thus: when the largest measure has been found, the smallest measure of that number is sought, the same number also being the smallest common measure of the original numbers. Here the smallest measure of fifty is found in two; therefore it is also the smallest measure of the original numbers.

[786] Of three numbers which are composite to one another, their largest and their smallest common measures are found in the following way:[157] First find the greatest measure of two of the numbers. If this is also a common measure of the third and smallest

---

[156] Cf. *ibid.*, 2. Here Martianus gives an imprecise account of what is now known as the "Euclidean algorithm."

[157] Cf. *ibid.*, 3.

number, then that which was sought has been found. If this is not the case, then the greatest measure of the middle and smallest numbers is sought in the same way, and this is common to all three. Take the numbers 350, 100, and 75. The greatest common measure of the numbers 350 and 100 has been sought and found to be fifty; let us consider whether this number also measures the third number, which is 75. If it does, then it is the common measure of all three. But it does not. Therefore we consider 100 and 75 together and we seek their greatest measure. I subtract 75 from 100, and the remainder is 25. As often as possible I subtract 25 from 75, which is twice; and the remainder is 25. This number is the greatest common measure of 100 and 75. It is also the greatest common measure of all three numbers. For twenty-five times three is 75, twenty-five times four is 100, and twenty-five times fourteen is 350.

Now let us consider what is the smallest measure of the number 25. It is not possible to find this in the numbers two, three, or four; but it is in the number five, and this same measure is the smallest one common to all three larger numbers. For two, which is the measure of 350 and 100, does not measure 75; and 3, which measures 75, does not measure 350 and 100; and 4, which measures 100, does not measure 350 and 75. The number 5 is the first that can measure all of them, because five times fifteen is 75, five times twenty is 100, and five times seventy is 350.

[787] Given two numbers, the least number which they measure is found as follows:[158] Take the numbers 2 and 3; they are prime to each other; let either multiply the other; twice three or thrice two is 6. Six is the least number which those two numbers measure. No one can say what the greatest number which they can measure would be, but the same numbers will measure any number which will be the product on multiplying by the number six.

Let two more numbers that are not prime to each other, 9 and 12, be given; the answer is not found in the same way, by multiplying them, because a smaller number than the one which is produced from multiplying these is able to have the least measure. Therefore another way must be found.

[788] Let us then see what are the least numbers which have

158 Cf. *ibid.*, 34.

the same ratio with them. With the number nine the smallest of the same ratio is 3; with 12, it is 2. Now let either of the smaller numbers multiply not its own number, but the number belonging to the other; that is, either 3 times 12 or 2 times 9. Thrice twelve is 36, and twice nine is 18. Of these let us consider whether the smaller number, 18, has a measure both in 9 and in 12. It has in 9 but not in 12. Let it be disregarded, therefore, and let us take the larger number, 36. This is the smallest number which both 9 and 12 can measure; for nine times four or twelve times three is 36. By similar calculation those two numbers will also measure any number which results from multiplying by 36.

[789] Given three numbers, the least which they measure is found in the following way:[159] Take the numbers 2, 3, and 4. Let the least number be taken which has a measure in duplication or triplication. That number is six. Now let us consider whether the third of these numbers (namely, four) measures this number. If it measures it, then that which was sought is found. But it does not measure it. Therefore let us see what least number 3 and 4 measure. It is 12; therefore 12 is the least number which all three can measure; for twice six or thrice four or four times three makes 12. And every other number which is the product of multiplying by 12 will also be measured by those numbers.

[790] If two numbers measure any number, the least number measured by them will also measure the same number.[160] Take the number 12; 2 and 3 measure it. The least number which those two numbers measure is six. But the same number also measures 12; for six times two is 12.

The same thing happens in the case of that number which any three numbers measure;[161] for the least number measured by these three also measures this number. Take the number 24; 2, 3, and 4 measure that number. Now the least number which is measured by those three is 12. But this also measures the number 24, for twelve times two is 24.

[791] If two pairs of numbers, larger and smaller, be set out of such a sort that there is the same ratio between the larger and smaller

---

159 Cf. *ibid.*, 36.
160 Cf. *ibid.*, 35.
161 Cf. *ibid.*, 36.

pairs of numbers, as often as the larger measures the larger, the smaller will measure the smaller.[162] Take the numbers 2 and 3, and 8 and 12. There is the same ratio between the larger and the smaller numbers. For both 3 and 12 have the ratio of superdimidius to two and 8. Moreover, 3 measures 12 four times, for four times three is 12; and two also measures 8 four times, for four times two is 8.

[792] If a unit measures any number as often as another number measures a fourth number, it will happen that, as often as the unit measures the first number of the second pair, the number which had its measure in the unit will measure the last number.[163] Take the numbers 1 and 5 and 6 and 30. The unit measures the number five five times, and six does the same for the number 30. Again, the unit measures the number six six times; and five also measures the number 30 six times.

[793] If two numbers multiply each other, and some prime and incomposite number measures the product, it must also measure either of the original numbers.[164] Let the number eight multiply the number ten; the product is 80. Now two measures this, for twice forty is 80. But the same number also measures 8 and 10, since twice four is eight and twice five is 10.

[794] Let as many numbers as you may wish, in continued proportion, which the Greeks call *analogia*, be placed in order; if the first measures the last, it measures the second as well, and all others following it; if it measures the second, it also measures the last and the intervening ones; if, finally, it measures any one, it measures all.[165] Conversely, if it does not measure the last, it will not measure the second, or any other; if it does not measure the second, it will not measure the last, or any other; and if it does not measure any intermediate one, it will not measure another.[166] Take the numbers 3, 9, 27, 81, and 243; between all of them there is the ratio of the triple; moreover, the number three measures 243, for three times

162 Cf. *ibid.*, 20.
163 Cf. *ibid.*, 15.
164 Cf. *ibid.*, 30. Martianus says "either of the original numbers"; Euclid says "one of the original numbers."
165 Cf. Euclid *Elements* 8. 7.
166 Cf. *ibid.*, 6.

eighty-one is 243. Thus the same number measures the number nine, since three times three is 9; and because it measures nine, it also measures the last number; and because it measures either, it also measures the others; and because it measures any intermediate number, it also measures the numbers at the extremes. But because two does not measure 243, it will not measure 9 or the intermediate numbers. And because it does not measure 9, it will not measure 243 or the intermediate numbers; and because it does not measure any of the intermediate numbers, it will not measure numbers at the extremes.

[795] If as many numbers as you please, beginning with the unit, are in continued proportion, the same quantity of prime numbers as measure the last number, will measure the number which is next to the unit.[167] Take the numbers that increase by duplication: 1, 2, 4, 8, and 16; of these, 2 measures 16, and it also measures itself. Or take the numbers 1, 12, 144, and 1,728; the prime numbers 2 and 3 measure 1,728, for twice eight hundred and sixty-four is 1,728; likewise thrice five hundred and seventy-six. But 2 and 3 also measure 12, which is next after the unit, since twice six or thrice four is 12.

[796] If as many numbers as you please, beginning with the unit, are in continued proportion, the smaller always measures the greater by some one of the other numbers that are in the same proportion.[168] Lake the numbers 1; 2, 4, 8, 16, 32, and 64. Of these, 2 measures 4, 4 measures 8, 8 measures 16, 16 measures 32, and 32 measures 64, by duplication. And 2 measures 8 by quadruplication. In the same way, 4 measures 16, 8 measures 32, and 16 measures 64. Likewise, by octuplication 2 measures 16, 4 measures 32, and 8 measures 64. Nor will there be a number found that does not also measure a larger number; and no other measure does this than the one which is in the same numbers.

[797] If as many numbers as you please, beginning with the unit, are in a continued proportion, and the number next to the unit is prime, the greatest will not be measured by any except those that will belong in the same proportion.[169] Take the numbers 1, 3, 9, and 27. Among these the ratio is triple, and the number closest to

167 Cf. *ibid.*, 9. 12.
168 Cf. *ibid.*, 11.
169 Cf. *ibid.*, 13.

the unit is prime. Therefore no number can measure 27 except 3 or 9, because they are in the same proportion; this would not be the case if the nearest number to the unit were not prime. Take the numbers 1, 4, 16, and 64. The nearest number to the unit is not prime; therefore the last number, 64, admits of other measures than those which are in this series—namely, 2, 8, and 32, since twice thirty-two, eight times eight, or thirty-two times two makes 64.

A number that is the smallest number that two prime numbers measure will be measured by no other prime number.[170] Take 5 and 7; these numbers measure no smaller number than 35; for five times seven or seven times five is 35, and no other prime number can measure this; not 2, nor 3, nor 11, nor 13, nor 177, and much less any number beyond.

[798] If a square number measures a square number, the measure of a side will also be the measure of another side.[171] Take the two square numbers 4 and 16. The number four measures 16, for four times four is 16. And on the side of four is two, on the side of 16 is 4; 2 measures four, for twice two is 4. It also becomes clear that, given two square numbers, if the measure in the side of one is in the side of the other, the measure of one square number is also in the other square number.[172]

[799] And if a square number does not measure a square number, the side of one will not measure the side of the other.[173] Take the square numbers 4 and 9. The number four does not measure nine; therefore neither does two, which is in the side of four; but 3, which is in the side of the number nine, does measure it. It also is clear that, given two square numbers, if the measure of the side of one is not in the side of the other, the measure of one square number is not in the other.[174]

[800] If a cubic number measures a cubic number, the side of one will also measure the side of the other. Take the cubic numbers 8 and 64. The number 8 measures 64, since eight times eight is 64. And if on the side of the cubic number 8, the number 2 is found; on the side of the cubic number 64, 4 is found. Two is the

[170] Cf. *ibid.*, 14.
[171] Cf. *ibid.*, 8. 14.
[172] Cf. *ibid.*
[173] Cf. *ibid.*, 16.
[174] Cf. *ibid.*

measure of four. Hence it is clear, in the case of two cubic numbers, that if the side of one is the measure of the side of the other, the one cubic number will also be the measure of the other.[175]

But if one cubic number does not measure another cubic number, the measure of the one side will not be in the side of the other.[176] Take two cubic numbers 8 and 27. The number 8 does not measure 27. The side of the cubic number 8 is 2, and the side of the cubic number 27 is 3. The number 2 does not measure 3. From this it becomes clear that if the measure in the side of one cubic number is not the measure in the side of the other cubic number, the one cubic number does not measure the other cubic number.[177]

[801] Any number that is measured by another number gets the name of the measure from the same number that makes the measure.[178] Take the number 9. The number three measures this, and a *third* part of the number nine is three. Take the number 16. The number four measures this; and 4 is a *fourth* part of the number 16. The same is true of all other numbers.

It follows, moreover, that if a number has a part, it will be measured by a number that has the same name as the part.[179] For example, the third part of the number nine is three; and three measures nine.

[802] Let this briefly suffice for numbers and measures.

Further discourse would befit the Attic sages,
If any exhalations still remain upon our altars,[180]
Or if the doubled cloth[181] still is worn in ancient style. But

---

[175] Cf. *ibid.*, 15.

[176] Cf. *ibid.*, 17. It should be noted that although Martianus states many theorems in the theory of numbers, and that he gives specific instances illustrating these, he fails to provide mathematical proofs such as are found in the *Elements* of Euclid.

[177] Cf. *ibid.* There is a lacuna in the text of Martianus here; the words "in the side of the other cubic number" have dropped out.

[178] Cf. *ibid.*, 7. 37.

[179] Cf. *ibid.*, 38.

[180] Remigius *ad loc.* (ed. Lutz, II, 236) explains: "If there is any flame left in our breast, which is the altar of wisdom, where we bring our offering of learning."

[181] The *abolla*—which, according to Remigius, was the garment of philosophers. He says that they wore the garment doubled.

Time warns me to bring my discourse to a close,
Lest boredom steal upon the heavenly throng,
And I, old 'Number-Keeper,' be driven from the sky."

Thus spoke Arithmetic, and in silence she joined her sister standing by.

BOOK VIII

Astronomy

[803] Meanwhile the august company of the gods were amazed at the intricacies of the harmonious and discordant [odd and even] numbers, and acknowledged the lady herself, a majestic, exalted, and awe-inspiring figure, to be in very truth the procreator of the gods. And the host of philosophers, too, who stood nearby—in particular, Pythagoras, with all his disciples, and Plato, expounding the cryptic doctrines of his *Timaeus*[1]—worshiped the lady with words of mystic praise. Pallas, casting frequent glances at the bride, queried her about her commendation of the handmaid's learning and joined her in nodding her approval. The Cyllenian [Mercury] took more pride in the brilliance and clarity of Arithmetic than in that of any other bridesmaid, and was elated with her grandiloquence. As Phoebus was delaying the introduction of another bridesmaid for a little while, for fear of detracting from admiration of the previous speaker, a reverential silence came over the audience for a time.

[804] In the meantime wrinkled Silenus, as an attendant of Bacchus,[2] had been standing behind, leaning for support. Perhaps the weariness of age was too much for him; then again it may have been the strain of concentrating on the remarkable discourse of the learned lady; or perhaps the occasion of the marriage ceremony had gotten the better of him, swollen from earlier drinking bouts, and he had drenched himself in an overdraught of wine. For some time now he had been relaxed in slumber and quietly snoring, when suddenly he belched like a croaking frog. Several of the gods, shaken by this frightening and raucous sound, turned round, and as those who were standing about noticed the profuse sweating of

[1] The key work of Latin science into the Renaissance. It is the book depicted in Plato's hand in Raphael's *School of Athens*.

[2] Remigius explains that the drunken Silenus here refers to the poets, who are considered mad because of their imaginings; and that Bacchus here personifies wine. Cf. Vergil's charming description of Silenus in *Eclogues* 6. 14-26.

the old man "breathing forth his slumber"[3] and soaked with intoxication, they burst into laughter, the more explosive as they tried
to suppress it. Then, since a marriage ceremony is not supposed to
inhibit banter, the attendants of Venus and the maidservants of Bacchus served up such merriment to those who were already convulsed with hiccups that several others who were trying to suppress
their laughter broke into violent and wanton ribaldry and unrestrained mirth. Finally, Cupid, unruly as ever and saucy and impudent in his affronts, nimbly and merrily ran up to Silenus and, as
the old man had settled his ruddy bald head upon his staff, he gave
him a resounding clap with his palm, and the reverberating sound
revived the laughter, which was more or less universal.

[805] Then the old man, his eyes scarcely opened and his vision
blurred, looked about him and saw the gods laughing at him.
When someone pushed him, he was annoyed, looked around
stupidly, and wiped his moisty mouth with the palm of his hand.
Bacchus chided him to action, and he grasped his staff. As he
sought to take a step, at the encouragement of Lyde,[4] the haze
lifted and he beheld the conclave of the gods. Of a sudden he was
aroused and, shaking his corpse-like body, he tried to stir it to
motion. His efforts unavailing, he stood there, more baffled than
before. His feet refused their office and went the wrong way in
fear; reeling, struggling, he stood still, retreated, and came back.
Then his bloated, quivering old body gave up, and he fell to the
floor. A louder uproar than before ensued; Pleasure knew no
bounds. Finally, on orders from Bacchus, Satyr[5] raised the besotted
Silenus to his shoulders and, draping his limp body like a wine sack
about his neck, he brought him back.

[806] While this animated mirth was at its height, Satire, who
always considered it her responsibility to edify and reprove my
thoughts, said: "You, Felix, or Capella, or whoever you are, with a
sense to match the beast's whose name you bear,[6] are you going
out of your mind with the intrusion of this unseemly jesting? You
must realize that you have brought raucous laughter into a heavenly
assembly and that it is a reprobate act in the eyes of the gods, and of

---

[3] Vergil *Aeneid* 9. 326, of a drunken man in a heavy sleep.
[4] Silenus' wife, according to Remigius.
[5] Servant of Bacchus, according to Remigius.
[6] *Capella* means "she-goat."

Pallas in particular, to represent someone prating nonsense like a madman. [807] And on such an occasion to have Cupid and Satyr prancing about like impudent wantons, at the very time that the maiden of the sky [Astronomy], one of the more beautiful of the handmaids, is about to present herself to the august senate and the view of the gods! Enough of that, and hereafter do not try to defend your nonsense or justify your conduct as license appropriate to a wedding ceremony. At least give ready heed to the Prienian maxim, and if you are not 'an ass listening to a lyre, know the proper time.' "[7]

Soundly cudgeled by such stern and fell reproaches from Satire —a charming lady at other times—and condemned by my own apologies for my impudent conduct, I asked her which of the girls was being prepared for introduction. Satire, the wrath that she had vented upon me not yet subsided, began as follows:

[808] "The time is now at hand to speak of the path of the starry sphere, the course of the poles and of the region where the hallowed planets trace their diverse and winding courses. I see the canopy of heaven gleam, now struck by a bolt of lightning from the sky. From one direction, Herdsman Boötes, brilliant in the northern light, is wont to watch Septentriones [Ursa Major and Ursa Minor]; in the other direction, where the earth verges out of sight beneath the inclined sky, bright Canopus ranges imperceptible. And now I think I see Phoebus' team, swiftly coursing, and the blazing horns of the ever-changing moon; and what is more, the middle circle that is bound by the diagonal girdle,[8] along which a path is traced by glittering planets. You would rather fashion cheap and silly fictions than listen to a girl discoursing on the stars."

[809] As Satire was reciting these lines, I succumbed again to the mood to banter, despite her prohibitions and stern rebukes. "A fine performance, my Satire," I said. "Has your choler made a poet out of you? Have you begun to thirst for Permessian waters?[9]

---

[7] Martianus is attributing the maxim to Bias of Priene, one of the "seven wise men" of ancient Greece. The proverb was well known: cf. Aulus Gellius *Attic Nights* 3. 16. 13; Aristides Quintilianus 2. 16; Menander *Misoumenos* [The Hated Lover] 41.

[8] I.e., the celestial equator, intersected by the inclined zodiac.

[9] A reference to the Permessus River, a stream rising on Mount Helicon, abode of Apollo and the Muses.

Are you already anticipating the flashing countenances of the gods?[10] What has suddenly happened to your ever-ironical and subtle contempt for the bombast and conceits of the poets, whereby you content yourself with chaffing and witticisms while consigning their poetry to the realms of absurdity? Is there any reason to rage madly at me and to chide me in a superior and contemptuous way for being amused at the slumbering Silenus? Am I to dispense with all imaginary creatures and introduce no pleasantry or mirth to relieve the boredom of my readers? Come to your senses, Satire; leave off your tragic ranting, and take a hint from the young Pelignian poet: 'Young lady, take my advice and smile.' "[11] [810] Satire and I were soon done with our abusive quarreling, and Apollo stepped out to introduce another of the handmaids.[12]

Before their eyes a vision appeared, a hollow ball of heavenly light, filled with transparent fire, gently rotating, and enclosing a maiden within. Several planetary deities,[13] especially those which determine men's destinies, were bathed in its glare, the mystery of their behavior and orbits revealed. Even the fabric of the celestial sphere shone forth in the same flashing light. Lesser deities—ethereal, terrestrial, marine, and subterrestrial—were astounded at the miraculous sight, supposing that Astraea, Themis, or surely Libyan Urania had appeared before them, and they offered the maiden a seat of honor. [811] Decked with gems and decorously arrayed in every detail, she stepped forth nimbly from the sphere. Her brow was starlike and her locks sparkled. The plumage on her wings was crystalline, and as she glided through the sky her whirring wings repeatedly took on a golden hue. In one hand she held a forked sextant, in the other a book containing calculations of the orbits of the planets and their forward and retrograde motions together with the poles of the heavens. These were delineated in metals of various colors. As she came into their midst many of the gods smiled at her; the others admired her radiant beauty. She began her discourse as follows:

[10] Perhaps a reference to the celestial bodies, the next subject to be presented.

[11] Martial *Epigrams* 2. 41. 1, recalling a verse of the Pelignian poet Ovid. (*Inuenis* in Dick's text appears to be a misprint for *iuuenis* [RJ]).

[12] Astronomy.

[13] A reference to the baleful or beneficial effects of the planets upon events on earth.

[812] "In the presence of great and venerable learning it would be fit and proper for me not to disclose whatever fruits have come from my diligent study. For I do not consider it modest or becoming to expound their characteristic motions and orbits to the very ones who perform those motions or to presume to instruct the gods in what they are doing. Moreover, matters which over the vast span of ages have been reposited in the sanctums of Egyptian priests, I was keeping secret, not wishing to divulge and profane them. In fact, for almost forty thousand years I kept myself in seclusion there, in reverent observation. And well might I wish that following the disruption caused by the Flood and the restoration of Athens[14] after a long lapse of time, no worldly allurements, no vainglorious speculations of philosophers had known that I was in Greece, destined not to be kept hidden by a philosopher's cloak, but to be divulged to all. Never, to be sure, would the understanding of your journey and of your return reach mortal intelligence and the taint of mortal cares.[15]

[813] Inasmuch as I have at one time or other in my peregrinations come to be known by the Greeks, whatever has been written by Eratosthenes, Ptolemy, Hipparchus, and other Greeks ought to suffice here and relieve me of the burden of discoursing at greater length. However, because a sense of obligation toward the Cyllenian, the one who reared and educated me, does not permit me to keep silent, and because the sagacious bride also invites me to disclose the secrets of my studies, I shall not keep silent in the presence of you celestial ones, who will be surveying the courses of your own heavenly bodies.

[814] The universe is formed in the shape of a globe composed entirely of four elements.[16] The heavens, swirling in a ceaseless and rotary motion, set the earth apart in a stationary position in the middle and at the bottom.[17] I would not disdain, at the very outset of my discourse, to give heed to the physical philosophers who do not believe that the softness of rarefied bodies is drawn and divided

---

[14] Plato *Timaeus* 23c speaks of an earlier Athens, before the great flood. See also Cora E. Lutz, "Remigius' Ideas on the Origins of the Seven Liberal Arts," *Medievalia et Humanistica*, X (1956), 34-39.

[15] The text here is corrupt, and the meaning can only be conjectured.

[16] Cf. Plato *Timaeus* 32c-d; Pliny 2. 5.

[17] Cf. §§ 584, 599.

by its very condensations into certain set paths and intervals of circles;[18] but rather that the natures of these bodies, coalescing by their own surgings, are diffused the entire way around in globular layers.[19] The physical philosophers declare that the first envelopment is that of water, the second of air, the third of fire, arranged about a midpoint which they call the center. And coming next is a fifth agglomeration[20] of corporeal matter, in which the shining heavenly bodies have their courses, in a region where the inclined paths of the sun, moon, planets, and zodiac are drawn; in the philosophical schools the last is referred to as the 'circular billow.' The very calm of that realm keeps its position outermost and its course an encompassing one; it is called 'starless' from the fact that it is studded with no constellations.

[815] If each belt of the encompassing substances is found to be homogeneous, no circle can waver from its ethereal orbit. When we use the word 'circles' we do not intend to convey a notion of corporeal demarcations of a fluid substance; we are merely illustrating the risings and settings of planetary bodies as they appear to us. I myself do not consider an axis and poles, which mortals have fastened in a bronze armillary sphere[21] to assist them in comprehending the heavens, as an authoritative guide to the workings of the universe. For there is nothing more substantial than the earth itself, which is able to sustain the heavens. Another reason is that the poles that protrude from the hollow cavity of the perforated outer sphere, and the apertures, the pivots, and the sockets have to be imagined—something that you may be assured could not happen in a rarefied and supramundane atmosphere.

[816] Accordingly, whenever I shall use the terms axis, poles, or celestial circles, for the purpose of gaining comprehension, my terminology is to be understood in a theoretical sense, the distinctions applying not to transitory conditions in the heavens but

[18] Martianus' enigmatic and turgid style here makes the reader wonder whether he was seriously trying to convey an intelligible conception of the heavens. His *circulorum intercapedines* [intervals of circles] here seems to have no relation to the intervals of circles in § 837.

[19] Cf. Pliny 2. 10-11, 160.

[20] Counting the earth at the middle as one of the four lower elements.

[21] In a passage which contains a phrase distinctly similar to Martianus' expression here, Varro is quoted by Gellius (*Attic Nights* 3. 10. 3) as he points to another limitation of the armillary sphere.

to calculations of intervals.[22] And so also should my remarks be understood when I shall speak of the world as verging upward or sloping downward, although it is alike in all its regions and is elevated or lies hidden from view according to the position of the horizon or the situation of the lands.

[817] So much by way of preface. I now point out that whereas a certain Roman author,[23] well known to me, derives the words *stella* from the verb *stare*,[24] *sidera* from the verb *considere*,[25] and *astrum* from Astraeus,[26] and whereas the Greeks have filled the sky with mythological figures, I prefer to discuss the precepts of the discipline itself. And indeed I shall assert that there are ten so-called circles of the universe. Some of these are parallels, which we can refer to by their Latin designation as 'equidistant circles,' having the same poles as the universe itself.[27] The poles are defined as equally dividing the segments, if a line is drawn through the center of a circle to the circumference.

[818] The first of the parallels is the one which is always visible and looms above, never plunging below the horizon, and just grazing the edge of the northern horizon.[28] This is called the arctic circle, from the fact that it encompasses, along with the other constellations which will be mentioned later, the constellations of the twin Septentriones [819]. The second of the parallels is the solstitial [or tropic], the limit which the sun reaches in summer and from which it is then turned away.[29] [820] The third, or equinoctial, parallel—the middle and greatest of all—marks the measure of the equal length of day and night.[30] The sun, in its middle position in the universe, crosses this

[22] Cf. § 837.

[23] Astronomy is probably referring to Varro, whose *De lingua latina* originally consisted of twenty-five books, of which only Books V-X survive, V and VI being in complete form. Cf. Cassiodorus 2. 7. 2.

[24] *stella* [star]; *stare* [to stand]. Isidore (*Etymologies* 3. 71. 4) gives the same derivation.

[25] *sidera* [constellations], *considere* [to set]. Varro (*De lingua latina* 7. 14) derives *sidera* from *insidere*.

[26] *astrum* [star, constellation]. Aratus (*Phaenomena* 98-99) reports that Astraeus was considered the father of the stars.

[27] Cf. Geminus 5. 1.

[28] Cf. *ibid.*, 2.

[29] Cf. Geminus 5. 4-5.

[30] *Ibid.*, 6.

parallel twice, when it is rising to its summer heat or descending to its winter quarters. [821] Next after this comes the winter tropic, upon reaching which, at the winter limit, the sun is turned back and begins rising again in its northward course.[31] [822] The fifth and last parallel is called the *australis*, or the antarctic circle. This is plunged beneath the surface, and its upper edge barely touches the southern horizon.[32] The powers of reasoning show it to be of the same extent as the arctic circle, which is situated diametrically opposite it.

[823] It is fitting now to explain the colures, portions of which are overhead, other portions of which are hidden beneath the surface.[33] I am aware that these circles are traced differently by different writers. For some assert that one colure is traced from the north pole into the south, and then passing beneath the earth is elevated again in the arctic pole. Others maintain that the circle has its beginning at the south pole, passes through the arctic pole, and returns to its point of origin. These writers, tracing another colure at right angles, cut the girth of the universe into four equal parts. [824] But I propound a view which my dear Hipparchus, a ranking authority, adopts, maintaining that these circles originate in signs of the zodiac and cross each other twice; and, cutting all the parallels at equal angles, they pass through the poles. One colure, originating in the eighth degree of Aries,[34] traverses the universe, passing through the poles, and returns to the same point; the other girdles the universe in a similar manner, arising in Cancer. We shall explain this more clearly later.[35]

[825] And now we must describe the oblique circles. Of these the zodiac, marked off in twelve segments, is tangent to two of the parallels, the Tropics of Cancer and Capricorn. It intersects the equator twice, but the angles produced are not equal. The zodiac furnishes a path for the sun, the moon, and the five planets. [826]

[31] *Ibid.*, 7-8.

[32] *Ibid.*, 9.

[33] *Ibid.*, 49.

[34] Otto Neugebauer, *The Exact Sciences in Antiquity* (2d ed., Providence, R.I., 1957), p. 188, points out that the adoption of Aries 8° as the vernal point (the vernal point of System B in Babylonian lunar theory) corroborates the view that astrology was introduced into Greece at a rather late date. The earliest use of Aries 8° in Greece was around the time of Hipparchus. Earlier writers used Aries 15° as the vernal point.

[35] Cf. §§ 832-833.

Among the oblique circles the Milky Way is plainly visible as extending with a much greater girth,[36] since it rises in the borders of the arctic circle and sets on the horizon of the antarctic region, and appears to traverse almost the entire heavens. Those who have refused to include this one among the celestial circles seem to me to be foolish.[37] There is now one circle left for mention, a circle which I am at a loss to name, since it varies with all times and places. This circle demarcates for us the upper and lower worlds; and, lying upon the surface of the earth in a line that curves completely around, it is called the horizon, or 'boundary circle.'

[827] Now that I have briefly and clearly described the celestial circles, I shall discuss their intervals, starting at my original point. I shall again begin with the sublime arctic circle. Here, following a geometrical procedure, I have set two points for drawing a circle: the one to mark the center, and the other the circumference. At the very pole of the universe I[38] have set a brilliant star, and from it to the head of Draco, which I had previously noted stretches to the circle of the horizon, I have drawn a line.[39] About this line, with the center fixed, I have drawn, in my mind, a circle encompassing an equal space on every side. The circumference extends through the following constellations: beginning at the head of Draco, to the right foot of Engonasis [Hercules], through the middle of the breast of Cepheus, through the front feet of Ursa Major,[40] and back to the head of Draco.

[828] Closest to this circle is the summer tropic. By extending another line from the celestial pole to the eighth degree of Cancer, a point which the sun reaches at the solstice, we produce the same sort of circle, but with larger girth, passing through the following signs: beginning with the eighth degree of Cancer, whose entire body it cuts through lengthwise, the circle next comes to the chest

[36] Note Martianus' naiveté in supposing that one great circle is of much greater extent than another because its course is more oblique and extends farther north and south.

[37] The Milky Way is frequently omitted from the list of celestial circles in the ancient popular handbooks.

[38] The celestial handmaiden Astronomy is speaking.

[39] This would be an arc extending from the polestar to the head of Draco.

[40] The tracing of the arctic circle depends upon the latitude of the observer. Geminus *Introduction to the Phaenomena* 5. 3 says that at Rhodes the front feet of the Great Bear mark the arctic circle. Cf. Hyginus *Astronomica* 4. 6.

and belly of Leo; then to the shoulders of Ophiuchus [Serpentarius], the head of Cygnus, the hoofs of Equus, and the right arm of Andromeda, then to the left shin and the left shoulder of Perseus, then to the knees of Heniochus [Auriga, the Charioteer] and, close by, the heads of Gemini, and back again to the eighth degree of Cancer.[41]

[829] The celestial equator, measured twice, from either pole, traces its circle in both Aries and Libra, with a line passing through the following constellations: from the eighth degree of Aries, through its entire body, to the retracted hoof of Taurus, thence to Orion's Belt, next through the elevated coil of Hydra, through Crater and Corvus to the eighth degree of Libra, between the two brilliant stars of that constellation; then to the knees of Ophiuchus, then through Aquila to the head of Pegasus, and back again to the eighth degree of Aries.[42]

[830] The winter tropic, with its location marked in a corresponding manner in the eighth degree of Capricornus, passes through the following constellations: beginning at the eighth degree of Capricornus, through its entire body, to the feet of Aquarius, thence to the end of the tail of Cetus, then to Lepus and the front paws of Canis; then through Argo and the back of Centaurus to the sting of Scorpio; next through the last part of Sagitta, and back again to the eighth degree of Capricornus.[43]

[831] The last of the celestial parallels, called the antarctic, encompasses as much space as the arctic circle. I could reveal which constellations are marked by its circular course, for no part of the celestial sphere is unknown to me. But since the circle stretches through regions not known or visible to men of the upper hemisphere, I shall omit mention of them, lest my unverified statement appear to smack of falsehood.[44]

[41] Martianus' tracing of Cancer corresponds to that in Aratus *Phaenomena* 480-500.

[42] Martianus' tracing of the celestial equator corresponds with that of Hyginus *Astronomica* 4. 3, and generally conforms with that of Aratus *Phaenomena* 511-24. Aratus, however, says that the circle has "no share in Aquila."

[43] Martianus' tracing of the Tropic of Capricorn corresponds with that of Aratus 501-6 and Hyginus 4. 4.

[44] The true reason for Martianus' withholding the names of the antarctic constellations is that he was a compiler, using the stock materials of popular authors. It should not be supposed that as a North African he would have been familiar

[832] Let us indicate the colures more clearly. They too conceal part of their circles and do not reveal themselves entirely to our view; yet our assumptions about them are reliable, and it is possible to trace their courses. The first of these[45] takes its beginning at the equinoctial point (that is, the eighth degree of Aries); it touches the far angle of Deltoton [Triangulum]; next it touches the top of the head of Perseus and his right arm; next, cutting his hand, it crosses the arctic circle and reaches the celestial north pole; from here it goes through the tail of Draco to the left side of Boötes, and then to the star of Boötes;[46] next to the right, and then the left, foot of Virgo; to the eighth degree of Libra; and from here it goes to the right hand of Centaurus, in which he holds Panthera; not far distant from the place where it touched the left hoof of Centaurus, it disappears from sight, in a region below the horizon; emerging again below Cetus, it passes through his body and shoulder to the head, and returns to the eighth degree of Aries.[47]

[833] A second colure, which is called the tropical colure, originates at the eighth degree of Cancer, passes to the left front paw of Ursa Major, through his chest and neck; then it reaches the celestial north pole; from here it goes through the hind quarters of Ursa Minor, on through Draco and the left wing and neck of Cygnus, touches the tip of Sagitta and the beak of Aquila, from which point it descends to the eighth degree of Capricornus; not far from here it plunges from view and rises again below Argo; it cuts through its rudder and upright stern and returns to the eighth degree of Cancer.[48]

[834] It is evident that two circles remain to be discussed, those which, as I mentioned above, are called the oblique circles. One of these, the zodiac, is not like the others, which I have drawn as lines; it obviously is the broadest of all the circles. When I was dividing this belt into 12 segments, I was aware of the reason for my assigning 30 degrees to each part. Moreover, I stretched the breadth of this belt across twelve portions, so that it covered in

---

with the southern constellations. The latitude of Carthage is actually slightly higher than that of Rhodes, where Hipparchus, Posidonius, and Geminus lived.

[45] The equinoctial colure.
[46] Arcturus.
[47] Cf. Manilius *Astronomicon* 1. 603-17.
[48] Cf. *ibid.*, 618-30.

latitude as much space as twelve of the degrees of the belt's longitude.[49] It will be easy to point out the reason for this when I come to
speak about the sun. The sun (sol) is the only (solus)[50] body to
be borne in its course along the middle line of this belt. [835] It
is also quite clear that this belt stretches across twelve very conspicuous constellations. For the existence of the Milky Way is con-
firmed as much by eyesight as by reasoning powers. Its breadth
frequently diminishes below the regular extent[51] but is compen-
sated by its great expanse in the stretch between constellations of
Cassiopeia and the sting of Scorpio.

[836] One circle remains to be mentioned—the horizon, which,
by reason of the fact that it always varies with the rising and
descending of the celestial sphere, cannot be traced through a definite
sequence of stars.[52] [837] Now it is appropriate to explain what interval of distance or space has been admitted between the celestial
circles by nature's intervention. Between the arctic circle, which I
have cut into eight spaces,[53] and the summer tropic, there is as
much difference in space as between 8 and 6. Similar interjacent areas
are contained in similar spaces; thus it follows that one belt is
larger than the other by one and a third times. Another intervening distance, between the summer tropic and the equator, is
smaller than the belt above it as is the ratio of four to six. From the
equator to the winter tropic there is a corresponding distance; from
the winter tropic to the antarctic circle there is the same amount of
space as between the arctic circle and the summer tropic; and the
antarctic circle has the same distance to its pole as the arctic circle
has to its pole.[54]

[838] Now that we have briefly discussed the circles and the
spaces lying between them, let us deal cursorily with the bodies
which are called fixed stars. It is an accepted fact that there are 35

[49] Cf. Geminus 5. 53.

[50] In placing sol [sun] and solus [only] in close proximity, Martianus implies
an etymological connection. Macrobius (Commentary 1. 20. 4) derives sol from
solus.

[51] Geminus 5. 69.

[52] Ibid., 62.

[53] I.e., from the celestial north pole.

[54] Martianus often has his handmaids speak in turgid and ambiguous phrase-
ology to conceal his ignorance. That is not the case here, where he could have
explained the matter in very simple terms. See above, Vol. I, pp. 181-82.

resplendent constellations spread across the entire heavens, unless one wishes to include their burdens, which are known by the names of animals: these are Capra [the Goat], which rests upon Henio-chus; and Haedi [the Kids], which he holds on his shoulders; or Serpens, which Ophiuchus grasps; or Panthera, which Centaurus carries. These constellations ought rather to be considered as parts of their more prominent constellations.

The thirty-five constellations[55] then are divided by a circle that cuts across them; some are northern constellations, others southern.[56] The northern constellations are found in the region of the zodiac toward the Septentriones; the southern constellations are further in. The northern sector is occupied by the two Septentriones; by Draco, which winds about and glides between them; by Arcturus, also known as Boötes; by Corona Ariadnes and Nixus [Hercules], which some call Engonasis [the Kneeler]; by Lyra, Cygnus, Cepheus, Cassiopeia, Perseus, Deltoton, Heniochus, Andromeda, Pegasus, Ophiuchus, Delphinus, Aquila, and Sagitta.

The southern constellations are as follows: Hydrus, Crater, Corvus, Procyon, Orion, Canicula, Lepus, Eridanus (which flows from the foot of Orion), Cetus, Centaurus, Argo, Piscis Australis, Caelulum, and Ara.

We consider Aqua, which flows from the cup of Aquarius, as more appropriately a part of that sign; and the star which some call Canopus and others Ptolemaeus (which is not visible to inhabitants of the northern hemisphere and begins to appear in the vicinity of Alexandria), I shall consider as part of the river Eridanus.[57]

[839] These constellations are kept separate by the zodiac, which maintains twelve equal divisions of signs but has only eleven constellations. For Scorpio occupies its own space with its body and the space of Libra with its claws; the feet of Virgo also occupy the upper

[55] It is hard to account for Martianus' total of 35. He goes on to enumerate 19 northern constellations and 14 southern, omitting 4 lesser constellations as parts of more conspicuous ones. To bring the number to 35, he must be counting Aqua and Canopus, which he specifically says are minor. Then again, one should not be disturbed about such discrepancies in a compilation of this sort. Martianus may have gotten his figure for the total from one author, and his list of constellations from another.

[56] Cf. Geminus 3. 1.

[57] On these constellations and their listing by various ancient authorities, see the eleventh edition of the *Encyclopaedia Britannica*, s.v. "Constellation."

part of Libra's space,[58] but the greater part is occupied by Scorpio. What we call Libra, the Greeks refer to as Chelae [the Claws]. I pass over the names of the twelve signs, since these are common knowledge.

[840] I realize that the topic coming next in order is the discussion of the circles or zones to which the constellations are assigned. But this calls for considerable elaboration, contrary to my plan of brevity; moreover, because the limbs of several signs are cleft in pieces—into halves or thirds—by various fixed circles, I leave this subject in darkness. Merely to cite a few examples, so that we may pass on to other matters: the left hand of Boötes is located within the arctic circle, the rest of his body is assigned to another zone; the body of Cepheus is divided in the middle, at the chest, and assigned to different celestial belts. Nixus, trampling with his left foot upon the head of the arctic Draco, rises with his own head to the summer tropic, giving one arm to Lyra and the other to Corona; and there are other unpleasant and melancholy details such as these.

[841] A more fitting subject for discussion is the question of which constellations are rising or setting when other constellations are rising. When Cancer is rising, Corona Ariadnes and a half part of Piscis Australis are setting; also Ophiuchus, feet first, as far as the upper arms, and Serpens, which he is holding (that is, except for the jaws and the entire head); also half of Boötes. But all of Orion is rising, as well as the beginning of Eridanus, and the bright star[59] in the tongue of Canicula. When Leo is rising, the remainder of Corona becomes hidden, and Piscis Australis, and portions of Ophiuchus, Serpens, and Boötes; likewise Aquila and the right part of Nixus; but the head of Hydra, Lepus, and Procyon, and the first part of Canicula are rising. While Virgo is rising, Lyra, Delphinus, and Sagitta are setting, as well as the greater portion of Cygnus, the last part of Eridanus, and the head and neck of Pegasus; at the same time the first part of Hydrus as far as Crater, and all of Canicula, and the [842] stern of the ship Argo are rising. When Libra is rising, the remaining portions of Pegasus and Cygnus, the head of Andromeda, the shoulders of Cepheus, Cetus, and the meanders in the river Eridanus are setting; at the same time, half of Corona, the

---

58 Cf. Geminus 1. 5; Macrobius *Commentary* 1. 18. 13.
59 Procyon.

right foot of Nixus, Boötes, all of Hydrus except the end of the tail, and the equine part of Centaurus are rising. When Scorpio is rising, the remainder of Andromeda, and the part of Cepheus which lies outside the arctic circle, and portions of Cassiopeia and Orion are setting; and, at the same time, all of Corona Ariadnes, the head of Ophiuchus, the entire body of Nixus except the left hand, the end of the tail of Hydrus, and all of Centaurus except the front feet are rising. When Sagittarius is rising, Orion, Canicula, and the feet of Heniochus are disappearing. But all of Ophiuchus, and the left hand of Nixus, and Lyra, and the head and shoulders of Cepheus, and the front feet of Centaurus are rising.

[843] When Capricornus is rising, all of Heniochus with Capra and Haedi is setting, together with the left part of Perseus, and the stern of Argo, and Procyon; at the same time, Cygnus, Aquila, Sagitta, and Altarium are rising. When Aquarius is rising, the equine portion of Centaurus and the head of Hydrus are setting; and the horse Pegasus is rising. When Pisces is rising, all of Hydrus, and the rest of the equine portion of Centaurus, and Crater are setting; moreover, the right part of Andromeda and Piscis Australis are rising. When the sign of Aries is rising, the feet of Centaurus and Altarium are setting; but the left part of Andromeda and the upper part of Perseus, as far as the belly, and Deltoton are rising. And when the sign of Taurus is rising, the feet of Boötes, and the lower part of Ophiuchus, as far as the knees, are setting; but the remaining part of Cetus and the left foot of Orion are rising. When Gemini is rising, Ophiuchus, as far as his knees, is setting; and Eridanus, Cetus, and Orion are rising.[60]

[844] The differences in times required for risings and settings must be explained. Those constellations that rise transversely and set vertically have swifter risings than settings; conversely, those that rise vertically and set transversely have slower risings than settings.[61] Cancer rises vertically and sets at an inclination, even though it has only a slight curvature in Capricornus. Cancer rises in 2½2 hours and sets in 1¹¹⁄₁₂ hours. The difference here is minimal.

---

[60] Dick omits this sentence from his text, following Petau, who rejected it as an inept gloss. But Aratus *Phaenomena* 724-31 observes the same risings and settings.

[61] Cf. Geminus 7. 10-12; Cleomedes 1. 6. 31.

Leo rises in 2⅓ hours and sets in 1⅔ hours. Virgo rises in 2⅔ hours and sets in 1⅓ hours. The same holds for Libra. But Scorpio's rising time is less [than Virgo's], and the duration of its setting is greater: it rises in 2⅓ hours and sets in 1⅔ hours. Sagittarius rises in 2 1/12 hours and sets in 1 11/12 hours.

[845] Conversely, those constellations that rise transversely and set vertically have shorter risings than settings. Among these, the sign of Capricornus, which rises in 1 11/12 hours, sets in 2 1/12 hours. The next sign, of Aquarius, rises in 1⅔ hours and sets in 2⅓ hours. Pisces rises in 1⅓ hours and sets in 2⅔ hours. Aries consumes the same amount of time for risings and settings as Pisces. Taurus rises in 1⅔ hours and sets in 2⅓ hours. And Gemini rises in 1 11/12 hours and sets in 2 1/12 hours.

[846] This underlies the inequalities in the duration of days and nights. When the sun begins to enter those signs which rise slowly, and as the signs following after are rising, a lengthening of days occurs; when it enters those signs which rise quickly and set slowly, it causes nights to become longer and days shorter. Again a puzzling question is raised,[62] and the accompanying answer will serve to explain. If all the signs comprise equal amounts of space, and if, at all times, night and day, six signs must be above the earth's horizon, then all days and nights ought to be of equal duration. There is no doubt that six signs are above the earth and that six are hidden, and also that days and nights do differ in their duration. For a day at the summer solstice has 14⅙ hours, and a day at the winter solstice has 9⅚ hours;[63] conversely, winter nights are prolonged, to the length of days at the summer solstice, and summer nights correspond in length to winter days. With such discrepancy in the length of the periods, the natural assumption is that the signs are not to [847] be considered equal. But such a conclusion is refuted by

[62] Cf. Geminus 7. 12-13.

[63] Professor Otto Neugebauer, in correspondence, has kindly drawn my attention to the fact that the figures Martianus gives here for daylight hours are in exact agreement with the figures given for rising times in §§ 844-45, and that the observations are correct for a latitude slightly above Alexandria. The source of Martianus' observations is not known; but of this we may be sure, that Martianus did not make his own observations or computations. See above, Vol. I, p. 185.

obvious facts and by our measurements. For the setting out of multiple clepsydras⁶⁴ proves that all the signs do occupy equal amounts of space. Although the signs do consume varying amounts of time in their risings and settings, nevertheless, if you balance the risings and settings of all of them, pairing them up, you will see that they correspond to the full measure.

[848] Now that this difficulty has been resolved, there is another, more elusive problem with regard to the inequality of spaces. Our dissenters will say: 'If the spaces occupied by the signs are equal, either the sun traverses some signs at a retarded speed or your accounting of the discrepancies of daylight is proved to be faulty. It is a recognized fact that thirty-two days elapse during the sun's course in Gemini, and twenty-eight days in Sagittarius, with the number of days varying between those amounts in the other signs. This would surely not be the case if the sun were borne at a uniform speed and the signs occupied equal amounts of space. But if the sun's velocity is always uniform, it must follow that the signs do not occupy equal spaces.'

[849] But a long-standing misconception is responsible for this confusion, a notion which all men have believed until now,⁶⁵ that, inasmuch as the earth is the center of the universe and the outermost sphere, it is also the center of the sun's orbit; but this is manifestly not true. For just as the spaces encompassed by the celestial circle and the middle orbit are different, so the points about which they revolve are different. Consequently, the earth is not the center of the sun's orbit, but is eccentric to it.⁶⁶ In alternate periods the sun depresses its course to a closer position to the earth and again elevates it, depending upon its juxtaposition with the signs of the zodiac; and although the equipoised sun moves along the middle line of the zodiac belt, the obliquity of its course causes it to be depressed or elevated. Would anyone doubt that Cancer and

⁶⁴ Macrobius (*Commentary* 1. 21. 11-22) discusses in detail the procedure of measuring the signs of the zodiac by the use of clepsydras. Martianus refers to them later (§ 860) in attempting to measure planetary orbits. Geminus (7. 12-17) raises the same question as Martianus and gives the same explanation, but he bases the proof of the division of the zodiac into twelve equal parts on dioptral measurements (1. 4).

⁶⁵ It is characteristic of a Latin compiler to give his readers the impression that his own ingenuity is responsible for a startling discovery.

⁶⁶ Geminus 1. 31-35.

Gemini are elevated in the so-called steeper[67] regions of the universe and that Sagittarius and Capricornus are depressed where they curve away? Whereas the zodiac and the signs that are fixed in the sky are equidistant from the earth in all directions, the solar orbit, which has a lower course, is either elevated or depressed. Hence it comes about that the signs seem to be traversed by the sun in varying numbers of days.

[850] So much for the discussion of the celestial signs and circles. Now I shall take up the orbits of the planets. Not because of their errant motions—for their courses are defined in the same way as the sun's, and they do not admit of any error[68]—rather, because their peculiar behavior confounds mortals' minds, I shall call them not 'errant bodies' (*planetae*) but 'confusing bodies' (*planontes*), as Aratus declares.[69] They have their proper names, and they are also called by other names.

[851] Saturn is called 'the Shiner' (*Phaenon*), and Jupiter 'the Blazer' (*Phaëthon*), and Mars 'the Fiery' (*Pyrois*), Venus 'the Lightbringer' (*Phosphoros*), and Mercury 'the Twinkler' (*Stilbon*).[70] But the races of mankind have given countless names to the sun and the moon. A distinction must be noted between these seven bodies and the fixed stars; the latter move only with the rotation of the celestial sphere, being set in their own fixed positions, whereas the planets are borne along in their own proper motions, in addition to their being swept along with the celestial rotation.

[852] For in varying amounts of time the planets strive to make up the distance that they are carried backward by a single diurnal rotation: the moon in a month, the sun in a year, Saturn in thirty years, and the others in periods of time proportional to the amount of space that they traverse.

[853] Although all these bodies are seen to move toward the eastern horizon, they do not move counter to the universe in a straight

[67] Macrobius (*Commentary* 1. 6. 51) and Cleomedes (113) speak of the steeper ascent in Gemini.

[68] The Latin *errantes* is a common designation for the planets, being a translation of the Greek word *planetae*.

[69] See Jacques Fontaine, *Isidore de Séville et la culture classique dans l'Espagne wisigothique*, II, 510.

[70] See Klibansky, Panofsky, and Saxl, *Saturn and Melancholy*, p. 137. See also above, Vol. I, p. 187, n. 51.

and direct line; rather they plod along with sideways motions across the fixed stars of the zodiac. It is well that they do, for the universe could not endure a contrary motion of its parts.

Again the doctrines of the Peripatetics maintain that the planets do not move counter to the motion of the celestial sphere but are out-distanced by the speed of the latter and cannot keep up with it.[71] Even if this were true, it could not disturb my calculations. For whether Saturn, with its excessive speed, vies with the celestial sphere and is scarcely outdistanced by it, the difference in their courses being slight, whereas the moon, which moves more slowly, is over-taken in the same sector of the sky in less than thirty days; or whether the moon is swifter than those other bodies that strive in contrary motion to the celestial sphere, because its orbit is over a shorter distance, and Saturn is slower because of the great extent of its far-flung orbit—take your choice; it is not contrary to my models, since, indeed, the motion of those bodies is regulated by relationships between themselves.

[854] There is one motion that is common to all seven planets —an easterly one. Another point to be noted is that they all differ in the times and circumstances of their periods. For five of the planets undergo stations and retrogradations, but the sun and the moon are propelled in a steady course. Moreover, these two luminous bodies eclipse each other in turn; but the other five are never eclipsed.[72] Three of these, together with the sun and the moon, have their orbits about the earth, but Venus and Mercury do not go about the earth.

[855] This general observation must be made, that the earth is eccentric to the orbits of all the planets (that is, it is not located at the center of their circles); and a second observation must be made about all seven, that although the celestial sphere rotates with the same uniform motion, the planets make daily changes in their positions and orbits; for no planet rises from the same position from which it arose on the previous day.

[856] This being the case, it follows that the sun has 183 circles[73] which it describes as it goes back and forth from the summer tropic

---

[71] Cf. Geminus 12. 19-22.

[72] Little or no mention of the occultation of planets is made by popular writers on astronomy, although Aristotle (De caelo 2. 292a) reports an eclipse of Mars by the moon.

[73] Geminus (5. 12) says 182.

to the winter tropic; it alternates its course over the same circles. While the sun is traversing this number of circles, Mars describes twice as many, Jupiter twelve times as many, and Saturn twenty-eight times as many. These circles are also referred to as parallels. All of the planets have forward motions, together with the celestial sphere, and they go about the earth with their risings and settings.

[857] Now Venus and Mercury, although they have daily risings and settings, do not travel about the earth at all; rather they encircle the sun in wider revolutions. The center of their orbits is set in the sun. As a result they are sometimes above the sun; more often they are beneath it, in a closer approximation to the earth. Mercury's and Venus' greatest elongation from the sun is one and one half signs. When both planets have a position above the sun, Mercury is closer to the earth; when they are below the sun, Venus is closer, inasmuch as it has a broader and more sweeping orbit.[74]

[858] As to the moon, which is closest to the earth, I shall speak later about its coursings. Immediately above the moon's orbit some authorities place the orbits of Mercury and Venus; others argue that the sun's orbit comes next.[75] Then come the orbits of Mars, Jupiter, and Saturn. To ascertain the dimensions of all these orbits—an undertaking which astronomers consider a difficult one—a basic assumption must be drawn from geometry, one which the bridesmaid Geometry herself offers in the present work and which has been approved by Eratosthenes and Archimedes; namely, that there are 406,010 stadia[76] in the earth's circumference. By irrefutable reckonings it is found that the moon's orbit is one hundred times greater than the earth's

[74] It is interesting to note that Copernicus (*De revolutionibus orbium caelestium* i. 10) singled out Martianus with high praise for making this observation of the epicyclic motions of Venus and Mercury, although this was a commonplace feature in the popular handbooks. See above, Vol. I, pp. 189-90.

[75] On the difficulties that popular authorities encountered in trying to reconcile epicyclic motions for Venus and Mercury with a fixed order of the planets and on the confusion that existed in antiquity and the Middle Ages, see Macrobius *Commentary* i. 19. 1-13 and the footnotes to my translation of the work (New York, 1952). Geminus (i. 28-29) places Mercury and Venus below the sun.

[76] This is one of the most astonishing discrepancies in the work. Martianus here refers to Geometry's earlier calculation of the earth's circumference, yet there (§ 596) he gave the correct figure for Eratosthenes' estimate (252,000 stadia). Cf. the figure given here with that in a fragment in the appendix of Ludwig von Jan's edition of Macrobius' *Commentary*; Berger, *Eratosthenis fragmenta*, p. 121.

circumference. This orbit is also found to be six hundred times as great as the moon itself. [859] During repeated eclipses of the sun, by comparing the extent of the shadow which the moon, lying directly beneath, casts upon the earth, with the size of the moon itself, we obtain these two accurate dimensions. If this subject is not tedious, I shall explain how I obtained these measurements.

It often happens that an eclipse of the sun occurring at the latitude of Meroë darkens the entire orb, but at a nearby climate—that is, one passing through Rhodes—the obscuration is partial, and at the latitude of the mouth of the Borysthenes [Dnieper] there is no obstruction and the full orb shines forth.[77] Since the correct distance in stadia at which the latitude of Rhodes is located is known, I have found that the breadth of the shadow which the moon casts is one eighteenth part of the earth. Now since the body which casts the conical shadow is larger than the shadow itself, it has been ascertained from the latitudes on either side at which the sun was partially obscured, that the moon itself is three times as large as its shadow.[78]

Thus it has been determined by the foregoing calculations that the moon is one sixth as large as the earth. [860] That the moon's diameter is one six-hundredth of its orbit is determined by the use of clepsydras. [Place two copper vessels in position, an empty one below, one full of water above. Mark the rising of the moon and that of a fixed star rising simultaneously with it. At the moment when the upper edge of the moon begins to appear above the horizon, quickly release the stopper from the upper vessel, the one containing the water, and let the water flow until the moon's entire orb appears. At this point remove the first vessel into which the water has flowed and put another in its place, into which the water may flow until, on the following night, the very same star rises which rose together with the moon on the previous night. Remove the upper vessel, from which the water flowed out in the space of twenty-four hours. Compare it with the amount which flowed out into the first vessel while the orb of the moon was rising, and you will find that the entire amount increased six hundredfold. Hence it is clear that the orbit of

[77] Cleomedes (2. 95) has the sun totally eclipsed at the Hellespont and partially visible at Alexandria.

[78] In what Martianus must have regarded as one of the most impressive mathematical procedures in his book, he is comparing a measurement of the earth's circumference with the moon's diameter.

the moon surpasses the diameter of the moon by six hundred times.]⁷⁹ We conclude, then, that the lunar orbit is one hundred times as great as the earth.

[861] After this demonstration, let us turn our attention to the other orbits. Will anyone doubt that the sun's orbit is 12 times as great as the moon's, if the latter completes its orbit in a month and the former in a year? The orbit of Mars is then found to be twenty-four times as great, Jupiter's one hundred and forty-four times as great, and Saturn's three hundred and thirty-six times as great. If the calculations are carried farther, we find both the number of stadia in the orbit of Saturn and how many times greater it is than the entire earth. For if the moon's orbit is 100 times as great as the earth and Saturn's orbit is three hundred and thirty-six times as great as the moon's orbit, then the orbit of Saturn is thirty-three thousand six hundred times greater than the earth's size.

[862] Now let us consider the moon's course, which is closest to the earth. Natural philosophers are agreed that its light lasts for a month. This may be so, but there is no doubt that the full moon is always illuminated. For if, on that side which lies directly facing the sun, it is illuminated over the entire hemisphere,⁸⁰ even when, on the thirtieth day, it reveals none of its light to us, yet on the upper side, which is facing the sun, it beams in full light. Then, as it leaves its conjunction with the sun and begins to be observed from the side, it becomes partially illuminated on the underside, until, reaching a position opposite the sun, it is illuminated on the side which is visible to us. [863] The brightness of the sun encircles the lunar orb and bathes with light the entire part which faces it. These brilliant rays also reach the earth, like an image of light reflected in a mirror. When the moon receives the light in the phase of its first rising, it is obscured from us; and as it draws away from the sun in the west, it begins to grow light. [864] Its appearance at first

⁷⁹ Petau rejected the bracketed passage—nearly the whole of § 860—as a gloss drawn in substance from Macrobius *Commentary* 1. 21. 12-21. The gloss is quoted from Remigius. Macrobius describes this procedure as used to measure the signs of the zodiac; the feasibility of that means of measurement was noted by Martianus (§ 847). Cleomedes (*De motu circulari corporum caelestium* 2. 75) gives a brief account of the procedure as used to measure the apparent diameter of the sun, and attributes the method to the Egyptians.

⁸⁰ Cf. Geminus 9. 5ff.

illumination, encircled by horns, as it were, is called *mēnoeidēs* [crescent-shaped]; at an eastward elongation of 90 degrees, when the sun's rays have illuminated its orb half way, it is called *dichotomos* [halved]; when it has progressed another 45 degrees, it is called *amphikurtos* [gibbous], that is, larger than half, smaller than full; and when the moon is 180 degrees removed from the sun, in a position of opposition, and is illuminated over the entire portion which faces the earth, it is called *panselenos* [full moon]. Gradually diminishing from this point, it repeats the names that are applied to the aforementioned phases.[81]

In one day and night the moon courses through 13 degrees of its orbit, while the other planets, in keeping with the great extent of their orbits, during the same interval course through the following portions of their orbits: Mars, one half of a degree; Jupiter, one twelfth of a degree; and Saturn, one twenty-eighth of a degree.

[865] The moon completes its circuit of the zodiac in 27⅔ days, but it requires 29½ days to overtake the sun. The reason for the larger period is that while the moon is completing its orbit, the sun has gone on from the position where it previously gave its light to the moon, and is found in the next sign or even the one following that. For if the moon receives its light in the last degree of Libra, Scorpio, or Sagittarius, it does not catch up with the sun in the sign immediately following but in the one after that. Thus the sun sometimes passes through these three signs unaccompanied, and, in the signs diametrically opposite, the moon will often be in conjunction with the sun twice. Inasmuch as the sun tarries in these signs for 30 days, in Gemini for 32 days, the moon, which overtakes the sun in 29½ days, will surely be able to find it in the same sign.

[866] The moon attains the full phase sometimes on the 14th, sometimes on the 15th, and more frequently on the 16th day; but a compensation occurs on the waning side.[82] For if it attains the full phase on the fourteenth day, it loses its light on the 15th day, so that the full number of days elapses. The moon completes its year in 354 days, for 12 conjunctions of the sun and the moon occur in this period. As a result, a solar year exceeds a lunar year by 11 days, but the difference is made up by intercalations.

[81] Cf. *ibid.,* 11-12.

[82] Cf. *ibid.,* 14: at the earliest, on the thirteenth day; at the latest, on the seventeenth.

[867] Let us discuss the degrees of latitude through which the moon courses. I pointed out above that there are 12 degrees of latitude in the belt of the zodiac, through which the planets have their various deviations. Some planets deviate through three degrees of latitude, some through four, others through eight, and some through all 12. The sun's course does not depart from the ecliptic except in the sign of Libra, where it is deflected to the north or the south by half a degree.[83] But the moon, ranging through all 12 degrees, is at times borne upward toward the north and at times verges downward toward the south, deflecting its course on either side to the extent of 6 degrees, as Hipparchus also acknowledges.

[868] A name has been given to the moon's oblique motion; it is spoken of as *helicoides* [spiral-shaped]. As it ascends or descends it cuts across the line of the ecliptic—which, as I indicated above, is a middle line with 6 degrees on either side—in sharp or broadened angles. The moon is not able to return to its former position in the same month with respect to the sun (that is, in the same degree and in the same position in latitude) until the two hundred and thirty-fifth month, which is in the nineteenth year.[84] Fifty-five years are required for it to return to the same place on the same day, in conjunction with the same fixed stars; and a lapse of a 'great year' is required for the fixed stars and the planets to return to their identical respective positions.[85]

[869] When the moon cuts across the ecliptic in its northward ascension, it is said to be in ascending elevation; when it is returning to the ecliptic from the north, it is in descending elevation; when it is moving from the ecliptic in a southerly direction, it is in descending declination; and when it is returning from there to the ecliptic, it is in ascending declination. These ascents and descents cause the eclipses of the two bodies. When the moon, in its ascents or descents, touches the ecliptic, if it happens on the thirtieth day—that is, when it lies directly beneath the sun with its entire body—it causes an eclipse of the sun upon earth; for by interposing its body, it darkens regions lying beneath it, while other parts of the earth, which are not

[83] See above, Vol. I, p. 193, n. 74.
[84] See *ibid.*, p. 194, n. 75.
[85] On the "great year," see above, Vol. I, p. 194. A fifty-six–year eclipse cycle was provided for at Stonehenge.

covered up, are illuminated by the sun.[86] The moon does not cause these eclipses every month, because it is not always found on the ecliptic on the thirtieth day; it is then passing above it or below it, so that it is not in an obstructing position.

[870] Similarly, an eclipse of the moon occurs when it is located along the line of the ecliptic in a position of opposition; that is, on the fifteenth day.[87] It is darkened by the conical shadow of the earth. For the sun sends the shadow of the earth along its ecliptic line; when the moon's orb reaches this line, since it will not be able to receive the light of the sun with the earth standing in the way, it will become darkened, the customary light being taken away. At other times, when it is in a position of latitude above or below the ecliptic, it will shine forth with an appearance of full light.

[871] Eclipses cannot recur within six months,[88] since the moon courses through 12 degrees of latitude and cannot be found on the ecliptic on the fifteenth or the first day. If, in returning to the ecliptic from the north, it comes into close lateral proximity with the sun but does not move into an obstructing position, it is said to produce an approximation in transit; but, if, in coming from the north, it does move into conjunction and obstructs the sun, it is said to produce an eclipse in northern transit. If it comes from the south and does not move into conjunction, it produces an approximation in southern transit; and if, in returning to the ecliptic from the south, it crosses the path of the sun, it produces an ascending eclipse node. These phenomena and vagaries of the moon confound mortals with their variety.[89]

[872] Now the sun, as we remarked above, moves with a twofold motion; namely, it is either swept along from the east with the celestial rotation or it moves obliquely in its own motion along its own course in a direction contrary to that of the universe. It daily changes the line of its rising from that point where it revolves with the uni-

---

[86] Cf. Geminus 10. In § 869 Martianus frequently uses Greek terminology.

[87] Cf. *ibid.*, 11.

[88] A. Pannekoek, *A History of Astronomy* (London, 1961), p. 46, points out that this fact was known to the ancient Babylonians, and he gives an explanation for the phenomenon.

[89] Cf. Ammianus Marcellinus *Res gestae* 20. 3. 4. The last sentence of § 871 here follows the version of several manuscripts, rather than Dick's emended version.

verse; we refer to the lines along which it moves as circles; therefore there is no doubt that there are 183 of them. For, whether the sun is descending in its course from Cancer to the winter tropic or coming to the summer tropic from the winter solstice, it is revolving along the same circles each time. These circles cut across the zodiac twice, and are always drawn through signs that are opposite each other; the first circle of Aries is also the first of Libra, and the thirtieth of Aries is the thirtieth of Libra; similarly, the first of Taurus is the first of Scorpio, and so on. Thus 183 circles are produced from 366 points. The circles are referred to as parallels and, as I have indicated, they intersect the zodiac at corresponding degrees of opposite signs. The sun traverses these circles annually in 365¼ days, whether it is moving in the direction of the summer tropic or returning to the winter tropic.

[873] We must not overlook the fact that although the two hemispheres are of equal dimensions—one from the equator to the north pole, the other from the equator to the south pole—and although, as I have mentioned, the signs on either side are equal, the sun nevertheless courses through them in unequal periods. It completes its ascending course to the summer tropic in 185¼ days, and its descending course to the winter tropic in 180 days.[90] The obvious cause of the discrepancy is that, as I have said, the earth is eccentric to the sun's orbit, which is more elevated in the upper hemisphere and draws closer to the earth in the lower. There is no doubt that the sun courses over its shorter curve more swiftly and over its more extended curve more slowly.

[874] The sun, when it climbs upward to Cancer from the equator, brings summer to mortals who are known to be living between the summer tropic and the arctic circle; while it is descending from Cancer to the equinoctial sign of Libra, it brings autumn; and when it retires to the winter tropic, winter holds forth, because chill invades when the warmth of the sun is remote; again, as it rises from wintry Capricornus to the equinoctial sign of Aries, the season of spring smiles upon us; and as it moves from there once again, the scorching heat of summer is renewed in Cancer. Dwellers in the antipodes undoubtedly experience these seasons at opposite times:

90 Theon of Smyrna (ed. Hiller, p. 153) has 187 days elapse during the northern course and 178¼ days during the southern course. Cf. Geminus 1. 13-17.

Capricornus brings their summer; Cancer, winter; and the sun at the
equator brings temperate conditions to either zone.

[875] There still remains for discussion the matter of the increase
and decrease of the duration of night, since winter nights correspond
in length to summer days, and summer nights to winter days; and
twice a year the equinoctial day is equal to its night. For, while the
sun is going from the vernal equinox to Cancer, all the days are
longer than the nights; likewise, from the autumnal equinox to the
winter solstice the days are shortened and the nights lengthened.

[876] The shortest day of the year, at the winter solstice, has 8
hours; and the longest day, at the summer solstice, has 16 hours,[91]
although it is true that the number of hours varies with the latitude.
There are 8 latitudes or climates. The closest to the summer tropic is
the one through Meroë;[92] then comes the one through Syene; the
third through Alexandria, extending on through Cyrene to that portion of Africa to the south of Carthage;[93] the fourth and middle climate is the one through Rhodes,[94] which is drawn through the
middle of the Peloponnesus and Sicily and extends to the mouth of
the Baetis River; the fifth climate goes through Rome and Macedonia
and, in the other direction, through Gaul and Lusitania, touching
down at the Tagus River; the sixth goes through the Hellespont and
Thrace and Gaul bordering upon Germany; the seventh, through
the mouth of the Borysthenes and the Black Sea and, in the opposite
direction, through Germany and Britain; the last climate is above the
Maeotis [Sea of Azov] and below the Rhipaean Mountains.[95]

[91] I follow the figures adopted by Dick in his edition, because they are in
agreement with a statement made in § 877. Other figures are adopted by Kopp
(9 and 15) and Eyssenhardt (9 and 14). It must be admitted, however, that there
is no strong reason to be influenced by considerations of consistency when dealing with compilations.

[92] Martianus makes an egregious blunder here. All the handbook authors place
the climate of Syene beneath the summer tropic.

[93] Mentioned here because Martianus was a native of Carthage.

[94] The climate through Rhodes was regarded, from the time of Eratosthenes,
as the middle one, but of a total of seven, not eight. See Vol. I, p. 197, n. 83.

[95] Ernst Honigmann, *Die sieben Klimata und die* ΠΟΛΕΙΣ ΕΠΙΣΗΜΟΙ
(Heidelberg, 1929), p. 51, believes that Martianus derived his climates from
Varro, for, unlike Pliny, who uses other expressions for *klimata,* Martianus uses
the Greek word several times and uses Greek names for the climates. Honig-
mann also believes that this list of the climates had been revised from the
Eratosthenean tradition by some Latin authority.

[877] The length of days is determined by the climates: the longest day at Meroë has 13 equinoctial hours, the shortest day 11; the longest day at Syene has 14 hours, the shortest 10; at Alexandria the longest has 14, the shortest 10; the longest day at Rhodes has 14 hours,[96] the shortest 9; the longest day at Rome has 15 hours, the shortest 9; the longest day at the Hellespont has 15 hours, the shortest 8; the longest day at the mouth of the Borysthenes has 16 hours, the shortest 8; in the Rhipaean Mountains the longest has 16; the shortest 8. Then, as you draw nearer to the pole, the day becomes ever longer, and the night shorter; consequently, it is to be assumed that there is perpetual daylight directly under the pole.

[878] However, at each climate the days lengthen and again shorten each year; and you must understand that from winter solstice the days increase in length in such a manner that in the first month a twelfth part of the increase to midsummer is added, in the second month a sixth part, in the third month a fourth part, in the fourth month another fourth part, in the fifth month a sixth part, and in the sixth month a twelfth part. The reason for the difference is that the zodiac winds around Cancer and Capricornus but cuts across the equator almost directly.

[879] So much for the sun's course. Now it is appropriate to consider the courses of the planets, and especially of those that orbit around the sun as it makes its celestial revolution. Stilbon (Mercury], completing an orbit in nearly a year, has a motion in latitude of 8 degrees, and is impelled in alternating directions. The circles of this planet and Venus, as I have said above, are epicycles; that is, they do not encompass the globe of the earth within their orbits, but describe an orbit to one side, in some way. The fact that they are seen to have risings and settings is caused by their being swept along by the motion of the celestial sphere.

[880] This same Stilbon, though it accompanies the sun in its varied epicycles, will never be able to depart from the sun by more than 22 degrees[97] of elongation; never will it be able to be two signs away, as at times it passes by the sun, then comes to a halt, and then retrogresses. This varied motion assumes different figures. Although its risings are inconspicuous and of short duration, it nevertheless has

96 Geminus has 14½ hours.

97 Pliny 2. 39 gives a maximum elongation of 22 degrees; Pliny 2. 73 gives 23 degrees.

risings and settings. Indeed, when the elongation permits and the planet is not obliterated by the sun's rays, it puts in a glimmering appearance, risen above the horizon, just ahead of the brilliance of the rising sun.

This planet can never have acronical risings, something that can happen only to planets that are situated diametrically opposite the sun (opposition is counted in the seventh sign). Consequently, a planet that cannot get farther than a sign and a portion of the following sign away from the sun cannot have acronical risings.

[881] Again, it does not experience settings in opposition to the sun; but it assumes its phase as an evening star when it grows bright upon being released from the brilliance of the sun, after the latter's setting.[98] Likewise it has two last visibilities: one phase when, as is its habit, it appears ahead of the sun and is then obliterated by the brilliant rays that overtake it; another when, as a result of its retrogradation, it moves into the vicinity of the sun and fades from sight in the west. It cannot be removed from the sun's light within 20 degrees, although it may have greater elongations; it cannot be found beyond the second sign. These last visibilities and clear risings will occur in the fourth month, and not always then.

[882] Now Venus, which is sometimes called Phosphoros, was manifestly thoroughly investigated by Pythagoras of Samos and his pupils. It has been shown to complete its orbit in a period of about a year. For in 300 and some days it ranges, like the moon, through all 12 degrees of latitude in the zodiac, getting 50 degrees distant from the orb of the sun, although it cannot have an elongation of more than 46 degrees.[99] Located on its own epicycle, it goes about the sun, varying its course; sometimes it passes ahead of the sun, sometimes it follows after it, and does not catch it; again at times it is borne above the sun and at times beneath it; and it does not always complete an orbit within a year. [883] For at a time when it is in retrograde motion, it takes longer than a year to traverse its orbit; but when it is going in direct motion, it completes its course even in

[98] This is contrary to Dick's preferred text, which would say "rising," not "setting." The manuscripts say "rising or setting" or "not setting but rising."

[99] Pliny (2. 38) has 46 degrees; Theon (ed. Hiller, p. 137) and Chalcidius (70) have 50 degrees for the maximum elongation of Venus. Chalcidius and Theon have 12 degrees of deviation in latitude for Venus; Cleomedes (*De motu circulari corporum caelestium* 2. 125) has 10 degrees.

eleven months. When it makes its risings in the early morning, ahead of the sun, it is called Lucifer; when it blazes forth after the setting of the sun, it is called Vesper or Vesperugo. Venus is the only one of the five planets, like the moon, to cast a shadow, and it is the only planet to be clearly discernible and not yielding for a long period of time to the splendor of the rising sun. Venus frequently lingers for four months in early morning rising, but in the west, as an evening star, never for more than 20 days. Its risings and settings are renewed in 10 or 9 months.[100]

[884] Pyrois, or Mars, has its own course, beyond the sun, and revolves about the earth, which is eccentric to its orbit, in almost two years. Mars has five degrees of deviation in latitude. Although it appears to have risings, settings, stations, and retrogradations in common with the two planets lying above it, it has its own apogee, first station, and exaltation apart from the others. Its apogee (that is, the point where its orbit reaches its highest elevation above the earth) is in the sign of Leo;[101] its first station is a unique one. Inasmuch as Mars is in close proximity with the sun, it feels the effect of the rays even from a position of quadrature and undergoes a station ninety degrees away from the sun on either side.[102] Mars has its exaltation or apsis in the twenty-ninth degree of Capricornus.[103]

[885] The propitious planet Jupiter, being higher than the others, completes its orbit in 12 years and has a deviation in latitude of five degrees. Its apogee occurs in Virgo, and its exaltation in the fifteenth degree of Cancer.[104] Its ascents and descents prove that its orbit is eccentric with respect to the earth.

[886] Phaenon—that is, Saturn—being situated above all the other planets, completes a revolution in slightly less than 30 years and has a deviation in latitude of 3 degrees or even only 2 degrees. Its apogee is in the sign of Scorpio, and its exaltation in the twentieth degree of Libra.[105] The risings of Saturn are like those of the two planets beneath it, in that the rays of the rising sun do not obscure it beyond 12 degrees. The terms 'morning rising' or 'setting' are applied to

---

[100] Cf. Martianus' discussion of Venus with Pliny 2. 36-38.
[101] Cf. Pliny 2. 64.
[102] Cf. *ibid.*, 60.
[103] Cf. *ibid.*, 65, where Pliny says the twenty-eighth degree.
[104] Cf. *ibid.*, 64, 65. See also above, Vol. I, p. 200, n. 99.
[105] Cf. Pliny 2. 64-65.

these planets when they are able to appear in the sky at that distance from the submerged sun.

[887] There is another rising, called acronical, which occurs when the clear orb of a planet rises in the east as the sun is plunging beneath the western horizon. Last visibilities of the superior planets occur when their shimmering light disappears as the rays of the sun overtake it. These planets make their morning stations 120 degrees away from the sun, and then, at opposition, 180 degrees away, they make their evening risings;[106] likewise, on the other side, they make their evening stations 120 degrees away. The latter are also called 'second' stations, and the former 'first' stations. At a distance of less than 12 degrees the rays of the sun overtake and obliterate these planets. The powerful effect of the sun's rays is responsible for the anomalies in the orbits of all the aforementioned planets and for their stations, retrogradations, and progressions. The rays strike the planets, causing them to rise aloft or to be depressed, or to deviate in latitude or to retrograde.[107]

[106] Cf. *ibid.*, 59.

[107] Cf. *ibid.*, 69-70. This book ends abruptly, perhaps in a lacuna, lacking as it does the closing scene that is found at the end of the presentation of each of the other six disciplines. It may be that nothing is omitted from the subject matter of the discipline itself, since Martianus, either here or in Book VI, has dealt with all the conventional topics found in an elementary book on astronomy.

BOOK IX

Harmony

[888] Seeing the flames in the marriage torches flickering and growing dim, Venus called for a renewal of festivities. "Will there be no end?" she asked. "Will learned teachers ever thwart conjugal pleasures? Lovely Pleasure, used to pampering, sits benumbed, and Cupid has a pale and glowering look. Comely Flora, whose wont it is to deck the marriage couch with garlands, sits anxiously with the Graces three. Sweet Melpomene has grown quiet; she plays no lyric tune upon her flute, nor tries to sing. In short, all revelry and youthful mirth that customarily prevail, are muffled now in awe of learned utterance. Persuasion seduces not the bridal couple's hearts, nor does Stimulation incite them with sharp goads. Nay, she who delights in loosing maiden girdles and in caressing maiden hearts with fond desires,[1] repressed her suggestive glances, all affrighted, and cannot bear to look upon the features of the grim Gorgon.[2] If erudition is desired at a celestial wedding, Calliope at least should sing the learned songs. Her melodies delight the mind, and she will banish boredom with her dulcet strains. I must confess, I weary listening to those laborious maidens, and I am saddened by unaccustomed delays. Juno Pronuba, if it be your pleasure to give ear to serious discourses and you have no concern about this heavenly wedding, then I succumb. Gay choruses are my way of life, and I cannot bear to look upon somber maidens steeped in Attic lore."

[889] Thus Venus spoke and, lying backward, leaned into the embrace of Pleasure, who was standing by her.[3] All the earth and sea gods approved her remarks, and several of the heavenly gods as well; in particular, Venus' husband, Mulciber of Lemnos [Vulcan],

---

[1] Presumably a reference to Juno Pronuba, goddess of marriage, invoked a few lines below.

[2] Presumably the Gorgon's head represented on the aegis of Pallas Athene.

[3] The wording of this sentence recalls a passage at the opening of Lucretius *De rerum natura*, in which Mars falls back into the embrace of Venus.

master of so many crafts, was quick to offer commendation. Then, as she reclined gracefully, and her relaxed attitude added to her charm, Mars gave her a tender and admiring glance from afar, and in a faltering and feeble voice he too commended her,[4] and then was seen to draw a deep breath. Bacchus was not to be outdone in the graciousness of his compliments. Atlas's descendant [Mercury], in truth, was so overcome by passionate desire for Venus that he wanted to leave off the elegant preparations which he had arranged for the ceremony. Such attentions were never displeasing to Venus.

[890] But the father of the gods had been advised by his sister[5] to hasten the proceedings. Nevertheless, so as not to scrimp the wedding preparations or dispense with the performance of so erudite a lady, pleasant as it would be to speed the marriage, Jupiter refused to be rushed: he asked how many bridesmaids remained to be heard from. [891] The Delian [Apollo] suggested that Medicine and Architecture were standing by, among those who had been prepared to perform. "But since these ladies are concerned with mortal subjects and their skill lies in mundane matters, and they have nothing in common with the celestial deities, it will not be inappropriate to disdain and reject them. They will keep silent in the heavenly company and will be examined in detail later by the maiden herself. But it would be a grave offense to exclude from this company the one bridesmaid who is the particular darling of the heavens,[6] whose performance is sought with joy and acclamation.

[892] "But first of all I would like to inform you that the mother of the maiden has brought along other young women, endowed with lavish gifts, to be added to the dowry;[7] she has agreed to submit them to that test of knowledge. These young women are of the same number and are equally attractive, and in the impressiveness of their erudition few of the maidens standing by them are on a par with them.[8] They have been instructed in the more mystic and holy

[4] Remigius suggests that Mars adopts this manner here to conceal his illicit affair with Venus.

[5] Juno.

[6] I.e., Harmony, because the motions of the spheres produce harmony.

[7] The mother of Philology is Phronesis. The translation "endowed" is based on the manuscript reading *collocatas*, rather than on Dick's *collocatur*.

[8] The reference is to the prophetic arts—like the liberal arts seven in number. Remigius says that Augustine gives the names of these maidens.

secrets of the maiden. With what displeasure or with what delight or weakness on the part of the celestial senate these girls would be passed over, I leave it to you, in the strength and majesty of your judgment, O Jove, to decide."

[893] To this the Tritonian [Minerva] replied: "To be sure, the maidens whom Phronesis has reared have zealously guarded the secrets privy to divinities, nor did any of you fail to entrust to them the interpretation of your hidden desires. Besides, several of them profess to be priestesses of the gods, and they avow that it is an impious deed to offer sacrifices to the holy divinities on earth except through them, and that a favorable outcome under such circumstances is surely denied. The maidens who have appeared have given a remarkable demonstration of their ancient learning; these maidens bear testimonials of your intimate relationship with mortals; for, in the cleavage that exists between the divine and mortal realms, they alone have always maintained communication between the two. [894] You will recognize them when they enter, and you will put them to the test, O gods."

In the course of this conversation between the Delian and Pallas, someone asked the names of the maidens. Phoebus then answered: "The first to appear will be Genethliace.[9] She shares in the knowledge of the heavenly order and covertly declares the lots of Lachesis and the things to be produced in approaching ages. Next will come Symbolice,[10] who compares future events with prognostications, and reconciles the conclusion of omens with happenings. The third maiden will be Oeonistice,[11] through whom the tripod declares those future events and every oracular cauldron has given clear responses. Furthermore, as evidence of their foreknowledge the crow is suggestive of me and the swan is associated with me, for the color of their plumage, which corresponds to the nighttime and the daytime, indicates that we get our premonitions of events of day and night from the birds. The tripod itself offers the divinations of the triple time sequence—present, future, and past. [895] Next will come the triple sisterhood, always bowed in prayer, who, by assuring mortals of your generally favorable decisions, first induced their wavering minds to hope for divine aid, and brought a nation

9 Lit., "having to do with birth dates (horoscopes)." Cf. § 228.
10 Lit., "symbolic, riddling."
11 Lit., "having to do with omens from birds."

that was in need of your protection into religious worship. Who of us would refuse to grant this sisterhood an opportunity to perform in heaven, whether this is a threefold female or three sisters acting under one name, when it is undeniable that we move freely upon earth through their intercession? [896] After them a beautiful maiden will appear, radiant in celestial light, who has been approved and designated by you, Jupiter, as your messenger. It is stoutly maintained, Father, that you have entrusted to her your lightning and thunderbolts and the flashes of triple-tongued light. She is familiar with the paths, tracks, approach, and outcome of omens that travel as fire. Are you going to deny a hearing to this woman through whom the warnings of your decrees become known to mortals? Why, then, best Father, do you not introduce these maidens forthwith and put them to the test?"

[897] After Latona's son [Apollo] had spoken thus, Jupiter ordered Harmony to appear, as it was suggested to him, the last of the learned handmaids that remained. The other maidens he then ordered to form into line. At this point Luna, reminded by the two parts of the day that had passed, spoke up: "Straightway I shall be able to examine with you the maiden who is about to enter, but with nightfall approaching I shall not be able to allot time to the maidens who follow. Indeed, I still have to traverse Plaustrum [the Wain] and Taurus and the downward course of the sky, and the goal of my celestial course does not permit me to listen to the discourse of the other maidens. And, I confess, I would like to learn the doctrines of such celebrated erudition if there is authority to defer the examination of the maidens, especially since a postponement until the day after tomorrow is a reasonable delay; thus might tedium and distaste, occasioned by the fatigue of learning and the effort of concentration, not preclude all discourses of a subtle nature; and the keenness required for seeking and demonstrating knowledge not be blunted and turned into an aversion by complexity and prolixity. I consider it fitting to defer such discourses until the audience is wide awake and thirsting to hear."

[898] As Luna was making these remarks, all the gods gave their hearty approval. Then the question was raised whether a recompense could be offered, and whether the day for bestowing the dowry could be postponed according to the public law. At this suggestion,

that cryptic authority on ancient law[12] was besought by the entreaties of his numerous descendants; and he replied that, according to custom, once the couple had been joined in marriage, there was no statutory objection to the wife's constituting the dowry for her husband.[13] Then Jupiter, prompted by the expert knowledge of his father, said: "My children,[14] I have reason for rejoicing, since whatever I know you are wishing for, is pronounced to be lawful. I shall not avoid the issue, inflexible and prideful in my estate, nor shall I be reluctant, under pretense of sloth and indifference, to hasten your plan or to test the skills of the learned maidens, since they, who have been summarily expelled from the earth, ought to find a place among the stars.

[899] "Now, therefore, let us give audience to that most eminent of ladies, Harmony, who is the last of Mercury's maidens to be heard. She indeed, above all others, will be able to soothe the cares of the gods, gladdening the heavens with her song and rhythms; and she desires only to make our palaces resound, detesting the ever-increasing dullness and spiritlessness of the earthborn, resulting from their lack of skill in melic verse. Having long since taken her departure from earth, Harmony has rejected mortals and their desolated academies; and now, barely overtaken by the Cyllenian [Mercury] in eager pursuit, she is being brought back after a long period of oblivion from her remote hiding place. [900] It will be both a pleasure and a profit to listen to this maiden, rediscovered after so many generations and restored to the melic arts. But the other learned and reverend sisters, when another day has dawned, will be introduced and given a thorough examination."

[901] Prompted by these remarks of Jove, Phoebus stepped outside in order to introduce the maiden, who was especially appropriate to him. The Paphian [Venus], startled by the warm reception for her returning daughter, gave a sign to Hymen to begin the wedding song. And he, brightening up, with animated spirit and with an approving nod from the Tritonian thus began:

[902] "When golden Moon has raised her blazing orb, I shall

---

12 Saturn, as will be revealed in a moment.

13 The legal language in §§ 892 and 897-98 supports the view that Martianus was a practitioner of law.

14 Apollo and Mercury are being addressed here, according to Remigius.

mingle lilies with roses.[15] The maiden and the god will consummate their vows on the sacred couch. Bring fragrant garlands for the bedposts. Though Evening Star may keep the maiden pure until then, you, Morning Star, will look upon her wedded. A mother's tears and firm grasp will not avail to break the bonds of wedlock. Fear not the marriage chamber, maiden. You too will be what Juno is to the Thunderer. She is now sweeter than a sister. If the venerable knowledge of your learned spouse has afforded you pleasure, his kisses will please you more. Coming Dawn with roseate eyes will see the rewards of a severed flower. I too in morning light shall spy the bashful bride concealing herself from view. [903] And now, Woodland Nymphs, prepare fresh garlands, appurtenances of Venus, and sprinkle saffron on the couch; and with a will pour violets upon it from conch shells; decorate the couch of happiness. You, Cupid, eager to let down the maiden's hair, draw forth the bridal spear[16] from your quiver. You, Juno, patroness of marriage, wont to cover a maiden's modesty with a bridal veil, now remove it. And beautiful Venus, alone familiar with the tender pangs of love, will caressingly console you. Obstinate maiden, knowing not how to yield to a new love, Venus will prepare your heart. And, as you cast your beauteous eyes demurely downward, keep my precepts locked deep in your mind. Embrace that learned youth in your shapely arms, and bestow on him a numerous progeny."

[904] While Hymen, in a sportive mood appropriate to the occasion, was singing this hymn repeatedly and for some length of time, thinking that he had brought pleasure to the gods, a large company of bystanders followed the Tritonian and Dione out of the hall. In the excitement over the return of Harmony, a throng quickly gathered. A crowd of maidens who had followed after the goddesses and were standing close by them, and of heroes, under orders to be present, bustled in expectation; the former to learn the theme of the songs, the latter to confirm their recollection of Harmony's features.

[905] Immediately a sweet new sound burst forth, like the strains

---

[15] Cf. § 726; Ovid *Amores* 2. 5. 37.

[16] *Caelibaris hasta*, a small spear, the point of which was used to divide the locks of the bride's hair. Cf. Ovid *Fasti* 2. 560, and the note in the Frazer edition (London, 1929).

of auloi;[17] and echoing melodies, surpassing the delight of all sounds, filled the ears of the enchanted gods. For the sound was not a simple one, monotonously produced from one instrument, but a blending of all instrumental sounds creating a full symphony of delectable music. As this melody soothed the breasts of the mortal bystanders and the gods for some time, the throngs of those who had gone out a little while earlier, anticipating the arrival of the maiden, were seen again in the van, walking ahead of the vast retinue. But their return was not unaccompanied by sweet and melodious sounds. For Eratine, daughter of the Cyprian, and Himeros, attendant of Cupid, and Terpsis, one of the household servants of Dione, were the first to enter, singing in pleasing harmony; but the lad[18] was [906] playing on a single aulos. Next came Persuasion, Pleasure, and the Graces, singing to the accompaniment of a lyre and dancing hither and thither with the rhythmic beat. At the same time companies of heroes and of philosophers with flowing locks were moving along in the van, to the left and the right, all chanting in soft and sweet tones, many of them singing hymns and praises of the gods, others singing melodies they had just learned. In the middle were some rustic and tuneful demigods, playing on appropriate instruments, the Goat-Footed one [Pan] on a pandura,[19] Silvanus on a reed pipe smoothed of knots, and Faunus on a rustic flute. A company of heroes that followed after, attracted great wonder and surprise; for Orpheus, Amphion, and Arion, most skillful musicians, were harmoniously playing a moving melody on their golden lyres.

[907] The same song with which the forgetful Thracian bard[20] invaded the realms of grim Erebus and gained his dear Eurydice; with which the wrath of the dumb-struck tiger sub-

[17] Martianus uses a derivative of the Greek term *aulos*. Though generally called a flute, the *aulos* was a double-reed instrument more like the oboe than the modern-day flute.

[18] Hymen, according to Remigius.

[19] Authorities do not agree on whether this was a stringed instrument or a wind instrument. See *The New Oxford History of Music*, Vol. I, index, s.v. "Pandore, Pandoura," and cf. Cassiodorus (*Institutiones* 2. 5. 6), who classifies it among wind instruments.

[20] Orpheus. He had been instructed not to look back upon Eurydice as he was leading her out of Hades; but, as he was approaching daylight, he looked back, and she disappeared from sight.

sided; with which Orpheus is said to have subdued fierce beasts; with which Mount Ismaros saw the foliage on her trees[21] grow stiff and her forests course up and down her sides; with which the Strymon checked the flow of her waters and the Tanais was often reversed; with which the lamb lay down securely beside the ravenous wolf and the hare drew near to the cruel hunting dog—with this song Orpheus now delighted his audience, adding hymns of praise to Jove.

[908] And so with song Amphion brought life again to bodies stiff with cold, made mountains animate, and gave to hard rocks sensibilities, teaching them to follow his refrains. The walls of Thebes, obedient to his song, were raised to the strains of his sweet lyre, and he provided a protection. And the billows were not deaf to Arion's lyre, when he in desperate straits cried out for help. Though the frothing waters of Scylla's strait churned about him, blasted by a dreadful storm sent by the unbridled south wind, Arion attracted dolphins from all the seas, and one accommodating creature heeded his tuneful song. O Harmony, verily surpassing the great divinities whose praises you have sounded; you have been able with your song to subdue Erebus, the seas, the stones, the wild beasts, and to bring sensation to rocks.

After them the even more honored chorus of fount-sprung maidens [the Muses] poured forth the nectar of Pierian song; accompanied by the twin pipes of the Phrygian,[22] they surpassed all the sweetness of the delights that had gone before.

[909] Harmony walked along between Phoebus and Pallas, a lofty figure, whose melodious head was adorned with ornaments of glittering gold. Her garment was stiff with incised and laminated gold and it tinkled softly and soothingly with every measured step and movement of her body. Her radiant mother the Paphian—who followed her closely—though she too moved with graceful measure and balanced steps, could scarcely match the gait of her daughter. In her right hand Harmony bore what appeared to be a shield, circular over-all, with many inner circles, the whole interwoven with re-

---

[21] Dick's text reads *glandibus* [on the acorns] where the present translation prefers *cladibus* [lit., on the branches]. See Alexander Souter, ed., *A Glossary of Later Latin to 600 A.D.* (Oxford, 1949), s.v. "cladus." *Cladibus* (Gr. *klados*) = *ramis*, according to Remigius.

[22] Olympus, pupil and favorite of Marsyas.

markable configurations. The encompassing circles of this shield were attuned to each other, and from the circular chords there poured forth a concord of all the modes. From her left hand the maiden held, suspended at equal length, several small models of theatrical instruments,[23] wrought of gold. [910] No lyre or lute or tetrachord appeared on that circular shield, yet the strains coming from that strange rounded form surpassed those of all musical instruments. As soon as she entered the hall, a symphony swelled from the shield. All other music—which, by contrast with its sweetness, sounded dissonant—now became silent. Then Jupiter and the other heavenly beings, recognizing the grandeur of the more exalted melodies, which were pouring forth in honor of a certain secret fire and inextinguishable flame, reverenced the profound ancestral song, and one by one arose in homage to extramundane intelligence.[24]

[911] Concluding this stirring symphony,[25] impossible to describe, Harmony turned to Jove and, lending her voice to a new melody and meter, began the following hymn:

"I worship you, O Jupiter, resounding with heavenly song; through you the sacred swirling of the heavens has set the glittering stars in predetermined motion. You, all-powerful Father of the multifarious gods, move and bind kingdoms beneath your scepter-bearing diadem, while Mind, which you instill with heavenly force, revolves the universe in ceaseless whirl. [912] The gleaming stars recall your scattering and kindling of the seeds of fire. Phoebus' light beneficently restores the luster of lovely daylight to the earth, bearing witness to your majesty. And Cynthia [Diana], jewel of the night, moves on ahead in her monthly course, a beautiful ornament with gilded horns. Under your dominion the Dragon[26] tears asunder the Parrhasian beasts,[27] rivaling the Bears in brilliance. The earth, yielding its solid body to soft envelopment, is pierced by an axis, and controls and is in turn controlled by the poles. Thus Nereus can know the limits of the seas, and the fiery bodies

[23] Remigius says that the term *effigies* refers to musical instruments made by mortals, as contrasted with the divine music symbolized on the shield.

[24] Pierre Courcelle, *Les Lettres grecques en occident de Macrobe à Cassiodore* (Paris, 1943), p. 204, interprets this as mystic silence.

[25] *Egersimon;* cf. § 2.

[26] Draco.

[27] The Great and Little Bears.

of the sky can draw nourishment, so that dissonant elements may not teem with strife, that parts remote may cherish lasting bonds and always dread the ruptive forces of Chaos. Ruler of the heavens, best Father, gathering the stars in fond embrace, you quicken your offspring with eternal bodies. Hail! For you our lyre is attuned, for you the gamut of our song resounds in double diapason.

[913] I pray you, venerable offspring of the heavens, who know how to play upon the barbiton [cithara][28] of many sounds, make your hearts propitious to our song, as the mixed[29] harmonies of the heavenly senate are being presented to gladden your company. And I in turn will celebrate you next in order of gods after Jupiter with my divided fiction,[30] and my song will attract and delight all of you with its tones, and will goad and stimulate emotions in places, and again will gently soothe them.

[914] And now, you benevolent luminaries that crown the senate of the gods with venerable crest, although Etruscan rituals celebrate you as the twelve divinities[31] and honor you with sacrificial offerings, nevertheless the two lights that gleam in twin courses, bearing Phoebean names, have been elevated to high rank by their nature: flashing Phoebus and Latona's comely daughter [Diana].[32] Indeed the lunar partner is coming in this direction; the blazing Delian will mount the chariot of Phaëthon. I shall beseech you now, chaste pair, our celestial crown, let not what the songs may tell to the divine couple bring a frown to your revered faces, and let not Hymen offend us with his lewdness. The wedding will be celebrated in lyric song; the wanton banter will come forth to the accompaniment of the lyre.

[915] And now, alluring Dione, enjoy my melody.

Stern primness yields to love.

The tossing sea that bore Cytherean Venus knows how to com-

---

[28] On the barbiton and the cithara, see W. D. Anderson, *Ethos and Education in Greek Music: The Evidence of Poetry and Philosophy* (Cambridge, Mass., 1966), pp. 3-7.

[29] *Miscilla;* cf. § 997.

[30] In the form of Menippean satire.

[31] Cf. § 42.

[32] The sun and the moon. Dick has Pallas, not Phoebus, but Eyssenhardt emends to Phoebus, which clearly makes more sense in the context [RJ].

mend my tender song; while Galatea stirs the Muse with Nereus' lyre, flaming passion draws the swimming Tritons, blowing on their conch shells, and the chorus of Phorcus; and love ungovernable prevails in the frothy billows.

[916] And now, alluring Dione, enjoy my melody.
      Stern primness yields to love.

Maenalian pines have borne[33] my song, and the Arcadian grove, old haunt of shepherds' pipes, resounds with Lycaean modes. The swift mistress [Syrinx] of half-beast Pan, is turned into speaking reeds and gives out sound, and as the god presses her with his lips she sighs forth song as if from kisses.

[917] And now, alluring Dione, enjoy my melody.
      Stern primness yields to love.

Cupid, changeable boy, is eager for the strings. Binding his sweetly strung bow with shoots of roses, he lays his weapons to rest as the Muse prepares the reeds. Entranced by song, he disregards his arrows and leaves his tender quiver[34] at our melody. Ardor and song combine to delight our breasts. Pleasure and beauty in turn: let us sing and let us love.

[918] And now, alluring Dione, enjoy my melody.
      Stern primness yields to love.

The mother of the Spartan beauty was a discreet girl;[35] but, lured by song, she knew not how to protect herself from guile. For a swan, assuming snow-white plumage (aware that silvery wings were less attractive and could not greatly please her beautiful eyes), prepared his plot, and feigning imminent death, suddenly began a tender song, invoking Apollo's Muses. Then, drawing close to the face of the perplexed girl, he stole a kiss from her rosy lips and, holding her in firm embrace, took away her chastity.

[919] And now, alluring Dione, enjoy my melody.
      Stern primness yields to love.

The goddess of the second light[36] preferred Endymion's song to life among the stars. Leaving the summit of the sky, she sought

---

33 Cf. § 11, where the tones correspond to the height of the trees.
34 See Souter, *Glossary:* s.v. *harundinetum.*
35 The reference is to Leda, mother of Helen.
36 Selene, goddess of the moon.

out her lover's cave and, burning with passion, gave her prize to his shepherd's pipe. Casting off her golden splendor, she entered the sheepfold, and covering herself with a sordid garment, she delights in the rustic life. By night, Cynthia feeds the mountain goats and, looking up at the stars, lashes at them vigorously with her crook. The seductive charm of his ampler song compelled the lovesick goddess to give no heed to tasks assigned by the gods and to endure their whispering. She spurns the honor that she holds by night, preferring the grotto of a swineherd, and rests her head upon a hard rock. After leaving the Thunderer's kingdom, she finds the grass a sweeter bed."

[920] Harmony's songs delighted and soothed the spirits of all the gods; and the strains that poured forth from her stringed instruments were no less sweet than the melody of her voice. Hereupon a discussion ensued, to which Jupiter listened with admiration, regarding the pains and labor involved in the production of that music and the effort and unabated concentration that must have gone into the mastery and attainment of harmonies so soft and caressing as to enthrall the innermost emotions of their hearts. Then, when Harmony perceived that those present were seeking the precepts of her art by way of putting her learning to test, refraining somewhat from songs and with encouragement from the Delian and Pallas, she thus began her discourse.

[921] "A loathsome and detestable creature to earthborn mortals,[37] I have been striking against the star-studded heavenly spheres, where I am forbidden to discourse on the precepts of my art—this despite the fact that the swirling celestial mechanism, in the swiftness of its motion, produces a harmony which it recognizes as concordant with the gamut of all proportions. But inasmuch as a maiden has risen up from the earth who is about to be wed, it behooves me now with my celestial powers to dispel the darkness, which is beginning to lift after a long intermission. I shall run through my precepts in accordance with your request, if you will first permit me to call to your attention the boons accruing to ungrateful mankind from the knowledge that is being restored.

[922] From the time that the limitless universe of the ineffable Creator begot me as the twin sister of heaven, I have not forsaken

---

[37] Adopting the reading *terrigenis* of Remigius.

numbers;[38] I followed the courses of the sidereal spheres and the whirling motion of the entire mass, assigning tones to the swiftly moving celestial bodies. But when the Monad[39] and first hypostasis of intellectual light was conveying to earthly habitations souls that emanated from their original source, I was ordered to descend with them to be their governess. It was I who designated the numerical ratios of perceptible motions and the impulses of perfect will, introducing restraint and harmony into all things, [923] a subject which Theophrastus elaborated upon as a universal law for all mankind. The Pythagoreans too assuaged the ferocity of men's spirits with pipes and strings and taught that there is a firmly binding relationship between souls and bodies. [924] I deigned to have numbers underlie the limbs of human bodies,[40] a fact to which Aristoxenus and Pythagoras attest. At last, with a generous outpouring of my favor, I revealed the concepts of my art to men, in a manner which they could understand. For I demonstrated the use of stringed instruments at Delphi, through the Delian's cithara; flutes were blown by my companion the Tritonian and by the Lydian Marsyas; the Mariandynians and Aonians blew upon reed pipes their hymns to the heavenly deities; I permitted the Egyptians to try their skill with the pandura; and I did not deny myself to shepherds imitating on their pipes the calls of birds or the rustling of trees or the gurgling of rivers. I invented the art of cithara players, of players on stringed instruments, on sambukes, and on water organs[41] throughout the world, for the benefit of lowly mankind. [925] Through me, in fact, men have inveigled the support of you deities and have quelled the anger of the underworld deities through mournful songs.

And were not military campaigns and victories in all parts of the world accomplished through my songs? The Cretans used to engage the enemy to the strains of the cithara; the Lacedaemonians,

[38] Remigius offers two explanations: harmony is inherent in the heavens; Harmony is a twin sister to Arithmetic, because there are numerical ratios in harmony.

[39] The Neoplatonic One, identified with the Fabricator of the Universe.

[40] Cf. § 739.

[41] On the prominence of the hydraulic organ as a musical instrument in Roman imperial times, see *Oxford History of Music*, I, 398; J. F. Mountford, "Greek Music and Its Relation to Modern Times," *Journal of Hellenic Studies*, XL (1920), 38.

to the sound of the aulos—the latter would not advance to the test of battle until they had made propitious sacrifice to the Muses. And did not the Amazons make a practice of brandishing their weapons to the tune of reed pipes? One of these women,[42] who had come to Alexander in the hope of conceiving by him, when she greeted him, was given a flute and went away as elated as if she had received a great gift. Is anyone unaware that the Spartans in Greece and the Sybarites in Italy are led into battle by aulos players? It has recently been learned that trumpets rouse the spirits of prancing steeds and battle [sic] and also sharpen the keen edge of wrestlers and other competitors in public games.

[926] And were not peacetime functions performed to the accompaniment of my songs? In many Greek cities, laws and public decrees were recited to the strains of a lyre. I have frequently recited chants that have had a therapeutic effect upon deranged minds and ailing bodies; I have restored the mad to health through consonance, a treatment which the physician Asclepiades learned from me. When an unruly mob of the common people were raging at the city fathers as they were deliberating, the sound of music that rose above their obstreperous clamor held them in check. Some young men in a drunken condition who were behaving in a rowdy manner were brought to their senses by the musicianship of Damon, one of my disciples. He ordered them to sing some spondaic measures to the accompaniment of a flute, and brought their noisy brawling to an abrupt halt. Have not I myself brought healing to diseased bodies by prolonged therapy? The ancients were able to cure fever and wounds by incantation. Asclepiades healed with the trumpet patients who were stone deaf, and Theophrastus used the flute with mentally disturbed patients. Is anyone unaware that gout in the hip is removed by the sweet tones of the aulos? Xenocrates cured insane patients by playing on musical instruments. Thales of Crete is known to have dispelled diseases and pestilence by the sweetness of his cithara playing. Herophilus checked the pulse of his patients by comparing rhythms.[43]

[927] The Thracian lyre player[44] was one who demonstrated that animals are sensitive to my songs and are drawn to follow

---

[42] Queen of the Amazons, according to Remigius.

[43] According to Remigius, if the beats were rhythmic, the patient was well.

[44] Orpheus.

is the *nete synemmenon,* or ultima coniunctarum [highest tone of the conjunct tetrachord]. The twelfth is the *paramese,* or prope media [tone next to the middle tone]. The thirteenth is the *trite diezeugmenon,* or tertia divisarum [third tone of the disjunct tetrachord]. The fourteenth is the *diezeugmenon diatonos,* or divisarum extenta [extended tone of the disjunct tetrachord]. The fifteenth is the *nete diezeugmenon,* or ultima divisarum [highest tone of the disjunct tetrachord]. The sixteenth is the *trite hyperbolaion,* or tertia excellentium [third tone of the highest tetrachord]. The seventeenth is the *hyperbolaion diatonos,* or excellentium extenta [extended tone of the highest tetrachord]. And the eighteenth is the *nete hyperbolaion,* or ultima excellentium [highest tone of the highest tetrachord]. These, then, are the tones that are comprised in a properly proportioned musical system.[52]

[932] Moreover, all musical movement (*modulatio*) consists of lower- or higher-pitched tones. A low pitch has a soothing effect because of the slackening of its sound; a high pitch, on the other hand, is due to the tightening and raising of the music to a thin and shrill sound.

[933] Among the aforementioned tones which rightly occur in each and every mode, there are three consonances (*symphoniae*). The first of these is the *diatessaron,* in Latin called *ex quattuor* [from the four].[53] It consists of four notes, three steps, and two and a half *productiones.* (By *productio* I mean a whole tone.[54]) It also consists of five semitones, which are equivalent to two and a half whole tones, or of ten dieses; but I am referring to the diesis which, as I noted above, is a quarter tone. This consonance is in the epitritic ratio. The epitrite is the ratio of the number three and a number one third greater—that is, 4 to 3.

[934] The second consonance is the *quinaria* [fifth], called in Greek *diapente.* It consists of five notes which are separated by four steps. It has three and a half *productiones;* that is, three and a half whole tones, or seven semitones, or fourteen dieses. It has the hemiolic ratio; that is, of a number and another number half again as great, as the ratio of three to two. The third consonance is that of the *diapason,* in Latin *ex omnibus* [through the entirety]. It has

52 See above, Vol. I, pp. 208-9.
53 The interval of a perfect fourth.
54 Cf. § 940.

eight notes, seven steps, six whole tones, twelve semitones, and twenty-four dieses, and is based upon the diplasic ratio; that is, the double.

[935] There are fifteen *tropi* [octave species]:[55] five principal ones, and a pair of *tropi* attached to each of them. There is the Lydian, with which the hypolydian and the hyperlydian are conjoined; the Ionian, with which the hypoionian and the hyperionian are conjoined; the Aeolian, and with it the hypoaeolian and the hyperaeolian; the Phrygian, and with it the hypophrygian and the hyperphrygian; and the Dorian, with the hypodorian and the hyperdorian.

A certain compatibility or kinship exists among these *tropi*, drawing them to each other, as in the case of the kinship between the hypodorian and the hypophrygian, or between the hypoionian and the hypoaeolian. Likewise there is a compatible relationship between the hypophrygian and the hypolydian. These are the only pairs that are joined together. The middle tone (*media*) of the lower *tropus* becomes the proslambanomenos of the higher *tropus*.

Each of these *tropi*, moreover, comprises five tetrachords. A tetrachord is a pleasing relationship of four tones arranged in order, in which the two bounding tones are consonant. But more of this later. Let us return to our original order of dealing with the fundamental topics. These preliminary remarks have been introduced in order to make the ensuing discussion more intelligible.[56]

[936] When Lasus, a man from the city of Hermione,[57] first taught the principles of harmony to mortal men, only three aspects were recognized: *hylikon* [subject matter], *apergastikon* [practice], and *exangeltikon* [exposition], also called *hermeneutikon*. Hylikon refers to things that sound together in a continuous and similar manner—

---

[55] See the article by J. F. Mountford and R. P. Winnington-Ingram in *The Oxford Classical Dictionary* (Oxford, 1949), p. 586.

[56] Martianus' discussion of music apparently is drawn from two main sources. From this point on, his discussion of music and metrics is largely a translation of the work *Peri mousikes* by Aristides Quintilianus (2d-3d cent. A.D.). Cf. above, Vol. I, p. 210.

[57] A dithyrambist who lived in the sixth century B.C., pioneer of the classical movement (*The New Oxford History of Music*, I, p. 382); teacher of Pindar and—according to the Suda (a Greek lexicon and encyclopedia of the tenth century A.D.)—author of the earliest work on the theory of music. See Macran, ed., *Aristoxenus*, p. 226.

melody, measures, and words: those that pertain to melody are called harmonics; those that pertain to measures, rhythmics; and those that pertain to words, metrics. *Apergastikon* has to do with the handling and exercise of the materials of the above subjects: it likewise is subdivided into three parts: *melopoeia* [musical composition], *lēpsis* [choice of pitch], and *plokē* [relation of pitches]. *Exangeltikon* is seen to refer to exposition, and it has three divisions: *organikon* [instrumental music], *ōdikon* [vocal music], and *hypokritikon* [recitation]. Each of these will be explained later in its appropriate place.[58]

Let us now deal with the voice as the parent of all sound, so to speak. [937] All voice production is divided into two categories: continuous and discrete. The continuous is found in flowing conversation; the discrete is used in music. There is an intermediate form, having elements of both; for it neither adheres strictly to the continuous variation of the one nor is discretely varied in modulation like the other. It is the form which is used in the recitation of all poetry.[59] The form that is subject to precise variations is called *diastematica* and is appropriate to the branch called harmonics.

[938] The subject of harmonics has seven aspects: tones (*soni*), intervals, systems, genera, keys (*tonoi*), changes of system, and melody construction (*melopoeia*).[60]

First, about tones, which are the basic elements of my discipline. [939] The tone has the same significance for us that the point has for geometers and the unit for arithmeticians. We also call tones *phthongi;* but the term *phthongus* refers to a particular musical production of the voice effected through a corresponding tension. Tension, called *tasis* in Greek, is what causes voice to be produced and to continue. The term *phthongus* is applied both specifically and generally. For general applications the word itself is used; for

---

[58] A promise not fully kept. Three of the terms are discussed later: *lēpsis* (§ 994); *plokē* (§ 958); and *melopoeia* (§ 965).

[59] See D. B. Munro, *The Modes of Ancient Greek Music* (Oxford, 1894), pp. 116-17.

[60] The remaining sections on music are devoted to a discussion of these seven aspects, as follows: tones (939-47), intervals (948-53), systems (954), genera (955-59), *tonoi* (960-63), changes of system (964), and melody construction (965-66). This division of harmonics probably is the standard one. It is used also by Cleonides *Introductio harmonica*. See Manfred Fuhrmann, *Das systematische Lehrbuch: Ein Beitrag zur Geschichte der Wissenschaft in der Antike* (Göttingen, 1960), p. 34.

specific applications the Greek word *idiaitata* is used. If we should consider how this term ought to be defined, the pronunciation of the word *phthongus* itself serves as an example of the raising and lowering of the pitch of the voice.

[940] Now in the case of tones, some terms are active and some are passive. Tension and relaxation are active; highness and lowness of pitch are passive. *Productio*—that is, *epitasis*—is the movement of the voice from a lower to a higher pitch; *anesis* is the opposite, for here the voice descends from a high pitch to some low and grave pitch. Deepness of tone is produced when the breath is drawn from deep within; sharpness of tone is produced from the forepart of the mouth.

The varieties of tone are countless, but in our special sense of the word there are only twenty-eight appropriate tones in each of the *tropi*. I have mentioned their names above.[61] [941] The first of these is the adquisitus [added tone]; it gets its name from the fact that it harmonizes with none of the tetrachords but is, as it were, an extraneous addition taken on because of its relationship with the mese, with which it is consonant.[62] This adquisitus is separated from the principalis principalium [*hypate hypaton*] by a whole tone. The principalis principalium is so-called because it has the first position in the [first] tetrachord and is, as it were, a 'ruler.'[63] Next the sub-principalis gets its name from its position directly beneath[64] the principalis. [942] In the principal tetrachord the enharmonic and chromatic (our Latin term *colorabile* is perhaps hard to justify; the term is derived from the fact that whatever lies between the principal colors, white and black, is designated by the Greek term for colorable [*chromatike*])—I repeat, the enharmonic, chromatic—and diatonic genera (we call the diatonic the 'extended') are terms that indicate the changes of systems.[65] Indeed, several varieties of

---

[61] In § 931 Martianus enumerated eighteen tones, but he was following a different authority; here he is translating Aristides Quintilianus, who lists twenty-eight. See above, Vol. I, pp. 211 ff.

[62] I.e., the adquisitus is an octave lower than the mese.

[63] The term "principalis" is derived from the Latin *princeps*, meaning "ruler." Cf. § 931.

[64] Actually above in pitch. See n. 50, above.

[65] See *The New Oxford History of Music*, I, p. 344: "Each tetrachordal skeleton is filled by two 'movable' notes. The possible ranges of their motion were

tetrachords are formed. The principalis mediarum [*hypate meson*] is so called because it is the highest tone of the tetrachord of the middle; the tone directly below it is called subprincipalis mediarum.[66] The three remaining tones correspond to those in the principal tetrachord. The 'tetrachord of the middle' gets its name from the fact that it is located between the highest tetrachord and the conjunct tetrachord.

[943] The tone that follows the two aforementioned tetrachords is called media [Gr. *mese*, 'middle']. This name is given to it because it is both the last tone of the lower tetrachord and the first tone of the next higher tetrachord in all modes. Both the lower and the higher are joined by the bond of the identical tone—which, in the case of the Lydian mode, has the symbol of an upright letter iota. One semitone step beyond the *media* is the tertia coniunctarum [third tone of the conjunct tetrachord]—which, in the same mode, namely the Lydian, has as its symbol a supine lambda. Next after this come [those three notes which have been mentioned above: the enharmonic, the chromatic, and the diatonic],[67] also known as the *paranete,* or in Latin *paene ultima* [next to the last]. Following this comes the ultima [*nete synemmenon*], which is called the 'last of the conjunct tetrachord' because it marks the end of this tetrachord. This tetrachord is called 'conjunct' because it is conjoined to the media itself, which is the first tone to complete a perfect consonance.[68] Advancing beyond the media, the following tone is called the *paramese* [next or counter to the middle], because the tone of the adjacent note is discordant with this neighboring note. [944] Next comes the tertia divisarum, which completes the full system of the diapason; hence it is called the 'third tone of the

---

classified in three genera . . . (a) enharmonic; (b) chromatic; (c) diatonic." Martianus (like his source Aristides) is considering the variable in each of the three genera not as one note but as three. This gives two additional notes in each of the five tetrachords and accounts for the discrepancy between the lists of eighteen and twenty-eight notes.

[66] This statement and the following are literal translations of the Latin text, which describes the positions with reference to fingering, not pitch. Cf. § 931, where the English designations of the tones are given in brackets.

[67] The words in brackets may be a gloss, not part of the original.

[68] I.e., the octave.

disjunct tetrachord.' After this the other tones follow in order. The name 'disjunct tetrachord' is explained by the fact that it is separated from the bounding media by one and a half tones. After this comes the 'tetrachord of the high-pitched tones,' so called because in each of the modes the tone is raised to a high pitch and reaches its culmination in each of the modulations (*in singulis modulationibus*).

[945] Of these tones or *phthongi*, some are necessarily firmly fixed and continuous, others are movable; some are called *barypyknoi*, others *mesopyknoi*, still others *oxypyknoi*, and still others *apyknoi*. Three groups of tones have a certain compact quality which is referred to as *spissum* [crowded or compact].[69] The *barypyknoi* are compactly clustered tones that occupy the low ranges of each tetrachord; the *mesopyknoi* occupy the middle ranges; and the *oxypyknoi* occupy the upper ranges. The *apyknoi* stand in the place of the three compact groups of tones, but are not joined together by any genus or rule.

[946] Fixed and continuous tones are called either *apyknoi* or *barypyknoi*. These take on a certain species and form, as it were, of the principal notes; consequently, some authorities refer to them as stationary (*statarii*), for they are unable to undergo extensions or changes.

The other type are called 'movable' and 'wandering,' because they admit sometimes larger and sometimes smaller steps. Of these, some are called *parhypatoeides* [like that next to the lowest], and others *lichanoeides* [like the index-finger note]. The former get their name because they lie immediately beneath the first note of the highest tetrachord.[70] The *lichanoeides* get their name from the finger which moves as the servant of the art to each musical sound —namely, the finger next to the thumb [*lichanos*].

[947] Some of these tones produce concords, others are dissonant and jarring. Those that are consonant are called *symphonoi*; those that are dissonant when struck are called *diaphonoi*. Those that

---

[69] Crowded intervals are defined in § 950 as pertaining to dieses; *spissum* (Gr. *pyknon*) is the name given to a close arrangement of three tones.

[70] Again, this is a literal translation of the Latin text and refers to finger positions, not pitch.

have a different designation of tone, but the same pitch, are called *homophonoi*.[71]

There are still other aspects to tones. The first is according to tension, resulting in a difference between high and low pitch. The second is according to the interval between them when tones are conjoined over one or more steps. The third is according to the conjunction of systems, when a tone belongs to one or more systems. . . .[72] the fifth is according to ethos; high-pitched tones indicate one kind of ethos, low-pitched tones another.[73]

[948] Now we must discuss the diastem. A diastem is an interval of sound which is determined by a higher-pitched and a lower-pitched tone. Among the diastems there are some smaller intervals, which are found in the enharmonic diesis; and there are larger ones, which double each interval in the octave, the largest interval that can be found in the modes. [949] Among the intervals some are composite, others are incomposite and asynthetic. Incomposite intervals[74] are those which run consecutively; composite intervals represent combinations of intervals that vary from each other. Some intervals are rational, others are irrational. Those are rational whose combinations, when sounding together, we can represent as proportional; those are irrational which do not have a numerical ratio underlying them. Some intervals are consonant, others dissonant. Some are enharmonic, others chromatic, and still others diatonic. Some are even, others are excessive or odd. I shall first mention even intervals and then excessive intervals. Those are even which can be divided into equal parts, as a tone into two semitones [i.e. parts]; those are odd or excessive which are divided into three semitones.[75]

[950] Some intervals are crowded, others are more extended. The crowded ones are held together by dieses, the more extended are

71 See Macran, ed., *Aristoxenus*, p. 237: "The term *homophonoi* is applied to notes which differ in function but coincide in pitch. Thus the Dominant of the key of *D* and the Subdominant of the key of *E* fall alike on *A*."

72 The fourth aspect is missing in a lacuna in the Martianus manuscripts. Aristides gives it as according to the region or locus of the voice.

73 On ethos and pitch, see Macran, ed., *Aristoxenus*, p. 73; Munro, p. 66.

74 See Macran, p. 237. Incomposite or simple intervals are so called because, in a given scale, no note can occur between them.

75 Aristides here has dieses. It would appear that Martianus failed to understand the discussion.

held together by tones. Among these, some are consonant, others dissonant; and the number of dissonant intervals is very great. The consonant intervals in each mode are six in number: the *diatessaron*, which we call *de quattuor* [the fourth]; the *diapente*, or *de quinque* [the fifth]; next the *diapason* [octave], which is a consonance 'throughout the whole' tonal space. Other intervals are consonant that consist of an octave and a fourth, an octave and a fifth, and a double octave, which is called the *disdiapason*.

[951] The interval of the diatessaron—that is, the fourth—has four notes, three steps, two and a half tones, five semitones, and ten dieses or quarter tones. It is in the epitritic ratio, as 4 is to 3. The diapente—that is, the fifth—has five notes, four steps, three and a half tones, 7 semitones, and 14 quarter tones. It is in the hemiolic ratio, which is as 3 is to 2. The diapason has eight notes, seven steps, six tones, twice as many semitones, and four times as many quarter tones. It is said to be in the duple ratio (*in diplasia ratione*); that is, as one is to two. [952] The interval of the octave and a fourth consists of eleven notes, ten steps, eight and a half tones, twice as many semitones, and four times as many dieses. It is in the *diplasie-pidimoirus* ratio, which is as 8 is to 3. The interval of the octave and a fifth has twelve notes, eleven steps, nine and a half tones, twice as many semitones, and four times as many dieses. It is in the triple (*triplasia*) ratio, as four is to twelve. [953] The interval called the disdiapason has 15 notes, fourteen steps, twelve tones, twenty-four semitones, and 48 dieses. It is in the quadruple (*tetraplasius*) ratio, as 12 is to 3. The whole tone is in the *epogdous* ratio.[76] Everywhere in the enharmonic genus we are obliged to admit the diesis, which is one quarter of a tone.

[954] Now we must explain what a system is. A system is a multitude of tones arising from the several modes. It contains many kinds of subdivisions, but I pass over this subject because I have dealt with it in the discussion of intervals. There are in all eight absolute and perfect octave systems.[77] The first begins at the adquisitus,[78] which we call the proslambanomenos and is completed at the

[76] Nine to eight.

[77] *Systema teleion* in Greek. See Munro, pp. 35-40. Martianus means eight octave species of the "greater perfect system." See above, Vol. I, p. 215.

[78] The ensuing terms have been translated above (§ 931). Martianus here confuses some of the terms.

media, which we have called the mese. The second extends from the principalis principalium to the paramese; the third, from the subprincipalis principalium to the tertia divisarum; the fourth, from the extenta principalium to the divisarum diatonus; the fifth, from the principalis mediarum to the nete divisarum; the sixth, from the subprincipalis mediarum to the tertia excellentium; the seventh, from the mediarum extenta to the excellentium diatonus; and the eighth, from the media to the ultima excellentium.

[955] Next in order I shall briefly discuss the genera of tetrachords and of movement. A genus is defined as the division of tetrachords in a certain way. There are three genera of movement: enharmonic, chromatic, and diatonic.[79] [956] The enharmonic genus has the smallest steps and crowded notes; the diatonic is roomier and has whole tones; the chromatic consists of half tones. Just as whatever lies between black and white is called color, so the name chromatic is applied to the genus lying between the other two.

[957] Since the enharmonic is encompassed by fixed tones, it observes in ascending order a modulation by diesis, diesis, and incomposite ditone; in descending order the entire modulation is reversed. The chromatic receives its melody in ascending progression[80] in this way: by half tone, half tone, and three incomposite half tones; in descending progression the order is reversed. The diatonic, composed of whole tones, receives its modulation in ascending order through semitone, tone, tone (its full complement); and in descending the order is reversed. At present the diatonic genus is in greatest use.

[958] We modulate some diatonic genera by *agōgē*, others by *plokē*. *Agōgē* refers to tones progressing consecutively; *plokē* is the term used when tones progress diversely.[81] Thus, in modulation one progression is called *eutheia* (that is, 'straight,' or 'direct'); another is *anakamptousa* (that is, 'bending backward'); still another is *peripherēs* (that is, 'surrounding'). *Eutheia* is a progression from

[79] *harmonia, chroma,* and *diatonon.*

[80] The words "in ascending progression," omitted in a lacuna in the Martianus manuscripts, are supplied here from the text of Aristides Quintilianus.

[81] *Plokē* is zigzag progression, when every second interval is ascending, and alternate intervals are descending. See Macran, ed., *Aristoxenus*, p. 267. See also above, Vol. I, pp. 216 ff.

a low to a high pitch; *anakamptousa* is the reverse; *peripherēs* is the progression which accommodates itself to, or serves, both.[82]

[959] Although the tetrachords, which we call *quadrifidi* [divided into four parts], have innumerable divisions, there are six familiar ones: one in the enharmonic genus; three in the chromatic, of which the first is soft and slack [*malakos*], the second hemiolic, the third tonic [high-pitched]; and two in the diatonic—one soft [flat], the other shrill [sharp, *suntonos*].[83] The enharmonic genus gets its modifications from the *tetartemoria diesis;* that is, a quarter part of a tone. The chromatic, which we called flattened, is produced by the *tritemoria diesis.*[84] The hemiolic chromatic is produced from the *hemiolia diesis,*[85] which belongs to the enharmonic genus.

[960] And now about tones. A tone is a magnitude of space. It is called a tone because the voice was the first of all sounds to be 'stretched' over this space;[86] that is, from a given note to another note, as from the media [mese] to the paramese; as, for example, in the Lydian genus, if the progression is from a note whose symbol is an upright iota to one whose symbol is a zeta or a supine pi.[87] Since I have explained what semitones and dieses are, their value and their nature, and have indicated the names and varieties of the octave species, we shall now take up the tetrachords.

Each octave species retains five tetrachords, as I have not failed to observe above. There is no doubt that the bounding notes of each tetrachord must be consonant. [961] A tetrachord is a coherent and faithful concord of four sounds arranged in a sequence. Tetrachords are classified as follows: principal, middle, conjunct, disjunct, and extreme or highest. The first tetrachord, which is lowest in pitch, begins with the principalis principalium tone and ends with

---

[82] According to Aristides Quintilianus, *agōgē* is divided into three species: *eutheia,* ascending by consecutive notes; *peripherēs,* ascending by conjunction and descending by disjunction, or vice versa; *anakamptousa,* descending by consecutive notes. Se Macran, ed., *Aristoxenus,* p. 267.

[83] See J. F. Mountford, "Greek Music and Its Relation to Modern Times," *Journal of Hellenic Studies,* XL (1920), 25.

[84] I.e., , 1/3, 1/3, 1 5/6.

[85] I.e., 3/8, 3/8, 1 3/4. See *ibid.*

[86] *Tonus,* from the Greek *tonos* (verb *teino,* "to stretch").

[87] For the representation of these symbols in the Lydian scale, see Macran, ed., *Aristoxenus,* pp. 50-51.

the principalis mediarum . . .[88] but the binding connection between
the principal and middle tetrachords is called the conjunct tetrachord, the tetrachord extending from the mese to the nete of the
conjunct tetrachord. The fourth tetrachord, that of the disjuncts,
is widely separated from these, and extends from the paramese
to the nete of the disjunct tetrachord. In the various octave species
this tetrachord is conjoined with the one next higher in pitch, and
the fifth is referred to as the extreme or highest tetrachord. So
much for the tetrachords.

[962] Now let us examine the pentachords. There is no doubt
that the pentachords also are five in number. The first is called the
'lowest of the principals' because it begins with the added tone and
ends with the principal of the middle tetrachord. The next in
ascending progression of this kind begins with the extended tone
of the principal tetrachord and ends with the note of the middle
tetrachord, which in the Lydian genus has the symbol of an upright
iota.[89] The third is the pentachord of the conjuncts, which goes
from the extended tone of the middle tetrachord to the highest tone
of the conjunct tetrachord. The fourth extends from the media to
the nete of the disjunct tetrachord. The fifth, in ascending progression, begins with the extended tone of the disjunct tetrachord and
ends with the nete of the extreme tetrachord.

[963] These classifications which I have just mentioned are approved by the best authorities of my discipline; but I am aware that
certain authorities maintain that pentachords can begin with semitones, which is the case in the diatonic scale, about which I have
had much to say above. I would like to have it clearly understood
that the adquisitus finds a place in all the other groups, but cannot
be found in those which do not start with a whole tone; that is,
in the tetrachords; these always begin with semitones. In the others,
which are called pentachords and which do not move in this way,
the adquisitus is added, so that they begin with a whole tone; the
second step in a pentachord is a semitone.

[964] And now we come to change melodic modulation. Modulation is the shifting of the voice to another figure of sound. The

[88] There is a lacuna here where Martianus must have given the bounding
notes for the middle tetrachord.
[89] The media, or mese. Cf. § 960.

change is accomplished in any one of four ways: by genus, say from the enharmonic to either the chromatic or the diatonic genus; by system, if, for example, we pass from the principal of the principals [i.e., the Greater Perfect System] to the subprincipal [i.e., the Lesser Perfect System] or another of the systems, or when we make a transfer from the conjuncts to the disjuncts; by mode, when the melody is transferred from the Lydian mode, say, to the Phrygian or other mode; or by melodic movement, when we shift from one species of melody to another, or when we modulate from a virile melody to a feminine one.

[965] Next in order I shall discuss the styles of melodic composition. Melopoeia is the effect of completed musical motion. *Melos* is the result of high and low tones. Musical motion is the expression of many tones. There are three styles of melopoeia: *hypatoeides*, *mesoeides*, and *netoeides*. *Hypatoeides*, which is called tragic, consists of deeper tones; *mesoeides*, called dithyrambic, uses equable tones in the middle range; *netoeides*, called nomic, consists largely of tones in the higher range.[90] There are also other varieties which are called erotic, others comic[91] and some that are encomiological. But these more appropriately belong to the previous classifications and cannot claim separate divisions. These styles are also referred to as modes (*tropi*).

[966] There are several varieties of melody construction, as follows: in genus, one may be enharmonic, another chromatic, and another diatonic; in style, too, because one is hypatoid, another mesoid, and another netoid; then also in mode; for example, Dorian, Lydian, and others. . . . so that anyone who undertakes musical composition ought to consider the system before anything else and then mingle and compose his notes. Let this discussion of the seven divisions of my art suffice.

And now let us briefly discuss the subject of rhythm (*rhythmos*, or *numerus*), since it too certainly is a branch of my discipline. [967] *Rhythmus* is a grouping of times that are perceptible to the senses and are arranged in some orderly manner. Or we may also define *numerus* as the orderly arrangement of different measures. It is subordinate to time, in accordance with a proper control of

---

[90] See Munro, pp. 63-64. See also above, Vol. I, pp. 218 ff.

[91] The words "others comic," omitted from Martianus' text, are supplied from Aristides 1. 12.

modulation, by which the voice is raised or lowered and which restrains us from melodic license, in accordance with my discipline and art.

There is a difference between rhythm and that which has become rhythmic (*rhythmizomenon*). [968] The latter is indeed the implementation of rhythms, whereas rhythm is considered to be the artificer or a form of motion.

All rhythm is divided into three categories: visual, auditory, or tactual. An example of the visual is in bodily movements; of auditory, in an appraisal of a vocal performance; of tactual, when a doctor looks for symptoms by feeling the pulse. The most important categories for us are the auditory and the visual.

[969] The art of rhythmics is entirely in measures; it admits certain measures with appropriate variations and selects legitimate substitutions. The difference between rhythm and meter is no small one, as I shall explain later. Now since, as I have said, rhythm involves the visual and auditory senses, these too may be divided into three types: into motion of the body; into proper regulation of sounds and melody; and into words, which are grouped by suitable proportions into measures and which, when combined, produce a perfect song. Rhythm in public speaking is divided by syllables; in modulation, by arsis and thesis; and in gesture, by patterns and determinate motions (*schemata*)[92] that have been designed.

[970] There are seven[93] genera of rhythm, arising from: first, times; second, enumeration of those words which can fall into measure, those that are considered rhythmic and those which are distinguished by three terms—*enrhythmon* [in rhythm], *arrhythmon* [not in rhythm], and *rhythmoides* [rhythmical]; third, feet; fourth, kinds of feet; fifth, *agōgē rhythmica* [rhythmic progression], as we refer to it, the genus according to which rhythms and measures proceed; (6) substitutions; and (7) rhythmical composition, or how rhythm can be produced.

[971] First let us take up the *tempus* [the basic unit of time], which, like the atom, admits of no cutting into parts or particles. It is comparable to the point of geometricians or the monad of

---

[92] Explained in § 971.

[93] Aristides Quintilianus has five classifications of rhythm. Martianus, in order to make the number of genera of rhythm correspond to those of harmonics, divides Aristides' first two categories into two parts each.

arithmeticians. The *tempus* is found in words, in the syllable; in modulation, in the sounds or intervals, which are indivisible; and in gesture, in the very first movement of the body, which we refer to as the *schema*. This will be the briefest point of time, which, I have said, cannot be reduced. There is also composite time, which can be divided and which, from the beginning, is either double, triple, or quadruple; for all time of rhythm extends that far. Its boundary is that which is the termination of a full proportion, and in this respect time is found to be like tone; for just as a tone is divided into four parts or dieses, so a time is comprised of a fourfold scheme of times.

[972] Of those times which are combined in measures, some are called 'enrhythmic,' others 'arrhythmic,' and still others 'rhythmoid.' Enrhythmic times are those which keep a definite proportion in their arrangement, as in the case of those combined in the double, the hemiolius, or other ratios. Times are arrhythmic which have no rule at all in their parts and are combined without a definite ratio. Rhythmoid times observe rhythm in some feet and spurn it in others. [973] Some of these times (*tempora*) are called *strongyla* (that is, 'rounded,' or 'well-turned'); others are called *periplea* [very full]. The 'rounded' ones rush along more precipitately or readily than a legitimate order and pace demands; the 'full' ones, however, unduly retard the rhythm and are held back in a slow pronunciation. There are both simple and complex types of times; the latter are also called *podica* [belonging to a foot].

[974] The foot is the first progression of rhythm, a combination of proper and related sounds. A foot has two parts, arsis and thesis. Arsis is a raising, and thesis a lowering and slackening, of the voice.

[975] There are seven differentiating aspects of feet. First, by magnitude, since we reckon some feet as simple, others as composite. An example of a simple foot is the pyrrhic; of a composite, the paeons or their equivalents, the epitrites. Those are called simple that are divided into times (*tempora*); those are composite that are in turn resolved into simple feet.[94] . . . others are called *alogoi*;

[94] This whole paragraph is badly corrupted in the manuscripts, and the second, third, and fourth aspects are missing in a lacuna which begins at this point. The sense may be restored by comparing with the text of Aristides Quintilianus; cf. above, Vol. I, p. 221, which so uses Aristides.

that is, irrational. No ratio is found in these, and an ill-formed combination is produced. [976] Another aspect is by division, where the question arises of what sort (*poia*) of thing is being produced when the elements that have been combined are separated in various and manifold ways, and composite feet are able to become simple. Another aspect is by figure, which customarily is dealt with by division. And a seventh aspect is by opposition; that is, when two feet have been taken together and the first has a longer quantity, the second becomes shorter; or, if the order is contrary, the quantities are reversed.

[977] There are three genera of rhythm: they are sometimes called dactylic, iambic, paeonic; sometimes equal, hemiolic, double.[95] Then, too, the epitritic is included, for the unit, when joined to itself, is always conformable because of its ratio of equality. The double type (two to one) preserves the double ratio of syllables as well as of quantities; the hemiolic type of rhythm exhibits the ratio of three to two. The ratio of four to three produces the epitritic measure. Those which we have referred to as equal we shall call dactylic. In the dactylic genus elements are joined together in a rule of equality: one quantity goes with another quantity, or two with a doubled quantity, in a numerical equality, as it were. Next comes the genus of iamb, which I have indicated above as in the double category. In this form the quantities of the feet preserve the double ratio, whether of one to two, or of two to four, or any other double ratio. The hemiolic, called paeonic above, occurs when the quantities of the feet follow the ratio and rule of the hemiolius—that is, two to 3. Often a measure is found in the ratio of epitritus, when a foot is introduced which bears the ratio of 3 to four.

[978] Now let us take up the series of each genus. The equal genus of rhythm begins with a dissyllabic foot (*disemus*), and goes up to sixteen syllables. This so-called *disemus* is the first to consist of an arsis and a thesis, as illustrated by the word *leo*. The double genus begins with a foot of three syllables (*trisemus*), and continue to 18 syllables. The hemiolic genus begins with a foot of

95 The text of Martianus gives the order incorrectly; the correct order is *aequalia, duplicia, hemiolia.* See *Webster's New International Dictionary of the English Language,* 2d ed., s.v. "rhythm," 2.b. Cf. above, Vol. I, pp. 221 ff.

five syllables and reaches the number of 25. The epitritic genus begins with a foot of seven syllables and ends with a foot of 14,[96] whose use is complicated. I have mentioned all these sequences of feet so that the laws governing each may be observed at all times. others mixed. There are two or more kinds of composite measures.

[979] Some rhythms are composite, others incomposite, and still Incomposite measures consist of only one kind of foot, as in the case of the tetrasyllabic feet. Mixed measures are those that are resolved sometimes into quantities (*numeri*) and sometimes into feet, as we ought to understand to be the case with a measure of six syllables. Of those measures that are said to be composite, some are joined in pairs, others in periods. A syzygy or copula[97] is the joining of two feet that are seen to be dissimilar, into one. A period is a grouping together of several feet which, though dissimilar, are taken together in a relationship of equality.

[980] There are three different kinds of dissimilarity: magnitude, genus, and opposition. A different in magnitude occurs when a measure consists of a dissyllabic as against a tetrasyllabic foot; in genus, when a diplasic and a hemiolic foot are joined together, or when there is a joining of several feet on an equal basis; in opposition or antithesis, when dissyllabic feet in the first position are placed with far longer feet, or tetrasyllabic feet are placed with dissyllabic feet, following them. It will be fitting to note that one foot can suffice to complete a period if it is introduced alone, without a relationship of equality with the others.

[981] Of those that belong in the class of the single foot, the dactylic is the first genus. In this type the feet are incomposite and are 6 in number. There are the proceleusmatic (lesser and greater), the simple spondee, the greater spondee, and the anapaest (lesser and greater). The proceleusmatic is a foot that has both a short thesis and a short arsis. The proceleusmatic occurs more frequently, however, in tetrasyllabic feet. The proceleusmatic that is dissyllabic and composed of two quantities is called the lesser proceleusmatic; the

---

[96] The manuscripts are corrupt here, or Martianus was mistaken in using 28 rather than 14. Meibom corrected the error, and the Dick text follows that emendation.

[97] On the meaning of copula, see Fanny J. Le Moine, *Martianus Capella: A Literary Re-evaluation* (Munich, 1972), pp. 22-25.

greater proceleusmatic is composed of four short quantities. The lesser or dissyllabic proceleusmatic is called *synechēs* [continuous], because the frequent occurrence and close proximity of mutually bounding syllables does not extend to any magnitude or measure with an opportunity for division. Therefore it is fitting to introduce this foot sparingly, so that continual use of the short syllable does not interrupt the flow of the verse, which ought to be recited with some dignity. It is fittingly used, however, in combination with other feet that are longer, in order to compensate by its swifter movement for the slower pace of the longer syllable. Therefore, an appropriate application of the proceleusmatic to measures ought to begin with a tetrasyllabic foot.

[982] The anapaest which is called greater receives an arsis of one syllable and a thesis of two. A quantity is called *monochronos* [of one time] even when it is a long syllable which customarily receives two times, or when three short times are taken together, or when there are four times in the combination. All of these are taken into account in reckoning equivalence to a long syllable. Thus the greater anapaest will receive an arsis which is called *monochronos*, but it is seen to have a *dichronos* thesis. With either part which is in the thesis equal to the other, it is necessary for the arsis to have a doubled time, that is to say that each time in the following syllable be equal to a time in the preceding syllable. Thus we call a greater anapaest (*anapaistos apo mizonos*) dactylic; but the lesser anapaest (*anapaistos ap' elassonos*) is a combination of two shorts in the arsis and one long in the thesis.

[983] The simple spondee will be a combination of both a lengthened arsis and a lengthened thesis; but that foot is called a greater spondee which is seen to admit not only an arsis of four quantities but also a thesis of four quantities.

Double measures are formed by copula; one of these will be the greater Ionic, the other the lesser Ionic. The greater Ionic will consist of a simple spondee and a proceleusmatic, obviously of the dissyllabic type. The reverse combination is found in the lesser Ionic.

The rhythms, incomposite and composite, that belong to the dactylic genus are eight in number. [984] The dactyl gets its name from the fact that its arrangement of syllables is like a human finger;[98] the anapaest, because it is arranged in reverse order.[99] The pyrrhic, or proceleusmatic, gets its name because of its repeated use in contests or children's sports; the spondee, because it is generally used at sacrifices.[100] The ionic is so called because of the uneven sound of its measures: for it has two long and two short syllables. Many listeners are often restrained at hearing such meters.[101] This is a sufficient discussion of dactyls.

[985] Now let us discuss iambs.[102] In this genus there are four incomposite measures, two composite by copula, and twelve composite by period. The incomposite measures are a random group: the iamb, consisting of a short arsis and a thesis double in length; the trochee, consisting of a doubled thesis and a short arsis; the orthius, consisting of an arsis of four syllables and a thesis of eight, so that this foot seems to comprise twelve quantities and has some kinship with the iambic foot; for in the first four quantities it corresponds with the iamb, the other eight quantities being additional. Lastly, there is the so-called semantic trochee, the reverse of the orthius, consisting of eight short quantities in the thesis and four short quantities in the arsis.

[986] Then come composite measures that are, to be sure, joined by a copula. They are classified as follows: trochaic bacchic, beginning with a trochee and ending with an iamb; iambic bacchic, beginning with an iamb and having the reverse of the feet just mentioned.[103]

Then there are also measures composite by period, which proceed, so to speak, along a definite path. Although the measures in this genus are twelve in number, we must recognize four in each period. The first contains one iamb and three trochees. With regard to the first period, the measure which has the iamb first is called the iambic trochee. The one which has the iamb in the second position is called the bacchic trochee. The one that has the iamb third is called

---

[98] Gr. daktylos [finger]; the dactyl has one long member and two short members.

[99] Gr. anapaistos [struck back, rebounding].

[100] Gr. pyrrichē [a war dance or competitive dance]; prokeleusmatikos [rousing to action beforehand]; spondē [libation].

[101] See Vol. I, p. 225.

[102] See § 988 for Martianus' derivation of "Iamb."

[103] See Vol. I, p. 224.

the trochaic bacchic; and the one that has the iamb fourth is called the epitritic iamb.

Of those measures that have one trochee and the rest iambs, the first is called the trochaic iamb. The second is called the bacchic iamb, another name for which is middle bacchic. The measure that has the trochee in the third position is called the iambic bacchic; and the one that has it in the fourth position is called the epitritic trochee.

[987] So far we have enumerated eight measures. Now of the twelve measures that we said are classified by periods, four keep two trochees and two iambs in each period. The measure that has the trochees in the first position is called the simple trochaic bacchic. The one that has them in the second position is called the simple iambic bacchic. But when the trochees are found in the middle position it is properly called the middle trochee. When the iambs are found in the middle, it is called the middle iamb. The total number, including measures that are joined in periods or by copula, is eighteen.

[988] The iamb gets its name from the Greek verb *iambizein*, which means 'to detract.' The ancients used this meter for lampooning; the name is also used because the iamb pours out the poison[104] of malice and spite. The trochee gets its name from the fact that it makes a swift turn, like a wheel.[105] The orthius is so called because of the uprightness of its thesis; the semantic trochee, being retarded in pace, gives indication of that drawn-out and halting character. The bacchics get their name from the fact that they most resemble the cries of bacchants and that the sport of Bacchus is suited to these measures.

[989] In the genus called paeonic there are two rhythms that are incomposite. One of these is called *paeon diagyius* from the long and the short in the thesis and the long arsis; the other, called *epibatus*, combines two long quantities in the thesis and a long arsis. These, then, are the measures of the paeonic genus; we have noted that they are incomposite. In this genus rhythm does not depend upon either copula or period. Thus the name *diagyius*[106] is given to one of them, having, as it were, two separate members;

---

104 Gr. *ios* [poison, or venom].

105 Gr. *trochos* [wheel].

106 A Greek word, meaning "two-limbed."

the term *epibatus* is given to the other because it consists of four members, a combination of a doubled arsis and two distinct theses.

[990] When these genera have been combined in various kinds of rhythms, the first species will be those called dochmiacs. Of these the first dochmiac comprises a combination of an iamb and a diagyian paeon. Later authorities have called this a diagyian cretic. The second species consists of an iamb, a dactyl, and a paeon. [991] These rhythms are called 'drawn out' (*deducti*), clearly because their sounds are continual and composite.

There are also rhythms that are called 'prose-like' (*prosodiaci*). Some of these have three feet (a pyrrhic, an iamb, and a trochee); others have four (an iamb in the first position, joined to the above three). Others consist of two syzygies or copulas (a bacchic and a greater ionic).

[992] There are also, to be sure, irrational rhythms, which we call *alogoi;* another name for them is choreics. There are two of these: one resembles the figure of a diiamb, and consists of an arsis that is long and two theses. In its number of times it is like the dactyl, but in its parts[107] it is related to the ionic and iambic rhythms. There is still another rhythm, which is called *trochaeides;* that is, which seems to have a certain form and species of trochee, consisting of two arses and a long thesis, just the reverse of the previous choreic.

[993] There are 6 types in the mixed genera: the cretic, the iambic dactyl, the trochaic bacchic dactyl, the iambic bacchic dactyl, the iamboid choreic dactyl, and the trochaeoid choreic dactyl. . . .[108]

[994] Rythmopoeia is the manner of composing rhythms and working out all the figures to full perfection. It is divided into the same parts as melopoeia, which are as follows: *lēpsis*, or 'perception,' by which we understand how much use to make of a certain rhythm; *chrēsis*, or 'use,' according to which we adjust our theses and arses appropriately; *mixis*, or 'mixing,' by which, as opportunity arises, we mix rhythms artistically.

There are three *tropi* in rhythmopoeia, as there are in melopoeia:

---

[107] The parts of its delivery, according to Aristides Quintilianus 1. 17.

[108] There is a lacuna here; the missing section seems to have contained an analysis of the six mixed forms.

there is the so-called *systaltikos*. . . .[109] We have mentioned this above in the section on harmony.

[995] We recognize that rhythm is masculine and melody feminine. For melody is the subject which, lacking a particular form, is judged on its own; rhythm, however, as a result of the manly activity involved in it, produces form, as well as various other effects, by sounds."

[996] Harmony was discoursing in a manner both stately and charming to an attentive audience of gods and heroes. Now she gracefully drew back, and her voice grew silent in the chorus of sweet song. Jupiter arose, and as he and the gods walked ahead, Harmony, humming a lullaby, came to the marriage chamber, to the great delight of all.

[997] And there, Martianus,[110] you have an old man's tale, a mélange sportively composed by Satire under lamplight as she strove with difficulty to teach the Pelasgian arts dear to Attic fleshhooks.[111] The work is complete in nine books. [998] Our garrulous Satire has heaped learned doctrines upon unlearned, and crammed sacred matters into secular; she has commingled gods and the Muses, and has had uncouth figures prating in a rustic fiction about the encyclopedic arts. [999] Herself distressed by awareness of the triviality[112] of her composition, and swollen with gall and bile, she said: "I could have come forth in a grand robe, to be admired for my learning and refinement, decorous in appearance, as if just coming from the court of Mars.[113] Instead I have been inspired by Felix Capella—whom ignorant generations have observed ranting as he passed judgment on barking dogs, giving to the high office of proconsul a bumble bee[114] long

---

109 The last two *tropi* are missing in a lacuna here, just as those of melopoeia are missing in the lacuna at § 966. The lacuna here may be supplied from Aristides' text (40. 14-15).

110 The author is here addressing his son.

111 The reading of the manuscripts, *creagris*, is unclear in meaning. Morelli conjectured *cathedris* [seats of learning]. The Greek word *kreagra* means "fleshhook."

112 Following the reading *nauci* of Remigius.

113 According to Remigius, this is a reference to the Areopagus, where Greek philosophers met and debated.

114 Remigius sees in the word a suggestion of one speaking pompously. The

separated from his blossoms[115] by the sickle, and in his declining years; a man whom the prosperous city of Elissa[116] has seen as a fosterling settled in a neighborhood of slothful herdsmen, barely managing on a small income, drowsy by day and blinking his eyes with effort—when I could fittingly quaff the Pegasean draught." [1000] And so, my son, in accordance with the testimony of an old man, show indulgence, as you read, for the trifles which he has produced.

---

text is very corrupt at this point; the translation gives what appears to be the meaning.

[115] *Flosculo*. This word often referred also to ornaments of speech.

[116] Dido, queen of Carthage.

Index

References to Jupiter and Mercury are not indexed, since they occur with great frequency throughout the work.